PRACTICAL HOME MAINTENANCE

Practical HOME MAINTENANCE

Macdonald

A Macdonald Book

First published in Great Britain in 1984 by
Macdonald & Co (Publishers) Ltd

This edition published in Great Britain in 1986 by
Macdonald & Co (Publishers) Ltd
London & Sydney

A member of BPCC plc

British Library Cataloguing in Publication Data

Practical home maintenance
1. Dwellings—Maintenance and repair—
Amateurs' manuals
643'.7 TH4817.3

ISBN 0-356-09749-8
ISBN 0-356-12314-6 Pbk

Illustrations: Raymond Turvey

Filmset by Text of Orpington

Made and printed in Great Britain by
Hazell Watson & Viney Limited,
Member of the BPCC Group,
Aylesbury, Bucks

Macdonald & Co (Publishers) Ltd
Greater London House
Hampstead Road
London NW1 7QX

Contents

Chapter 1
ROOFS

Steeply sloping roofs – 'pitched' roofs – are the type from which rainwater drains most easily. They also cause snow to slide off before it overloads the structure. Pitched roofs, however, are expensive to construct, so it is standard practice on outbuildings such as home extensions to fit flat roofs; and even flat roofs are made to slope slightly, so that water can drain off.

Major roofing repairs are beyond the scope of the do-it-yourselfer, not least because of the hazards of working at heights. There are, however, many minor jobs that can be done safely.

GETTING UP THERE

Roofing work is not particularly difficult or skilled, but working high above ground can be extremely hazardous so do be cautious if you ever climb up to a roof.

Confidence comes only from working with the right tools and knowing exactly what you are doing. This applies equally to all types of job – not just those carried out at heights. If you are unsure of your competence, then opt out and employ a professional.

Provided you are careful, however, you should be safe. The appliances for access to a roof are: ladders, roof ladders, and access towers or proper scaffolding.

Ladders

Ladders made of aluminium are preferable to the traditional wooden ones. Aluminium ladders do not rot (unlike wooden ladders), so there is less risk of a rung collapsing under your weight. Even so, you should always examine a ladder before use to make sure it is sound. Aluminium ladders are also lighter, so are easier to carry around and less likely to topple as you position them.

When carrying a ladder, keep it vertical and securely supported by your body. Raising a ladder from the horizontal is easier if someone helps you. Ask your helper to place a foot on the bottom rung. Then, after lifting the other end,

1.1 *Jam a ladder under the sill of a door when you want to raise it.*

1.2 *The safe way to carry a ladder*

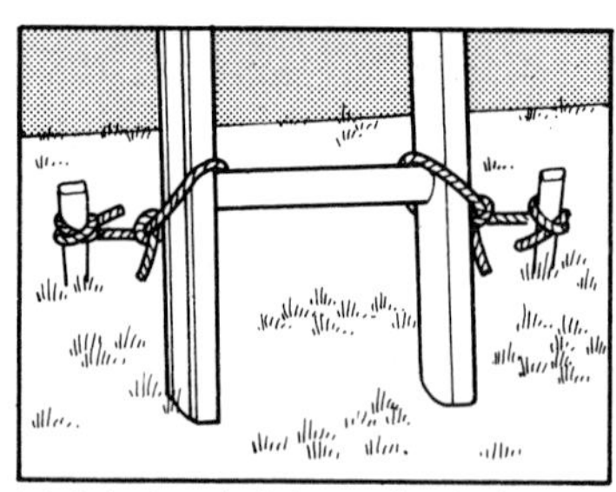
1.3 *At its foot, lash it to stakes in the ground..*

walk towards the helper, raising the ladder over your head as you go until it is vertical. If you have no one to help you raise it, jam the foot of the ladder against a wall, or under the sill of a door (Fig. 1:1). Lower a raised ladder in the reverse order.

Most right-handed people will find it easier to support a vertical ladder on their left side. To do this, extend your right arm to hold the rung just above your head, and curl your left arm round the other side to hold a rung just below waist level. If you find it easier to support the ladder on your right side, put the left hand above the head and the right hand below the waist (Fig. 1:2).

When positioning the ladder, make sure its distance from the bottom of the wall is at least a quarter of its height up the wall. If the ladder is extendable, stand on the ground, not on the ladder, while you extend it in two or three stages. Between stages, rest the hooks attached to the bottom of the upper section on to a rung of the lower section. Watch out that the top of the ladder does not hit any obstructions as you raise it. If you need to go higher than you can extend the ladder while standing on the ground, extend the ladder before raising it.

A rope-operated ladder can be extended fully while it is leaning against the wall. Grasp a rung of the lower section just above your head and pull the top of the ladder away from the wall. At the same time pull on the rope with the other hand. Some extending ladders have wheels at the top to make it easier to raise them when they are against a wall.

You must always raise a ladder sufficiently high to allow you to work in safety. It is dangerous to stand on the uppermost rungs, for you need something to hold on to. The fourth rung from the top is about as far as you should safely go. Also do not extend an extendable ladder too far. Allow at least a two-rung overlap on a 4 m (13 ft) ladder; three rungs on a 5 m (16 ft) one. If the ladder you own is not tall enough for the job in hand, hire one that is rather than risk serious injury just to save yourself a hire fee.

For access on to the roof, the ladder should extend beyond the eaves. Provided that they are sound, cast iron gutters will support a ladder, but in general plastic ones will not. In any event, a ladder can easily slip along a wet gutter, so the safest course is to fit ladder stays. These are metal or wooden brackets near the top of the ladder to support it on the wall away from the eaves.

Make sure the ladder is secure at the bottom. Ask a helper to keep it steady with a foot firmly placed on the bottom rung. If you do not have a helper, lash it to stakes driven into the ground (Fig. 1:3). If you are working near a front door you can pass rope through a letter box and tie it to a stick that cannot be pulled through (Fig. 1:4). On concrete, place sacking under the base of a ladder that does not have rubber feet or tie it to a heavy object; on soft ground, stand it on a board so that it cannot sink – otherwise there is a danger that one stile might sink farther than the other. Do not tie the ladder to the base of a drain pipe, which may not be fixed securely enough, and always make sure the ladder is standing evenly. On uneven ground, place a wedge under one foot.

Lash the ladder at the top, too. It is a good idea to fix stout, rust-proof ring bolts permanently just below the eaves (Fig. 1:5). Where a window has two opening sashes side by side you can tie a ladder to the transom (Fig 1:6).

To climb the ladder, hold the stiles not the rungs. Wear stout shoes with a good instep to support your weight and prevent you tiring quickly. If you have to carry only one or two small tools, wear overalls with pockets in which to put them, leaving your hands free to climb and work. But never put in your pockets sharp tools that could cause injury if you fell. Sharp tools or large numbers of items should be placed in a bag or bucket, which you hold well clear of the ladder in one hand, while gripping a stile with the other. Hook the bag or bucket, or a paint can, on to a rung while you work.

Never be tempted to lean out that little bit farther just to save yourself the trouble of climbing down and moving the ladder along: it is too dangerous.

When you come down an extending ladder, be prepared for the misalignment of the rungs of the upper and lower sections, which can cause you to miss a rung and be thrown off balance.

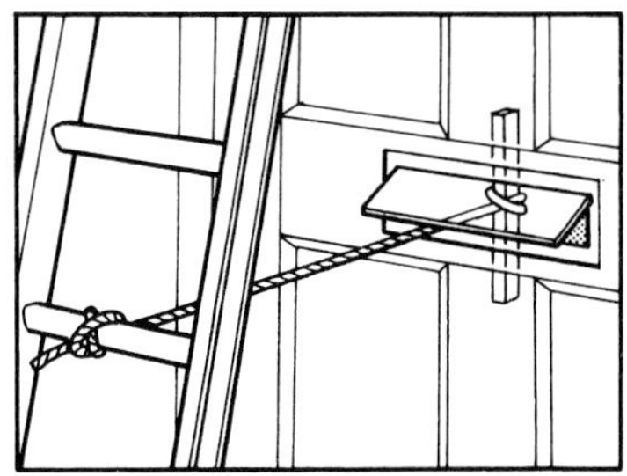

1.4 *A ladder tied to a stick on the other side of the letter opening...*

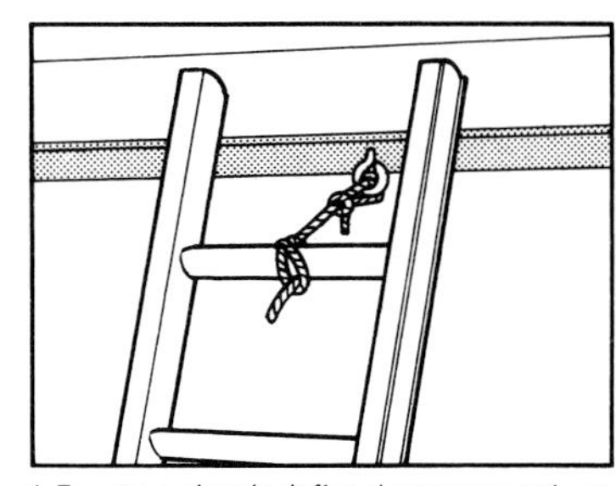

1.5 *...to a ring bolt fixed permanently at the eaves...*

Roof Ladders

To climb from the eaves and up the slope of a pitched roof you need a roof ladder. It is dangerous to dispense with this and walk across the roof, because you risk breaking the roof tiles and slipping off.

It is not easy to manoeuvre a roof ladder up from the ground. Probably the best way is to tie a rope to it, climb up the ordinary ladder, then, with a helper down below to guide it, haul it up. Aluminium roof ladders are easier to handle.

A roof ladder has wheels at one end, so you can push it across the tiles to the ridge. When it is there, you turn it over, and it hooks on to the ridge. You can also lash it at the base – to the top of the ordinary ladder, for instance, which must in turn be lashed securely. If you have any doubts about the security of the fixing of your roof ladder, do not climb it, but seek the advice of a professional.

1.6 *...and round the transom of a window frame.*

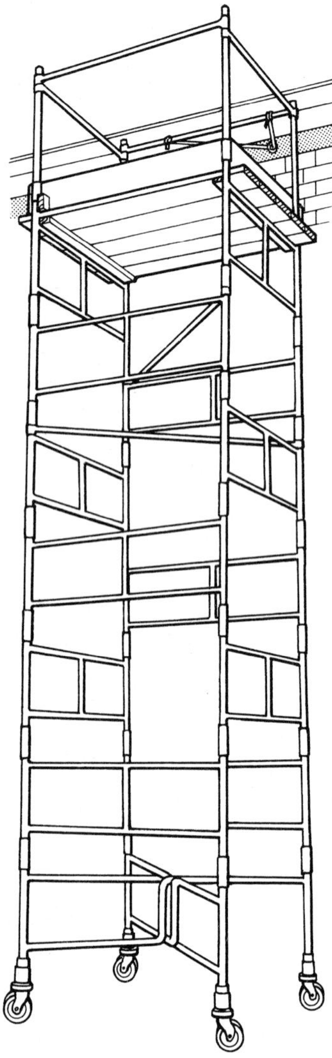

1.7 *It is easier, safer and less tiring to work from an access tower.*

Access Towers

Working from an access tower (Fig. 1:7) is much easier, safer and less tiring than from a ladder. It is, however, expensive to buy or hire an access tower, but the expense is easily justified for some jobs – when you wish to finish a job quickly in bad weather, for example, or to support large quantities of heavy material, such as bricks and mortar for a chimney stack.

Access towers are delivered as metal frames, which you lock together, without nuts and bolts, to form a rigid structure. A platform of boards is fitted, and toe boards should be used, too, so that tools and materials cannot fall over the sides. Various types of feet are available for the bottom frame. For example, you can have metal plates for grass or soft ground; or castors for easy mobility over firm ground; and for uneven ground, the feet can be adjusted to different lengths.

Before buying or hiring an access tower, ensure that it is tall enough for your use. In general, the maximum height available is only about 4.9 m (16 ft), although outriggers can be added to raise it to 6.1 m (20 ft). That gives a reach of about 8 m (26 ft). To the tower can be fitted a ladder with which you can climb on to a roof, and some can be built cantilevered, for instance, over an extension.

Some precautions are necessary when you work from a tower. If the base of the tower is of the usual size – 1.2 m (4 ft) square, and the tower is taller than 3.7 m (12 ft), it must be lashed to the house at the top. If the base is only 1.2 × 0.6 m (4 × 2 ft) the tower should be lashed in place when it reaches a height of 2.4 m (8 ft). Ensure that the tower is level and sits squarely on the ground. If it has castors, ensure that these are locked before you climb up. Never move a tower on which there are people or tools and materials.

Scaffolding

For some types of job there is no satisfactory alternative to scaffolding. Typical examples of such jobs are the renewal of a section of the roof, and the repair of a chimney stack high up on a gable wall. The need to erect scaffolding appears to place most roofing work out of the scope of the do-it-yourselfer.

In fact, if you have a relatively minor job to do that nonetheless requires scaffolding, it is probably better to employ professionals. If there is a large and costly job, which you think you have the skills to carry out competently and safely yourself, you might consider having the scaffolding erected professionally.

PITCHED ROOFS

Pitched roofs are normally clad with slates or tiles. Such roofs have to be strongly constructed to support the immense load of the slates or tiles as well as any snow that settles. Moreover, the roof is exposed to the wind, which can exert a large force in exposed areas.

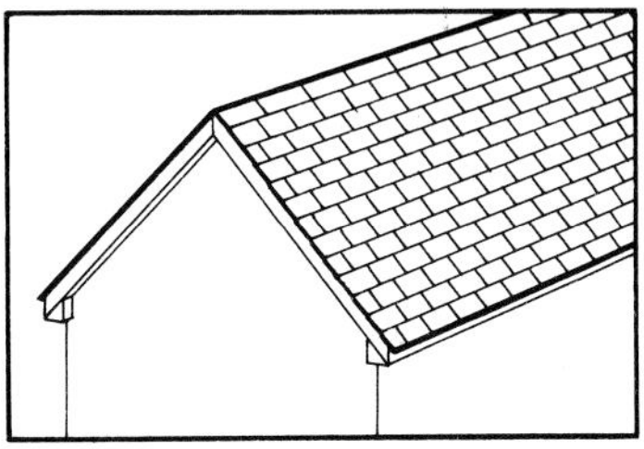
1.8 *Types of roof: two-way pitched*

How they are built

There are two common shapes for a pitched roof. If the roof has just a simple slope on each side, meeting in a ridge like a tent, it is said to be two-way pitched (Fig. 1:8). The walls at the ends of a two-way pitched roof are the gable walls, and are often triangular in shape at the top. It is usual for the roof to project slightly beyond, and be supported by, the gable wall. The end of the roof is concealed behind bargeboards, which are nailed to the end rafters. The roof projection beyond the gable is the verge which shields the top of the wall from the rain.

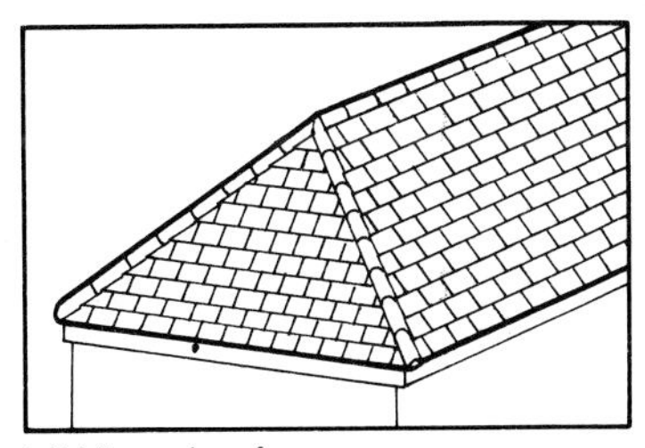
1.9 *Hipped roof*

On some houses, the gable wall extends higher than the ridge. In such cases the gable is square at the top, capped off with a stone coping or rendering. This type of wall, against which a roof abuts, is an abutment wall. The other common type of roof shape is called a hipped roof (Fig. 1:9). It is formed when the roof has a third slope, rising from the end walls to the top like the side of a pyramid.

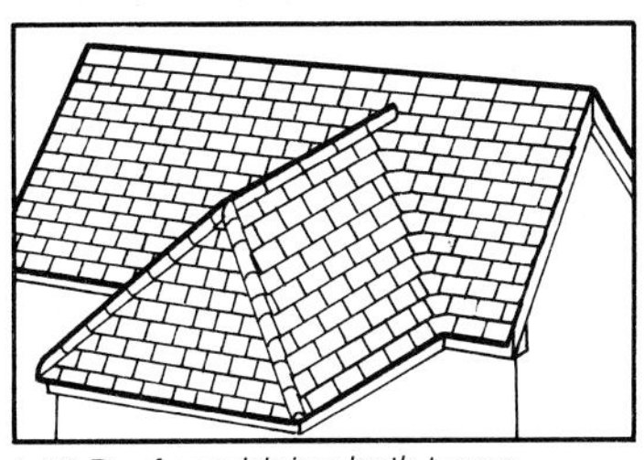
1.10 *Roof combining both types: two-way pitched and hipped*

Some houses have both types of roof joined in one: for instance a house that is L-shaped in plan may have a two-way roof on one leg of the L, but a hipped roof on the other; a T-shaped house, too, may have hips at the two ends of the roof covering the top cross-member, but a two-way pitch at the end of the main T-section (Fig. 1:10); a hipped roof may have a dormer window with a two-way pitched roof; and there are other variations.

1.11 *Mansard roof*

Another type of pitched roof you may see occasionally is the mansard (Fig. 1:11). In this the pitch is at two angles – a gentle one at the top and a steeper one below, nearer the outer wall. Often, these roofs were designed to allow a room in the attic. They were, in fact, a cheap way of getting an extra storey, for the lower parts of such a roof are more easily and cheaply built than a brick wall.

Lean-to buildings, verandahs and porches often have a single-sloped roof covered by tiles and slates. These are known as mono-pitch roofs (Fig. 1:12).

1.12 *Mono-pitch roof*

Traditionally, the frame for a pitched roof was built up on site by skilled joiners (Fig. 1:13). On pitched-roof houses built since about 1950, however, the triangular frame is of a trussed rafter construction. With these, the triangular frames are constructed as a whole in a factory, and brought to the site looking much like giant coat·hangers (Fig. 1:14). They are strengthened by lengths of timber known as trusses. The difference between a trussed frame and the traditional type is crucial if you ever think of building a loft extension. It is impossible to erect a room in an attic formed by trussed frames, for you cannot remove any of the middle trusses to clear a space for a loft conversion without seriously weakening the whole structure. It is possible, however, to remove sections from an older-style roof, provided that compensating support is added elsewhere. But the subject of loft conversions is complicated and you should never attempt it without expert advice.

Whichever construction method has been used, the frames are broadly similar. The lower member of the triangle is the joist, to the underside of which the ceilings of upstairs rooms are fixed. These joists are fixed to wall plates at the top of the main walls of the house. The two sides of the triangle are the rafters, and these are joined both to the wall plates and to the sides of the joists. At the top end, the rafters are joined to a horizontal length of timber known as the

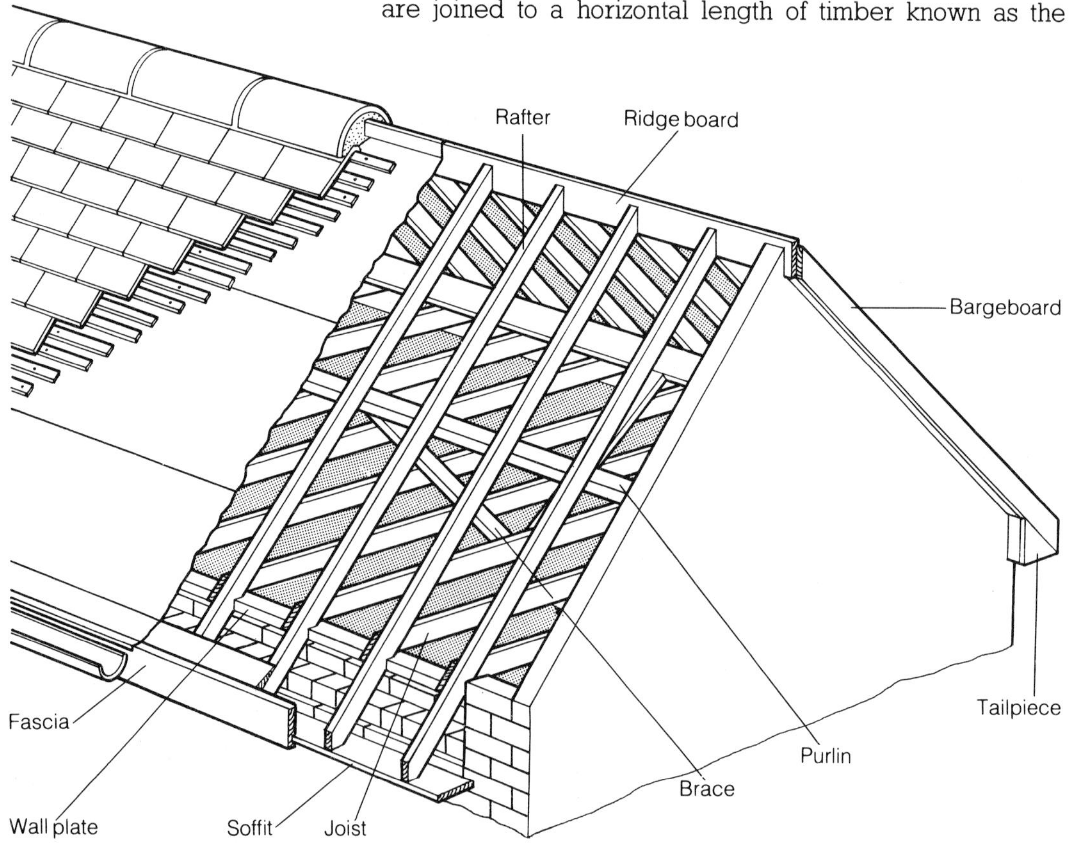

1.13 *Traditional method of roof construction*

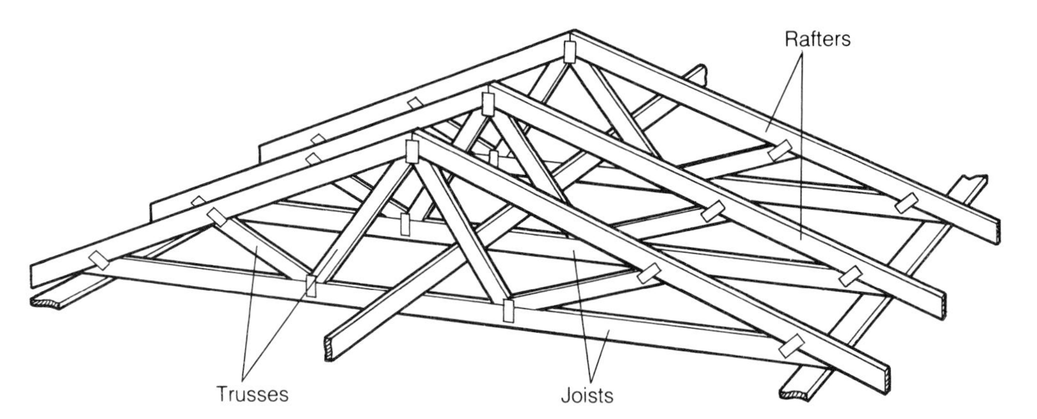

1.14 *Trussed rafter roof*

ridge board. Intermediate support for the rafters is provided by purlins, which are usually braced. Two methods of bracing are used. There may be struts supported on an internal load-bearing wall, or hangers fixed vertically to the joists and further strengthened by runners extending vertically between the hangers. The purlins may be notched into the rafters, or just bevelled to suit the angle at which they meet. (For general construction of a pitched roof, see Fig 1:13.)

The rafters project well beyond the eaves and are finished off by two lengths of timber. The one underneath the rafters is the soffit board, and the other – to which the gutters are fixed – is the fascia. Sometimes the eaves are left open. Never block off open eaves as a draught-proofing or insulation measure. They are left open to keep the loft well-ventilated and dry. Blocking off might encourage condensation, which will dampen and rot the roof timbers and saturate any loft insulation, rendering it ineffective. Houses built with blocked off eaves have compensating ventilation elsewhere.

Older houses often have a front external wall extended to form a parapet. This is sometimes topped with a stone coping. The parapet has a damp-proof course (see Chapter 3) two or three courses from the top to stop moisture being conducted from the parapet to the main walls of the house. In such instances, a gutter as such is not installed; gutter boards are used to form one artificially.

A parapet wall hides the roof from view. Often the roof behind it consists of two small pitched roofs which are joined to form a valley (Fig. 1:15), which serves as a gutter to collect water from the two inner pitches. The two parts of a valley roof do not need to be as high as would a single, pitched roof covering a house of the same size. This, with the fact that they are concealed behind a parapet, ensures that they are sheltered from some of the effects of the weather. An unfortunate consequence of the lower height, however,

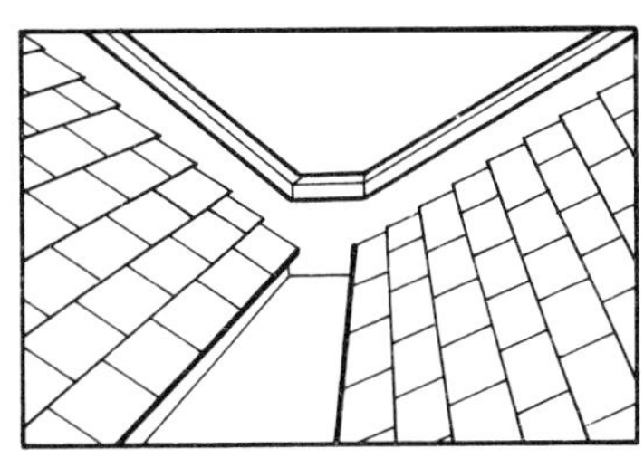

1.15 *A valley roof*

is that there is not much headroom beneath them should you ever have to do work up there.

Slates and tiles

The slates and tiles on a pitched roof are fixed to a series of battens that extend across the rafters. It is good practice to fit felt underneath the slates, and this, too, extends lengthwise across the rafters. The felt is there to catch any moisture that gets through gaps in the tiles, and to prevent it from falling into the attic. It should sag slightly between the rafters to form a small shallow channel into which the water can collect and run away. The felt is held in place by the tiling battens, and where an overlap is required, it should be at least 75 mm (3 in) wide with the layer nearest the ridge covering the one on its eaves side. At the eaves, the felt should project beyond the tiles so that water running down it will be carried clear of the roof and into the gutter. Extra layers of felt are sometimes fitted into valleys and eaves.

For a very strong, waterproof construction the rafters may have first been covered with boards, either tongued and grooved or square edged. The felt is nailed to the boards, and tiling battens are fitted as usual on top of the felt. The expense of this type of construction makes it rare.

The tiles or slates overlap each other by an amount determined by the space between the battens. This spacing is a crucial part of the building design, so do not increase it for any reason. Usually the overlap is between 60 and 90 mm (2½-3½ in).

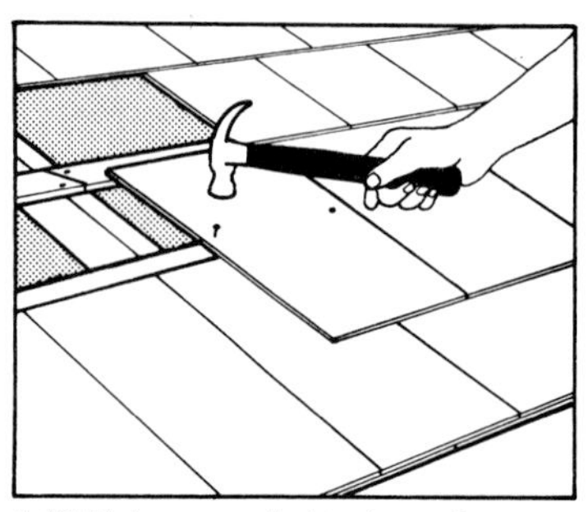

1.16 *Slates are nailed to the roofing battens.*

Slates are secured by nails, which should be of copper, aluminium or a non-corroding alloy, such as bronze. Never use ferrous nails; they are sure to rust. Two nails per slate should be used, preferably in the middle of the slate, so they are less likely to be levered up and broken by the wind (Fig. 1:16). Moreover, it is easier to replace a centre-nailed slate if it does break, than one nailed at the top edge.

Nails are also used in fixing tiles, but there is no need to nail every one. Tiles have nibs that locate on the battens, and the weight also helps to keep them in place (Fig. 1:17). It is usual to nail only every fourth or fifth row.

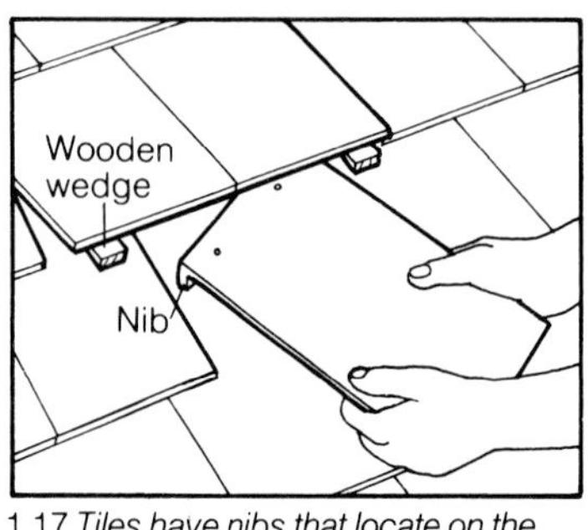

1.17 *Tiles have nibs that locate on the battens.*

It was once customary to fix slates and tiles to the battens by mortar, which also helped to seal the gaps between them. This process is known as torching, but it is now obsolete. You may, however, still see it on older houses. Never apply torching to a roof in which it is not already used.

Tilers usually start work at the eaves, where they lay two rows one on top of the other because this is where water is most likely to penetrate the roof. The double course projects well into the gutter, and it is lifted up either by the fascia board, or by a small triangular batten known as a tilting fillet, so that the tiles bed properly on the nails. Similarly a double course is laid on gable wall verges. Often the bottom tiles are bedded in mortar, and the gap between them and the wall is pointed so that high winds cannot get through and dislodge the tiles.

Ridges are usually finished off with V-shaped tiles, bedded in mortar, although dry fixing systems, which make use of metal clips and sealing strips, are being introduced. Sometimes a lead joint is applied. Similar tiles are used at hips. A piece of metal known as a hip iron (Fig. 1:18) is fitted to stop the tiles from sliding down the hip before the mortar has set. Valleys are lined with lead or zinc, or shaped tiles are fitted.

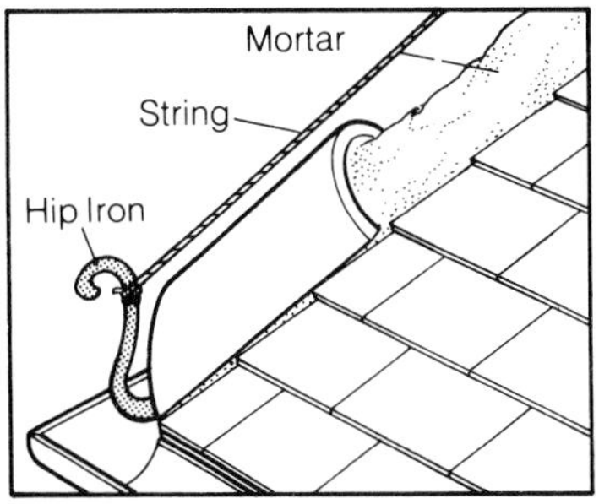

1.18 *A string line from the hip iron to the ridge acts as a guide when you are fixing hip tiles.*

Simple repairs to pitched roofs

As roofs are often out of view, we tend to think of them only when some defect shows, but you should check up on your roof from time to time. Perhaps you can get a good view of it from a neighbour's window or even from your garden or the road. Use a pair of binoculars to help you make a closer inspection. When you decorate the exterior of the house or maintain the gutter, take the opportunity to inspect the roof. Look for missing or cracked roofing tiles and slates, damage to the ridge or hip tiles and defects on the chimney stack. There might be some flaw letting in damp – which, though not showing through in the house below, is nevertheless attacking the structural timbers of the roof and attic, and could be causing rot that will lead to extensive (and expensive) repairs. Occasionally also you should look through the trap door to the attic for defects to the roof visible from the underside.

The roofs on some older houses are in such bad condition that re-roofing has become a major industry. Some slated and clay-tiled roofs built before 1939 are nearing the end of their period of usefulness. Many of the clay tiles with which houses in the 1930s were roofed are crumbling, due to weathering by water and frosts. Some slates too have started to delaminate. Many roofs were built with ungalvanized ferrous nails, which have started to corrode; the roofs are then suffering from what builders call nail fatigue.

When a roof deteriorates badly, complete renewal is the only option. Old slates can be replaced with new or second-hand slates, and clay tiles with new clay tiles. Concrete tiles are less expensive so they are more popular. A wide selection is available and you should be able to choose a style that suits your house. Re-roofing, however, is not a job for the do-it-yourselfer. You should employ a roofing contractor, having obtained at least three different estimates before placing your order.

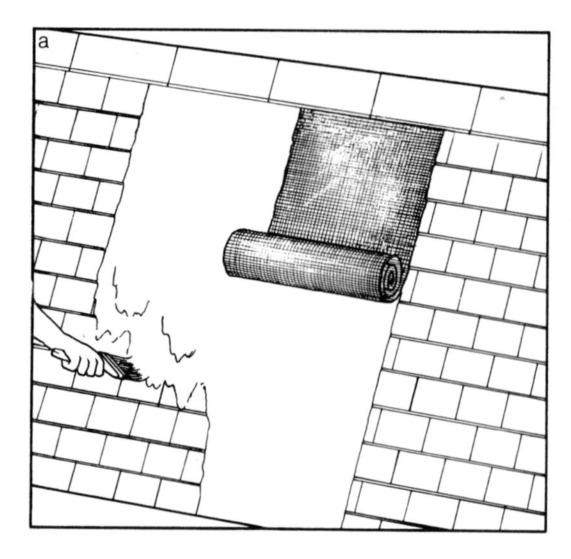

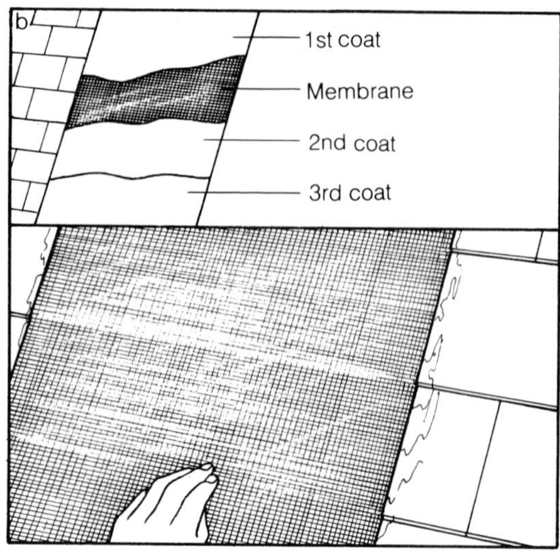

1.19 *Sealing a leaky roof: (a) Brush on a waterproofing liquid then (b) bed the membrane firmly in it.*

There remain, however, many minor repairs that you can tackle. Often a damp patch on the ceiling is the first sign of trouble. Should this occur, inspect the roof both from above and from the attic to pinpoint the source of the leak. Remember that the position of the patch is only a rough guide, because the water might have seeped across the inner surface of the roof or along the top of a ceiling after dripping through the roof itself.

Sealing a leaky roof does not need to be an extensive or an expensive job. In some instances it can be achieved by brushing on a waterproofing liquid. In others a reinforcing membrane is bonded to the roof (Fig. 1:19). These systems are supplied by firms that specialize in damp repellents, and are stocked at DIY stores and builders' merchants. Usually full instructions are provided with the product.

These systems provide an effective barrier against porosity and can be useful in an emergency to provide a temporary seal. Against major defects such as corroded nails, or rot in the timber structure, however, they are ineffective. Even when they do seal a leak, they have the disadvantage that they are noticeable, and draw attention to the fact that you have a problem roof, which could be a drawback should you want to sell the house. Nevertheless when funds are tight and a roof is leaking, they can be a solution, although perhaps only a temporary one until you can afford a new roof.

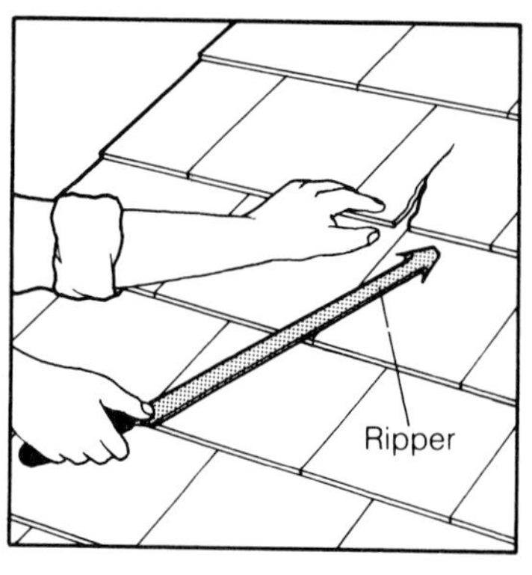

1.20 *Removing a broken slate with a slater's ripper*

Replacing a broken slate can be a straightforward DIY job. First remove the existing slate. It may be so loose that you can merely pull it away. If it is still held by nails, remove them with a slater's ripper (Fig 1:20). This is a long flat blade with a handle at one end and one or two hooks at the other.

Push the blade up under the slate and engage a nail with the hook. Give a short sharp tug, and the nail will break. Repeat the process for the other nail, if there is one, then you should be able to pull the broken slate clear.

You cannot nail the new slate into place, because the batten into which the nails should be driven is hidden under neighbouring slates. Secure the slate instead with a small clip, which you can make from a strip of lead, aluminium or copper about 225 × 25 mm (9 × 1 in). In the first instance, bend just one end of the metal, slip this end on the batten and fix it by driving a galvanized nail through it and into the batten below (Fig. 1:21). Take the new slate and ease it into place keeping it flat. When you are satisfied with its position, bend the end of the clip up and over it to hold it securely in place.

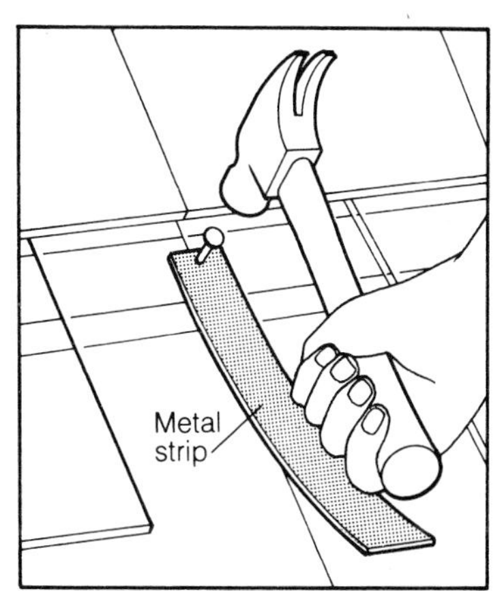

1.21 *First stage in forming the clip that will hold a replacement slate in place*

Replacing a broken tile is simple once you realize that roof tiles are held by slots or nibs in the tile which engage on the roof batten. Only every fourth or fifth row is nailed. If the tile to be replaced is not nailed, remove it by pushing a trowel underneath it, and lifting its nibs clear of the batten. Push the new tile into place under the surrounding tiles, engaging its nibs on the batten. Should it be nailed, loosen it with a tiler's ripper, as described above for slates.

Fitting underfelt

Many older houses do not have felt under the tiles or slates, so there is no second barrier to water or draughts that might penetrate the gaps between the slates or tiles. There is an improvised method for adding felt to the roof. It will not offer as good a protection as felt fixed before the slates were laid but it is well worth doing.

The method involves cutting strips of felt to go from ridge to eaves between the rafters. The strips should be just wider than the space between the rafters so there is a slight sag in the middle down which any moisture that collects can run. They should also project under the eaves so the moisture can drain into the gutter.

To fix the strips, nail or staple them to small-section battens, and screw the battens to the sides of the rafters. Use non-rusting materials throughout. If you cannot make up the strips from one length, so must use two pieces, allow a generous overlap of 150 mm (6 in) or more. The ends nearest to the ridge should be on top in the overlap!

Replacing ridge tiles

If a ridge tile becomes loose, it might slip out of place. Loosening can result if the mortar holding the tile has cracked, perhaps because of slight settlement of the roof, and water has got into the joint. Repairs should be carried out as soon as possible because the tile could slip further, or even be blown off in a high wind.

You can merely replace a loose or missing tile, but it is best to remove all the tiles and reset them. If one of the ridge tiles has been forced loose, there is a good chance that the mortar holding the others is weak. Since you have gone to the trouble of climbing up on the roof, taking tools and materials, you might as well do the job properly.

Using a hammer and cold chisel, chip away at the mortar holding the tiles. Remove the tiles and chip off the bedding mortar. Any tiles that are broken or cracked should be discarded. Shop around for second-hand tiles to match these and any that happen to be missing. If matching tiles are not available, it is probably as well to replace all the tiles. The appearance of the house is marred if all the ridge tiles do not match, because they are such a noticeable feature.

The tiles are bedded in mortar of three parts sharp sand to one part cement. Before laying the tiles, soak them in water so they will not absorb the moisture from the mortar and cause it to dry out too quickly with the consequent risk of shrinkage and cracking. Spread the mortar along the ridge, place each tile in position, and press it down on the mortar with a small trowel. Point the joins.

Some ridge tiles – the traditional pantiles, for instance – have an unusually large cavity. Do not fill this with mortar, because such a large amount of mortar might shrink and crack. Instead, fill the gap by mortaring in dentil slips, available at builders' merchants (tradesmen often use bits of broken tile for this purpose). Dentil slips should also be included in tiles at the verge.

Replacing hip tiles

The join where two pitches of a roof meet – the hip – is covered with hip tiles, which are similar to ridge tiles, and fixed in the same way. Any that are defective should be replaced as described for ridge tiles. The bottom tile, however, has to be cut at an angle on both sides to follow the line of the eaves, and is held in place by a hip iron. Make sure there is one on your roof, especially before you carry out repairs to the hip tiles. If not, replace it. It is screwed into the end of the hip rafter.

When replacing all the tiles on a hip, cut and fix the bottom tile first. Then stretch a string line from it to the ridge, so that all the tiles will be aligned (see Fig. 1:18). On a hip, just as on a ridge, deep profile tiles should be packed out with dentil slips.

Sealing verges

The mortar in the verge at the top of a gable wall can deteriorate and allow moisture to penetrate the roof. Fine cracks can be sealed with a mastic – the sort you squeeze out of a gun, for instance. If the mortar has deteriorated badly, chip it out and re-point. For repointing see Chapter 3.

Leaks in the valley

Leaks can develop in the valley – the internal angle where two roofs meet. The zinc or lead of which these are traditionally made can become porous or cracked. Seal cracks with a proprietary bituminous mastic, which is sold at DIY centres and builders' merchants. Spread the mastic to a thickness of 1.5 mm (1/16 in) and about 50 mm (2 in) beyond the crack on all sides. Cover the mastic with metal foil or thin roofing felt. Ensure the edges are well bedded-down in the mastic, and sealed by it. Cover with a further 1.5 mm (1/16 in) layer of mastic.

To make sure that no fine cracks have gone unnoticed, coat the whole length of the valley with a bitumen-based damp-proofing liquid, sold widely for such a purpose in builders' merchants and home improvement centres. A valley that is leaking because it is porous, but in which there are no cracks, should be treated with such a liquid.

If the valley has deteriorated beyond repair, replacement is a major job, probably best left to a professional. It involves stripping off the tiles or slates on each side, and taking out the old gutter. The timber supports underneath should be checked for signs of rotting and replaced as necessary, and any rusty nails should be replaced. Then the new valley is fixed in position.

A valley may also be formed from tiles, and these may need replacing from time to time. New valley systems, for professional installation, are also available from manufacturers.

Woodworm and rot

The cold, moist atmosphere of an attic is ideal for woodworm, which can infest the timber of the roof. Make periodic checks for signs of infestation. In particular, always treat any new timber you install with preservative.

Rot is usually more of a problem in the lower regions of the house, which are likely to be damper and less well ventilated. Should any of the roof timbers get wet, however, there is a risk of rot developing. Keep the roof in a good state of repair and well ventilated so the attic remains dry.

Wood that is badly damaged by worm or rot needs to be replaced, but beware of cutting out any of the structural

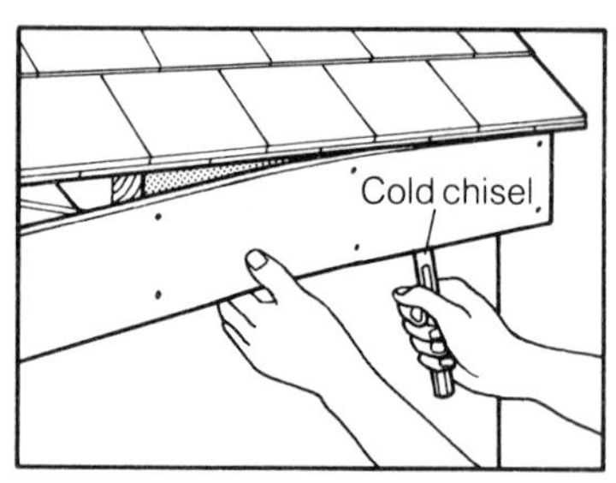

1.22 *Prise away the damaged fascia.*

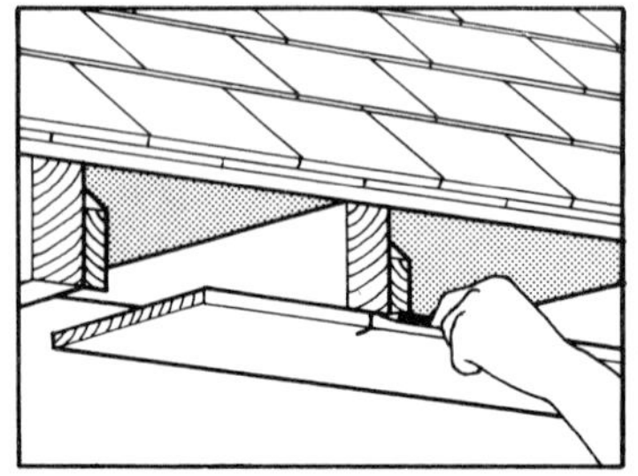
1.23 *Offer up a new soffit board and mark where it should be fixed to the bearer.*

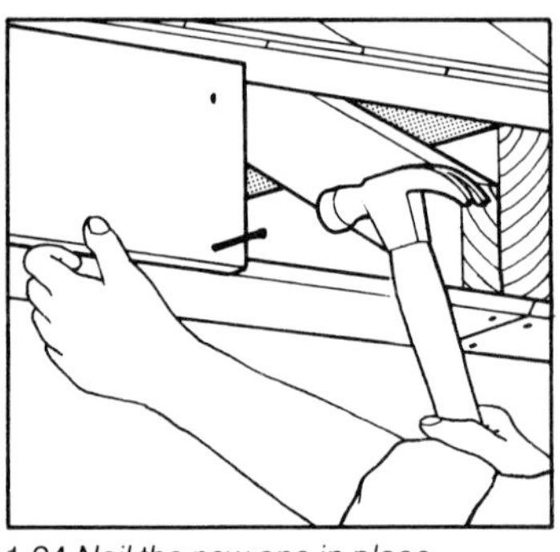
1.24 *Nail the new one in place.*

members of a roof without expert supervision. Techniques for dealing with woodworm and rot are discussed in Chapter 5.

Repairs to fascias and soffits

Just as with any other exterior woodwork, the fascias and soffits are likely to rot if they are not well maintained. Remove small areas of rot by chopping them out with a hammer and chisel, then fill them with an exterior-quality filler. Sand the filler when hard. Repaint the whole board, so the repair will not be noticeable.

If the fascia and soffits are in bad condition, they should be replaced. This involves removing the gutters, so a good time to do the work is when you intend to install new gutters and downpipes (see Chapter 2). You will need a helper, and scaffolding, which you can hire from a plant contractor.

The fascia and soffits (which often come in more than one length of board) are nailed into place. To remove them, prise them free with a lever, such as a crowbar or cold chisel (Fig. 1:22). Then remove the nails with a claw hammer or pincers.

If the joist and rafter ends and the soffit brackets are rotten, cut them back to sound wood and replace with new, otherwise you will not be able to get a firm fixing. Good timber need only be cleaned up, any old nails removed, and the holes filled with exterior-quality filler. Treat both old and new timber with preservative, then paint.

Cut the new soffit board to length and prepare it, then fix it in place with nails driven into the soffit brackets.

Where a run has to be made up from more than one length of board, you get a neater result if you use a mitre rather than a butt joint. Offer the board up into place, and mark on it the centre of the bearer to which it will be fixed (Fig. 1:23). Cut a mitre at this mark and in the next length of board so that the half-way point of the joint is at the centre of the bracket (Fig. 1:24).

The boards that make up the fascia are fixed next. As before, use mitred rather than butt joints where more than one length is needed. The fascia is fixed by being nailed to the rafter and the soffit (Fig. 1:25).

Punch home all nail heads, fill, then paint. The painting should consist of knotting, primer, undercoat, then two top coats. Parts that will be inaccessible once they are in place should be painted before they are fixed.

Bargeboards

Bargeboards that have deteriorated are replaced in the same way as fascias. The job is not so cumbersome, because there are no gutters to be removed and replaced.

Notice that the bargeboards are shaped at both ends – where they meet at the ridge and where they fit round the eaves. Use the old board as a template for marking out the new.

At the lower end of the bargeboard a shaped piece of timber is fitted. This is known as the tail piece. Use the old as a template for marking out the new, then fix with glue and screws or dowels.

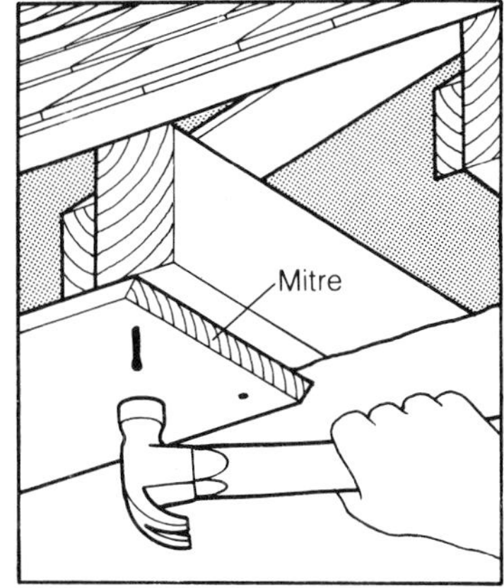

1.25 *A mitred end gives a neater fixing.*

CHIMNEY STACKS

A chimney stack is installed to carry the flue from the fireplace well clear of the roof, so that the flue gases cannot be sucked back into the house. The flue lining continues up the stack and ends in a chimney pot, set in a bed of mortar, which is known as the flaunching. The chimney pot may be fitted with a cowl, which is necessary to prevent some types of chimney from smoking.

The stack could need re-pointing, which can be done as for other external walls (see Chapter 3). Just as any other wall that butts up against a roof, the chimney stack has flashing, which can be renewed as described later in this chapter. There are two defects, however, that are specific to a chimney: the flaunching might become badly cracked and chipped, causing damp to enter the structure; and the pot might become damaged.

Repairs to the flaunching

Chip off the old flaunching with a hammer and cold chisel. Make sure you remove all loose material – it often helps to brush the top of the stack with a wire brush. Take care, though, that nothing goes down the flue – you can cover the top of it temporarily as a precaution. Place the debris in a bucket, and lower it on a rope to the ground. If the chimney pot is to be dispensed with, tie a rope round it and lower it to the ground. Take care as you do this – the pot is heavier and much bigger than it appears from the ground. In fact, throughout this job it would definitely be desirable to have a helper on the ground to untie buckets and pots as they are lowered, to tie a new pot to the rope and to mix cement for you and shovel it into a bucket so you can haul it up.

Place the new or existing pot in position over the top of the flue, and brush water round its base so that it will not absorb moisture from the flaunching. The mortar should be a mix of 1 part of cement to 3 parts of sharp sand. Apply it with a trowel, building up from the edge to a depth of about 75 mm (3 in) round the pot. The flaunching should be smooth and shaped so that rainwater will drain away and not llodge there. Clean off any mortar that has stuck to the pot.

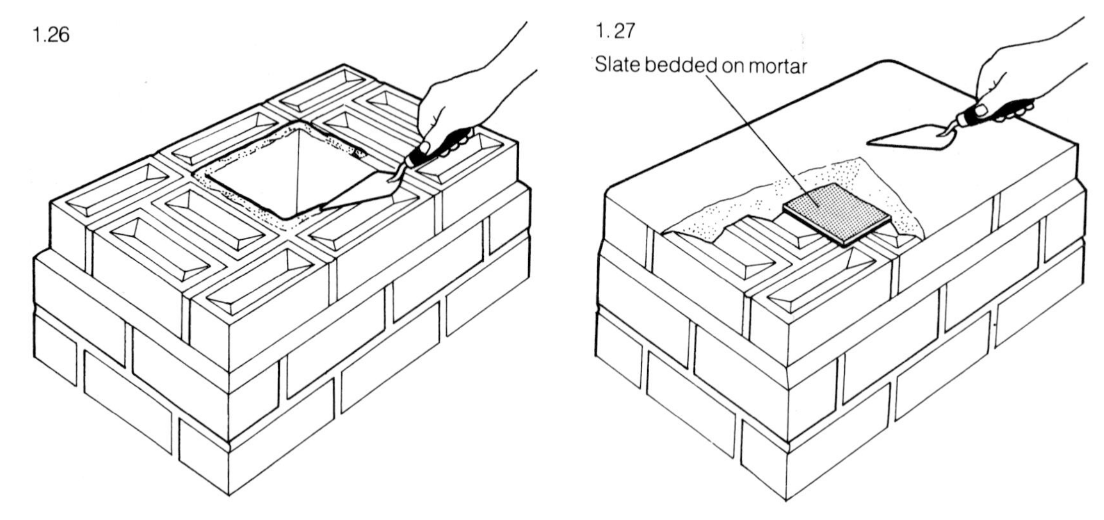

1.26 *Lay a band of mortar round the top of the flue.*
1.27 *Cover the top of the stack with mortar, sloping it downwards from a high mid-point.*

Blocking off a chimney

If you are certain never to use the flue again, the top of a chimney can be blocked off. If you choose to do this instead of renewing defective flaunching or a pot, remove the flaunching and pot as already described. Clean up and dampen the brickwork at the top of the stack. Lay a 25 mm (1 in) thick band of mortar round the top of the flue (Fig. 1:26), and bed on it a slate big enough to cover the flue mouth. Now cover the whole top of the stack with mortar, sloping it from a high point in the middle down to the edges, so that water will run off (Fig. 1:27). Alternatively, fit a capping pot (available from builders' merchants).

A blocked-off flue requires ventilation at fireplace level, to prevent condensation forming inside and passing through the chimney breast to affect the decoration of the room. If the fireplace is left intact, it will give all the ventilation required. But should you decide to remove the fireplace and block off the opening, you must incorporate a ventilation grille.

FLASHINGS

The line where a roof meets a vertical surface, such as a wall or chimney stack, is a vulnerable spot and needs to be well sealed off to stop rainwater getting through. The usual method of doing this is with flashing. Lead is ideal because it is impervious to water yet easy to shape and bend. Recently, however, it has become expensive, so bituminous felt is often substituted.

The lead or bitumen is dressed into a mortar joint, and bent down to cover the tiles, the felt being sealed on to the tiles with mastic.

Repairs to flashings

The flashings for the main roof are intricate. Where a two-way roof meets an end wall, for instance, a stepped flashing is required to follow the slope of the roof. Much more complicated is the arrangement round a chimney stack, with an apron flashing on the lower side, stepped flashing on perhaps two others, a back gutter, and perhaps even soakers – small pieces of lead, copper, zinc, or bituminous felt used to weatherproof the joints between these or bituminous felt.

Given all these complications, and considering the difficulty of access, it is perhaps better to employ a professional when renewal is necessary, although you might feel confident about tackling the minor repairs. Renewing a straight, horizontal flashing, however, especially on the roof of a small lean-to building where access would be easy, is certainly much simpler.

For the new flashing you could use lead, but bituminous felt is less expensive. Remove the old flashing (Fig. 1:28), and rake out the mortar joint to a depth of about 25 mm (1 in) (Fig. 1:29). Clean the brickwork and tiles – a wire brush is suitable for this. If there is a small mortar fillet where roof and wall meet, inspect it for damage, and repair it if necessary, as described in the next section. Bend the flashing over then push it into the join and wedge it there (Fig. 1:30). Next bend it over the tiles, sealing it with mastic to stop it from curling. Then repoint the mortar joint.

You may prefer to use a proprietary flashing, which is sold in home improvement stores and builders' merchants. The method of applying such flashing strips varies, so always follow the manufacturer's instructions. These strips usually have a backing tape, which you peel off to reveal an adhesive. Some are in grey plastic, to simulate lead; others have an aluminium foil covering.

The fault in a flashing may not be so drastic as to call for complete renewal. For instance, the flashing itself may be sound, but the mortar in the joint might have deteriorated, causing the flashing to fall away. In that case, rake out the joint, put the flashing back into place, and re-point.

Cracks in an old flashing can be sealed with bituminous mastic. The method for doing this is as for dealing with cracks in a valley (see page 19).

Mortar Fillets

A mortar fillet is sometimes used instead of flashing, particularly where a party wall in a row of terraced houses extends beyond the roof line to form an abutment wall. The effect of the weather and perhaps settlement of the roof may weaken

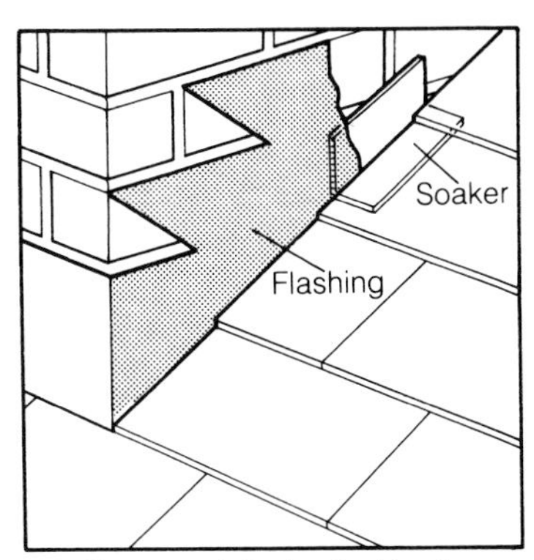

1.28 *To renew defective flashing first take out the old.*

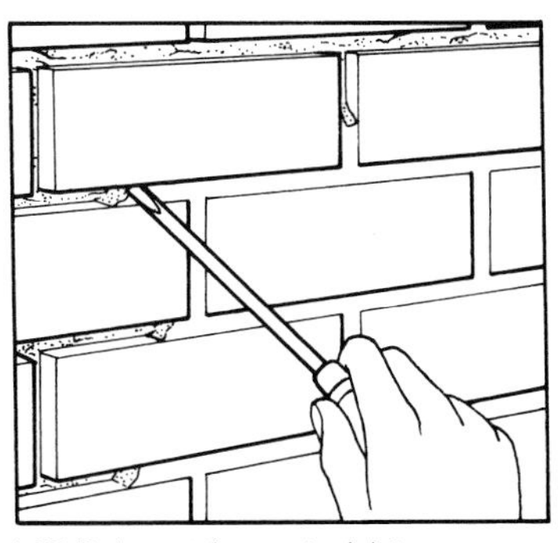
1.29 *Rake out the mortar joints.*

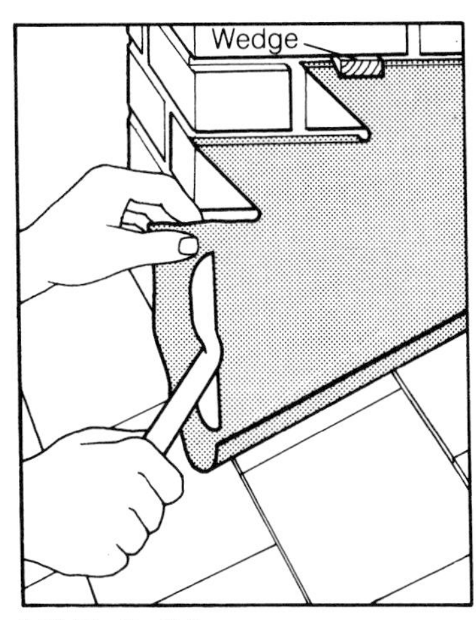

1.30 *Finally, fit the new.*

this fillet and cause it to crack or fall away from the wall. If the fillet is in a bad state just here and there, repair it as necessary with new mortar. Usually, however, the fact that it has deteriorated in one place can be taken as a sign that the whole lot may be ready to crumble. The best thing to do is chip it all away with a bolster chisel and club hammer, and renew it. Use a mix of three parts of cement to one of sharp sand, and apply it with a small pointing trowel, or filler knife. It is not easy to make the fillet as neat as the original builders left it, but it is worth the effort to try.

The line between a wall and a new or old fillet can be sealed with mastic applied with a gun.

INSULATING PITCHED ROOFS

About 20 per cent of the heat lost from the average house goes through the roof. So while you are considering your roof you should ponder on how well your loft is insulated. To minimize heat loss, a thickness of 100 mm (4 in) or even 125 mm (5 in) of insulation in centrally-heated homes is today more desirable than the mere 25 mm (1 in) that was recommended previously. If you insulate your loft or top up the insulation already there you should recover your outlay, by way of reduced fuel bills, in about a couple of years. Although it is an unpleasant task carried out in cramped conditions, doing it yourself will guarantee that the work has not been skimped.

Loft insulation is available either in the form of a blanket that is rolled out between the joists or a loose-fill material, that you pour from a sack. Both types are equally effective, but in an odd shaped loft with lots of nooks and crannies, it can be quicker and easier to pour out a loose material than to fit blanket. If you are starting from scratch use whichever you wish. When topping-up, it is better to use the type you already have.

Take care not to place any load – even a foot – on the ceiling while you are in the loft, or it might break through. It is a good idea to take a plank with you and stand on that.

Opinions vary about the clothes you should wear. Some people believe that if you wear as little as possible, you can take a shower afterwards and quickly wash away all the scratchy fibres. Others say you should protect yourself with long-sleeved shirts buttoned at the collar, trousers tucked into socks and sleeves into gloves. In any event, you should protect your hands with gloves, and wear a cap or something to cover your head.

Roll out the blanket, making sure it is well tucked down at the eaves so that wind cannot blow underneath it. If you use loose-fill, simply pour it into place. It is, however, surprisingly easy to misjudge the depth to which you have filled a gap, so make a gauge from a length of wood with a notch cut out of each end of the lower edge to form a T with a short stubby descender. The depth of this descender should equal the distance from the top of the joists to the required top of the insulation. Rest the cross-piece of the T on top of the joists, and drag it along to spread the granules to the correct depth.

A well-insulated loft is cold, so make sure the water pipes and tanks are well protected, either with lagging or, if the pipes are low enough, by laying the blanket over them and draping it on top of the tank. Leave the space under the tank clear, however, so that warmth can penetrate up to it from the rooms below, as a further aid to stop it from freezing.

One problem with attic insulation is that it can make the loft so cold that condensation develops and soaks the insulation, rendering it ineffective. Most lofts have sufficient ventilation to stop this from happening. If not, lay polythene under the insulation as a vapour barrier, or install ventilating grilles.

FLAT ROOFS

Flat roofs are usually covered with two or three layers of roofing felt. The top layer has embedded on it a covering of stone chippings, which may be added either at manufacture or during installation. The chippings reflect ultraviolet rays, which could damage the felt. Usually the first layer of the three layers of felt is laid lengthwise in the direction of the slope. The second layer is laid across, and the final one in the direction of the first. Some experts say it is better for all three layers to run lengthwise, provided the joins do not coincide (Fig. 1:31). To ensure that they do not, the roofer begins laying at one edge and works across to the other, where the final piece is cut to width. The second layer begins at this edge with a full-width roll until the first edge is reached, where the last piece will once again have to be cut to width. The third layer begins at the initial first edge, so the joins in this are kept apart from those of the first and second.

In two-layer coverings, the first usually goes across the slope of the roof, and the other one lengthwise. Alternatively, both can be laid lengthwise, using the method already described to ensure that the joins do not coincide.

The felt is laid on some form of decking, which can be made up of either planks (tongued and grooved or square-edged), exterior-grade plywood or chipboard, compressed strawboard, or a concrete screed on top of some other form of board. The decking is supported on rafters at centres

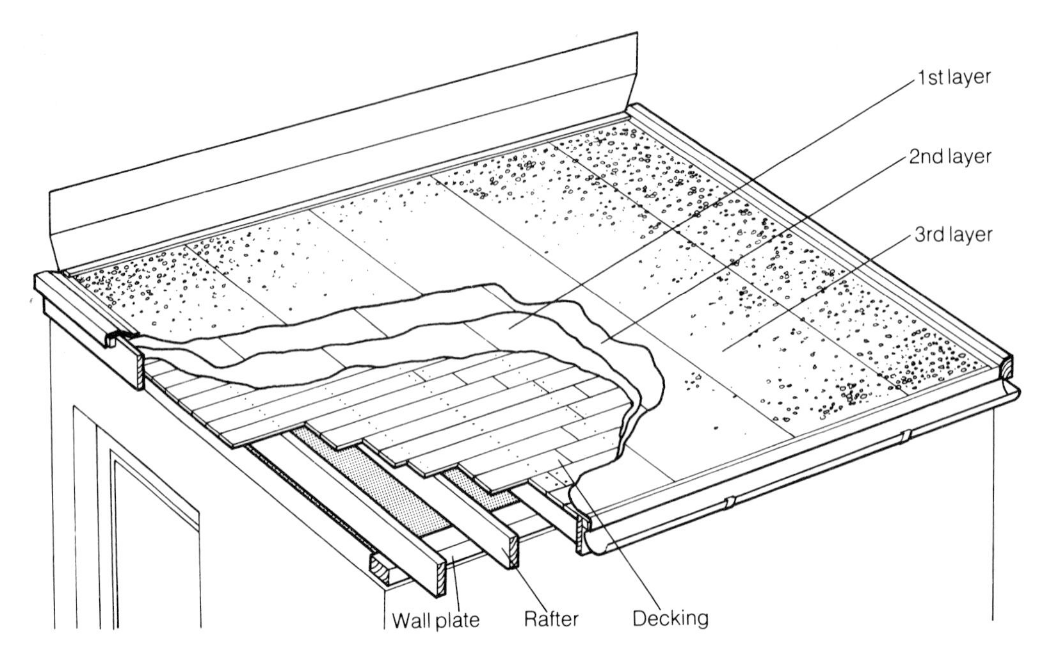

1.31 *Construction of a flat roof*

between 400 and 450 mm (16-18 in). Lengths of tapering small-section timber, called firring, are fixed to the top of the rafters to ensure the slope needed to allow the roof to shed rainwater. Insulation and a vapour barrier are incorporated in modern constructions. For general construction of a flat roof, see Fig. 1:31.

The rafters may be fixed in one of several ways. They can rest on, and be skew-nailed to, timber wall plates on the top of the external walls. Where the rafters meet a parapet wall, or where the walls of a lean-to join up with the house wall, the rafters can be fixed to a wall plate resting on a brick-work corbelled out of the main wall. They can be supported on a joist hanger, or let into a socket formed by the omission of bricks here and there. On extra-lightweight structures, such as garages and conservatories, they may merely be supported by wall plates bolted to the wall. As with pitched roofs, the ceiling is fixed to the underside of the joists.

Access to flat roofs

Flat roofs are often used on single-storey buildings. Reaching them is not much of a problem, and does not require such equipment as access to a pitched roof. For instance, you might climb on top of a single-storey extension from a large stepladder. Nevertheless, where appropriate, all the safety precautions outlined at the start of this chapter should be observed strictly. The flat roof of, say, a modern town house may not seem as daunting as the slate-covered pitched roof of, for example, a turn-of-the century building, but do not be lulled into a false sense of complacency: a fall from a flat roof can be just as serious.

The equipment for reaching the flat roof of a house is the same as for a pitched roof: extending ladder or access tower. Roof ladders are not required, however, and complex scaffolding is seldom necessary, but you will need sturdy boards across the roof.

Mending flat roofs

Most repairs to flat roofs should pose few difficulties, but the complete re-felting of the main roof of a house is a big job and not one to be undertaken lightly.

Just as with pitched roofs, you cannot assume that the source of a leak in a flat roof is immediately above a damp patch on a ceiling. Water can run a long way on top of the ceiling before finding a way down. Climb on to the roof to inspect it. The fault might be a local one. For instance, you could discover one or more thin cracks. Seal these with mastic sold for such a purpose at builders' merchants. If you notice bubbles, these are caused when moisture has penetrated underneath the felt and is warmed by sunshine. The moisture expands, and forces the felt upwards, forming the bubble. To remove a bubble, make two cuts across each other (Fig. 1:32), and peel back the four sections formed. Leave them for a short while to make sure all the moisture has evaporated, so this job should be done during warm weather. Bed the felt back in place in a bitumastic compound (Fig. 1:33). Press the cut felt down well, apply more compound on top, then sprinkle on a few chippings.

Holes in the felt can be repaired, provided that you can get hold of offcuts of felt – by no means easy, because it is sold by the roll. Cut a piece of felt about 50 mm (2 in) bigger all round than the hole. Bed it in bitumastic compound, apply more compound on top, and add a few chippings (Fig. 1:34).

Leaky felt may bear no obvious signs of damage. In old faded felt, the likely cause of leakage is porosity which requires waterproofing. At its simplest this consists of the application of a waterproofing liquid, of the type supplied by the companies that specialize in damp-repellents. A more thorough treatment involves bedding a reinforcing membrane in the liquid. These materials are sold at builders' merchants and DIY stores.

Clean the roof thoroughly with a stiff brush. If there is any moss or lichen present, scrape it off and apply a fungicide. Ensure that no debris falls into a downpipe, for it might cause a blockage: to be sure, bung up the top of the pipes. Give the roof a close inspection for small cracks. If you spot any, treat them as already described, then carry out the waterproofing.

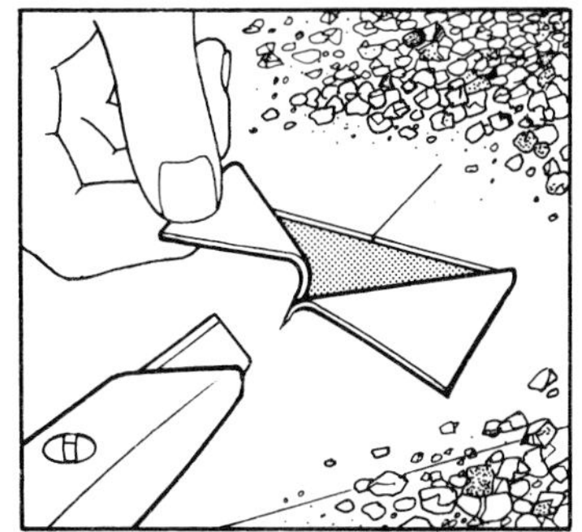

1.32 *To repair a bubble in felt, first make two cuts across it.*

1.33 *Peel back the triangles thus formed and bed them back in mastic.*

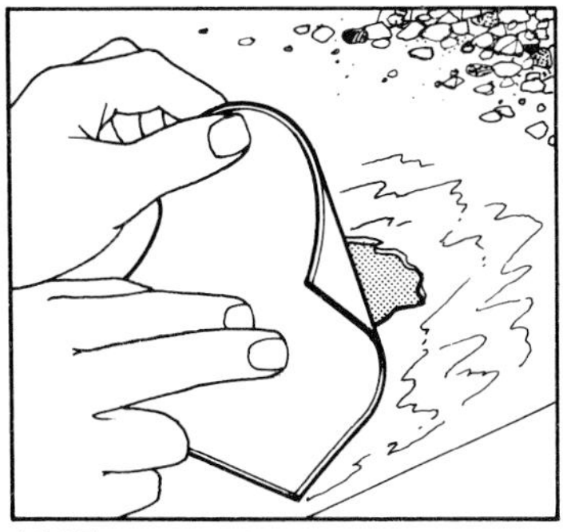

1.34 *To repair a hole in felt, cover with a felt patch, and bed it down in bitumastic compound.*

Re-felting a flat roof

To make sure you comply with local bye-laws, find out from your local authority what type of felt you should use and the fixing method (there are fire precautions as well as waterproofing considerations to take into account). Generally the procedure is to buy the felt in advance, cut it to size with a sharp knife, and let it lie flat for a day or two to uncurl. If you have the most common type of flat roof, one with a decking of planks, the old felt will be fixed with nails. Removing this will be a dirty job, so beware blocking the downpipes. Prise up the top layers of felt with a tough paint scraper, an old chisel, or a long-bladed knife. If you have any trouble, try a garden spade. Its sharp blade will probe under the layers, and the long handle gives plenty of leverage. The bottom layer is almost certain to be fixed with clout nails. Remove these with a claw hammer or a tack lifter (a tool that looks like a screwdriver, but with a V-shape cut in its blade) (Fig. 1:35). Once the nails have been removed, you should be able to lift the felt clear.

Inspect the timber decking for faults. You may have to replace missing nails – there should be two per board, per rafter. All heads, on old or new nails, should be punched well home.

Some of the boards may have swelled slightly, because water finding its way through the defective felt has soaked into them. If the swelling is slight, plane the board down flat. Where it is severe, the board may have to be replaced. Any boards that are damaged, or any areas affected by rot, should be removed and replaced. Treatments for rot are described in Chapter 5.

New wood should be treated with preservative; old wood may need this too. Do not use creosote, because this reacts adversely with the bitumen that is used both for the manufacture and the bonding of the felt.

On a flat-roofed lean-to, look at the flashing. If it is sound, roll it back carefully so that it can be re-positioned once the job is done. Should it be defective, remove it and install a new piece after the felt is in place.

The first layer of felt is fixed with galvanized clout nails (Fig. 1:36). Use 20 mm (¾ in) extra large-headed nails, spaced at 150 mm (6 in) centres. Begin nailing in the centre of each sheet and work outwards, to make sure that it lies completely flat and there are no air pockets, otherwise bubbling might occur later. Overlaps should be at least 50 mm (2 in) wide and here the nailing should be at 50 mm (2 in) centres.

Subsequent layers of felt are bonded in place. Professionals use a hot bonding method, but a do-it-yourselfer might

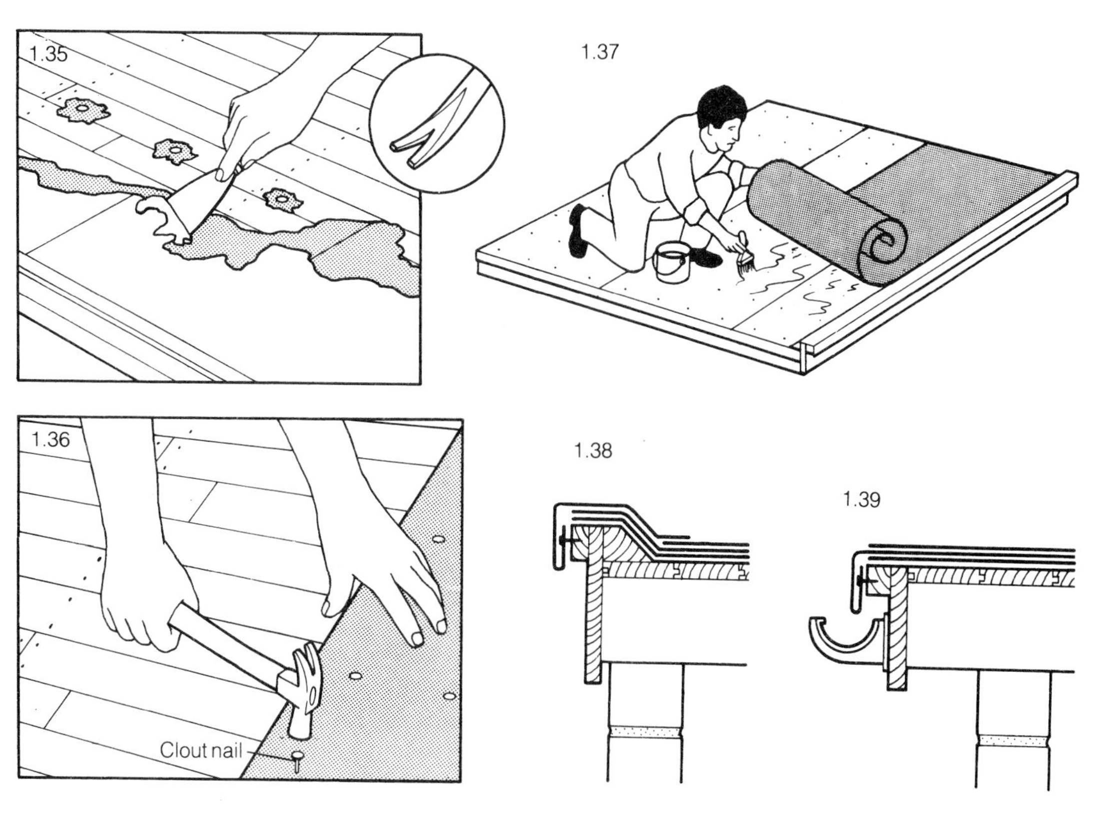

1.35 *Prise off top layers of felt with a paint scraper. Remove nails with a clout hammer or a tack lifter (inset).*
1.36 *Fix the first layer of felt with clout nails.*
1.37 *Apply the mastic to the roof, and roll felt on to it.*
1.38, 1.39 *Finish off the edges with welted aprons.*

prefer a cold bonding method, using a suitable mastic adhesive sold at builders' merchants. Each length is stuck down in two halves. With the length laid flat in position on the roof, take one end, and roll half back on the other half. Apply the mastic to the roof, and roll the felt back, carefully bedding it into position (Fig. 1:37). Work from the centre outwards to all edges to make sure no air pockets are trapped underneath. Now roll the second half back on this first one, apply adhesive to the roof and stick the felt down in position, using the same method. Carry on in this way with subsequent lengths, until the roof is covered.

The cap sheet, as roofers call the top felt, is fixed similarly. Make sure, though, that the joins do not coincide, as described in the introduction to this section.

The edges are finished off with welted aprons (Figs 1:38, 1:39). The apron at the eaves needs to project well into the gutter so that rainwater will be thrown well clear of the structure.

Do not try to economize by cutting these aprons across the width of a roll. Cut along the length so that the material folds easily.

Finish off by bonding chippings at the rate of 100 kg per 5 sq. m (122 lb per 9 sq. ft) of roof. The chippings should be about 13 mm (½ in) across and can be of limestone, granite, gravel, or calcinated flint. Do not skimp on these, for the sun will damage the felt if you do.

Other deckings may have been used on a recently built flat roof. Plywood or chipboard is treated in the same way as planks. Where other materials are used, however, some points are worth noting.

Joints between sheets of compressed strawboard need to be sealed by tape. If, when you remove the felt, you find that the tape has been damaged, you should renew it. The tape, which is 100 mm (4 in) wide, is sold at builders' merchants.

The surface of the board should be clean, dry and free from dust. Seal it with a special primer; do not fix this board with clout nails. Instead, nail the first layer with aluminium serrated nails; or bond it in the way described for the top two sheets on a plank decking. Top layers are bonded in this way.

A concrete decking needs a thorough brushing to remove any bits that are loose, and any holes or depressions should be filled. For this you can use an exterior-grade filler, or a sand and cement mix. The concrete should then be treated with a primer, which will be sold at the outlet where you buy the roofing felt. This seals the surface and ensures good adhesion. When the primer is dry, you can fix all the layers of felt by the cold bonding method already described.

Insulating flat roofs

Insulating flat roofs can present a problem if the insulation provided by the original builder is no longer satisfactory. It is difficult to remedy the situation because, unlike pitched roofs, flat roofs have no accessible loft you can insulate.

You can fix tiles to the ceiling, but these have only a limited effect. In severe cases the only course of action is to construct a false ceiling below the present one (see Chapter 8) and pack insulation between the two.

Should it ever be necessary to carry out major repairs that involve the lifting of decking, you should take advantage of the opportunity to insulate between the rafters.

GLASS AND PLASTIC ROOFS

Besides the materials already discussed in connection with pitched and flat roofs, there are various kinds of glass and plastic roofs.

Conservatories, verandas and many types of lean-to often have glass roofs. For purposes of repair and maintenance, these are generally treated as though they were horizontal or sloping windows. Such roofs are prone to excessive heat loss, and they promote condensation. In fact, the condensation can be so severe – with water dripping down continually – that it is sometimes difficult to distinguish between condensation and a leak. The best way to be sure is to observe when it happens. Leaks will occur only during rain; condensation can happen during cold, dry, as well as wet, weather. To carry out a diagnosis in warm, dry weather pour a little water on the suspect spot and see if it comes through.

Besides replacing the roof, there is little that can be done about the condensation, or the lack of insulation. In any event, such glass structures have undoubted advantages, and are part of the period charm of older houses.

Leaks can be cured. Keep the putty in good condition. It and the glazing bars should be well painted. Make sure the paint goes beyond the putty and on to the glass by 3 mm (⅛ in) in a neat line all round to effect a good seal. If leaks persist, a tape is available to seal off the joins between glass and frames.

Be wary of climbing on to a glass roof. Usually the glazing bars are simply not strong enough to support a person's weight. Place scaffold boards, which you can hire, across the roof so that they rest on the wall of the structure at each end. If the strength of the wall is in doubt, the scaffold board should rest on a large stepladder at each end. Take care not to overbalance, or step off the plank.

Even if the roof is strong enough to support you, do not put your weight on the panes of glass.

Corrugated plastic

The roofs of many home extensions designed as sun rooms and conservatories, but not intended as habitable rooms, are covered with corrugated plastic. This is a long-lasting material, but leaks can develop.

Physical damage to the plastic can be caused by heavy objects being thrown or blown on the roof during a gale. A heavy fall of snow cascading from the main roof could also cause cracks. If this occurs, take off the damaged sheet and replace it with a new one. Take a little of the old sheet with you when you go shopping to make sure the profiles match exactly. When fitting the new sheet, remember that each should overlap its neighbour by two corrugations, and that overlaps between the ends of sheets should be at least 150 mm (6 in) (Fig. 1:40).

Sealing washers may be defective. The sheets are fixed to wooden rafters with screws or nails, or to iron rafters with clips. Such fixtures should have a nail cap and a rubber or plastic washer between the head of each nail and the sheet, to stop the rain getting through (Fig. 1:41). These may have deteriorated, or might never have been fixed in the first place. Replace any defective washers; install them where

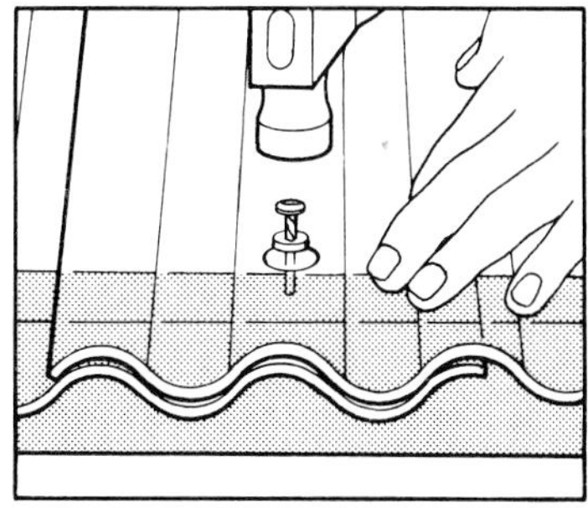

1.40 *Fixing corrugated plastic*

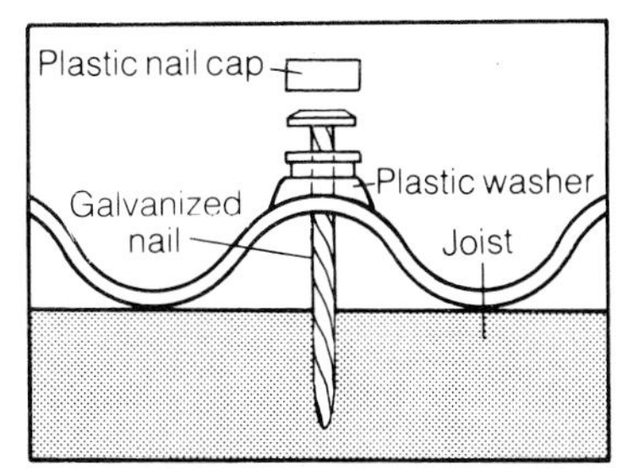

1.41 *Fixing nail, with cap and washer*

they are missing. You can buy replacement caps and washers, as well as nails if these need renewing.
The flashing may have come adrift from the wall, or be defective. You may be able to re-fix loose flashing back in the mortar joint as described in this chapter. If the flashing is defective, buy and fit a replacement. Flashing specifically for corrugated materials is available.
Support for the sheets may be insufficient, in which case they can buckle, causing gaps through which rainwater can penetrate. The only remedy is to provide extra support, and replace the affected sheets.

Chapter 2

GUTTERS AND DOWNPIPES

Gutters and downpipes, known collectively as 'rainwater goods' (Fig. 2:1), need to be kept sound and free of obstructions, otherwise house walls can become soaked and the structure damp. The ground can become waterlogged, leading to damp in the foundations as well.

MATERIALS

Traditionally rainwater goods have been made of cast iron, which is a strong, tough material. It is also durable if its tendency to rust is checked. Unfortunately, frequent preparation and repainting is tedious and expensive. In any event, you cannot paint the insides of downpipes, which are just as liable to rust as the outsides, and eventually, cast iron rainwater goods disintegrate under the attack of corrosion. Cast iron has the added disadvantage of being heavy and awkward to handle during installation. In the 1940s asbestos was sometimes used, but proved impractical. Today, rainwater goods are invariably made of plastic.

Plastic rainwater goods are made from upvc (unplasticized polyvinyl chloride). The material is light and easy to handle. It does not corrode or deteriorate from weathering, and it requires very little maintenance – you can choose whether or not to paint it. In fact, provided upvc goods are not damaged physically they are virtually everlasting.

MAINTENANCE

Cast iron rainwater goods should be kept well painted to contain corrosion. Remove rust by rubbing with emery paper or a wire brush (a wire brush on an electric drill is a useful aid). Another method is to apply a proprietary chemical rust remover.

Loose or flaking paint should also be removed by scraping or wire-brushing, or with a chemical stripper. Never use a blowlamp on metal – the heat will force it to expand and damage could easily result. If you are working on a bare metal surface, the first coat put on after cleaning should be a

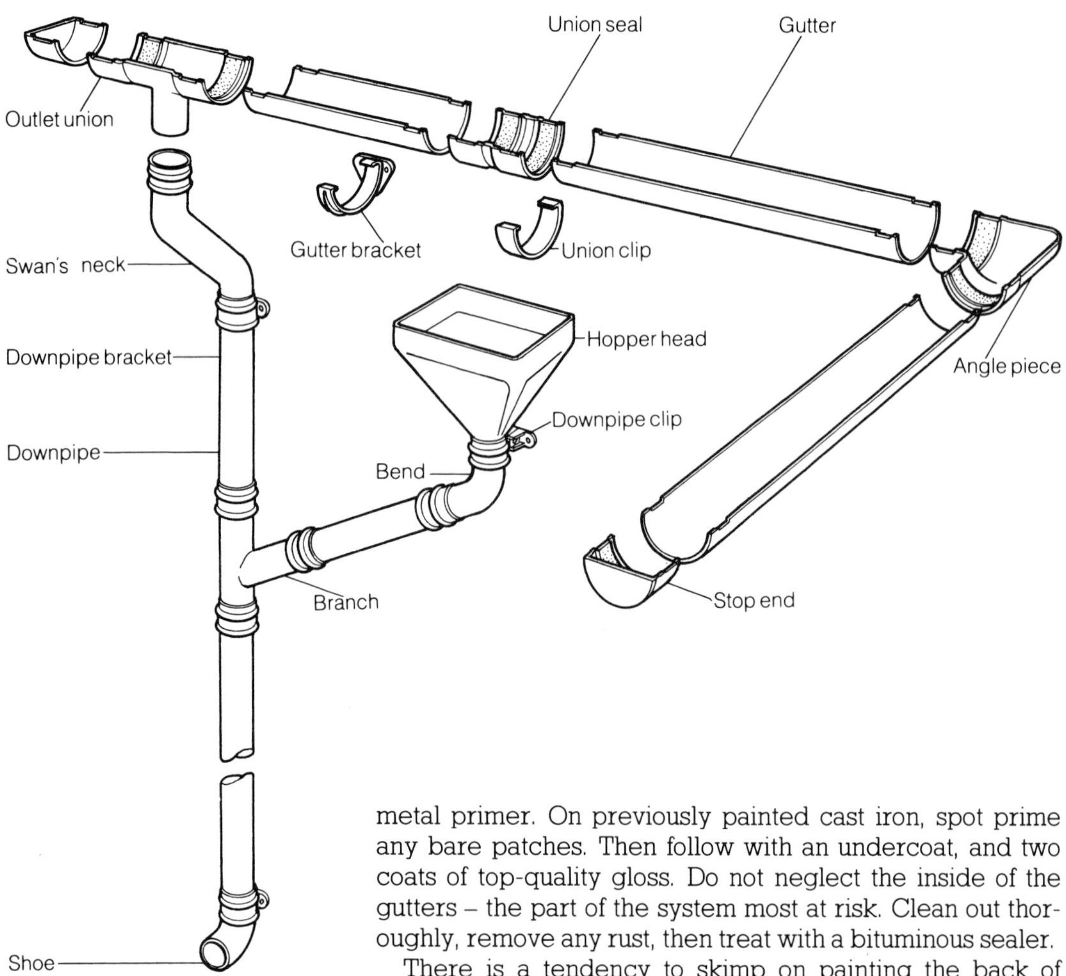

2.1 *Components of a typical gutter and downpipe system*

metal primer. On previously painted cast iron, spot prime any bare patches. Then follow with an undercoat, and two coats of top-quality gloss. Do not neglect the inside of the gutters – the part of the system most at risk. Clean out thoroughly, remove any rust, then treat with a bituminous sealer.

There is a tendency to skimp on painting the back of drainpipes. These areas are out of sight, hard to get at, and difficult to treat without getting paint on the house wall. Do not just ignore the problem, however, for the backs of pipes are just as likely to corrode as the fronts. To avoid defacing the wall, protect it with a small sheet of hardboad or card while you paint.

If yours is one of the rare houses with asbestos rainwater goods, then take care because the material is a health hazard. I suggest that you contact your local council's Building Control Department for advice.

Plastic rainwater goods require little maintenance. If you wish to paint previously unpainted ones, apply an all-surface primer, followed by an undercoat, then one or two top coats of gloss. If they are already painted and are in good condition, one or two coats of gloss will do. Flaking paint can be removed with a chemical stripper. Never use a blowlamp on plastic goods.

CURING FAULTS

Various problems can develop with a rainwater disposal system. These are the more common ones.

Overflowing gutters

One of the commonest reasons a gutter overflows is that it has become blocked, perhaps by dirt, leaves (in the autumn) or a bird's nest (in spring). The solution is straightforward – look for and clear the blockages. If the gutter is of cast iron, clear it with a garden trowel – its rounded shape will fit the inside of the gutters better than a bricklayer's trowel. For plastic gutters, make a half-round scoop in hardboard. If you are working near the outlet to a downpipe, block it off with a rag bung to prevent debris falling down to cause a blockage there. Scoop out the blockage from the gutter, and shovel it into a bucket suspended from one of your ladder rungs.

Flush the system through with buckets of cold water, and then clean out the insides of the gutters with an old brush or a cloth.

There is not much you can do to prevent a recurrence of the trouble. Atmospheric dirt will fall on the roof and, during a downpour, wash down into the gutters. If the house is surrounded by trees, however, it might be worth fitting netting on top of the gutters, to keep out falling leaves.

Another possible cause of an overflow is that a section of the gutter may have sagged, making it lower than the top of the downpipe, so that water cannot flow away. A pool of water in the gutter at one place is often a sign that the gutter is sagging there. On iron gutters, try to bend the brackets upwards to restore the correct slope. Otherwise drive small wooden wedges between the bracket and the guttering to achieve the same effect (Fig 2:2). Fill the gap with the aid of a glass fibre repair kit if you wish. Take care not to flex cast-iron guttering by more than about 25 mm (1 in), or you risk breaking the seal at the joints.

With plastic guttering, it is usually better to re-fix the brackets slightly higher up. Make sure you plug up the old screw holes to stop moisture entering the wood.

In either case, a new bracket might be necessary.

Leaking joints

Water may be escaping where two lengths of guttering join. Sections of cast-iron guttering overlap each other slightly, and are fastened together by a nut and bolt, the joint being sealed by a waterproof mastic. The joint can deteriorate because of age or movement. If it has, it will have to be re-made from scratch. Begin by unfastening the nut and bolt.

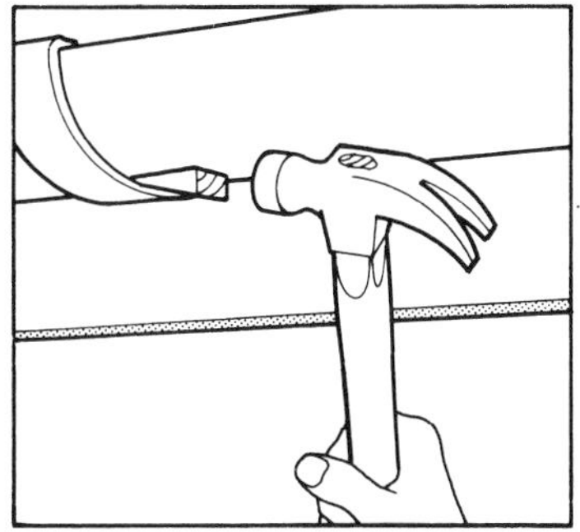

2.2 Wedging up a sagging gutter

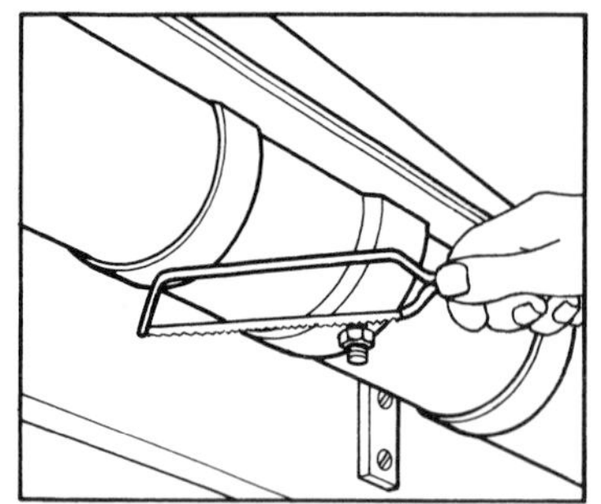

2.3 To repair a leaky joint in cast iron gutters, first remove the bolt (e.g. by sawing) that holds the sections together.

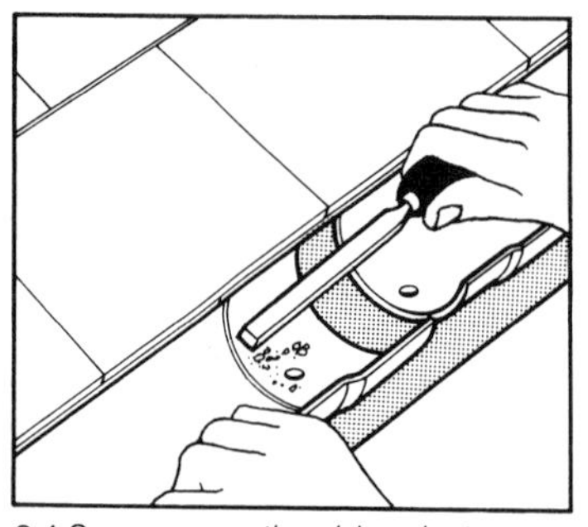

2.4 Scrape away the old sealant.

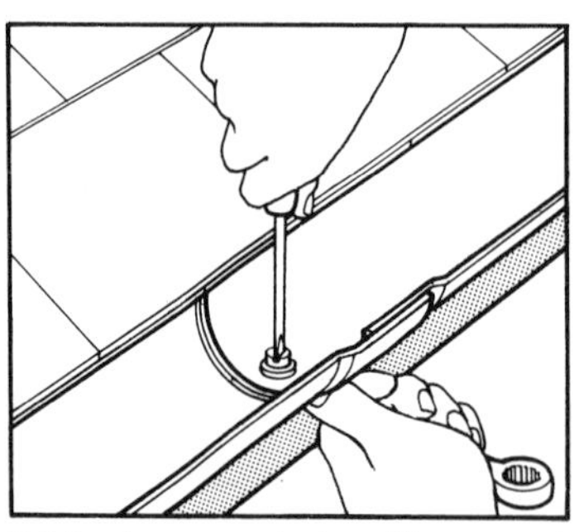

2.5 Apply new sealant and fit a new nut and bolt with washers.

That will not be easy because they would have corroded. Try to free them with penetrating oil, but usually you will have to cut through the bolt with a hacksaw, and perhaps drill out the remains of it (Fig. 2:3). Sometimes you can knock out the stub of the bolt with a hammer, but be careful not to strike the iron with too much force, for it can shatter dangerously. Lever the two sections apart, using an old chisel or screwdriver, and scrape away all the old sealant (Fig. 2:4), cleaning up finally with a wire brush. Apply a bed of sealant to the lower of the two overlaps, bring both together and fit a new nut and bolt, with a washer on each side (Fig. 2:5). Wipe up any sealant that oozes out. Treat the inside of the joint, or even a longer stretch of the gutter if need be, with a bituminous sealer.

Plastic sections lock together in various ways, according to brand. Some have a self-locking seal; others are welded together by solvents. Examine their joint to determine the method of sealing. Renew a failed seal with non-setting mastic, or apply fresh solvent to a loose, welded joint.

Leaks in gutters

The middle of a section of plastic gutter is unlikely to leak unless it has been damaged physically. Mid-section leaks usually occur on cast iron when the metal has rusted through. What you do about it depends on the extent of the damage. Repairs can be carried out with waterproof tape, or even a glass fibre repair kit. Such a leak, however, might indicate extensive rusting and that complete replacement of the section is required.

Damaged guttering can be replaced with a plastic section, even if the existing gutters are of cast iron.

Remove the defective section of guttering by dismantling the joints as explained above. If it is cast iron, take care how you get it to the ground. It can easily shatter, causing dangerous fragments to fly everywhere. Either fasten a rope to it and lower it gently, or carry it down. Always keep children and pets well out of the way when you are taking down old cast-iron rainwater goods. New plastic guttering can be cut to the correct length, if necessary, using a sharp fine-toothed saw, such as a hacksaw or carpenter's panel saw.

Adapter joints can be bought to connect plastic to cast-iron guttering. Since your present gutter is defective, it is likely that the brackets need replacing too. Buy new ones and fix them at the spacings recommended by the manufacturer. Your supplier should have leaflets giving such information. More detailed instructions on fitting new guttering are given later in this chapter.

Blocked downpipes

The dirt and debris that causes trouble in the guttering can also block downpipes. You will know there is a blockage when you see water standing in the gutter near the top of an outlet to a downpipe, or leaking from a joint between sections of downpipe.

To clear a blockage, push it through with a long stick or cane. In stubborn cases, tie a wad of rags to the end of the cane to make a sort of plunger.

On simple, straight runs of downpipe (such as on a garden shed or garage, or even a simple one-storey home extension) that end in an open gully, push the cane through while the pipe is still fixed to the wall. Make sure you cover the gully so that the blockage is not pushed there to cause more trouble.

Downpipe runs on houses tend to be more complicated. For instance, there are offsets – or 'swan's necks' – that take the pipes under the eaves of the house and there are bends and curves elsewhere. To clear curved pipes, you will have to dismantle them, but that does not mean taking down the whole pipe. The joins between sections of downpipe are unsealed so that you can tell at a glance in which section a blockage has occured. If rainwater pours out of a joint, then it is certain that a blockage lies below the joint.

Even a straight run may end in a sealed connection, and a blockage pushed down it would enter the drains, perhaps causing a blockage there, where it would be more tiresome to clear; so these pipes, too, should be dismantled for clearing. Remove the section of pipe from the two clips or brackets holding it in place. It should then be easy to poke through the stick or cane to remove the debris. Clean the pipe thoroughly by pulling through a rag wad tied to the end of a length of rope. To prevent further blockages cover the top of the pipe with a wire dome.

Leaks in downpipes

Small cracks or holes can appear in cast-iron downpipes because of rust. They can be repaired with waterproof tape, or a glass fibre repair kit. Holes in plastic goods should come about only because of damage, and they can be mended in much the same way. A section of downpipe – or indeed the whole run – may be so badly damaged, however, that replacement is the only course.

Damaged downpipes should be replaced with plastic. You should have little difficulty in joining up the new pipe to the existing outlet from the gutters. Take down the existing pipes from the bottom, working upwards, and fit the new ones from the top, working downwards. Details for installing new rainwater goods are given later in this chapter.

FITTING A NEW SYSTEM

Eventually, a cast-iron rainwater disposal system can become so corroded that the only course is to remove it completely and fit a new one. Installing a new system is not beyond the scope of a competent handyman. Try to finish the job as quickly as possible because, for a time, your home will be without the protection of gutters and downpipes. The work might take a do-it-yourselfer a few days.

Planning the new system

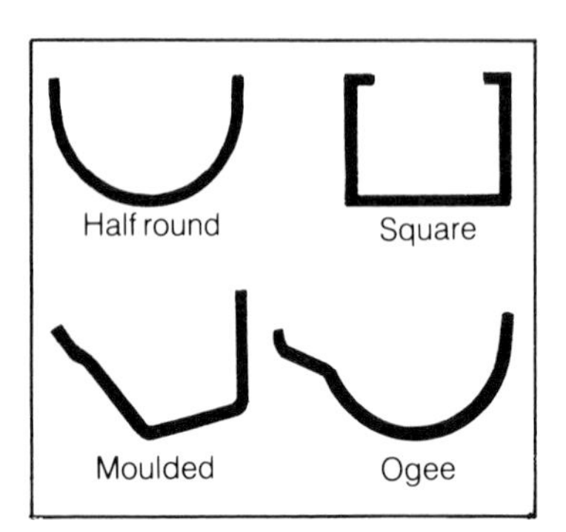

2.6 *Possible profiles for new gutters*

Plan the new system before ordering materials, and have all the components you will need to hand before taking down the old system. Study the instructions, both those given in this chapter and those in the manufacturer's manual. This way you will minimize the time when the house is without the protection of a rainwater disposal system.

Decide on the shape of the new rainwater goods. Plastic ones are available in the normal half-round, as well as square (although it is not exactly so) and ogee profiles. There is also a semi-elliptical shape that is deeper and more efficient than the half-round (Fig. 2:6).

Adaptors are available for connecting new plastic to neighbouring old cast-iron gutters if necessary. Should your system be on the point of collapse, then it is likely that your neighbour's is in a similar condition. Two or more of you might get together to renew a joint system at the same time. This would speed up the whole process, and reduce its cost.

Next, you must determine the size of the gutter from lip to lip. Three common ones are 75 mm (3 in), for extensions and outbuildings; 100 mm (4 in) for normal ,sized houses; and 150 mm (6 in) for larger house roofs. Ensure you buy the right size: too small, and it will not carry the rainwater away properly; too large, and you have spent more money than necessary.

Working out the amount of rainwater that will fall on a roof of a given size, and from that determining the size of gutter required to carry it away, requires the skill of an architect or surveyor. You can, however, simply specify the same size as the present one (assuming that it performs satisfactorily).

Finally, determine what components you need. Choose a brand that can be bought from a store near your home. Bearing in mind what your chosen manufacturer can supply, inspect the present system and try to buy a plastic equivalent. The guttering consists of one or more openings – called outlets – to connect up to the downpipes; a stop at the end of the run (if necessary); angles to take the guttering round corners; joints; support brackets; and the guttering itself, which will probably come in standard lengths.

Choose downpipes that are the same brand as the gutters,

and be sure to use a matching size. Besides the pipes there are the clips; the brackets; the offset, or 'swan's neck', that takes the pipe under the eaves or under or round some other obstruction; and some means of feeding the water into the drain – a shoe for an open gully, an adaptor for the connection to a closed drain. There may also be a hopper head if waste pipes in an upstairs room – the bathroom, for instance – discharge into a pipe.

Removing the old system

Dismantling the old system might take longer than you had imagined, so allow ample time when you plan the work.

Begin by removing the downpipes – start at the bottom and work upwards. The pipes should be in sections, joined by clips or brackets and screwed to plugs in the wall or the mortar joints. At the bottom will be a shoe or adaptor for directing the water into the drain. Pull out the pipes, and remove the brackets. If these are so corroded that you cannot move their fixing screws, cut through them with a hacksaw then prise out any short stubs left in the wall. Do not worry about damaging the metal, because it is only fit for scrap. Take care, though, not to damage the walls.

Most older houses, other than those with a single-stack plumbing system, have a soil pipe to carry waste from the lavatory. Do not confuse this with the rainwater downpipes. It should be dealt with entirely separately (see Chapter 11). To distinguish between the two notice that a soil pipe projects much higher than the gutters so noxious fumes and smells are carried well away from the house, and the joins between sections are sealed for the same reason. Moreover, you should be able to see where the outlet from the lavatory connects with the soil pipe.

Dismantle and remove the drainpipe in sections. Remove the fixing brackets next. Usually, these are screwed to the fascia, but occasionally you may come across gutters held in brackets fixed to the rafters of the roof. In either case, withdraw the screws with a screwdriver. It is likely that the screws have corroded, so removal is not easy. In that case, one of the methods suggested (on page 83) for loosening screws in door hinges may work. As a last resort, cut away as much as possible with a hacksaw, and prise out, with pincers or a claw hammer, any piece that remains in the timber, taking care to cause as little damage as possible.

This is a good opportunity to examine the fascia, for any signs of damage, and to carry out any repairs. You might be surprised to discover how much of the wood you have missed when painting behind the gutter. Take this chance to repaint thoroughly. Brush away all dirt and cobwebs and fill all holes and cracks through which damp might enter the wood. Remove any loose or damaged paint, wash down and rinse; then brush a primer over bare spots. Cover knots and other resinous areas with knotting, followed by an undercoat and two top coats of gloss.

Installing a system

A manual containing detailed instructions for installation can be obtained from a supplier or manufacturer. The general procedure is to install the gutters first – all else will be governed by the position of the outlets to the downpipes. To pinpoint this position, drop a plumb line from the gutter to the drain outlet at ground level. Then mark on the fascia the centre of the position for the outlet.

At the end of the run, fix a bracket to support the guttering as close as possible to the underside of the felt projecting from beneath the tiles or, if felt is not fitted, as close to the tiles as possible. Tie string to this bracket and stretch it taut to the position of the outlet. Use a spirit level to ensure that the string is level, then slant the string to give the correct fall (Fig. 2:7). This will be specified by the manufacturer, but it should be about 5 mm (⅕ in) for every metre (40 in) of gutter run. Mark the position and fit the brackets to support the outlet. Now fit all the other brackets in that run. Two brackets are usually needed for the outlet, plus one at each join and at the spacing recommended by the manufacturer, which is likely to be one bracket about every metre (40 in). Use the string, tied taut to a bracket at each end of the run, as a guide to setting all the intermediate brackets at the correct height, and mark the positions at the correct spacing on the fascia. Use non-rusting screws for the fixings. The brackets are normally screwed to the fascia, but if there is none, brackets for screwing to rafters can be bought.

Now fit the gutter to the brackets. Use a sharp, fine-toothed saw (a hack saw or a carpenter's panel saw) to cut standard lengths to size. The gutter should be cut squarely across its length. To ensure this, place it upside down on the bench and drape a sheet of newspaper over it. Bring the two edges of the newpaper together, and use the side of it as a guide for the saw (Fig. 2:8), or draw a guide line next to the newspaper. Remove the swarf with a medium-grade file. Fit the gutter to the stop end and outlet. On some brands this is done with clips; others use a sealing device, or solvent welding. If two lengths are to be joined to make a run of suitable length, follow the manufacturer's instructions. Leave gaps within the joints to allow for expansion or contraction during hot or cold weather.

When all the gutters are in position, install the downpipes. These are usually assembled from one or more standard lengths and are cut to size. As with the gutters leave expan-

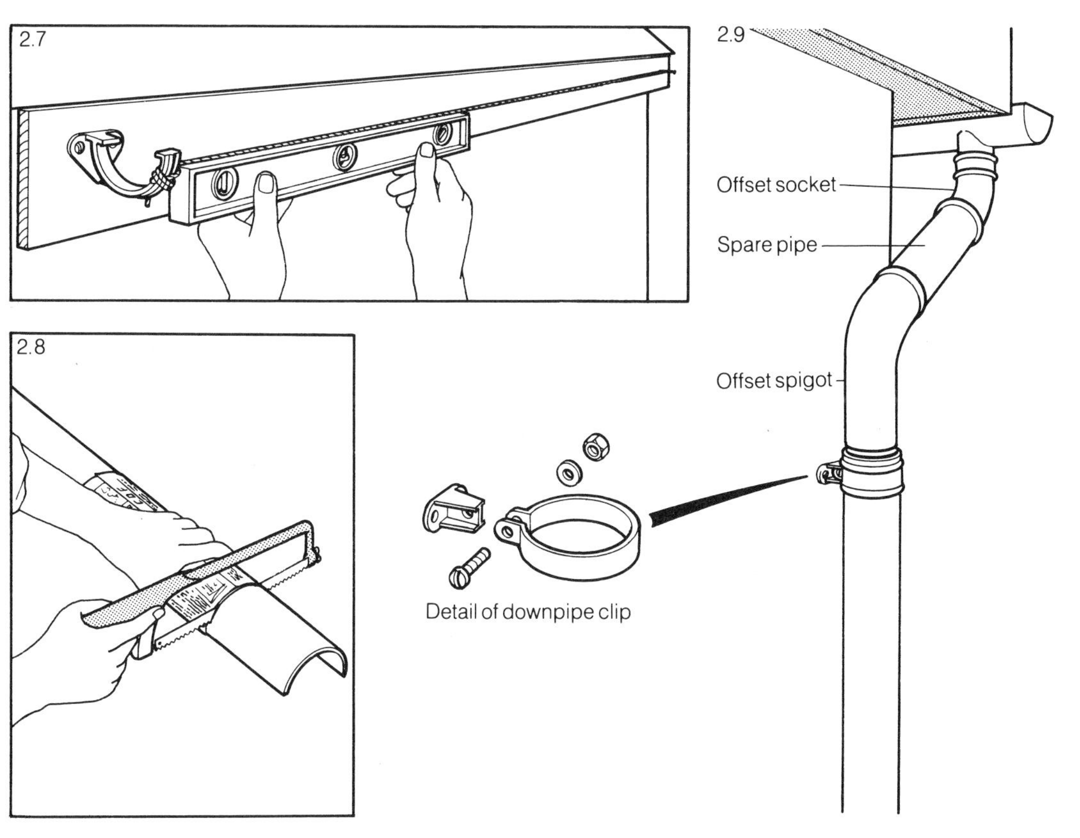

sion gaps. The pipes are held to the wall by clips (Fig. 2:9). Place a clip at each join, where provision will be made for the expansion gap, and at intervals as recommended by the manufacturer – probably every 2 m (6 ft or so). There is no need to drill into brickwork to make the fixings. The weight they carry is minimal, so fixings into mortar joints are adequate. Cut the pipes to lengths that allow such a fixing. Cut the pipes as described for gutters. Do not seal the joints: should a blockage occur later, water issuing from a joint helps to detect its position.

To take the pipes under the eaves, you need an offset or 'swan's neck'. Either buy one or make it from an offcut of pipe, an offset socket and an offset spigot. Seal also the joint between the gutter outlet and the offset socket, but not that between the spigot and the rest of the downpipe. Joints in pipes that are not vertical should be sealed, otherwise water will pour out of them regardless of whether there is a blockage farther along.

Position the fixing clips so that the main runs of the pipe are vertical. When the clip holding the offset spigot is in place, drop a plumb line from it to help you mark on the wall an accurate position for the clips lower down.

2.7 *Use a spirit level and string to get the correct fall between brackets.*
2.8 *Use a sheet of newspaper as a cutting guide.*
2.9 *Downpipes are held to the wall by clips.*

If the downpipes discharge into an open gully, install a shoe at the bottom (a clip will be needed here, too) pointing away from the house wall and no higher that 50 mm (2 in) above the grating of the gully. This ensures that water will enter the shoe and not splash up against the house wall. If an adaptor is needed for a direct connection to the drain, buy one from a supplier's catalogue.

As a final check, pour a bucket or two of water in the gutters at the highest point to make sure everything is functioning correctly.

Chapter 3
EXTERNAL WALLS

CONSTRUCTION

External walls can be of cavity or solid construction. Cavity construction is by far the better of the two in that it ensures a warmer, drier building. All homes built before 1914, and many built between 1914 and 1945, have solid walls, however. The only way to determine which type a house has is to measure the thickness of its walls at window or door openings, for the dimensions of cavity and solid walls are different. In taking such measurements, always remember to allow for the thickness of the internal plaster or any other internal or external wall cladding.

The foundations

The exact nature of the foundations will depend on the size and construction of the building, and the nature of the subsoil. The most common type for small buildings is known as the strip foundation, which is used where the soil is firm. It consists of a trench all round the perimeter of the house, filled with concrete in the case of modern homes, or with bricks or stone in older houses. The trench serves as a 'footing' on which the external walls rest. In older houses the walls may be thicker, or stepped at their base.

Similar, though less substantial, foundations are also constructed to support internal walls and the 'sleeper' walls – brick walls or piers only a few courses high – that provide intermediate support for the joists of a suspended timber floor.

On soft, sandy soil the foundation may be one large concrete raft, with an extra-deep perimeter and a central spine or spines to support internal walls. Such a raft may also be placed inside strip foundations to support internal and sleeper walls.

The substructure of a house needs to be extremely well ventilated to keep it dry and free from rot. For this reason air bricks are placed low down in external walls; below the ground floor, and internal and sleeper walls are built honeycomb fashion – bricks are left out here and there – so that air can circulate freely. It is most important that the ventilation holes are not blocked, otherwise you risk introducing damp into the foundations. If you see airbricks covered – either accidentally by, for instance, garden rubbish, or deliberately in a misguided attempt to stop draughts – unblock them immediately.

Cavity walls

A cavity wall consists of two separate walls, or leaves, each the width of a single brick, with a 50 mm (2 in) space in between. A leaf built today would be 100 mm (4 in) thick, whereas one built before metrication would be 113 mm (4½ in). The gap not only stops rainwater that might penetrate the outer leaf from soaking through to the inner one, but also provides a cushion of air that acts as an insulating material (Fig. 3:1). When cavity wall insulation is installed, it is this gap that is filled.

To make the whole construction stronger, the two leaves are held together by wall ties, which are bedded into the mortar on both sides. The ties are galvanized so they do not rust, and may be of wire, or of flat metal twisted so that any moisture collecting on them will be thrown off and not carried across the cavity.

When carrying out any work on a cavity wall that involves drilling or cutting through one of the leaves, it is essential not to allow any debris to fall into the cavity. It might lodge on one of the wall ties and collect in a pile, where it could cause a bridge that might introduce damp into the inner leaf. This is often the cause of a puzzling case of damp in the upper parts of a cavity wall.

Lightweight aerated concrete blocks, and building blocks made from clinker or clay, are used increasingly for the inner leaf. These are cheaper and better at conserving heat.

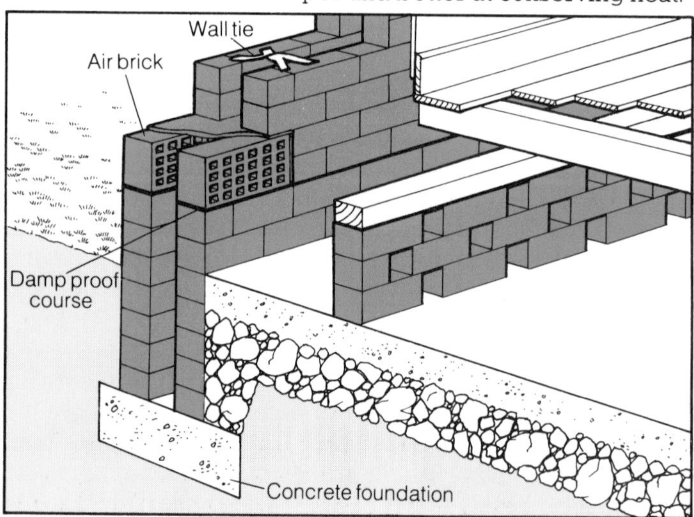

3.1 *How a cavity wall is built*

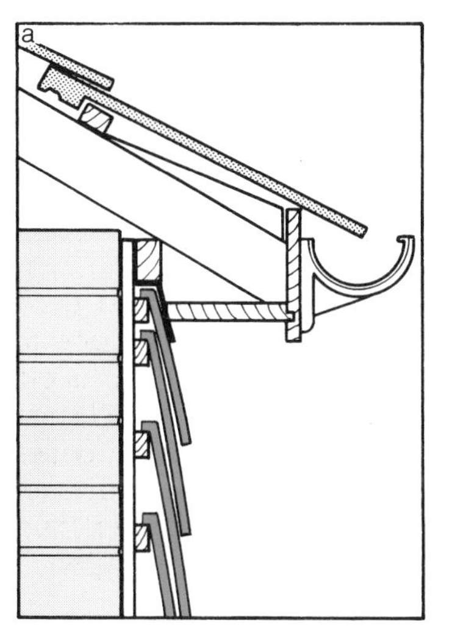

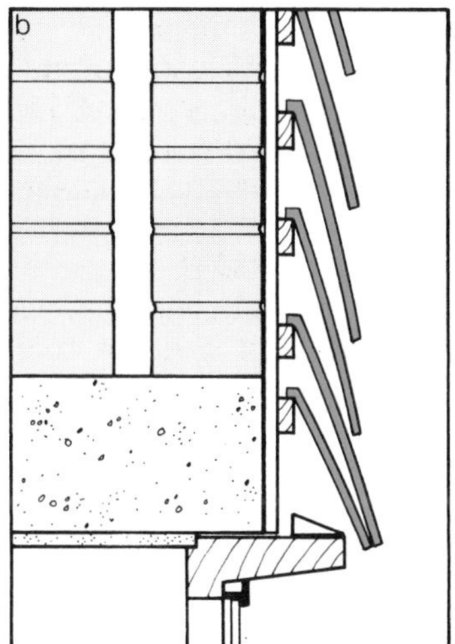

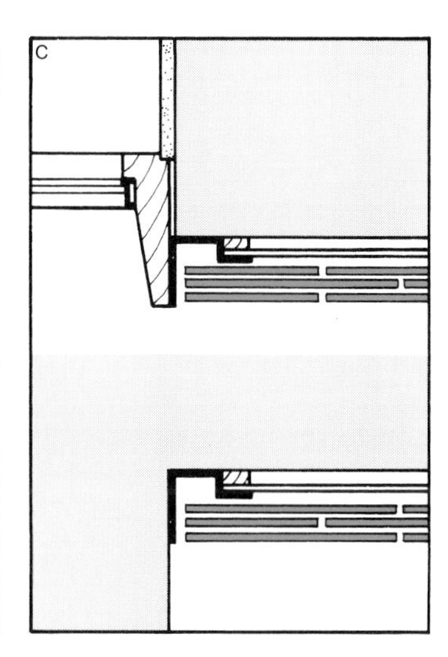

3.2 *Tiles cladding an external wall:*
(a) The tiles are nailed to battens.
(b) Detail, where the tiles meet the top of a window opening (c) Plan view showing how tiles meet the side of an opening.

Solid walls

Solid walls are usually as thick as the length of a brick, about 230 mm (9 in), although some houses have what are known as 'brick-and-a-half' walls, giving a thickness of about 345 mm (13½ in). In three- or four-storey houses, the lower floors may be 'brick-and-a-half' and the upper ones single brick.

A solid brick wall offers only limited protection against the weather, because rainwater can soak through it to the plaster and the decorations. It is also a poor insulator, but can be improved by a cladding of tiles or timber.

If your home has solid walls without cladding it is a worthwhile addition – for insulation and appearance. To add tiles, fit horizontal battens by screwing them into wall plugs, using brass or other non-rusting screws (Fig. 3:2). Then fix the tiles to the battens with galvanized nails. The battens should be spaced to allow a generous overlap on the tiles.

Timber cladding is fixed in a similar manner, but needs fewer fixing points – battens spaced at about 900 mm (3 ft) would be adequate. Both battens and cladding should be treated with a preservative.

REPAIRS TO BRICK WALLS

Many homes have bare brick walls, in which various faults can develop.

Efflorescence

Efflorescence is the name given to a white powdery substance that can appear on the surface of a wall. In modern homes it is nothing to worry about: it is simply caused by the salts in the brickwork drying out and crystallizing as they come to the surface. Eventually it will go away of its own accord, but if its appearance bothers you, remove it with a stiff brush. On no account use water, for that will only make matters worse by slowing up the crystallizing process.

On old walls, an outbreak of efflorescence could mean that the wall has suddenly become damp, so look for and remedy the cause.

Crumbling bricks

On a house built of soft brickwork, the face or edges of some bricks can begin to crumble. This is caused when moisture in the brickwork freezes and expands, shattering the substance of the brick. The condition is known as spalling. The best way to deal with a badly affected brick is to remove it, and replace it with a matching one.

Use a long, thin cold chisel and a hammer to cut away the mortar all round, then lever the brick away. Wet the surrounding brickwork thoroughly to make sure it will not soak up moisture from the new mortar. Place mortar on the bottom and sides of the opening and on top of the replacement brick, then lay it into place, cleaning up any mortar that oozes out. If a matching brick proves impossible to locate, you can always turn the damaged brick round, cleaning up the face now on view.

Repointing

The mortar in brick walls can become affected by the action of wind and rain. It may become loose and crumbling or be worn down below the level of the brickwork. Repointing is then called for.

Repointing consists of applying new mortar on top of the old to bring it to the correct level. It is not a difficult job, and requires only a few specialist tools, but if you are going to tackle any high places, get a good strong ladder or a scaffold tower.

You will also need: an old chisel or screwdriver for raking out loose or crumbling material, and perhaps a hammer to help dislodge difficult pieces; a hawk, which you can buy from a builders' merchant, or make yourself from a small square piece of board and a short length of dowel or broom handle; a small pointing trowel; a straight-edge; an old painting brush; a bucket; and a 'frenchman', which you can fashion from an old kitchen knife sharpened to a point and bent at right angles at the end.

Work on a small area of the wall at a time: you will probably find a square metre (10 sq. ft) about the right size. Begin by raking out the old mortar to a depth of 13 mm (½ in), then brush out any loose material. Use the brush to wet the brick-

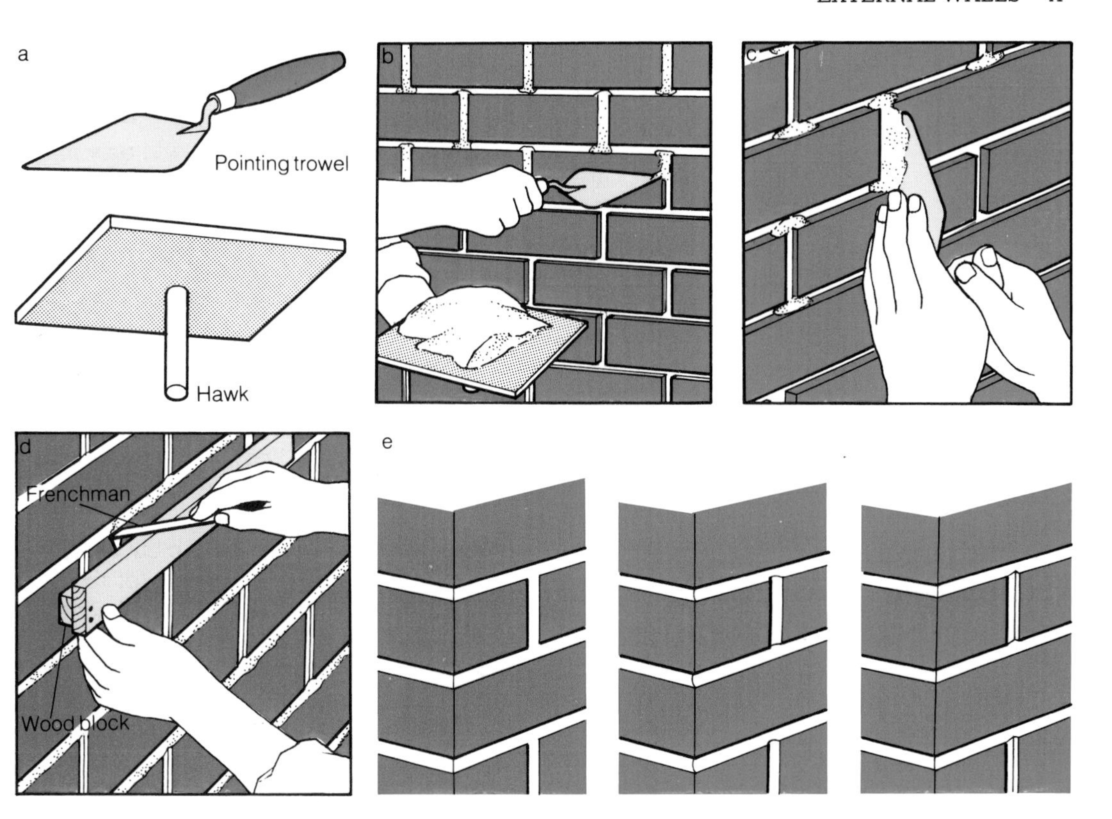

work thoroughly with water from the bucket, so that it will not draw out the moisture from the new mortar.

The mortar should consist of 1 part cement to 4 of sharp sand, and be mixed to a stiff consistency. Place some mortar on the hawk, and smooth it into a pat. Holding the hawk close to the wall, pick up some mortar on the back of the trowel and push the trowel forwards, tilting the front of the hawk upwards at the same time so that the mortar is lifted clear.

Point the vertical joints first, holding the trowel at a slight angle to press the mortar well into the joints. Using the frenchman with the straight edge, chop off the thick surplus at the outside of each joint when a section of verticals is finished.

Next, point the horizontal joints. Use a similar technique to fill each one roughly, then draw the trowel across it to form a smooth continuous band of mortar. Cut off the thick surplus at the bottom with the frenchman.

The horizontal joints must be formed so that rainwater will not lodge in them; there are several ways to do this (Fig. 3:3).

3.3 *Steps in repointing a brick wall: (a) Two of the tools – a pointing trowel and a hawk. (b) Point the vertical joints first, pushing the mortar well into the joints. (c) Chop off large amounts of excess mortar with the trowel. (d) Use a straight edge and a 'frenchman' to remove the surplus at the bottom edge. (e) Three ways of finishing the joints so that rainwater will not lodge: flush, keyed, and weathered.*

Painting bricks

Many householders, when faced with bricks that are past their best (dirty, slightly porous, perhaps crumbling a little), decide on painting as the cheapest, easiest way of covering up the defects. Certainly bricks are a suitable surface to receive masonry paints, but this is a solution to be adopted only as a last resort. Once you start painting bricks, you have to repaint them every five years or so, perhaps more frequently in exposed areas. Bricks are porous and the paint will soak into them so that it can never be removed. In any event, bricks are a beautiful building material in their own right, so cover them up only if the wall is a problem.

RENDERED WALLS

Rendering is a mix of cement, lime and sand (or other aggregate) that is applied to external walls to make them more weatherproof or to cover up poor quality materials. It is found mainly on solid walls, but modern homes, built of cavity construction, may also be rendered, either for protection or for decoration. Stucco, a form of rendering, was very often applied to houses in the eighteenth and nineteenth centuries as decoration.

The main problems with a rendered surface are that all sand and cement mixes shrink, and that all buildings move, even if only slightly. As a result, cracks can develop in the rendering. Rainwater can penetrate even the smallest cracks and work under the surface of the rendering, weakening the bond of the sand and cement to the bricks, and causing blisters of loose material or even patches of the surface to fall away. The damage can be especially severe if the water under the surface freezes.

Protecting the rendering

The main task is to make the surface waterproof, so that rainwater cannot penetrate. Top-quality exterior wall paints provide such protection, and cover hairline cracks too. They can also improve the appearance of the house. Alternatively, apply a coat or two of a clear silicone water repellent. This will not make the house look any better, nor will it disguise repairs, but it is easier to apply than paint, and much less preparation is required when you have to re-treat the wall.

Repairing cracks

Paint will not bridge cracks greater than, say, 1.5 mm (1/16 in), so any larger cracks will need to be filled. You can use an exterior-grade decorators' filler for this, but if the cracks are wide, a sand-and-cement mix would be better and more economical. Small packs of ready-mixed mortar to which you merely add water are available for such repairs. If you mix the mortar yourself, use 1 part cement to 3 of sharp sand.

Clean out the crack with the point of a trowel or filling knife, and remove loose material. Then push home the filler – in more than one application if the crack is big – and smooth it off flush with the surrounding surface.

Repairing patches

If a patch of rendering becomes loose and falls away, or a blister of loose rendering develops, repair it immediately, because the rendering is usually part of the weatherproofing of your home.

With a bolster chisel and hammer, hack away the loose, crumbling material back to the brickwork. Begin in the centre of the blister and work outwards towards the edges, until you come to sound material. Similarly, with a bare patch, hack away all round the edge of the hole until you reach sound rendering.

Make your own mortar for the repair – 1 part of cement to 5 or 6 of sharp sand with a proprietary plasticizer added is a suitable mix – or buy a bag of ready-mix and add water. In either case the mortar should be of a stiff consistency.

First, treat the bare bricks with a pva building adhesive, mixed and used according to the manufacturer's instructions. Apply the mortar in two stages. Place some on a hawk, hold it close to the wall and push the mortar into the damaged area with a steel float (Fig. 3:4). Just before this first application hardens, scratch its surface in a criss-cross pattern with a knife or the point of a trowel – builders call it the 'scratch coat' (Fig. 3:5).

Leave for 24 hours, then apply the finishing coat, making it as similar as possible to the finish of the rest of the wall. For instance, if the wall is smooth, spread out the top coat until it

Patching-up damage to rendering:
3.4 *Apply the first coat with a steel float.*
3.5 *Scratch it with the point of a trowel.*
3.6 *Remove surplus mortar from the final coat with a batten.*

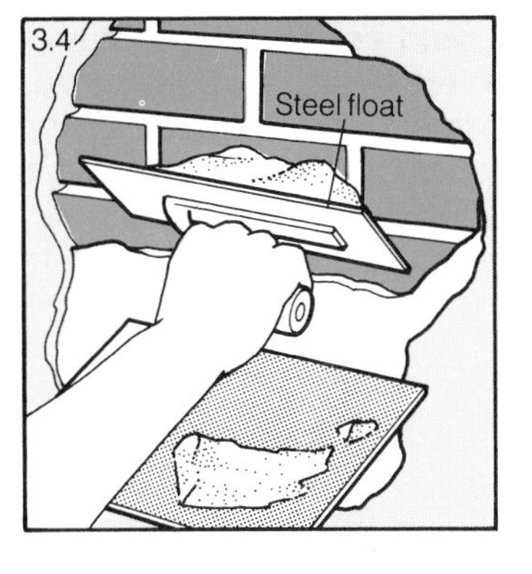

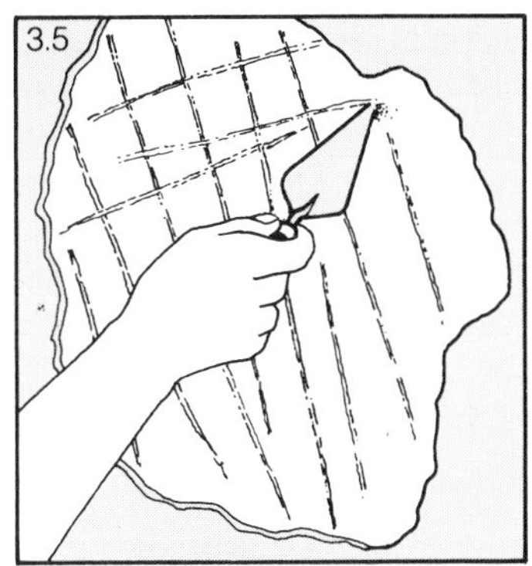

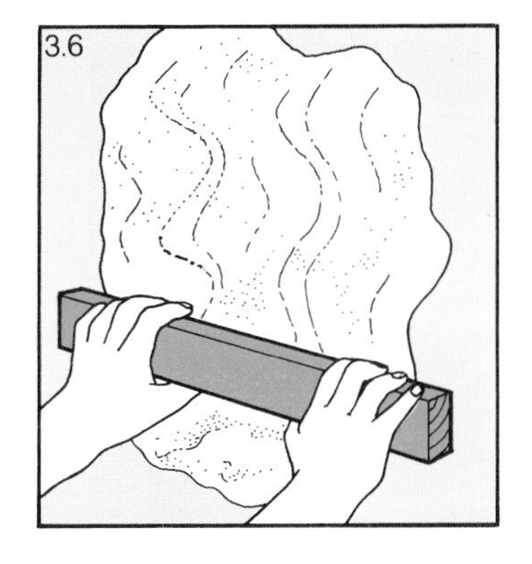

is slightly higher than the surrounding area. Then draw a batten across the surface of the patch in a sawing motion to remove surplus mortar (Fig. 3:6). Leave it for about an hour to dry, then dampen it with water – you can apply this with an old paint brush – and smooth it off with the steel float.

The other finishes you can achieve, which are listed below, should be worked while the finishing coat is still soft, a few hours after it has been applied.

Roughcast has a proportion of coarse aggregate in the final coat, which is thrown (literally) on to the wall as a wet mix, and left untrowelled.

Scraped finish is achieved by leaving the final coat to harden for several hours, then scraping it with a tool, such as an old saw blade.

Textured finish has the final coat worked with a trowel or even an old banister brush.

Stippled effect, too, is created with a soft banister or dustpan brush.

Wavy effect is produced with a piece of ribbed rubber.

Bold texture is achieved by dabbing with a fabric pad.

Pebbledash

Small cracks in pebbledash (a rendering containing small pebbles) should be treated with mortar just as those in the smoother forms of rendering. However, you will need to add pebbles to larger patches in order to keep the texture of the surface uniform throughout.

The pebbles can be mixed with the final coat, or added after it has been applied. In the latter case, carry out the repair as already detailed for smooth rendering. Then place the pebbles on a container, such as a small shovel, throw them on to the wet mortar, and press them into place with a wooden float.

New rendering

Defective walls, especially solid ones, are often rendered to make them more weatherproof, or to cover up faults in the brickwork. This job requires a high degree of skill, and is carried out by plasterers. It also demands a detailed knowledge of the sub-surfaces in order to decide on the preparatory work and the exact type of mortar mix needed. Without this skill and knowledge, the rendering simply will not adhere properly to the wall, and faults will develop quickly. So if you want a whole wall rendered, employ a professional.

DAMP IN WALLS

Damp is one of the worst defects that can affect a house. Even in its milder forms it is unpleasant, but a serious outbreak will first destroy the decorations, then in time attack the woodwork, and eventually strike at the fabric of the building; it will make the place dank and unhealthy.

There are three types of damp, each with its own causes and cures. Rising damp, as its name suggests, is damp rising up into the structure from the ground. Penetrating damp, caused by rainwater (or occasionally by water from a plumbing mishap), enters through defects in the shell of the building. The third type of damp is condensation, which originates inside the house.

It is not always easy to decide which type of damp your home is suffering from. In extreme cases it will take an expert to give a correct diagnosis. However, there are some general pointers. For instance, if the damp occurs low down on the wall near floor level, you can suspect rising damp. In, say, a bathroom that is prone to severe condensation, the paint can be lifted away from the wall by damp near the skirting, which is a symptom of rising damp, but the cause could equally be condensation streaming down to the bottom of the wall.

The effects of condensation can also appear misleadingly on many parts of the walls and ceiling, but this type of damp is usually easy to recognize. It occurs when most of the windows are closed (which reduces ventilation) and after water vapour has been released into the air by cooking, washing clothes, or bathing.

Rising damp

There is always moisture in the ground, even during dry spells, and it can find its way up walls like paraffin rising up the wick of an oil lamp unless there is something (such as a damp-proof course) there to stop it.

All modern buildings are built with a damp-proof course (dpc). It is near ground level and looks like an especially thick horizontal mortar course, with a thin, usually black line in it, going all the way round the house. In older homes the dpc might be of slate, lead, mastic, asphalt or bituminous felt; pvc is often used in modern buildings. Substitutes for a dpc include chemicals injected into the brickwork, or ceramic tubes drilled into the walls low down at regular intervals.

A dpc that is in good condition should keep rising damp at bay. If rising damp is evident despite a dpc, one of two things must be wrong.

First, something might be creating a bypass to the dpc

and introducing damp into the walls above it. The cause might be garden soil piled up against the wall, or a bulk delivery of builders' sand or coarse aggregate for concrete work. A garden wall meeting the house walls without a damp barrier in between could bridge the dpc, as could a porch or lean-to unless precautions were taken. Some wall claddings – tiles or timber – and rendering can have the same effect if not applied correctly.

The second possible cause is that there may have been a failure in the dpc. Settlement of the structure, for example, can fracture it. If you get rising damp in a home with a dpc, carry out a thorough inspection looking for a likely bridge. Should you find a simple bridge, such as garden soil, get rid of it immediately. A more complex bridge – a garden wall, or porch, for example – presents greater difficulties. Although a dpc for dealing with such situations can be bought at builders' merchants, inserting it once the construction is finished is a major task; you might have to demolish the offending structure – at least in part. If no bridge is apparent, seek expert help, as vetting and repairing a dpc is not work for the do-it-yourselfer.

Inserting a proper dpc in a house that does not have one is a job for trained operators. However, there are several methods of keeping damp at bay that can be employed by the practical do-it-yourselfer.

You can inject into the walls a silicone-based water repellent normally applied to the surface of exterior walls. To do this, bore a series of 16-19 mm (⅝-¾ in) holes into the middle of the bricks in two courses immediately above the floor or dpc level. Such large holes might overload an ordinary DIY electric drill, so it might be worth hiring an industrial drill and bit for a day. Slope holes downwards at an angle of about 15° and stop them about 20 mm (¾ in) from the other side of the wall (stick a strip of tape round the drill bit as an improvised depth gauge). In solid walls – the kind most likely to be affected by rising damp – bore the holes from inside the house. Treat each leaf of a cavity wall separately, boring holes from both inside and out.

Bung up each hole with a cork or rubber bung that has a hole in the centre: corks of this type are used in home brewing and can be bought at chemists or home-brew shops. You now need a garden pressure spray fitted with a lance. Fill it with water-repellent liquid and push the end of the lance through the hole in the bung. Operate the spray so that the liquid is forced into the hole. Continue until the liquid comes to the surface of the wall round the hole – it will look as though the wall is sweating – which will take from two to five minutes depending on the porosity of the brickwork. Treat each hole in the same way.

You might be able to hire an electric pressure pump, which would be better than a garden spray, speeding up the work, and forcing the liquid farther into the brickwork.

As soon as the treatment is finished fill the holes with a sand-and-cement mortar, and leave for 24 hours. Then brush the area round the holes with more water-repellent liquid. Leave for at least a week before replacing plaster and skirting boards, then redecorate.

Another method is to buy an interior damp barrier kit. This does not form a damp-proof course, but provides a barrier that stops damp in the wall from getting through to the inside and damaging the decorations. Normal paint and wallpaper decorations can be applied on top of it.

The kit consists of a waterproof laminate, a primer and an adhesive. Remove any wallpaper and loose or flaking paint, and take down the skirting board. Treat the wall with the primer, then fix the laminate in place.

A third method is to brush a water repellent made for interior application on to the wall. It will not last as long as the laminate barrier, but will give some protection.

Damp can also rise through solid floors (see Chapter 9). Treatments carried out on the walls should be continued on to any membrane fitted to a floor.

Penetrating damp

Penetrating damp is caused by water entering through defects in the structure of the house. The way to prevent and cure it is through a high standard of house maintenance. Keep the roof sound, and maintain the walls as described in this chapter. Repoint when it becomes necessary, and remedy any defects in rendered walls. Seal any gaps between window and door frames and the walls with a proprietary sealant; keep gutters and downpipes clear of blockages; deal immediately with any plumbing mishaps that soak a wall; and apply an exterior-grade silicone-based water repellent to porous walls.

Damp in basements is common because they are below ground level and are surrounded by soil, in which damp is present. There is no practical way to eliminate damp from basement walls, but you can keep the damp at bay.

Prepare the walls by fixing a polythene sheet to them or by applying a damp-repellent liquid. Then fix bitumen lath to the walls with galvanized clout nails (Fig. 3:7). Bitumen lath is a pitch-impregnated corrugated fibre. The corrugations create channels on both sides of the material: those on the wall side form ventilation corridors in which the dampness can evaporate. Those on the room side provide a key to recieve plaster (Fig. 3:8). Plasterboard can be used by do-it-yourselfers instead of plaster.

3.7 *One way of keeping damp at bay in basements: nail bitumen lath to the walls.*

3.8 *The lath's corrugations act as a key to receive plaster.*

Another possibility is to build a partition wall clad with plasterboard close to but not touching the main wall of the basement, creating in effect a cavity wall. Normally the framework for a plasterboard partition is screwed to the wall, but for damp-proofing it should be fixed to the ceiling and floor, in the way outlined on page 126 for constructing a non-load-bearing partition. It is a good idea to fit insulation blanket (of the kind used to line a loft) behind the plasterboard, so that the basement will be warm as well as dry.

The floor of the basement will also need a damp-proof membrane (such as clear polythene) to stop damp from rising through the floor. Overlap the membrane and the damp-proof treatment on the walls.

Condensation

Whereas rising and penetrating damp are becoming more and more easy to control, the problem of condensation is probably getting worse. Certain steps may be taken to ease the problems of condensation, but there is no lasting cure.

The trouble arises from the simple fact that the warmer air is, the more moisture it can hold. As air in a room is warmed, it absorbs extra moisture, and in some parts of the home – the kitchen, with cooking, washing-up and laundry going on, and the bathroom, when people take a bath or shower – there is a lot of moisture to be picked up.

Warming a room also causes the air in it to move. As it does so, it meets cold surfaces – glass, tiles, or plaster walls. Immediately it touches them, the water-laden air cools, shedding some of its moisture.

There are two ways in which you can combat condensation. The first is to reduce the amount of moisture in the air. Ventilation lets in more air and thus brings the humidity indoors into line with that outside, where there is much less moisture in the atmosphere. Leave a window open whenever the outside temperature permits. Where the problem is severe, have an extractor fan fitted. In kitchens, fit a cooker hood with a fan, ducted to the outside.

The second method is to turn cool surfaces into warm ones. Cork and timber cladding on floors and walls are warm. Soft, dull paints such as emulsions are better than the hard, brittle surface of gloss, and wallpaper is better than either, especially if it has expanded polystyrene beneath it. The more effective of these materials are, of course, the more expensive, but where the problem is severe it will be worth considering them, if only for the coldest parts of a room, which are the external walls. As a last resort you might install a de-humidifier – an electric device that removes moisture from the air.

Chapter 4
WINDOWS

Windows are not the only means of ventilation. This can also be provided by an air-conditioning system or an air brick. Some bathrooms and lavatories, especially in modern flats and conversions, have a fan instead of a window, but cellars and foundations have air bricks.

The minimum amount of ventilation required in a room is specified by the regulations. The rules governing ventilation would affect a planned conversion only if it would result in a room having smaller windows. For example, if you plan to enlarge a room by knocking down a wall, there should be no objection if the resulting room would have windows at both ends. If, however, there is a windowless adjoinment – such as a store room on one side of the wall – then you might not be allowed to make the alteration.

Your main concern with windows will be to see that daylight and ventilation are all that they let in.

The windows are among the most vulnerable parts of a house – not only to the weather but also to intruders. Most burglars break into houses through the windows. They do not like to break the glass, because of the noise it makes, so usually they force the catch, then climb inside.

Window catches are, in fact, the easiest to open. Fit security devices to them, and particularly to those that are out of sight yet easily reached, such as ground-floor windows and those accessible from a drainpipe, extension or lean-to. Do not think that a small window is secure against burglars – they can usually find a way through.

There is a great diversity of window locks. For casement windows, there are lockable catches and lockable devices that fit on to the window stays. For vertical sliding sashes, there are devices that lock the window either when closed or slightly open – to air the room while keeping out thieves. In extreme circumstances, there are iron bars, or security grilles fixed on a sliding track so they can be opened or closed.

FRAME STYLES

Glass cannot be connected directly to masonry. It needs to be housed in a frame, which is fixed to the wall, with an arrangement for opening to give ventilation. Over the years a wide variety of styles of window frame has evolved.

Casement Windows

Casement windows are the most common type (Fig. 4:1). The frame is made up of vertical sides (jambs), tenoned into a horizontal top (the head) and a sill at the bottom. Larger windows have intermediate vertical members (mullions) and subsidiary horizontal ones (transoms). The mullions and transoms are also fixed by means of tenons. The panes of glass are held in small sub-frames, or sashes. The word sash is used for a style of window fitted commonly in Georgian and Victorian houses. In fact a sash is any frame that holds a pane of glass.

The sashes in a casement window may be fixed or opening. Opening sashes are hinged either on the side or the top. Sashes with hinges at the top are called top-hung vents. Usually sashes open outwards, because that makes for a good weather seal when they are closed. Where a window is divided into several small panes, the glass is housed in a framework of small glazing bars. These bars may be joined by means of halving joints, or mortise and tenons.

Besides reglazing (dealt with later in this chapter) the maintenance of casement windows is as for doors. Opening sashes that stick should be dealt with as sticking doors. Hinges and sections of rotten frame should be repaired as rotten door hinges and frames. The similarity between

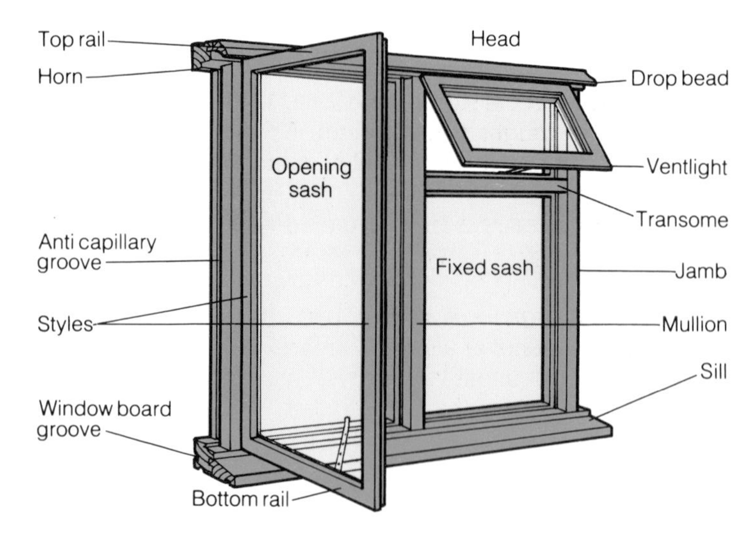

4.1 *A typical casement window*

opening sashes and doors extends even to the naming of the parts. The two sides of a sash are known as stiles, and the top and bottom are called rails. Should the join between the stile and rail become loose, repair it with dowels, as described for doors. Alternatively, use brackets or repair plates. Chisel out a groove in both stile and rail, then sink the bracket or plate in it and screw it into place. Fill the hole and re-paint.

If the window is badly rotted, replace it completely (see pages 77-9).

Vertical sliding sash windows

The correct term for the type of window referred to popularly as 'sash windows' is 'vertical sliding sash windows'. They consist of two sashes which might be sub-divided into small panes. Both sashes can be opened by sliding them up or down in grooves within the frame. When they are closed, the outer sash should be at the top. The sashes are kept closed by a catch.

The sashes can be left open in any position, because they are counterbalanced by weights attached by cords. They slide in channels formed by three sets of beading. From the outside inwards, these are termed the 'outer', 'parting' and 'staff' beads. Staff beads are sometimes called inner beads. The staff beads are fixed to the top and bottom of the window opening as well as to the sides, but usually a parting bead is placed only on the sides. The outer bead is usually part of the profile of the window frame, but the others are separate pieces nailed in place. The staff bead lies flat on the frame, but the parting bead is fixed on edge – usually lying in a small groove in the side of the frame, formed there as an aid to the correct positioning of the bead.

Each set of windows has four weights – one for each side of each sash. The weights are within a weight compartment on each side of the window and are attached to the sashes by cords nailed to the sides of the sash. The cords pass over pulleys in the weight compartment. Each compartment is divided in two by a parting slip, which keeps the two weights apart.

Sashes that rattle are too loose within the channel formed by the beads. A temporary remedy is to place rubber or plastic wedges (sold for just this purpose) between a sash and the beads. The wedges are inconvenient, however, because they drop out whenever a sash is opened.

To effect a permanent repair, prise away the staff bead (if the inner sash rattles), the parting bead (if the outer sash is at fault) or both beads (if both sashes are loose). Insert a screwdriver, chisel or paint scraper between bead and window frame to prise the bead away. Then re-fix the bead slightly closer to the sash, but not so close that it prevents free movement.

Repositioning the beading will damage the paintwork, so the job is best done just before you intend to decorate.

Sashes that stick may have absorbed moisture and become too thick for the channel, causing the beads to hold the sash in a vice-like grip. The immediate remedy is to prise away the affected bead, as explained above, and reposition it. Be careful, however, not to place it so far away from the sash as to cause rattles. Should the sash shrink and begin to rattle, it should be weather-proofed and the bead repositioned.

The other probable cause of sticking sashes is a build-up of paint. If you apply coat upon coat of paint each time you redecorate, the channel will eventually be narrowed sufficiently to stop the smooth running of the sashes. The only remedy is to scrape off, or sand down, the paint to an acceptable thickness, then re-paint.

Pulleys that squeak as the cords pass over them should be oiled. Apply the oil sparingly to prevent it soiling the panes and curtains.

Draughtproofing is one of the major problems with sliding sashes. A channel that is wide enough to let a sash slide will also cause air to enter. The only way to draughtproof them is to double glaze them by installing a secondary pane on the room side of the window. This solution is expensive, but it will make the house more comfortable. You may prefer instead to hang heavy curtains in front of the window.

Renewing the cords is necessary when one has frayed and broken (Fig. 4:2). When a cord breaks, renew all four, because if one has failed, it is a safe assumption that the others are beginning to weaken too. Aim to do the job when the weather is warm and dry.

First prise off the staff bead from both sides of the window – there is no need to bother about those at the top and bottom. Swing the inner sash clear. Cut the cords if they are still intact, but not so that the weight crashes to the bottom of its compartment. Remove any remnants of cord still clinging to the sash. Now place the sash away securely, so the panes do not get broken. Next prise away the parting bead, then free the outer sash as before, cutting any cord still intact. Remove any bits nailed to the sash and put the sash out of harm's way.

Renew each cord in turn, beginning with those on the outer sash. Each is dealt with in exactly the same way. First, retrieve the weight from the bottom of its compartment. Access to it is through a pocket piece – a piece of wood cut out of the side of the frame. Usually there is one piece covering two weights. The pocket piece may be held by a small retaining screw, but usually it is a push-fit in the

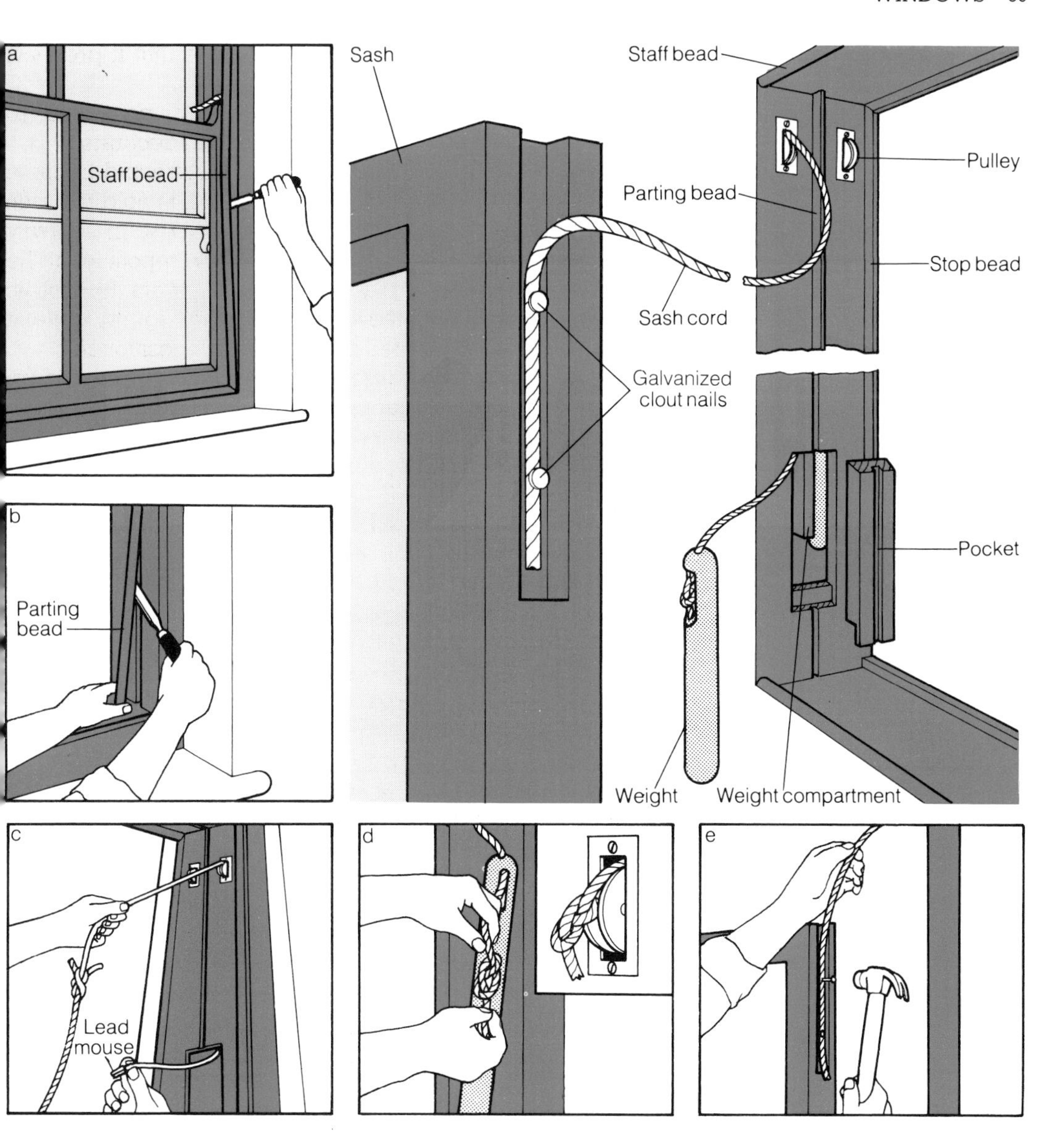

frame. Lift it out by pushing a thin-bladed knife down its side and prising it away. Lift out the weight and untie the cord. The weights are not painted, but it is not a bad idea to wire brush them to remove rust. Remove dust from the bottom of the compartment with a vacuum cleaner.

Pass a length of new cord over one of the outer pulleys at the top of the frame. The cord will probably not drop down under its own weight so improvise a 'mouse'; a small weight tied to the end of a length of string. The weight should be small enough to pass over the top of the pulley, yet sufficiently heavy to drop down into the compartment. Trades-

4.2 *Renewing sash cords: (a) Prise off the staff bead so that the inner sash can be lifted clear. (b) Prise off the parting bead to release the outer sash. (c) Drop a noose into the weight compartment to pull through the new cord. (d) Fasten cord to weight and tie knot at other end (inset) so it cannot be dragged over pulley. (e) Nail cord to groove in side of sash. The arrangement is shown in close-up (top/right).*

men use a small piece of lead, which they tap with a hammer round the end of the string. Drop the mouse down into one of the outer weight compartments and tie the free end of its string to one end of the new cord. Pull on the mouse to pull the new cord through, then fasten the end of the cord to the weight in this compartment. Cut the cord to length at the pulley end. To determine the correct length, pull on the cord until the weight is just clear of the bottom of the compartment. Cut it about 150 mm (6 in) from the top of the pulley. Tie a knot at the top of the cord to prevent it slipping through the pulley.

Deal with the outer weight on the other side in just the same manner.

Bring back the top sash to the window opening. Draw the knotted end of one cord clear of the pulley to give yourself a comfortable length on which to work. Untie the knot and fix this free end to the top of the side of the sash. The length of cord should be such that, when the sash is fully closed, the weight is just clear of the bottom of the compartment. There is usually a small groove to accommodate the cord, and it is fixed in place by small galvanized clout nails. Do not fix the cord right to the top of the sash, otherwise it will not close properly: the top fixing nail should be slightly farther from the top of the sash than the distance between the top of the pulley and the top of the window opening. Fix the cord on the other side in just the same manner, and put the sash carefully in place in the window opening.

Renew the cords on the inner sash in just the same way, then replace the pocket piece. Fix the beadings back in position.

Fixing new beads may be necessary either because of wear and tear over the years, or because they might have been broken during the repairs described in this section. The parting bead is a plain length of timber. Usually it is fixed only to the sides, so there is no need to match it. The staff bead is ornate and, since it is fixed to the top and bottom of the opening as well as to the sides, any new lengths will have to match those already there. If you cannot buy matching timber, replace all four lengths of this beading – it is neither expensive nor difficult to fix. The lengths of staff bead should be mitred at the corners, but the parting bead is cut square.

All the beadings are simply pinned in place. Do not use glue, otherwise it will be impossible to renew the sash cords without causing extensive damage to the frame. The beadings are fragile – especially the parting bead – so drill pilot holes for the fixing pins, to prevent the timber from splitting.

Horizontal sliding sashes require no balancing weights to keep them in a chosen position. Usually the frames are made of aluminium with very few mullions or transoms, so they admit a large amount of daylight. They are popular as one form of double glazing.

French windows and patio doors

French windows and patio doors give easy access to a garden or terrace. French windows are hinged and door-height. Patio doors are tall horizontal sliding windows. They are more convenient than French windows because they do not blow about in a wind and space need not be allowed on the patio or balcony for them to open. They are also much easier to operate than French windows. They usually have slender frames (nearly always in aluminium) with few, if any, mullions or transoms and no glazing bars, so they offer an uninterrupted view. As with all sliding doors or windows, however, one sash slides behind the other when they open, so they do not offer such easy access to the outside.

If patio doors have not been built into the existing structure, installation may involve cutting a new opening in an external wall. So that the structure of the house is not weakened, a lintel must be fitted before the opening is cut. The work is beyond all but the most adventurous of do-it-yourselfers.

For most home-improvers, installing patio doors will be a case of fitting them as replacement windows. Often they take the place of existing French windows, in which case installation is comparatively easy. They can also be fitted in locations where there is just a conventional window with its cill well above the floor, because chopping out the brickwork to extend a window opening downwards presents no difficulty. Widening an opening, however, is an entirely different proposition, for that involves removing the existing lintel, and installing a longer one in its place. If French windows have a conventional window on one or both sides, these, too, can be extended downwards, because a single lintel would have been used to cover all the openings.

There are several points to consider in deciding whether to have the doors installed professionally, or to fit them yourself.

First, many companies offering such doors give you no choice – they operate on a supply-and-fit basis only. Others install them for you or let you do the work yourself or have it carried out by a local builder.

Second, if you shop around, it is possible to buy doors and have them installed for only slightly more than it would cost if you install them yourself.

Third, the work of installing patio doors, even as a replacement for French windows – the simplest of all the jobs - means that there will be a gaping hole in the wall of your house during installation. The sooner the gap is plugged, the better. Preferably, the work ought to be finished in a day. (If it takes a weekend or more, cover the opening each night with, say, a sheet of polythene.) A professional could work quicker than a do-it-yourselfer, and the installation would be finished in a much shorter time.

Whatever you do, remember that the installation of patio doors has become popular and has attracted many firms into the business. Make sure you deal only with a reputable one. Study the advertisements and get quotes from a least three firms. Some will try to rush you into ordering by offering a discount if you sign on the spot: do not fall for that one. If eventually you decide to buy from a firm offering such a discount, give the order on condition of that discount.

Most patio doors are framed in aluminium, which has many advantages over wood. It is immensely strong, so the frame members can be of small sections, allowing larger areas of glass for more light and a better view of the outdoors. It is durable, does not twist, warp or rust, requires no maintenance, and comes in a range of anodized coloured finishes. There is, however, one big disadvantage. It is a good conductor of heat, so will carry the heat of the room to the outside rapidly, making the metal almost as cold inside as it is outside. Inside the room, warm air condenses on the cold frame and might even set up slight downdraughts. The way around this problem is to choose a brand that incorporates an insulation barrier inside the frame.

The doors run in a track set in a timber surround, which can be of either hardwood or softwood. Hardwood is more durable than softwood, and is usually sealed or varnished, requiring much less effort than the frequent painting required by softwood.

Patio door frames made from wood will not get as cold as aluminium, so condensation is not the same problem. Rot and woodworm might affect the wood, and the timber will require maintenance – painting if it is softwood, varnishing or sealing if it is hardwood. Hardwood patio doors, however, are expensive.

A recent innovation is plastic patio door frames. These, too, are durable, rust free and require no maintenance (they probably keep their looks better than aluminium). The only drawbacks are that the frames are bulky, and they come only in white.

Most patio doors are double glazed – a sealed unit is set into the frames. The few that have just a single pane are intended for indoor use. Never be tempted to install a single-glazed door on an outdoor wall: they are only slightly cheaper, and will make the room colder by setting up downdraughts.

Doors can be supplied with safety glass, which is highly advisable, especially where young children might bump into the glass as they play or hit a ball against it.

Normally two doors are needed to cover the window, but three or even four are better on a larger opening. The doors can all be sliding, or you may decide to have one fixed. On a two-door unit, for example, if both doors slide, one must in any event go behind the other, so only half the opening can be used at any one time. It might not, therefore, be worth paying the extra to have the choice as to which half opens. If you choose one fixed door, give some thought to how it will be used before deciding which door it would be more convenient to have as the opening one.

Sliding patio doors used to be a burglar's delight, because they were insecure. Some could be lifted out of their tracks from the outside, and that left no problem about wrenching the rest open. Modern designs have no such faults. High security locks are usually standard fittings and bolts can be ordered as an extra or fitted later.

Patio doors are an excellent means of supplying ventilation to a room during hot sunny weather. When the temperature is cooler, however, for instance during the evening after a warm day, ventilation through a patio door (even if it is slightly closed) can be too much. A better arrangement is to incorporate top-hung vents over the main doors.

Most patio doors are built to standard sizes. If the opening at your home is not of standard size, the doors will have to be made specifically to fit, and will be more expensive.

Installing patio doors yourself requires only a brief outline as manufacturers give full instructions.

Accurate measurements are the most important part of the job. In fact, even if you are doing the installation yourself, it is not a bad idea to let a company representative take the measurements, so that the company are responsible for any mistakes. However, if you take the measurements yourself take both width and length measurements at several points. If they vary, supply the smallest dimensions. Measure the actual opening – not the window frames you have at present, and take the measurements on the outside of the house, for you need to know the spacings between brickwork, not plastered walls indoors.

To carry out the installation remove the existing windows, then carry out any planned enlargement downwards. Install the new timber frame, and fix the sliding channel to it. Hang the doors into place, adjusting as necessary, then seal the gap between timber sub-frames and wall with mastic.

To make sure that the job is carried out as quickly as possible, read the maker's instructions thoroughly and make sure you understand them fully before you start. Assemble all the tools and materials that will be needed. If any cutting of the various members to size – or any removal of the projecting horns from a sub-frame – will be required, do this in advance. Make an early start on the morning that work begins.

Windows that increase room size

Bay windows can be installed to add a little more floor area to a room at minimal extra cost, either just on the ground floor or on the floor above as well. They also give a room wider windows than could be fitted flush with the existing external wall. The cost is less than for a full extension, because the bay does not usually extend the full length of the external wall, and it does not reach the full height of the ceiling – except where it is the lower window of a two-storey bay. In plan view, bays come in a wide range of shapes, including square, rectangular and semicircular. The roof can be either pitched or flat to match the style of the main roof.

Bow windows are a sort of bay, but in plan they form the shape of an archer's bow.

Dormer windows project from a pitched roof, but the panes – unlike those of a roof window (see below) – are vertical.

Oriel Windows are a form of bay on an upper floor that does not extend down to ground level. They are usually quite small, but are not generally found in modern homes.

Other types

Pivot-hung windows open on a central pivot, so that the face usually turned outwards can be cleaned from inside. Some windows pivot horizontally, and others vertically. The problem of cleaning is particularly acute in high-rise flats, but in any event it is something to be considered even on two-storey houses.

Louvred windows consist of narrow lengths of glass, held in a metal frame (usually aluminium) that allows them to be tilted open, similar to the wooden slats of a louvred door. At one time they were popular, especially in kitchens and bathrooms, because it is possible at a touch to increase the ventilation they provide – to expel steam and cooking smells, for instance. They are, however, draughty and the louvres tend to rattle in the wind. Worse still, they are the easiest windows for burglars to break into. As a result they have fallen out of favour.

Roof windows are fitted into the slope of the roof, instead of a section of slates or tiles. They give light and ventilation into a loft area and can be installed by any competent do-it-yourselfer. Various proprietary kinds are available – follow the maker's instructions for installation.

MATERIALS

Frames

Most window frames are of wood. Steel frames were once popular, until it was realized that protection from rust would be a problem. Aluminium has also been used – especially for patio door frames. Increasing use is being made of plastic.

Wooden window frames The timber used is usually softwood, which has to be painted, although in a few expensive houses hardwood may have been used, and the frames sealed or varnished. Even softwood frames, however, often have a sill made of hardwood – such as oak – which is extremely durable.

Window frames are not square in section, but consist of several mouldings. For instance, there is a rebate to receive the glass and to ensure that opening sashes fit snugly when closed. The top rail head has a shaped piece (a drip bead) to throw off rainwater, and there are 'anti-capillary grooves' within the frame and opening sashes to prevent water creeping through. The sill is sloping so that rainwater runs off it, and there are (or should be) drip channels underneath it to stop water running back and on to the house wall.

On the inside, keep the frames well painted or varnished. If you are starting from bare softwood timber, treat knots and other resinous areas with knotting. Prime the whole frame, then apply an undercoat and two top coats of gloss. If you paint regularly, and the top surfaces are in good condition, you can make do with just a couple of top coats – provided that you wash down and rinse the frames, then allow them to dry first. Beware, however, of a build-up of paint on the edges of opening hinged sashes, the rebates into which they close, and the grooves of vertical sliding sashes. If they are painted too thickly, they will not work properly. Hardwood frames should be sealed or varnished regularly.

Steel frames (consisting of sections of mild steel welded together) were very popular in the 1930s and just after the last war. Then it was thought that they had several advantages over timber frames – that they would not be affected by woodworm or rot, and they would not shrink or warp. In fact, experience showed that they are subject to something that is probably as bad, and may be worse – rust. They are no longer popular, but many are in use. The tendency to rust is especially noticeable in the earlier frames, which were protected only by painting. Later frames were hot-dip galvanized at the factory.

The frames are fixed by means of screws driven through pre-bored countersunk holes. Originally the fixing was direct to the brickwork, but later it became the practice to set the frames in a wooden surround.

Rust can eat right through steel frames. It can also cause them to twist so that gaps develop between fixed casements and the surrounding brickwork or timber, and opening casements will not work properly.

Regular re-painting of treated frames is most important. Provided that physical damage does not remove any of the coating it is possible to keep rust well under control. The problem is not so easy with untreated frames. Remove all rust before you paint, either with a wire brush or abrasive paper. (Use a power tool to make the work quicker and easier) or apply a chemical rust remover. Next apply a metal primer, followed by an undercoat and a couple of top coats. On no account should you remove paint from a metal frame with a blowlamp. Besides the hazard of the glass being broken, the heat could twist the frame out of shape. Besides re-painting, the only other maintenance required for steel frames is the occasional oiling of the hinges.

A steel frame that twists out of true needs to be repaired by an expert. Consult the manufacturer. If, however, the frame becomes so badly damaged that complete replacement is necessary, it can be removed simply, especially if it is set in a wooden surround. The fixing screws are probably jammed by corrosion, or so covered with paint that they will not turn. The procedure explained in the later section on removing old doors will work here – see page 83. Almost anything can be freed if you apply a little heat to the screw head – do not worry about damaging a frame that is to be replaced.

There should not be too much difficulty in finding a replacement steel frame of the right size. In any event, minor adjustments can be made to the thickness of the existing timber surround, if there is one, or a surround can be inserted where there is none.

The timber surround will be fixed by one of the methods described on page 67 for fixing timber frames. If this surround has to be removed, it should be taken out as described for such frames.

Aluminium frames are used for many modern windows – especially sliding ones. Aluminium does not rot or rust. It needs no painting, but should be kept clean and polished to prevent the surface tarnishing and becoming pitted.

Plastic frames are, as yet, rare and expensive, but keeping a house in good repair will be easier when these become universal. They do not deteriorate from rot or rust, will not warp or twist and need no maintenance.

The hole in the wall

The frame of a window fits an opening in an exterior wall, without supporting the wall above. Support is given by either an arch or a lintel, and sometimes a combination of both. In old houses, the lintel might be of stone, or it could be of timber and covered with bricks. Timber lintels might need to be replaced after many years but the work affects the structure of the house and should not be attempted by the do-it-yourselfer.

Modern buildings have reinforced concrete lintels. These may be visible on the outside of the wall, or they could be set back and hidden behind brickwork. They are either pre-cast, brought to the site and hoisted up into position, or they are cast *in situ*, with concrete poured into a framework. If an *in situ* lintel is faced with bricks, wall ties are usually inserted in the mortar courses, and these project into the concrete.

A damp-proof course (dpc) has to be fitted above a lintel, and it should project slightly so that any moisture collecting on the inner surface of a cavity wall will run clear to the outside. A dpc is also required across the cavity before a sill is fitted, to stop moisture crossing from the outside leaf to the inside.

In modern houses, the gap at the side of the opening between the two leaves of a cavity wall is bricked up; slate may have been used in older houses.

The wooden sill of the frame may rest on a stone lintel in older houses or on a reinforced concrete one in modern houses. A tile sill, resting on concrete, is also often found.

There are various ways in which a frame can be fixed to the brickwork round its opening. For instance, the frame will probably be delivered with the top rail projecting (just as a door frame) to form a horn on each side to offer protection during transit and on site. These horns may be embedded in the brickwork during installation or they may be sawn off. Lower down, screws or nails can be driven through the frame and into wooden plugs cemented into the mortar courses, or the screws can go into wall plugs inserted in the brickwork. Alternatively, fixing cramps – a sort of angle bracket – can be screwed to the side of the frame, and embedded into the mortar courses.

On the inside, the join between frame and wall is plastered over, and in addition may be neatened by some form of moulding. Outside, it can be pointed with mortar, or a non-setting mastic. Sometimes mortar is used to within 13 mm (½ in) of the surface, and the rest topped off with mastic.

This pointing needs to be well maintained to keep the

house weatherproof. Should it get worn down, repoint it with mastic – the type squeezed out of a tube is the most convenient.

Reglazing wooden windows

A broken window pane should be replaced as soon as possible to keep out the weather and prevent injury. Even if the glass is merely cracked it can fall out of a frame unexpectedly.

If the damage occurs after the glass merchant has closed, tack polythene sheet over the window to give overnight protection against the weather. Fix the sheet to the frame with drawing pins, then nail small battens around the polythene to complete the seal.

A new pane should be about 3 mm (⅛ in) all round smaller than the opening to give the glass room to expand or contract in hot or cold weather. The window frame may not be truly square, so measure the opening on each side and at the top and bottom. Order the glass to the smaller measurement.

You also need to specify the thickness of glass, although your supplier will advise you. For windows of up to 1 sq. m (about 10 sq. ft) use 3 mm thick glass. If the window is larger,

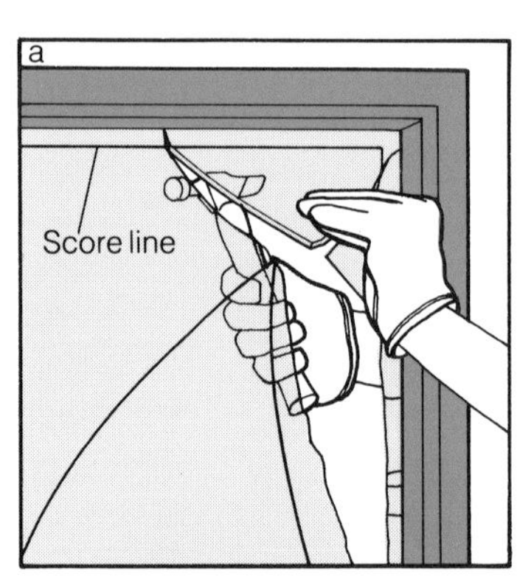

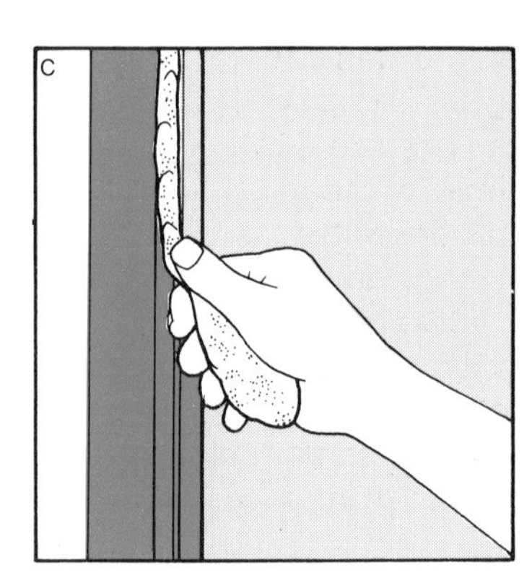

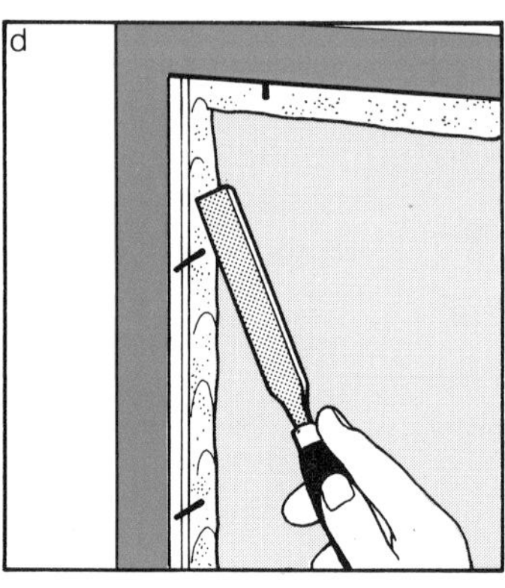

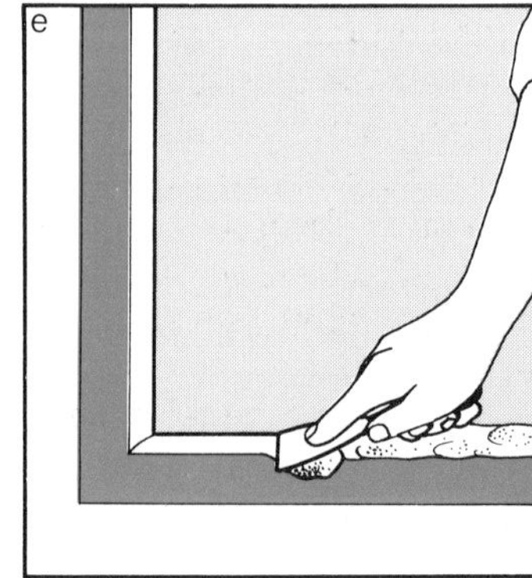

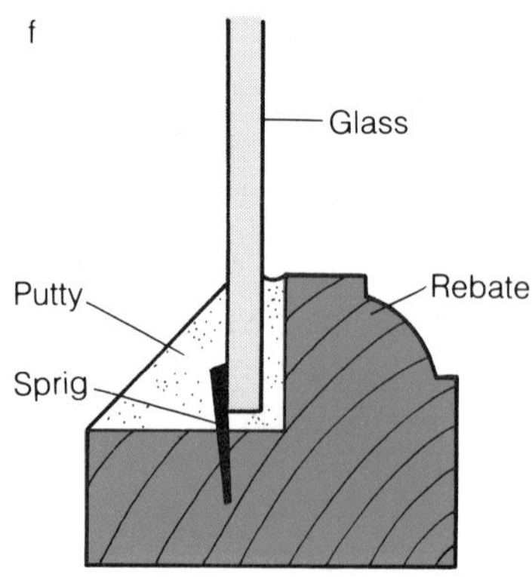

4.3 *Reglazing wooden window frames: (a) Tap out the broken pane with a hammer. (b) Scrape out the old putty. (c) Work the new putty into the rebate. (d) Tap in the new glazing sprigs with the edge of a chisel. (e) Smooth the putty. (f) A detail of how the glass is held by putty and sprigs.*

use thicker glass. For very large picture windows, you need glass twice as thick, but such a job is beyond the scope of do-it-yourselfers.

To carry out the repair (Fig. 4:3), remove the damaged glass. Always wear protective gloves. One of the safest ways of taking out the old pane is to score it with a glass-cutter on all four sides about 25 mm (1 in) away from the edge. If the window is hinged, open it fully and tap out the broken bits from one side with a hammer, pulling them away with gloved hands on the other. If the window is fixed, work from the inside, tapping out the glass, but trying to hold it so that it doesn't fall away dangerously. This is particularly important on an upstairs window.

Score the border of glass that remains, then tap it to break out the sections. Lever out the short stubs of glass that are left. With an old chisel, scrape out the putty from the rebate, then use pincers to remove the glazing sprigs. Dust out the rebate, and coat with a wood priming paint.

Take a handful of putty and knead it into a pliable ball, then work it into the rebate with your thumb. Place the glass in the rebate, and press it gently into position. To prevent the glass from breaking, press it at the edges, never in the centre. Fix glazing sprigs to hold the glass into place. Tap them into the wood with the side of the chisel, taking care not to damage the glass. Press putty on the outside of the glass and smooth it down with a putty knife. Make sure the line where the putty meets the glass lies slightly below the level of the rebate, so that the putty will not be visible from inside. Mitre the corners neatly. On the inside of the room, trim off any surplus putty.

Seal off all round the putty outside by brushing it gently with a damp brush. Clean the pane. The putty should take about a week to harden, then it can be painted. The paint should stray on to the glass by about 3 mm (⅛ in) to weatherproof the putty.

Reglazing metal windows

The technique is similar to the method for wooden ones, except that wire clips are used to retain the glass instead of glazing sprigs (Fig. 4:4). It is important to use a putty that is suitable for the frame. Ordinary putty is based on linseed oil, and it dries out and hardens as the oil is absorbed into the timbers. Metal frames cannot absorb moisture, so the putty must be self-hardening. Dual-purpose putty (suitable for either wood or metal) is available.

The wire clips are fitted into holes in the metal frame. There is no need to insert a clip into every hole – three or four on each edge are usually adequate. The clips are available from glass merchants.

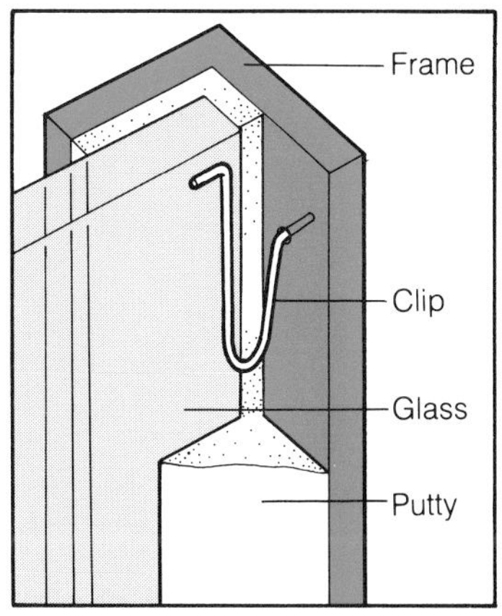

4.4 Wire clips used in glazing metal frames

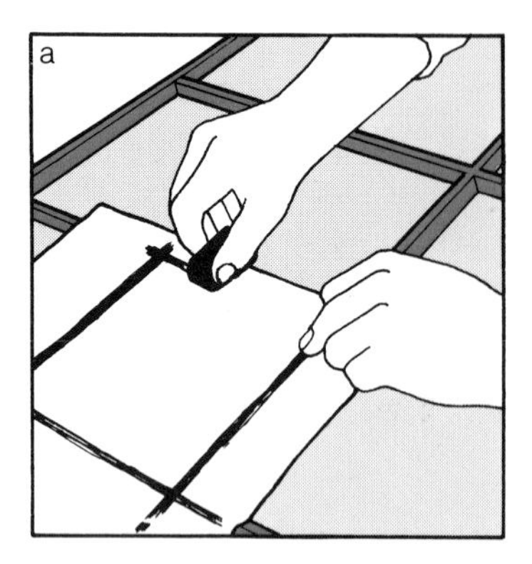

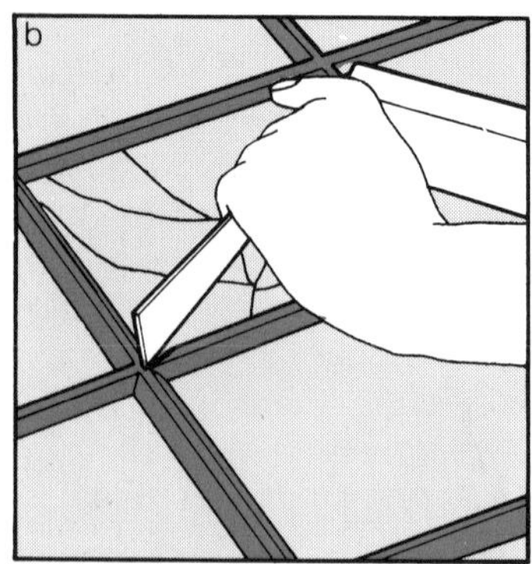

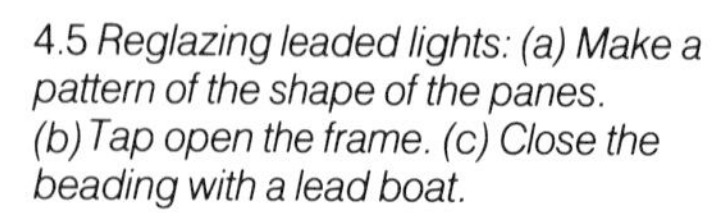
4.5 *Reglazing leaded lights: (a) Make a pattern of the shape of the panes. (b) Tap open the frame. (c) Close the beading with a lead boat.*

Reglazing leaded lights

Leaded lights require great care, because they are delicate and can easily be damaged. As a precatuion, cut a sheet of hardboard or thin plywood, and ask a helper to hold it against the back of the window while you work on it. An opening window should be taken down, and placed on a workbench. Support the back of the window with blocks of wood.

If the panes are not a regular shape, give the glazier a pattern with your order. To make this, place a sheet of paper flat over the broken piece, and take a rubbing of the lead pattern. Have the new glass ready before proceeding further (Fig. 4:5).

Gently tap open the mitred corners of the lead framing, with a putty knife or old chisel. Lever open the rest of the beading, using the broken pieces of glass still in it. Clean out the old putty.

The new pane should have its sharp corners nipped off – something the glazier might do for you. If not, remove them with the tip of a pair of pliers. Nip small pieces only so you do not break the pane. Close the beading so that it is parallel to the glass, but not touching. Glaziers use a wooden tool, called a lead boat (because at one end it is shaped like the bow of a boat) but you can make do with a scrap of wood. Take some putty suitable for metal, darkening it if possible with black lead powder. Push it into the gap between beading and glass on both sides, smoothing it off neatly.

The sill

Wooden window sills are among the parts of a house most vulnerable to the weather. If they are not well protected with paint or varnish they will rot. Small patches of rot are easy to repair. Deal with them instantly to prevent them spreading. Test for rot by pushing a sharp knife or other tool into the sill. The tool will meet resistance in sound timber, but pass easily through rotted wood.

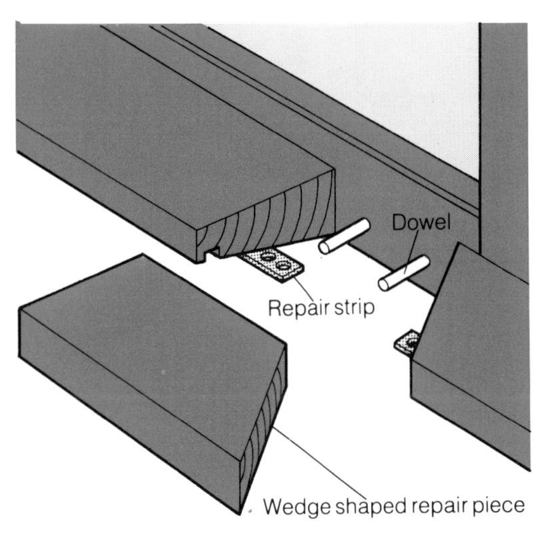

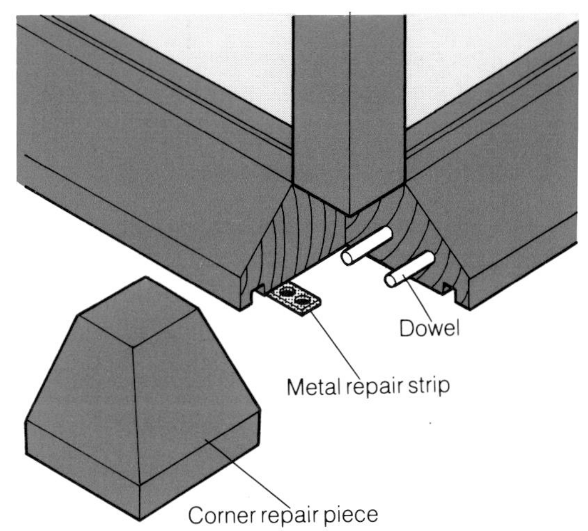

4.6 *Fixing new timber to a damaged sill in the middle and at the corner.*

Begin by cutting out the rotted section. Cut well into sound wood on each side to form a wedge-shaped section. Burn the rotted timbers. To repair modern sills, you may be able to buy a matching piece of standard sill moulding. For older sills, it might be necessary to plane down a piece of square timber to match. Remember that drip channels will need to be cut into the section (see below).

Brush wood preservative well into the cleaned edge of the sill and soak the replacement piece in it thoroughly.

Fix the new timber into place with dowels driven into the sill (Fig. 4:6). You need two dowels, no matter how small the repair, and extra dowels at 100 mm (4 in) intervals for longer pieces. To strengthen the repair, fix steel strips to the underneath of the sill. Corners can be repaired similarly.

Concrete sills can be repaired, too. Fill small cracks with a decorator's filler suitable for outdoor use. Paint the sill with either a masonry or gloss paint to conceal the repair.

Large holes and cracks should be filled with cement; buy a small bag from a DIY store. First, though, treat the crack with a pva building adhesive, and add some of the adhesive to the mortar to make it more workable, as recommended in the adhesive instructions.

A deep hole is best filled in two stages. Smooth the finishing coat down flush with the edge of the sill, then disguise the repair with paint.

A framework is required if a concrete sill needs extensive repair. Make it of stout timber at least 25 mm (1 in) thick. Hold the formwork in place by nailing it to blocks of wood fixed to the wall with masonry nails (Fig. 4:7).

Drip channels prevent rainwater from running over and under a sill back on to the wall under the window opening. The drenching that results could cause the foundations or

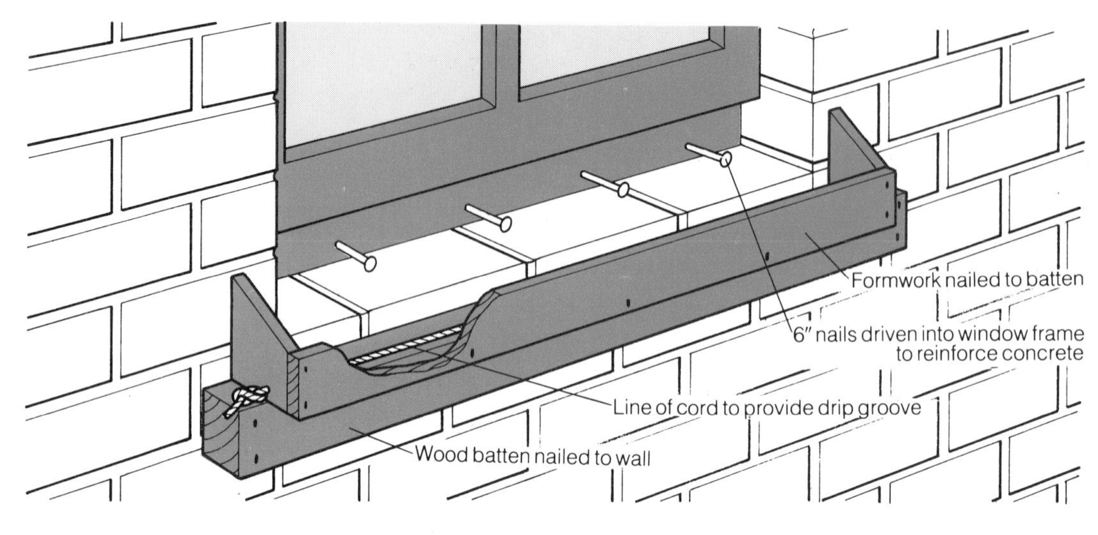

4.7 The formwork for extensive repairs to a damaged concrete sill

the interior of the house to become damp. Drenching is to be avoided especially under a window opening, where it could be conducted to the frames and eventually cause them to rot. One or more grooves formed, during manufacture, into the underside of a timber sill or moulded into a concrete one will prevent the rainwater reaching the wall, causing it to drip harmlessly off on to the ground instead.

It is important to keep drip channels clean, otherwise they will not function effectively. Dirt and spiders' webs tend to gather there, so scrape or brush them out regularly.

If there are no drip channels under your sill, it is worth fitting them. Using a router, you could cut out a couple of grooves in a timber sill while it is *in situ*. This, however, is not an easy task. An alternative that works just as well as a groove is to glue and pin a couple of lengths of half-round moulding underneath the sill (Fig. 4:8). A gap between the mouldings forms an effective groove. On concrete, merely glue the moulding into place.

Sill
Pin
Half-round moulding

4.8 Half-round moulding forming a drip channel under a timber sill

DOUBLE GLAZING

The commonest reason for installing double glazing is as a means of insulation. The cost can be recouped in reduced fuel bills. The 'pay-back time' – the time taken for reduced fuel bills to equal the cost of the system – is complicated by inflation, but it can be reckoned in years, rather than months.

At its best, double glazing can reduce the amount of heat lost through windows by half. In most homes, with average-sized window panes, however, the amount of heat lost through the windows is significantly less than the amount that escapes through an uninsulated roof, say, or badly built walls. So, unless you live in a house with enormous windows, you are unlikely to save at best any more than ten per cent of your fuel costs. When compared with the cost of double glazing, a mere ten per cent of fuel bills seems a meagre saving, but sound-proofing and cost saving are not the only reasons for double glazing.

Double glazing can add to the comfort of your home by cutting out downdraughts. These are produced as air is warmed and rises towards the ceiling, then cools and falls back towards the floor. This movement will always occur when there are areas of air of different temperatures in a room. A pane of glass in a window is like a large cold panel in the room. It will cool the air around it and cause it to move. The cold air from the glass can have the same effect as draughts entering through gaps between the edges of the frame and walls. Double glazing, because it makes the windows warmer, helps to eliminate such draughts, and make agreeable parts of the room that hitherto were too cold.

How double glazing works

Glass is a good conductor of heat – it conducts warmth rapidly from inside your home to the outside. By installing thicker glass you would reduce the flow of heat only slightly, but double glazing is a better alternative. It consists of two panes of glass between which air is enclosed. The insulation is improved if the enclosed air is rarefied – forming a weak vacuum. The amount of air – the spacing between the two panes – is important. The ideal is 19 mm (¾ in). A smaller gap would allow even rarefied air to conduct the warmth away. You can increase the gap without causing too much loss of heat, but beyond a certain limit movement of air inside it will negate the insulating effect.

Types of double glazing

There are various ways, in domestic situations, of providing insulation with two panes of glass. A 'sealed unit' of insulating glass is made in a factory. It consists of two panes of glass sealed hermetically during manufacture, with a gap between them (Fig. 4:9). The gap between the two panes is formed by a strip of metal or plastic, or the pane may be fused together. The double pane of glass permits the heat from the sun to enter a room, but stops it from getting out. The unit takes the place of an ordinary pane of glass. If the rebate of an existing window frame is not deep enough to take a sealed unit, you can get a stepped unit, which is thinner at the edges.

Sealed-unit double glazing works extremely well, because there can be no movement of air between the glass. Moreover, it is never dismantled, so it involves no more

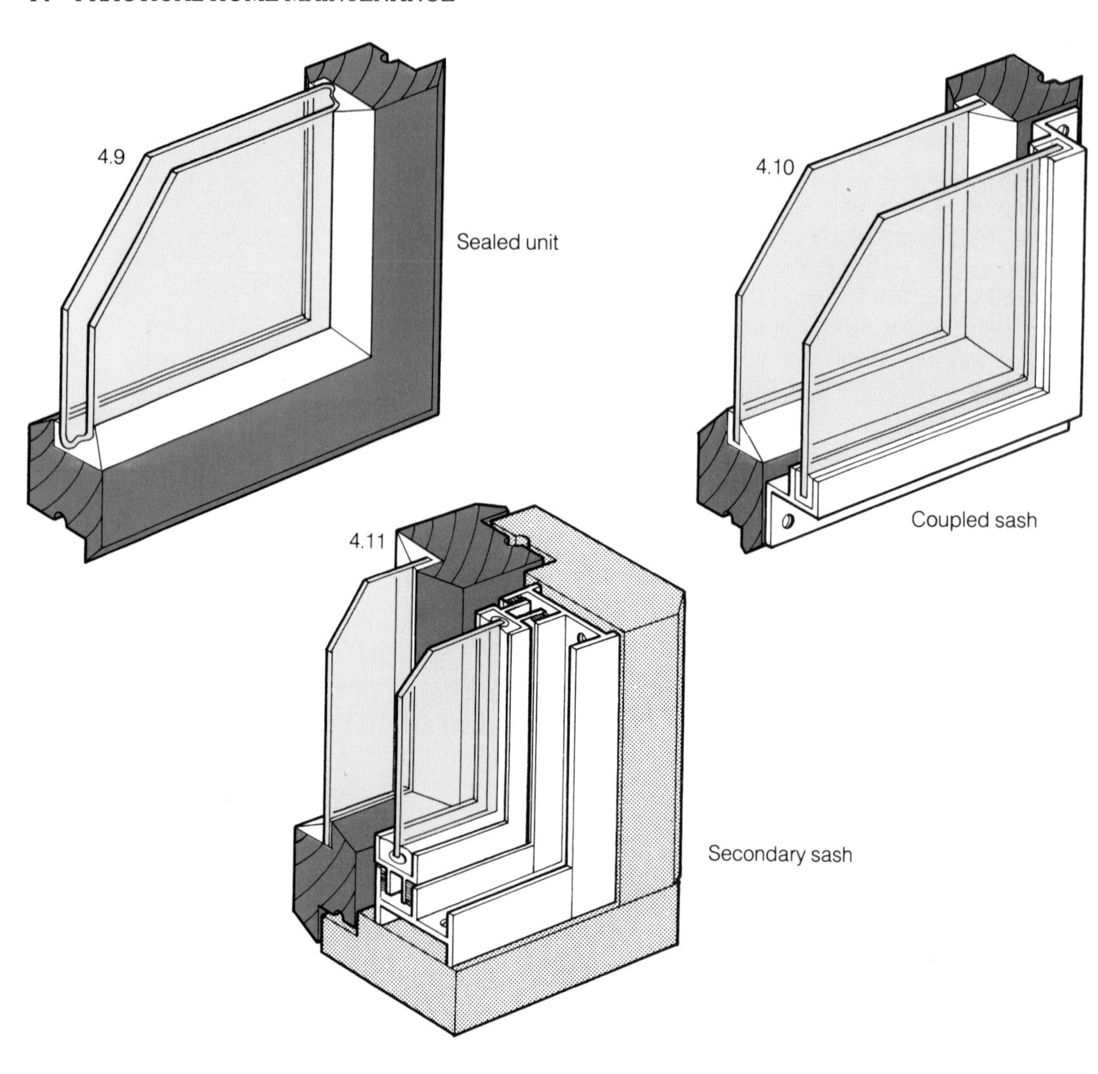

4.9 – 4.11 *Types of double glazing.*

window cleaning than does a single pane. It is also virtually unnoticeable. Make sure, however, that any gaps between the frame and the surrounding wall are sealed, and that opening sashes fit well so that draughts are not admitted.

The overwhelming disadvantage of sealed-unit double glazing is its cost. If you are building a house – or even just an extension – then plan to have standard units to simplify the job. The greatest expense is incurred when you have to order non-standard sizes for an existing window opening. Sealed units are not suitable for certain types of period architecture.

In existing locations, it is usual to fix one of the other types of double glazing – 'coupled sash' or 'secondary sash'. These two are similar, and many people group them under the same general heading. The coupled sash (Fig. 4:10) consists of an extra pane attached to each of the sashes already in the window, which might be either fixed or opening. Secondary sash is a separate installation of windows just inside the existing ones (Fig. 4:11). The secondary sash can comprise both fixed or opening sashes, but usually it consists of a series of horizontal sliding sashes – much like small patio doors.

Aluminium or plastic strip is used to hold coupled sashes in place (they may be screwed, clipped or hinged to the main frame) and to form the frames of secondary sashes. There should be no gaps between the channel holding secondary sashes and the surrounding window opening.

Secondary sashes can block off any draughts coming through the gaps round opening sashes and between the wall and the frame of existing windows. Even so, such draughts would set up movement of air in the gap between the two panes, and reduce the effectiveness of the air as an insulator, so always eliminate draughts before you install double glazing, instead of expecting double glazing to block them off.

A disadvantage with both coupled and secondary sashes is that they increase the amount of window area to be cleaned.

Coupled and secondary sash double glazing can be bought from a company that supplies and fits them. They will send a representative to measure the opening and estimate the cost of the job. The sashes will then be assembled to fit the window, as with patio doors. Remember to investigate what several suppliers have to offer, and get two or three quotes. Some firms will make the sashes ready for you to install yourself.

The alternative method is to buy a DIY kit. This consists of lengths of aluminium or plastic that you cut to size and screw to the window to hold each pane in place. Although these units are not as sophisticated as manufactured ones they work well and are easy to fit; the overwhelming advantage is the cheapness.

Double glazing to keep out noise

As well as retaining heat in the home, double glazing can also be used to reduce the amount of noise that enters it – from aircraft or a motorway, for example. This is called acoustic insulation. To be effective, the gap between panes should be about 200 mm (8 in) – much wider than for thermal insulation. That, at any rate, is what contractors who build hotels on, for instance, the edge of airports or motorways aim for. In most homes such a dimension is impossible, because the spacing between glass and wall is usually only between 100 and 150 mm (4-6 in). Nevertheless, good acoustic installation can be achieved with a set of secondary sashes. Place the sash as close to the inner edge of the window reveal as possible, making sure there are no gaps between the track and the reveal. Line the inside of the reveal – the window cill as well as the sides and top – with acoustic tiles. Such an installation will also give some thermal insulation.

MODERNIZING

Window frames are part of the architectural style of a house. Many people modernizing a period house want to change them, but beware of altering the style of your home too much; you might destroy its character and ultimately its value. Many charming old houses have been ruined by the insertion of huge, gaping windows. Anyone who wants an ultra-modern home ought to buy one, rather than modernize an older one. Nevertheless, some changes are essential, but they should be carried out with discretion.

Larger panes

It is possible to replace some of the smaller panes in a window with one large sheet of glass (Fig. 4:12). First, you have to remove the individual sashes. If they are opening ones, withdraw the screws holding the hinges. The fixed sashes are nailed into place. Tap them out by using a hammer to hit one end of a stout piece of wood while the other end is on the sash.

Be mindful of safety: you might well break the glass, which could fall outside. Make sure there is no one there to get hurt.

With the sashes out, you will still be left with the transoms and mullions. Saw these out as closely as possible to the main frame, without causing any damage to the rebates. Remove short stubs with a chisel. Clean up with a rebate plane, then sand the surfaces thoroughly.

Make sure the new pane of glass is sufficiently thick. A glazier will advise you, but here is a guide. For panes up to 3.5 sq. m (12 sq ft) with a maximum single dimension of 1300 mm (51 in) use 3 mm (24 oz) glass. For panes of between 3:5 sq. m and 8.5 sq. m (12 – 28 sq. ft) with a maximum single

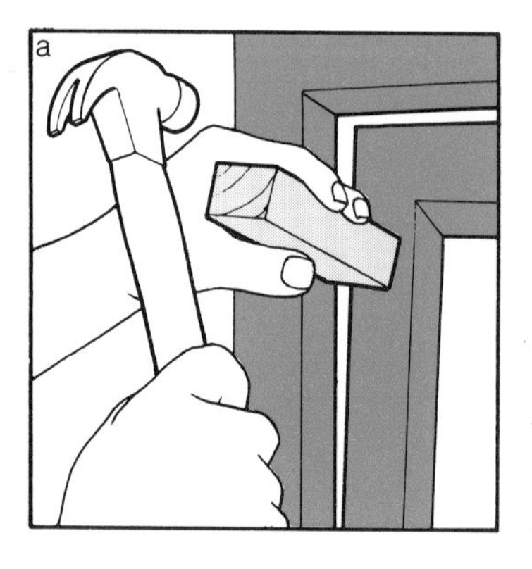

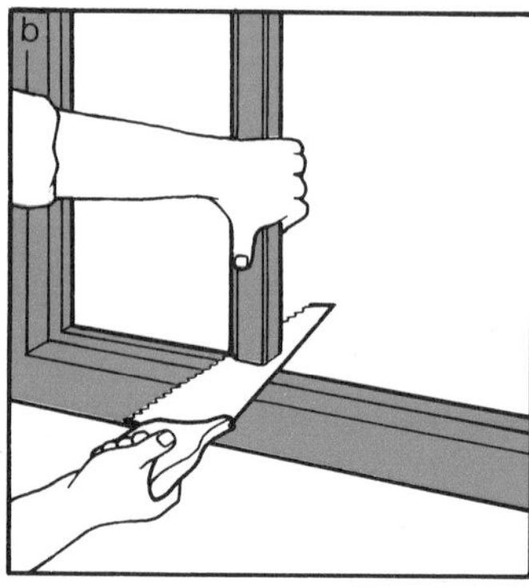

4.12 Adapting a casement window to take one large pane of glass: (a) Tap out a fixed sash. (b) Saw through a mullion. (c) Chop out the mullion stub so that the new pane (inset) can be fixed in the rebate.

dimension of 2100 mm (84 in) use 4 mm (32 oz) glass. Larger windows are unlikely to figure in DIY work.

If some of the original sash designs are to remain in the window, then it is as well to make up a new sash, nail it in the frame and glaze it. This gives a uniform look.

Beware of disposing of too many opening sashes during a conversion both for your own comfort, and possibly to comply with local building regulations.

Converting fixed sashes

A fixed sash that is merely nailed into place can be converted into an opening one, although you risk breaking the pane in doing so. Gently tap out the sash from its transoms and mullions, as described above. Fit hinges to the sash and to the frame, as described in the next chapter.

New windows for old

The time may come when your window frames are so rotted that complete replacement is the only course. When this happens, take the opportunity to install your choice of window, but in keeping with your home's outside appearance. When starting from scratch like this, the possibilities are enormous. For instance, you could ensure that the new frames have rebates sufficiently deep to take sealed-unit double glazing. The extra cost would be moderate at this stage. You might like to have extra opening sashes or you could have pivoted, instead of hinged, sashes. At the back of the house, consider extending the opening to make patio doors.

You have also to decide whether to do the work yourself or not. Often the extra cost of having the work done for you, instead of buying the components and carrying out the work yourself, is small. Moreover, the work will probably be done more quickly – an important point with regard to security and sudden changes in the weather.

Should you decide to do the work yourself, make sure you measure up properly. Measure each dimension in at least two places and take the smallest. Have all the components to hand, and all preparatory work completed, before you take out the existing window.

Begin by removing the individual sashes. Saw out the transoms and mullions. Cut out any external rendering that will prevent the main frame from being moved easily (Fig. 4:13). Then saw through the jambs on each side near the cill and the head, and prise out the jambs. Next, saw through the window cill and board, and prise these out. Remove the remains of the jamb at the bottom. Lastly, prise out the frame head. To do this, you may have to remove the brickwork holding the horns in position. Or you can just saw them off,

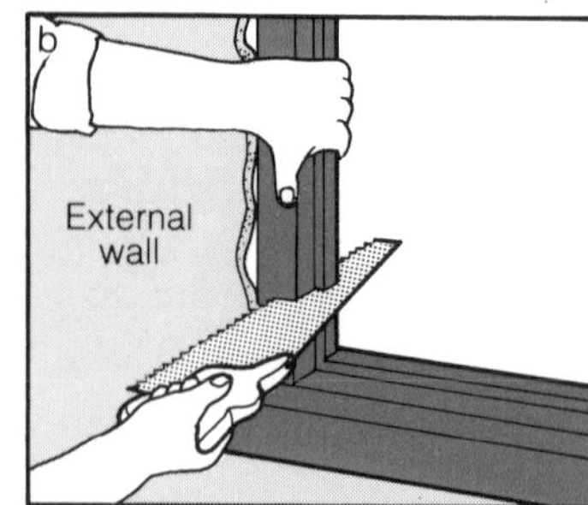

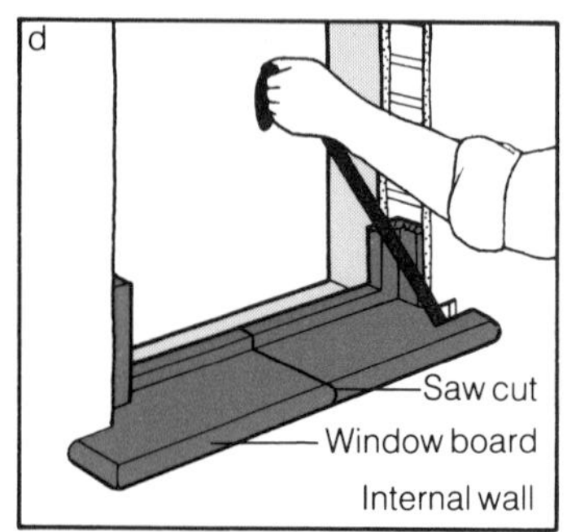

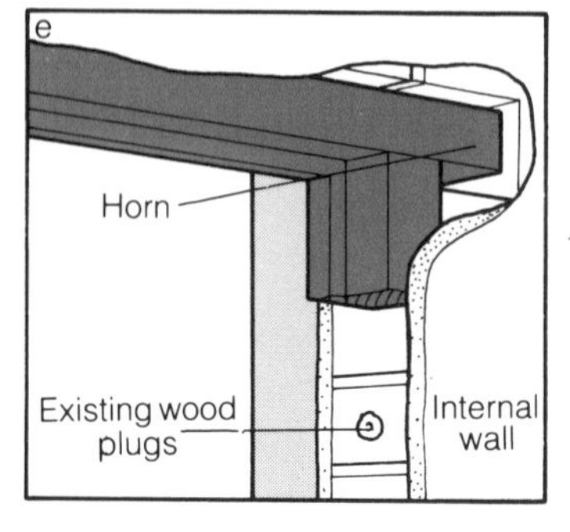

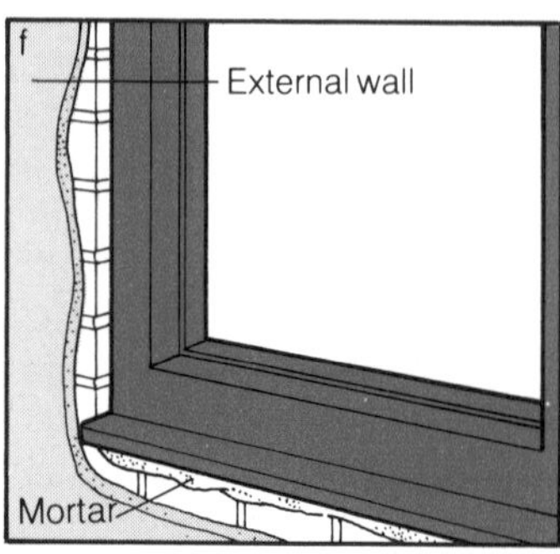

4.13 *Replacing a damaged timber frame: (a) Chop a border of rendering from round the opening. (b) Saw through a jamb. (c) Prise out the jambs. (d) Remove sill and remains of jambs. (e) The frame head (f) The new frame in position.*

and leave them *in situ*. If the fixing was by means of nails driven into wooden plugs, examine the plugs to see if they are in good condition. If they are, use them for fixing the new frame. If they show signs of rot, pull them out and point the gap with mortar. Fix the new frame with screws driven into wall plugs.

Clean out the old opening, removing dirt and debris, then place the new frame in position to try it for size. Adjust it with a plane if it is too big. Apply a bed of mortar to the bottom of the opening, and sit the frame on this. Fix the frame into place by driving screws through pre-drilled holes in it and into the original wooden plugs or into new wall plugs. Seal the gap round the sides and on top with mastic applied from a gun. Replace any brick to cover the horns.

Chapter 5
JOINERY

'Joinery' describes all work carried out with wood. This includes large sections of the floor and roof structure, however, which are more conveniently dealt with elsewhere. In this chapter we shall be looking at the finishing wood touches on the walls – skirtings, doorways, picture rails – and the doors.

If you have an old house, it is all too easy to rip out the joinery and replace it with something new, with the aim of modernizing your home. Remember, however, that the joinery is an important factor in determining the atmosphere of a period home. If you remove it, you risk destroying the house's character. It is a fact that houses with period features intact or sympathetically restored are the ones that attract the highest prices on the housing market. So, if you are not careful, you could be lowering the value of your most precious asset. Nevertheless warehouses selling appropriate mouldings are becoming increasingly common.

DOORS

It is impossible to make a door from one single piece of timber. You cannot get wood of sufficient width to span a door opening, and even if you could, it would be intolerably heavy and expensive. The methods used to solve this problem can be seen in the various styles of door that have been fitted.

Panelled doors (Fig. 5:1) are the most decorative. They are made up of two outer vertical members known as stiles. Joining them are horizontal members called rails. Usually there are three of these – the top, bottom and middle (or lock) rails – although there may be more. Traditionally, the rails were mortised into the stiles, but nowadays it is usual for them to be joined by means of dowels. The spaces between the main members are filled with panels that may be solid or of glass. Previously, solid panels were of natural timber, but recently plywood is likely to have been used instead. Solid panels are usually fitted into grooves in the stiles and rails, and the join is neatened by moulding. Glass panels cannot be recessed into grooves, because re-glazing would then be impossible.

The size of panels used in glazed doors varies enormously. Some doors are almost entirely of glass, with just a stile at each side and rails at top and bottom. Others have a number of thin glazing bars dividing the glass into small panes.

Solid panel door have become popular again and it is now fashionable to fit panelled and other period-style doors, particularly as the front door.

External doors are not interchangeable with internal doors: they have totally different functions. An external door has to be made of weather-resistant materials and must be strong enough to resist burglars. Internal doors need to be of a fire-resistant construction. Internal doors are usually about 35 mm (1⅜ in) thick whereas external doors should be about 44 mm (1¾ in). Hardwood is usually used only for external doors, and softwood for room doors, but practice varies.

Flush doors (Fig.5:2) evolved as an alternative to panelled doors, because of the soaring price of timber. They consist of thin sheet material – hardboard or plywood – fixed to both sides of a timber framework. This framework consists of a stile on each side edge and a cross rail at the top and bottom. There may be other cross rails and diagonal braces. The facing is glued and pinned to the framework. Alternatively, instead of the intermediate support battens, there may be a honeycomb of toughened paper, or curls of wood shaving, glued to both facings. Blocks of wood (called lock blocks) are fitted on both sides to take handles and latches.

5.1 – 5.3 *Three types of door.*

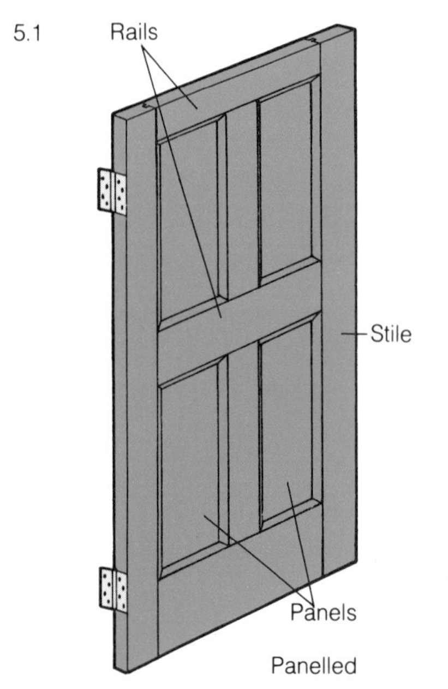

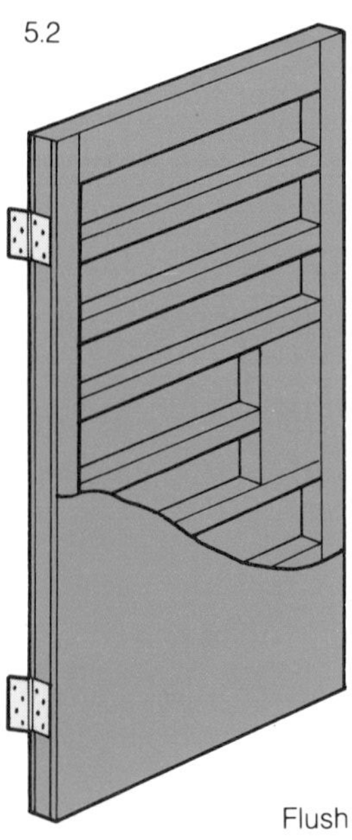

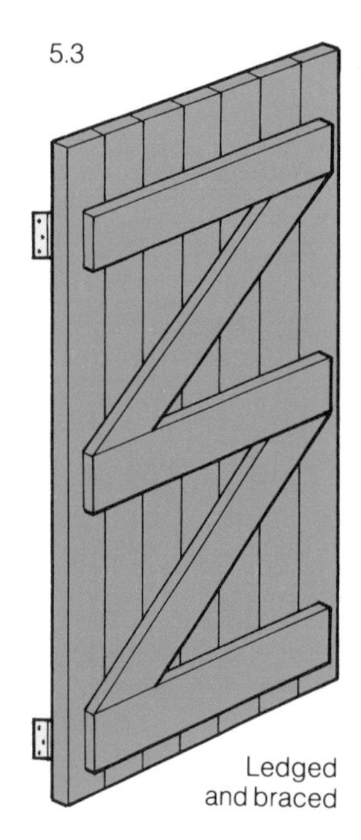

Some doors are designed to be fitted on to either the left or the right edge, so they have only one lock block. If you buy a door, be aware of the choices.

On exterior flush doors, there will be provision, too, for fitting a letter flap. The edges of a well-made flush door will have thin lengths of timber (lipping) to give a neater finish and protect the edges of the facing. The lipping may be fixed by means of a tongue and groove, or it might be glued and pinned into place. Lipping is particularly important on an exterior door and usually matches the facing. A flush door can also be partly glazed – it may, for instance, have a glass panel at the top.

Ledged and braced doors (Fig. 5:3) are nowadays used mostly on outbuildings – garden sheds, for instance – or as a full-height garden gate. At one time they were used also as house doors, and examples of this can still be seen in many period cottages. This type of door is based on tongued and grooved timber, or matchboarding with a V-shaped groove between the boards, as in some wall cladding. Ledged and braced doors are invariably made of softwood.

The timber is joined together and nailed to horizontal members known as ledges. Usually, there are three ledges – one is placed some way from the top, another some way from the bottom, with a middle one usually half-way up the door. To strengthen the door and prevent it from sagging, diagonal timbers – the braces – are fitted between the ledges. The braces should always slope upwards from the hinged edge – so when buying such a door bear in mind that there is a left and right hand choice. These doors are stronger when the braces are jointed into the ledges.

Ledged and braced doors do not have thick edges so they cannot be fitted with mortise locks or be hung by means of hinges recessed into a stile. You must use surface fixed hinges, which can easily be removed with a screwdriver. As a result, such doors are not secure.

Framed ledged and braced doors are variants of ordinary ledged and braced doors. A frame is made, similar to that for a panelled door, with a stile on each edge and a top, bottom and middle rail. The rails take the place of the ledges but braces are fitted, and the door is clad with tongued and grooved cladding or matchboarding. This construction is much stronger than that of an ordinary ledged and braced door. Furthermore, it will take mortise locks, and butt hinges can be fitted to the edges, so it is suitable where greater security is required.

Glass doors without any timber framing whatsoever can be bought. The glass is opaque, to ensure some measure of privacy with the door closed, and is toughened, so there is no fear of breakage. Such doors are very useful as a means of letting light into dark rooms. They are, however, more expensive than a timber door with glass panels, and cannot be reduced in size if they are too big for the opening.

Louvred doors originated in Mediterranean countries, where there is a considerable need for ventilation. They have become popular in cooler climes, however, as a decorative feature. The main disadvantage is that they cannot serve as draught excluders if necessary. Moreover, dust can pass through them. The louvred door is made up of two stiles and two or more cross rails. The louvres – horizontal slats – are set at an angle and overlap each other, so that although spaces are left between the louvres, you cannot see through them. A door can be louvred from top to bottom, or it may have louvres just in the top half, and be a panelled or flush door lower down. Mock louvres are made up of triangular slats fixed to a hardboard or plywood background, or to moulded plastic. These look like the real thing, but there is no space for air to pass through.

Aluminium doors are also available, but they are expensive, and thus rarely found.

Buying a new door

New doors are widely stocked – at DIY shops, builders' merchants, home improvement centres and joinery suppliers. Some large firms specialize in doors, and produce lavish catalogues of what is available. Many of them make a speciality of supplying feature doors.

Before you go shopping, find out what size of replacement door you need. Measure the opening, rather than the existing door, which may have shrunk over the years. Doors and door openings are made to standard sizes, so you should be able to buy one to fit into a modern house. Older houses might have non-standard openings.

If you cannot find a door of the right dimensions, you might be able to cut one down to size, but this is difficult to do without weakening the door.

Panelled doors, because of their wide stiles and cross rails, can be slightly reduced – by up to 19 mm (¾ in) all round. Flush doors should not be pared down at all if you can possibly avoid it. Remember there is a lipping on the side edges, and the top and bottom cross rails are too small to stand much of a reduction. You can, however, plane a little off them to get a good fit.

You can also, of course, have doors made to size, but these are much more expensive than standard-sized doors.

The thickness of the door can be a problem too. You might be unable to find one to match the rebate in the frame. The problem is easily solved with an internal door, because the door stop is usually just nailed into place, and can be prised off and re-positioned. On an external frame the rebate is usually an integral part of the moulding. To increase it, trim some of the timber away, but not too much or it will be weakened. To reduce the rebate you might be able to glue and pin extra timber to the frame. If either of these methods fail, then order a made-to-measure door. Tell your supplier whether you want an external or internal door.

Removing an old door

It is always advisable to hang a new door with new hinges. Remove the old door by withdrawing the screws that hold the hinges to the frame, not those fixing them to the door. Try every screw on all the hinges to make sure that they can be turned – it is likely that some of them have become so clogged with paint, or affected by corrosion, that they are stuck firmly in place. There are several methods for loosening these.

First of all, ensure you use a large enough screwdriver. The width of the blade tip should be almost the length of the screw slot, and the blade should be of a thickness that fills the width of the slot. The blade should be in good condition, not worn at the edges. Scrape all paint from the screw slot and the top of the head, then place the screwdriver blade into the screw slot, and give the handle a short sharp blow with a hammer – this will not cause damage to a modern plastic-handled screwdriver, in the way it would to an old wooden one. The blow should be sufficient to dislodge the screw from the wood. If the screw still does not turn, use a screwdriver blade inserted in a carpentry brace to give you a better purchase.

If you still have no success, try applying mild heat, from a soldering iron or a pencil flame blowlamp for example. The heat causes both the screw and the surrounding woodwork to expand – but at different rates, because they are different materials. When they cool, they will revert to the former size, but should no longer be stuck together. You probably intend to re-decorate in any case, so the damage caused by the heat to the paintwork will not matter.

Once you are sure every screw is freed, start to withdraw them. Starting from the top, take out every screw but one from each of the hinges. Now either get a helper to hold the door or place wedges underneath it, so that it cannot fall away from the frame. Take out the remaining screws, then lift the door clear.

Fitting a new door

Fit the hinges (see later sections) to the door before raising it into position. It is convenient to carry out other work, such as adding locks and – in the case of front doors – letter flaps

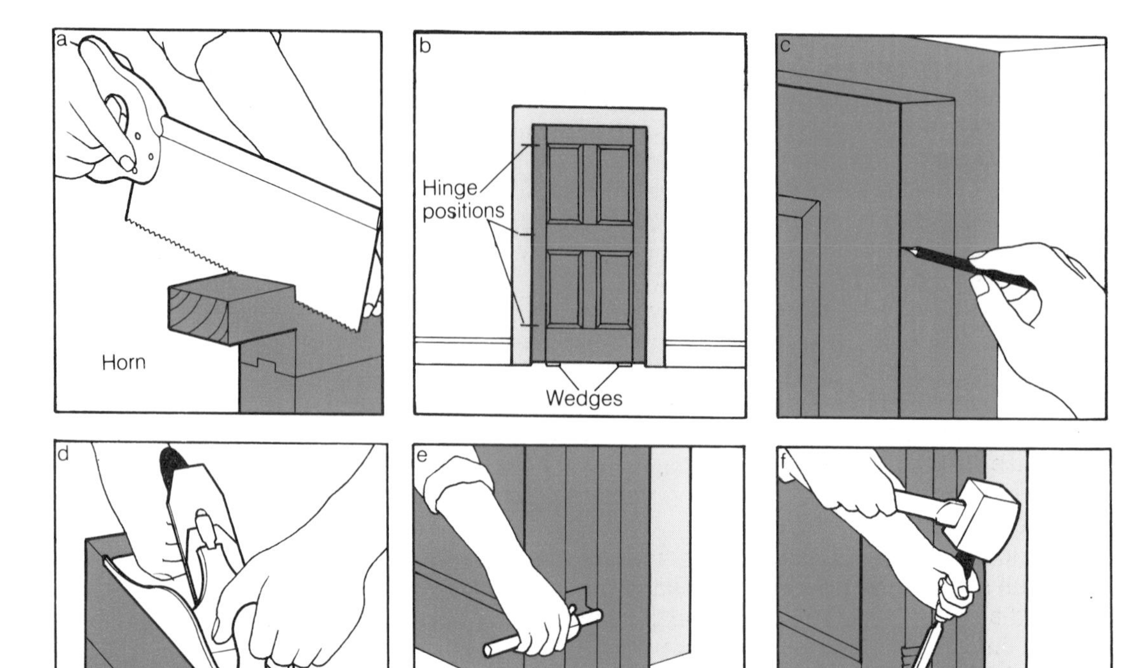

5.4 *Hanging a new door: (a) Saw off the 'horns'. (b) The door is wedged in position. (c) Mark where door needs to be reduced. (d) Plane it down to size. (e) Mark a hinge recess on a frame. (f) Chop out the recess on the frame.*

before the door is hung. The striking plate, into which the lock, bolt or latch locates, cannot be fitted until the door is hung, however. If the door is to be glazed, wait until it is hung before doing so. Then there will be less risk of breakage.

A panelled door will be delivered with the stiles protruding top and bottom. These 'horns', as they are known, are there to protect the door during transport. Saw them off with a tenon saw, working from the outer edges inwards, to lessen the risk of splitting (Fig. 5:4). If you need to saw any timber off the height or width of a panelled door, do so at this stage. Note though that you cannot just saw the excess from one edge, because the door will appear unbalanced. Remove equal amounts from both top and bottom or from both sides.

With the door roughly to size, stand it in the opening, on small wedges. Note how the door fits, marking with a pencil where it needs to be reduced in size, then take it down and plane it as necessary. To avoid splitting the ends of the stiles, work from the outer edges inwards when planing the top and bottom of the door. On a flush door do not plane too much off the lipping.

Size the door so that there is a clearance of about 3 mm

(⅛ in) at the top and sides; slightly more at the bottom where it has to clear the floor covering. Stand it once again in the opening, on wedges, and mark on the side of the door the position of the hinge recesses on the frame. Fit the hinges at these spots and hang the door. Initially, fix only one screw per hinge. Now see if the door opens and closes properly. If it is binding in places, shave the edges where necessary. If the recesses in the frame are slightly too deep for the new hinges, pack the hinges out with card. When you are satisfied, fix all the remaining hinge screws.

Fitting butt hinges The position of the previous hinges on the door frame will determine exactly where the new ones should be fixed on the replacement door. Assuming that the old hinges worked satisfactorily, fit new ones of exactly the same size, so that they will fill the recess neatly. If, however, you have replaced the doorway lining of the door frame, or you are hanging the door in a new site, there will be no hinges to guide you. Note then that you need three 100 mm (4 in) butt hinges. The top one should be placed a distance of one and a half times its length from the top of the door. The bottom one should be one and a half times its length, plus 50 mm (2 in) from the bottom edge. If both hinges were sited at equal distance from the edges, the bottom one would appear to be lower down than it actually is. The middle hinge should be halfway between the top and bottom ones.

To cut a recess for a hinge, place the door on edge on the floor. Have it held steady, preferably using a vice. Determine the distance of the first hinge from the top or bottom of the door, and mark the spot on the door in pencil. At this point draw a line across the edge, using a try-square, so that it is truly square to the face of the door (Fig. 5:5). Draw a similar line, with the aid of the square, the length of the hinge away from the first. Now set a marking gauge to the width of one leaf of the hinge. Mark a line this distance away from the closing face of the door. The knuckle of the hinge,

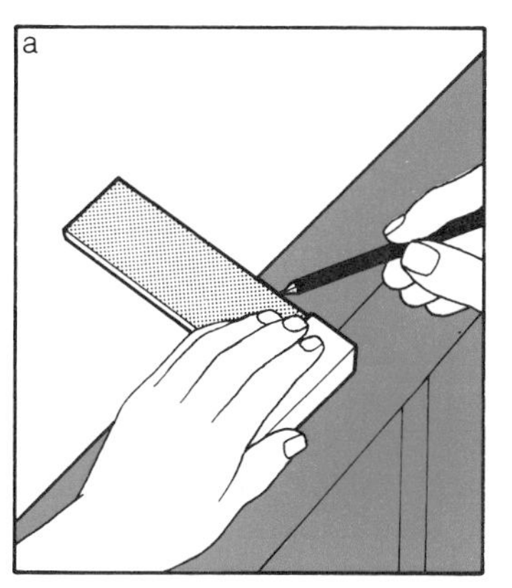

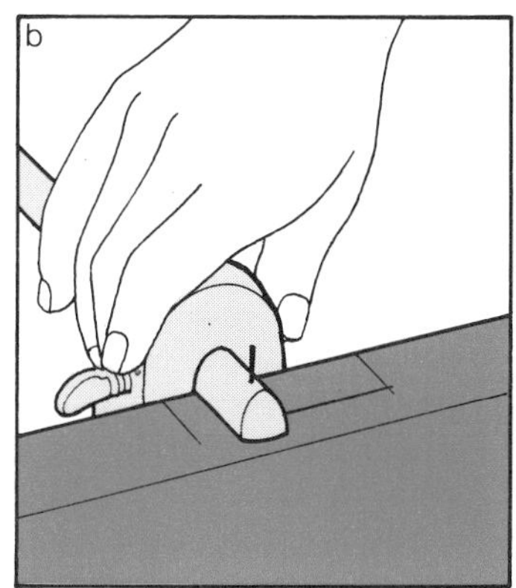

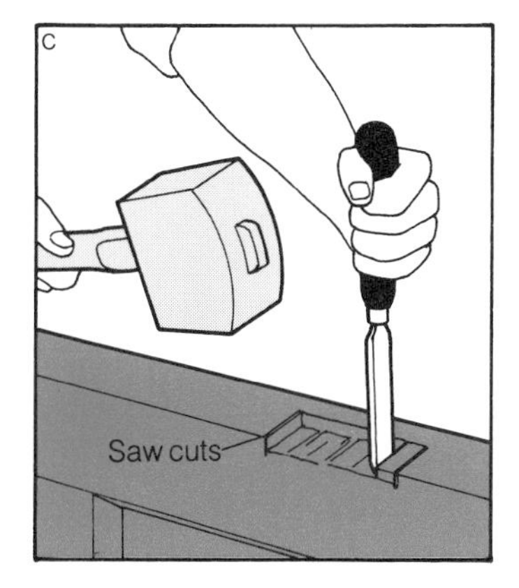

5.5 *Fitting butt hinges: (a) Mark out the top and bottom of the hinge recess with a square. (b) Complete the outline with a marking gauge. (c) Chop out the recess.*

when closed, should be just clear of the door face. Next, set the gauge to the thickness of one leaf of the hinge, and mark this on the face of the door. Make a saw cut, using a small tenon or dovetail saw, along the top and bottom lines, down to the thickness line on the face.

Chop out the recess with a chisel and hammer. Make a series of chisel cuts, 3 mm (1/8 in) apart, to the depth of the line on the door face and parallel to the saw lines on the edge. Clean out the waste with the chisel, working from the front edge. Position the hinge leaf in the recess, to check that it is a good fit, and that it lies flat. The door will not close properly otherwise. Make any adjustments needed. If the hinge is proud of the recess, shave off a little more timber with the chisel. If it is sunk too deep, pack it out with card.

Drill pilot holes for the fixing screws, and screw the hinge into place, taking care to position it accurately. Some hinges are pre-packed complete with fixing screws. If yours are not, test the gauge of screw required by test-pushing a screw into the hole. Use 25 mm (1 in) screws. Fix the other hinges in the same way, then hang the door.

Recesses for a hinge in the frame are cut in much the same way. The work will be more difficult because of the awkward working position, so take extra care to ensure accuracy.

Fitting rising butts Unlike ordinary butt hinges, rising butts raise the door as it is opened, and lift it clear of any carpet. You can remove the existing hinges of an ordinary door, and fit rising butts in their place. A door fitted with rising butts also tends to be self-closing.

The leaves of a rising butt are not fixed together as are those of an ordinary butt. Instead, one leaf can be removed from the hinge pin, which is fixed to the other leaf. The leaf with the pin is fitted to the frame and the other to the door. Provided you fix the pin leaf clear of the frame, the door can merely be lifted clear, should it ever be necessary to remove it.

Rising butts are available in right or left hand sets, so note the side on which your door is hinged before ordering. They are fitted in much the same way as ordinary ones, but there are two points to note. First, the two parts must be positioned on both frame and door with extreme accuracy, otherwise only one will be seated properly, and too much of a strain would then be imposed on it. Second, the top of the door must be bevelled off towards the frame, so that it can open properly.

Fitting a letter plate A new front door will need a letter plate. Aim to position this at a height that will allow the postman to push letters through without having to stoop. On a panelled door, set the plate in the middle rail; never the bottom one.

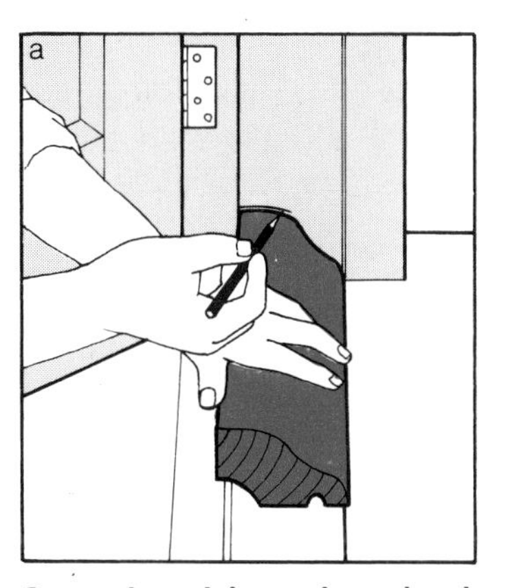

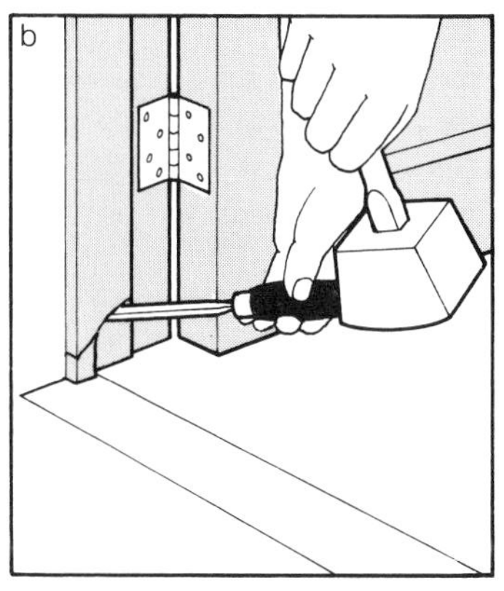

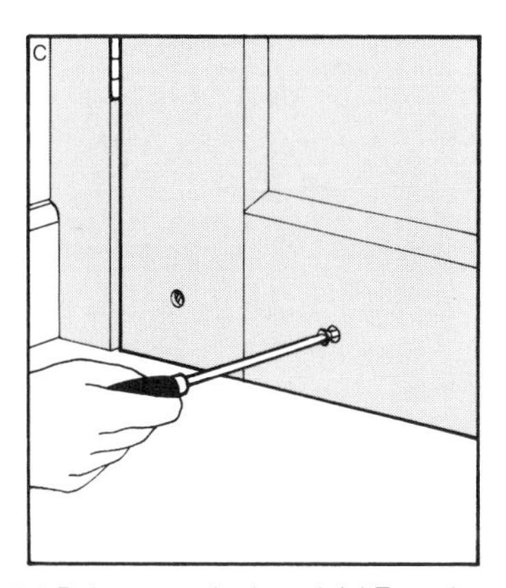

5.6 *Fitting a weatherboard: (a) Trace its outline on a door stop. (b) Chop out its shape from the stop. (c) You can nail the weatherboard in place or fix it with screws driven from inside.*

On a glazed front door that has no middle rail, fit a vertical flap in the lock stile. Provision for a flap to be fitted is usually made in an external flush door. In that case the position is decided for you.

Letter plates are usually fixed by means of bolts that pass through the door, and are held in place by nuts on the inside.

Place the door flat on a bench, and position the plate accurately and squarely. Mark in pencil on the door the outline of the opening. Drill a large hole at each corner of the opening, and cut out the shape with a padsaw or powered jigsaw. Clean up the edges of the cut with glass-paper. Now place the plate back in position, and mark the position of the fixing bolts. Drill clearance holes for these bolts. Place the plate on the front of the door, push in the bolts, and on the other side fit and tighten the nuts on the bolts.

An internal flap can be added to eliminate draughts. Normally this is just screwed into place.

Fitting a weatherboard A weatherboard is a shaped piece of moulding fitted to the bottom of an external door to throw rainwater clear. It prevents the door from becoming soaked, and so makes it less likely to rot. Some have a flatback, and are held to the door by nails. Others have a tongue, and this locates in a groove that has to be ploughed in the door.

To fit a weatherboard (Fig. 5:6), first cut it to match the exact width of the door. Take an offcut from the moulding making sure both ends are square and hold it in place at the bottom of the door stops on each side of the opening. Trace in pencil the outline of the moulding on both stops. Chop out this shape from the stops so that the weatherboard will fit snugly into them when the door is closed.

Treat the bottom of the weatherboard with an exterior quality sealer and brush a gloss paint on the back. You can also paint the underneath. To help you grip the timber drive one or two nails into the front. While the paint is still wet, place the weatherboard on the door, and nail it in place. Punch home the nail heads, fill them, and paint over. Do not forget to treat the bare wood which you exposed on the frame.

Security

One of the most important functions of an external door is that it should keep out burglars. In fact, the most popular point of entry for housebreakers is through a window, but it is still good sense to make it as difficult as possible for them to walk through a door.

One of the most common security devices for external doors is a night latch. Most people would refer to it as a lock, but there is a difference: both locks and latches have a bolt, but a latch bolt is sprung so it closes automatically. To open the latch, you turn a handle inside or a key outside. A lock can be closed or opened only by a key. A lock or latch that is actually housed in a hole cut in the body of the door is known as a mortise lock or latch. If it is fitted on the surface of the door, it is called a rim lock, or latch. A night latch is a rim latch. It is fixed to the back of the door, and the keep into which its bolt locates is fitted to the back of the frame (Fig. 5:7).

This latch is the easiest of all security devices to force. Although it has a catch to prevent the bolt from moving, the only value of this is to stop the latch from closing and locking you out if, for instance, you go outside for a moment without your keys. It is useful to have a latch on an external door. When you are at home, it keeps the door closed without your having to lock it, but when you go out you need greater security.

5.7 *Security devices for a door*

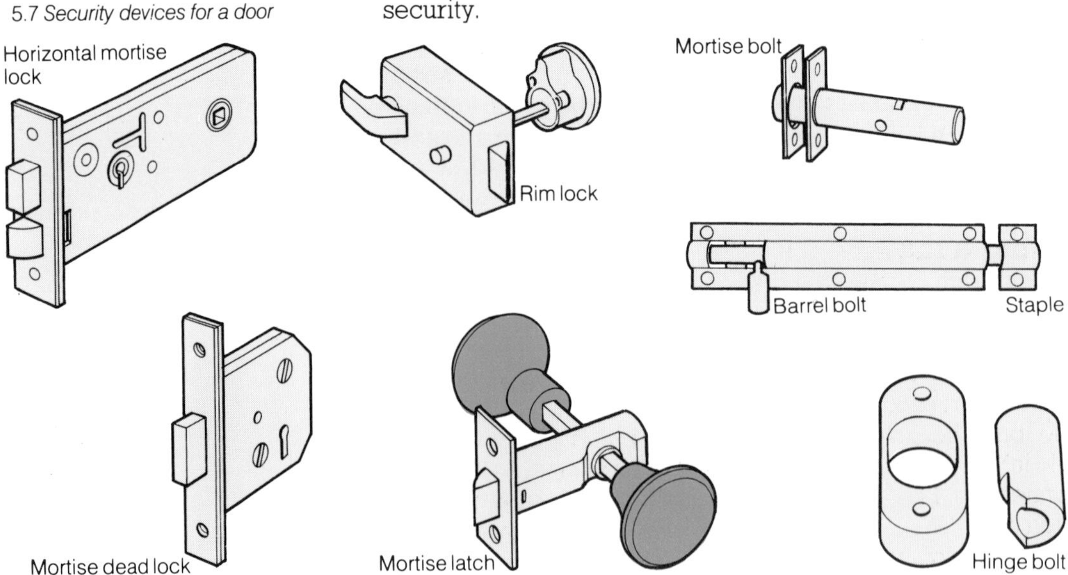

Some night latches can be deadlocked both from inside and out. These are more secure than the simple latch, but they are no substitute for a mortise lock on external doors. When you are out the only protection for the door by which you have left is the lock you close with a key as you go, so make sure it is a good one. Buy a good quality mortise lock, with five levers and steel roll bars inside the bolt, so that it cannot be sawn through.

If your home has two external doors, the back door can have bolts instead of, or in addition to, a mortise lock. If you fit it with both, it will be more secure than the front door. This can be an advantage because usually the back of a house is more vulnerable, as a burglar at work will be less visible there than at the front.

Cheap barrel bolts that have the staple (the part into which the bolt locates) fitted to the inside face of the frame are not very secure, for a door held by these can be pushed in. It is much safer to fit bolts with staples in a hole bored into the side of the frame. Better still, fit mortise bolts, which are like simplified mortise locks.

It is not just at the lock edge that a door needs protection. It is just as vulnerable to a determined thief along the hinge edge. If the hinges are weak, or not securely screwed in place, they can easily be broken off, if forced. So replace any that are in doubtful condition, and insert longer screws instead of the existing ones.

Another way to strengthen the hinge side of the door is to fit bolts there, making it less easy to force the hinges. These are variously known as hinge, stud, or dog bolts. They are fixed to the frame, and locate in holes bored in the door when it is closed.

You can also fit a spy hole as a means of checking on the identity of callers before you open the door. Alternatively, you can fit a door chain.

Another worthwhile device is some strong, wide metal trim around the letter plate, to prevent a determined thief from trying to saw the door in half.

Fitting a night latch

A night latch consists of a cylinder barrel, into which the key fits, and a latch case, mounted on a backplate on the inside of the door. To fit one of these latches you need to drill a hole through the door of sufficient diameter to take the cylinder barrel. Start drilling from the front of the door, using a brace and bit. The hole will probably need to be about 38 mm (1½ in) in diameter and should be positioned so that the connecting bar of the cylinder locates correctly into the latch case. The dimensions for aligning both parts of the lock are usually given with the fitting instructions. The connect-

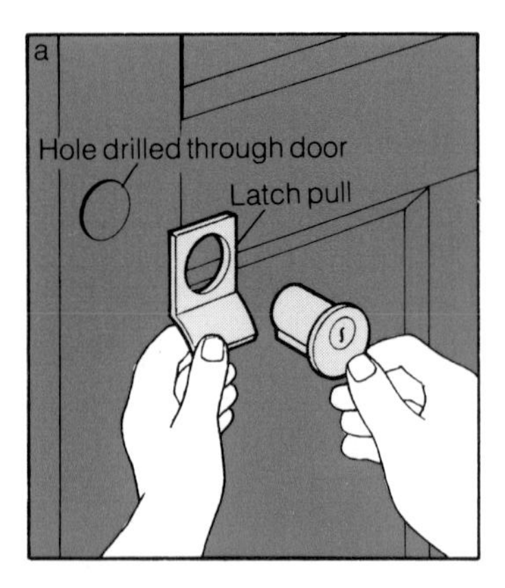

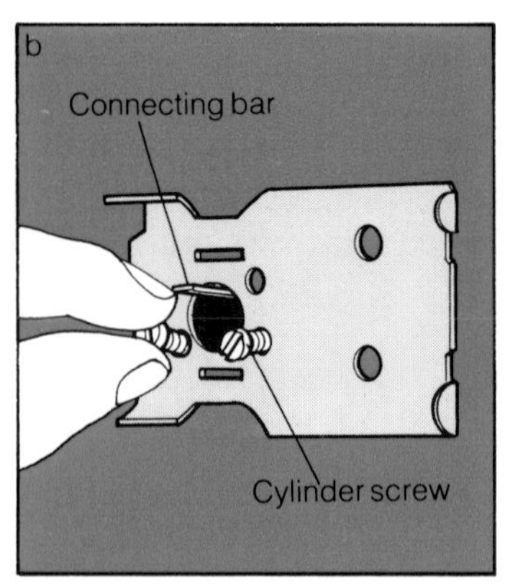

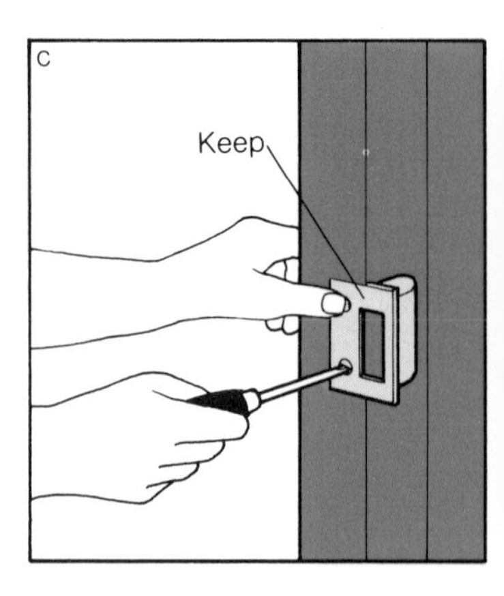

5.8 *Fitting a night latch: (a) The cylinder passes through the latch pull. (b) The back plate is fixed to the inside of the door. (c) Fix the keep.*

ing bar will also have to be cut to a length to suit the thickness of the door.

The cylinder passes through the latch pull (Fig. 5:8), a surround that incorporates a small handle with which you can pull the door closed. Screw the back plate into place on the inside of the door, aligning the hole in the plate with the hole in the door. Cut the connecting bar so that it protrudes about 13 mm (½ in) on the inside of the door into the latch case. Screw the latch case to the cylinder. Shut the door and slide the keep on to the latch. Mark the position of the keep on to the frame, then chisel out a small recess so that the edge of the keep fits flush. Fix the keep with screws.

Fitting a mortise lock

A mortise lock should be fitted to an external door to make it more secure. If the lock is to be fitted on an existing door, there is no need to remove the door from its hinges. Should the door be new, however, fit the lock before hanging it. The striking plate, which receives the lock bolt, cannot be fitted to the frame until the door has been hung.

In a panelled door the lock is fitted at the level of the lock rail; in a flush door it goes into the lock block, which is usually higher than a lock rail. Determine the position of the lock, and hold the casing on the front edge of the door. Mark the top and bottom lines of the mortise to be cut for the lock (Fig. 5:9). Push a pencil through the keyhole of the lock, to mark on the face of the door where the keyhole of the door has to be cut. Using a try-square, draw a pencil line on the stile edge, at right angles to the edge of the door, to mark the top and bottom of the mortise. To ensure that the lock will be positioned centrally, measure the thickness of the door, and subtract from this the thickness of the lock. Set a marking gauge to half the remaining thickness, and use it to mark lines from both the inside and outside faces of the door to complete the outline of the mortise. The easiest way to cut

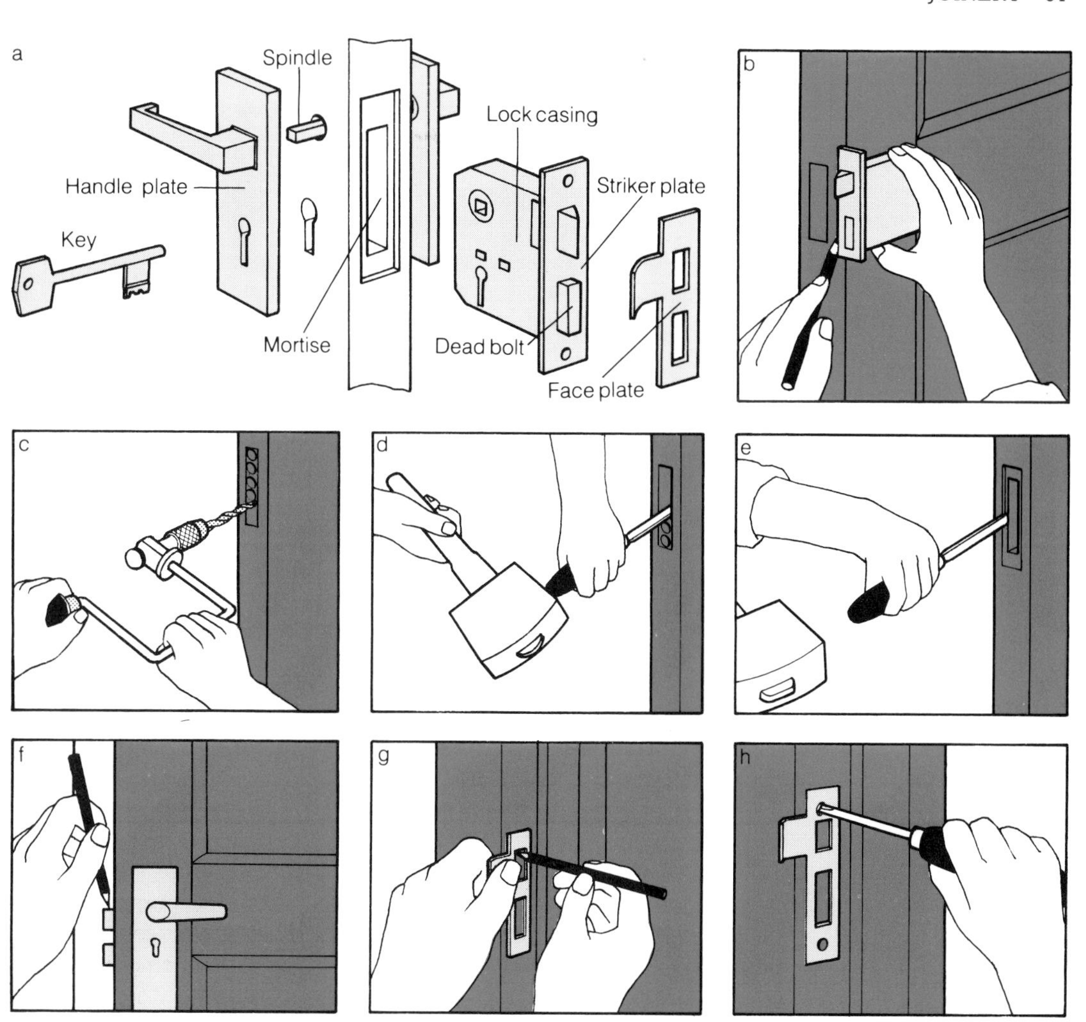

5.9 *Fitting a mortise lock: (a) The parts of the lock (b) Hold the casing on the face of the door to mark out for the mortise. (c) Bore holes for the mortise. (d) Clean out the mortise. (e) Pare out for the cover plate. (f) Mark the position for the striking plate. (g) Mark for the hole to receive the bolt. (h) Fix the striking plate.*

out the mortise for the lock casing is to bore a series of holes with a brace and bit, the diameter of which equals the thickness of the lock. The depth of the holes should be the same as that of the lock casing. Make sure that the brace is held square to the work. Clean out the mortise with a chisel, and push the lock casing into it to test that it is a good fit. If the fit is bad, withdraw the casing and examine it. Scratches in its paintwork and paint marks on the inside of the mortise will show where the mortise needs to be eased off slightly.

Push the casing into the mortise once again, then draw a line on the door edge around the face plate. Using a chisel, pare out a recess in the edge to take the face plate and the cover plate. When fitted, the cover plate must be flush with the stile edge. Since the closing edge of the door is usually slightly bevelled off, to allow it to enter the frame more snugly, the recess for the cover plate will need to be a little deeper along that edge.

Make the hole for the key; drill the top half, then complete the lower half with a padsaw. Neaten the keyhole by screwing an escutcheon plate (a small metal surround) on each side of the door. A small pivoted cover may be incorporated on both plates, or merely on the one intended for inside.

Now fit the striking plate to the door frame. To do this, close the door and turn the lock with the key. A slight force on the key will cause the position of the bolt to be imprinted on the door frame. If the mark is not clear, try pushing a sheet of carbon paper between door and frame, or smearing a little paint on the end of the lock bolt. Hold the striking plate on the frame, position its hole directly over the mark of the bolt, then draw on the frame the position of this hole and of the entire plate. Chisel out a mortise to take the bolt and a recess for the plate. Screw the plate into position.

Test that the lock works properly. If the bolt does not enter the hole in the striking plate easily, you might be able to enlarge the hole slightly with a metal file. Otherwise, the plate may have to be re-positioned. Marks on the sides, top or bottom of the bolt and hole will show where the bolt is binding.

Fitting a mortise latch

A mortise latch is fitted to a room door. It may, or may not, incorporate a lock. The catch is fitted in the same way as for a mortise lock, except that there is a handle on each side of the door. These locate on a spindle that passes through the door. A hole for the spindle is drilled through the door. When the latch case is in position in the mortise, the spindle is pushed through to engage in the hole for it in the case. The handles engage on the spindle.

The handles are merely screwed into place. When a combined lock and latch is fitted, there is no need to fit an escutcheon plate (to cover the keyhole) because this is incorporated into the handle.

Fitting a spy hole

A spy hole is a lens system in a solid door through which you can peer at callers before deciding whether you should open the door to them. The lens gives an exceptionally wide angle of view. The spy hole comes in two parts that screw together from opposite sides of the door. To fit it, bore a hole through the door (the instructions will tell you the correct diameter) at a convenient height for your eyes. Push the front half of the spy hole in from the outside of the door, and the back half from inside. Thread them together. There is a slot on the inside section to allow you to tighten it on the thread of the other half, so that the front portion cannot be extracted from the outside.

Faults with doors

One of the simplest faults that can develop in a door is that the hinges might start to squeak as the door is opened and closed. Apply a light oil sparingly to the top of the hinge pin, so that it will work its way down the knuckle. Applying it at any other part of the knuckle will be ineffective; and too much oil will merely drip onto the floor coverings.

Various faults can prevent the door from opening and closing properly.

The hinge may not be securely fixed to the frame. If this is the case, try fitting longer screws – the diameter of the hinge holes will prevent you from fitting thicker ones. Take out and replace only one screw at a time so that you do not disturb the door on the frame. If a new screw goes in too freely, remove it, then pack out the hole with a small dowel – tradesmen often use a matchstick or two. Then fit the screw again.

One or more of the hinges may be worn. Try rocking the door gently to see if there is play at the hinges. If so, fit new hinges. Fit the hinges one at a time, so that the door can remain hanging. If there are only two hinges, ask a helper to steady the door, or support it on wedges as you renew each hinge.

A door can be 'hinge bound' – a condition in which the door meets the hinge side of the frame before it is properly closed. One possible cause for this is that the hinge screws protrude, instead of fitting flush. If so, drive the screws fully home. A door can also be hinge bound if one or more of the hinges is recessed too deeply in either the door or the frame. If this is so, withdraw the screws holding the hinge, then place card or hardboard underneath it to pack it out level and flush with the surrounding timber.

An external door may become too tight to fit in its frame, particularly during rainy weather. This is a sign that damp is causing the door to swell – perhaps because it is not sufficiently protected against the elements. Wait until the door has dried out thoroughly, then paint or varnish it properly.

Binding or sticking can also be caused by a build-up of paint on the edges of a door. Open and close the door to see where it is binding. If the spot is not obvious, rub chalk on all the edges. The chalk will be removed where the door binds. Plane the door so that there is a clearance of about 3 mm (1/8 in) between the frame and the door when closed, then repaint. Do not take much off an external door in damp weather because when the door dries out the gap will be too much.

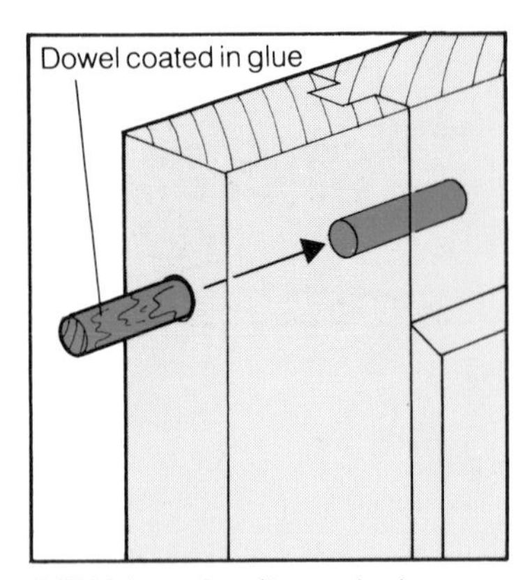

5.10 *Using a dowel to repair a loose joint between a stile and rail*

It is impossible to plane a door properly – especially at the top and bottom edges – while it is still hung. You will have to take it down, but before you do, make sure you know where it is binding. If the bottom binds, swing the door backwards and forwards several times over a sheet of coarse glasspaper placed on the floor. This might remove the cause of the trouble. Finish off with fine glasspaper so that there will be no rough edges to catch on any carpet.

If the door binds near the top of the lockstile and on the floor on the same side, the bottom hinge might be at fault, causing the door to sag. Pack the hinge out with card or board to bring the door upright, or fit a new hinge. If the binding is at the bottom of the stile and the top of the frame, look for the cause in the top hinge.

In both panelled and flush doors, the joint where the top or bottom rail meets the stile might work loose. You can often repair this by boring holes through both rails and stile, and inserting dowels on which you have smeared glue (Fig. 5:10).

A tongued and grooved door may sag because it is inadequately braced. In fact, although such doors are invariably described as being ledged and braced, there may be no braces – just ledges. Fit braces, after making sure the door is squared up properly.

Warped doors will not close properly, and if a lock is fitted it might not turn. Take the door off its hinges and remove all the door furniture. One way to cure the warping is to place the door flat on the ground with the bow uppermost, in an enclosure such as a garage or shed. Raise the door by sup-

Cures for warped doors: 5.11 *A brace between a ceiling and the door*
5.12 *Force a door flat with a batten screwed to the floor.*

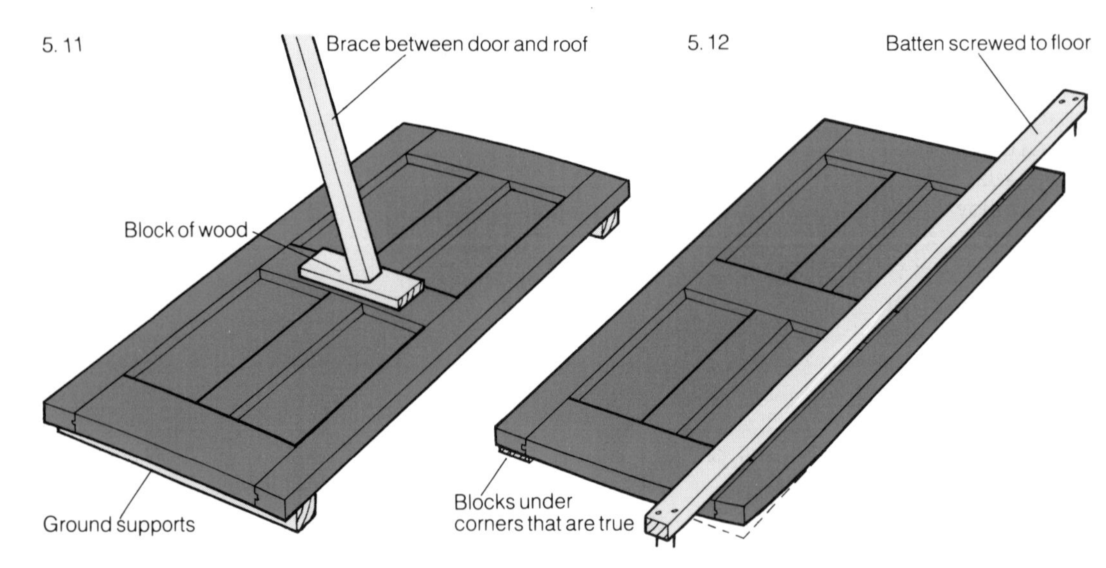

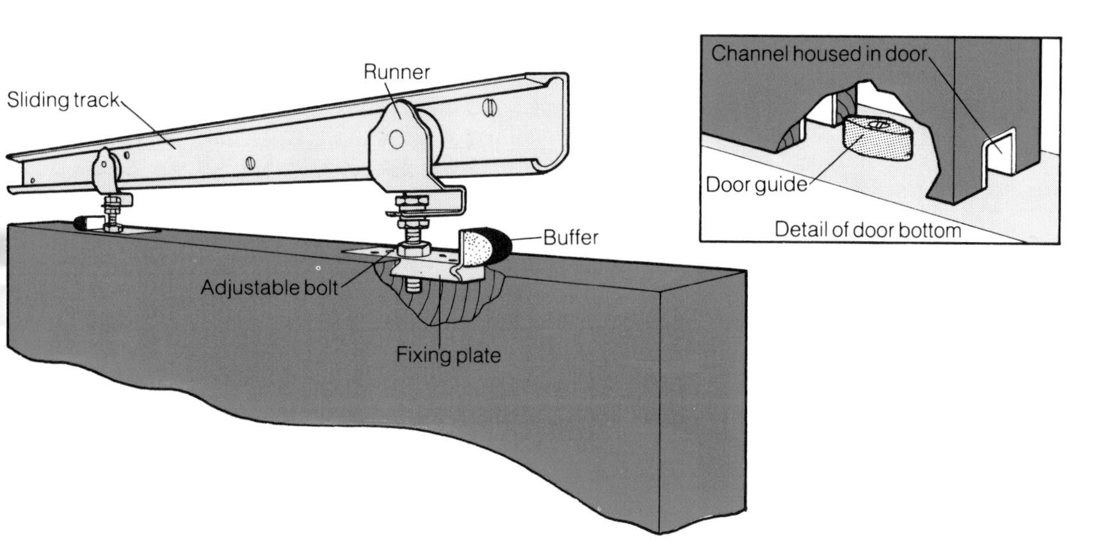

5.13 *Typical sliding door gear*

porting it at each end, then put a brace between the roof or ceiling and the face of the door (Fig. 5:11). The aim is to distort the door as far the other way as it is warped on its face. Leave the brace in position for a few days.

Another method is to lay the door on a boarded floor with blocks the thickness of the distortion under the corners that are true (Fig. 5:12). Force the door flat with battens screwed to the floor.

Fitting sliding doors

To allow sufficient space for the average room door to open and close you have to leave clear at least a square metre (about 40 sq in), of floor space. This is a large area to take out of the small rooms of today. To give more space, you could convert your present hinged doors to sliding doors. The conversion is simple for most doors, and you can buy kits for this purpose.

The kits come with complete instructions, which you should follow carefully. Basically you have to prise off the architrave on one side of the opening, fit a track over the opening, and add wheels (which locate on the track) to the top of the door (Fig. 5:13). Hang the door by its wheels on the track. A channel at floor level makes the whole thing work smoothly, and there is a pelmet to hide the mechanism. A different type of handle is required – usually it comes with the kit – so the present latch and its striking plate on the frame will have to be removed and made good.

DOORWAYS

Doorways are lined with timber to neaten the opening, give a stop against which the door can close, and provide a fixing point for hinges, locks and latches.

External door frames are usually fitted into a recess in the brickwork. They consist of two upright side members (jambs) into which a rebate is machined at the factory to form a stop for the door to close against. The jambs are nailed to wooden plugs set into the wall while it is being built. The timber at the top of the opening is known as the head, which may project beyond the opening and be mortared into the brickwork. The projections are known as horns. The jambs are mortised into the head. Some doorways have no horns: instead the jambs are dowelled into the head, which may also be nailed to wooden plugs. At the bottom the jambs may be tenoned into a wooden cill. Alternatively, they may be fixed with rustproof dowels cemented into the step, and bedded on a layer of mastic to protect the end grain.

At the foot there is often a threshold, against which the door closes, to make the opening more weatherproof. Metal thresholds incorporate a strip of rubber or plastic that seals against the bottom of the door.

Internal door openings (Fig. 5:14) usually have a wooden door lining at both sides and at the top. The lining is nailed to timber plugs, and its width is the thickness of the wall with the masonry and plaster on both sides. Linings machined to fit various thicknesses of wall are available at wood yards.

A stop bead, against which the door closes, is fitted. It is formed either by a rebate or (more usually) by a separate length of timber nailed into place.

An ugly join line between the plaster and the edge of the door lining can be covered and neatened with lengths of moulded timber known as architrave. These are an important feature of the room, and can add as much to the period quality of the room as the skirting and picture rails. The architrave is usually mitred at the top corners.

Sometimes the plaster is taken up to the edge of the door lining, and the architrave nailed to the edge of the lining. In better quality work, however, a batten the thickness of the plaster is fixed to the face of the brickwork, butting up against the lining on both sides and at the top. Then the plaster is taken to the edge of the batten, and the architrave is nailed to this batten. No threshold is normally fitted to the foot of an internal door.

Lengths of timber machined to form lining, stop bead and plaster bed in one profile are sometimes installed.

Fanlights may be fitted above both external and internal

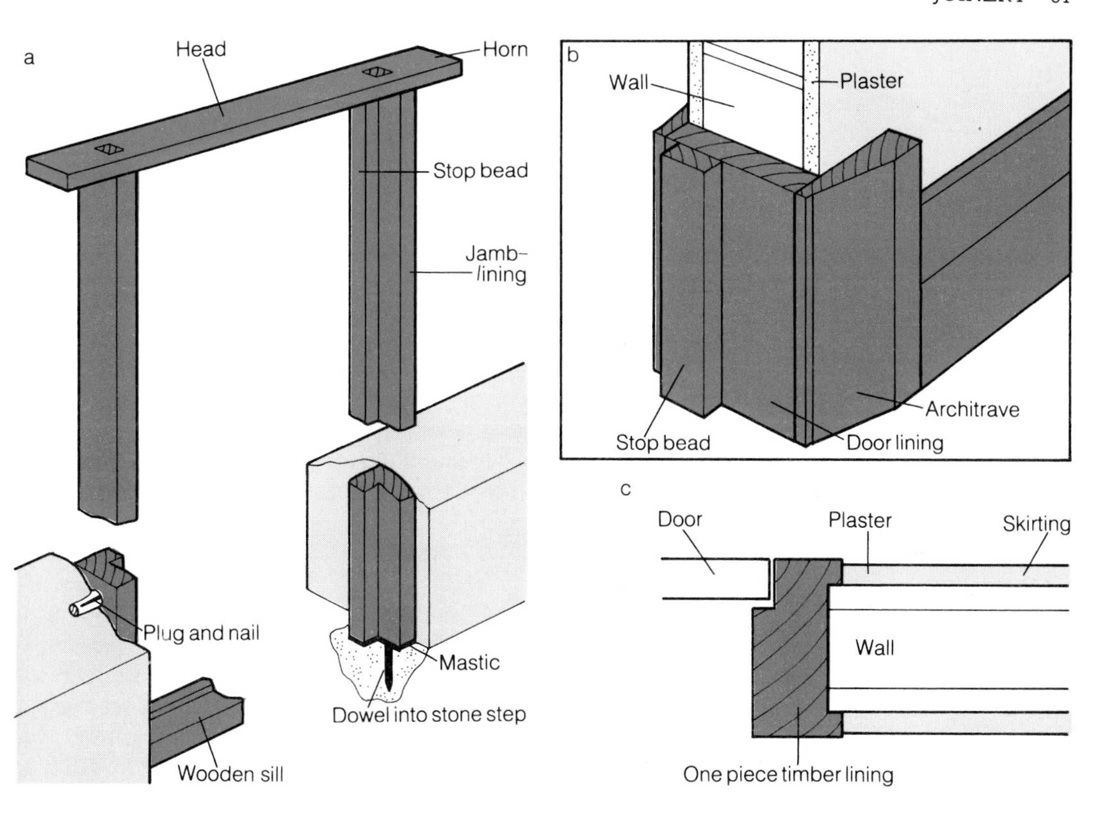

5.14 Construction of doorways: (a) How an external doorway is built up (b) How an internal doorway is formed with lining, stop bead and architrave (c) Plan sketch of an internal doorway

doors. On external doors – and occasionally on internal ones too – the fanlight can be opened for extra ventilation.

To accommodate a fanlight, the door opening is made extra tall, and jambs and head are installed in the normal way. A transom is fitted to form the bottom of the fanlight and the top of the door opening. In fixed fanlights over internal doors, the pane of glass is usually held merely by lengths of beading. On external and hinged fanlights putty is required, just as for any other window.

Doorway repairs

The jambs of an external door become exposed to the weather, particularly at the foot, when the step gets soaked. As a result they may rot. To repair them, cut out the damaged section, then beyond it into about 75 mm (3 in) of sound wood. If there is a wooden threshold, the jamb may be tenoned into it, and you will then have to cut through the tenon. Get a new piece of timber (it might be easier to use two pieces to form the rebate). Plane it down to size if necessary, apply preservative to the back, and fix it with screws. Join to the existing timber by means of a scarfe joint.

Shrinkage of the timber and settlement of the wall may cause gaps to develop between external door frames and the wall. These can be filled with mastic – the type squeezed from a tube is easiest to apply. To save on the amount of mastic needed, a large gap can first be packed out with rags or rope.

The architrave is the part of an internal doorway most likely to suffer damage. It is virtually impossible to patch up a damaged architrave because of the difficulty of buying new mouldings to match the old. The only course is to remove it totally (on both sides and the top) by prising it off. Then buy new architrave from a timber merchant.

Stop beads, too, are easily damaged. These can be patched, in the manner described for external door jambs, or you can prise the whole length off and replace it. Since this is usually a straight piece of wood, and not moulded, matching up presents no problem. A damaged lining can be repaired or replaced similarly.

Jambs and lining may shake loose from the wall, even though the timber is sound. The traditional way to re-fix them is to remove them, cement new timber plugs into the wall, then nail the pieces back in position. Sometimes, however, it is possible to re-fix sound jambs or lining without removing them from the wall. Drill through the loose section and into the wall, using a masonry bit. Twist a plastic wall plug on to the end of a wood screw, and insert the wall plug into the hole. Tap the screw head with a hammer, and the plug should pass into the wall – you will feel when this has happened. Tighten the screw, cover its head with filler, and re-paint. Do this at sufficient spots on the frame to ensure a firm fixing.

Linings and jambs can become so damaged that they have to be renewed completely. If you attempt this job, make sure the sides are truly upright, and the opening square, otherwise it will be more difficult to fit the door and get it to work properly. It is difficult to make the sides vertical using the brickwork as a guide. A more reliable method is to drive extra long plugs into the wall, leaving them sticking out well proud. You can make the plugs from 50 × 25 mm (2 × 1 in) softwood. They should be propeller-shaped at the end so they lock into place when driven into the mortar. For extra security, place mortar into the hole before fitting the plugs. Now drop a plumb line from the top of the opening and saw the plugs level with the line. Screw the lining to the plugs and it will be vertical.

SKIRTING BOARDS

Skirting boards are lengths of decoratively shaped timber, fitted to neaten the gap between floor and wall. The plaster does not normally extend down to floor level. In period houses, skirtings can be as high as 300 mm (1 ft) or more – and moulded ornately. Today skirtings are much plainer and smaller – perhaps only 100 mm (4 in) in height.

Modern skirtings are usually fixed by means of cut nails driven through the timber and into timber plugs in the masonry. In period houses, where the skirting is deep and elaborately moulded, it is more likely to be nailed to wooden grounds fixed to wall plugs. Rarely, the skirting is of two sections; a bottom piece with a tongue located in a groove in the floorboards, and a top piece joined to the bottom, also by a tongue and groove.

Plugging the gaps

As the timber shrinks, gaps appear between skirting and wall at the top, and between skirting and floor at the bottom. Draughts can enter through these gaps, particularly the one at the bottom. In any event, gaps are unsightly, so it is as well to cover them. The gap where the skirting meets the wall can be stopped up with ordinary decorator's filler. It is quicker and easier to pin lengths of moulding to cover the gap between floor and skirting. Use either quarter-round or triangular-section mouldings (Fig. 5:15). The moulding should be pinned to the skirting (never the floor) to prevent it shaking loose by the vibration of the floor. Mitre the mouldings at the corners.

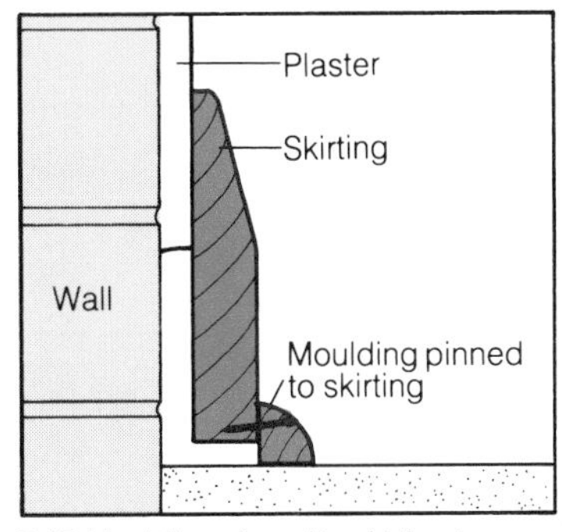

5.15 *Moulding pinned to skirting to keep out draughts*

Removing skirting board

Badly damaged skirting board should be completely replaced. If you are fitting built-in floor-standing cupboards – kitchen cabinets, for instance – to a wall, it is often easier and quicker to remove the skirting, then cut it to length and refix it to any part of the bottom of the wall that remains on view, than to trim the cupboard base to fit round the skirting.

Prising off the skirting is easy. Take an old carpentry chisel, and wedge it behind the skirting, preferably near one of the fixing nails. It is worth scraping off the paint to locate one of these nails. Pull hard on the chisel handle and the skirting will start to come away. You can now push timber wedges behind it while you wrench away near the other nails to free the whole length of skirting.

Fitting new skirting

First get your skirting. Choose with care, because skirting contributes to a room's character.

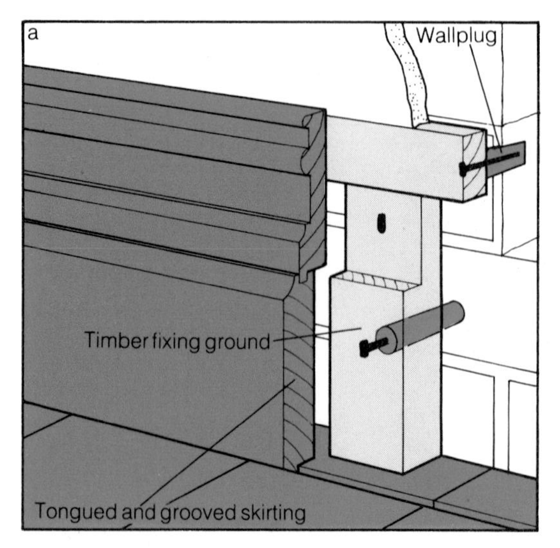

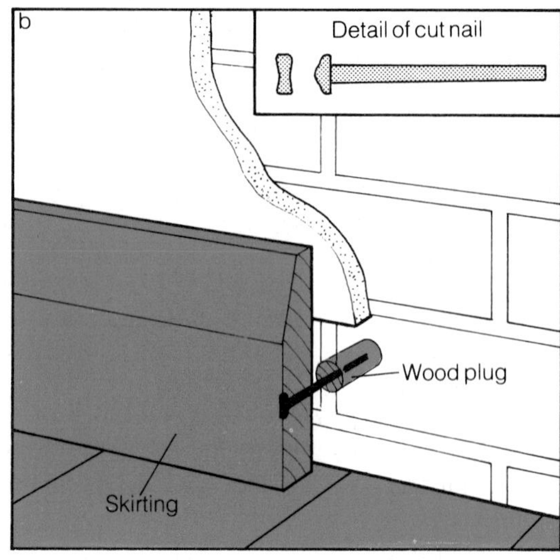

5.16 *How skirtings are fitted:*
(a) Ornate skirting of a period house
(b) Modern skirting.

If you are fitting skirting to just one wall of a room, the problem will be to match it to the rest. This should present no difficulty in recent houses, for skirting with the right profile will be readily available. Older skirting, however, might have to be replaced completely, so that the entire room will look the same.

Modern skirting, as sold widely in timber yards, would not look out of place in a house built, say, since World War I, but it is worth trying to match the period appearance of skirting on buildings earlier than that.

Finding matching skirting need not be difficult now that the importance of period fittings is recognized. Many firms specialize in salvaging such fittings from buildings due for demolition, then offer it for sale. Ask around locally, or look at advertisements in local newspapers to find out if there are any near your home.

The other possibility is to buy separate pieces of small-section moulding, and join them together to form something that looks like your skirting.

Aim to buy skirting in lengths that will cover the whole wall in one span, because joins in the middle never look as neat. Fix the skirting by driving nails through it and into the plugs on the wall (Fig. 5:16). It is worth the effort to position the nails accurately enough to allow you to drive them into the original fixings. All you have to do is cut the skirting to length, then lay it flat on the floor in front of the wall where it will be fixed. Make pencil marks on its face where the nails should go. Drill clearance holes for these nails so that there is no chance of splitting the timber. This is particularly important if you have bought expensive period skirting, or are using lengths of thin moulding. Punch the nails home, cover the heads with filler, and paint the skirting.

Patches for skirting

Where a part of a length of skirting board is damaged, it may be possible to insert a patch. To repair damage in the middle of a length of skirting, begin by cutting out the defective portion. Cut at an angle so that the skirting is wider at the front than at the back. One method of cutting is to push wedges behind the damaged section to force it away from the wall (Fig. 5:17). Now set up a small, fine-toothed saw (preferably a dovetail) in front of the skirting, and in a mitre box. Saw through the skirting at an angle of 45°. This is difficult, because it requires many short movements with the saw, but it can be done. You may have to finish off with a thin bladed saw, such as a keyhole saw.

If you find this method too difficult, there is another, but it is not as neat. This involves making a series of holes with a drill (you will get greater accuracy with an electric one) from the front to the back of the skirting. As with the saw cuts, these should slope, but you do not have to aim for an accurate 45°. It is more important to make all the holes at exactly the same angle. Chop out the waste with a chisel.

5.17 *Patching damaged skirting: (a) Cut through the damaged section with either a small saw and mitre box, or bore holes with an electric drill. (b) Mark the new skirting if you have cut out the old with a drill. (c) Make fixing points. (d) Nail the new skirting in place. (e) Deal with corners – external (bottom inset) and internal.*

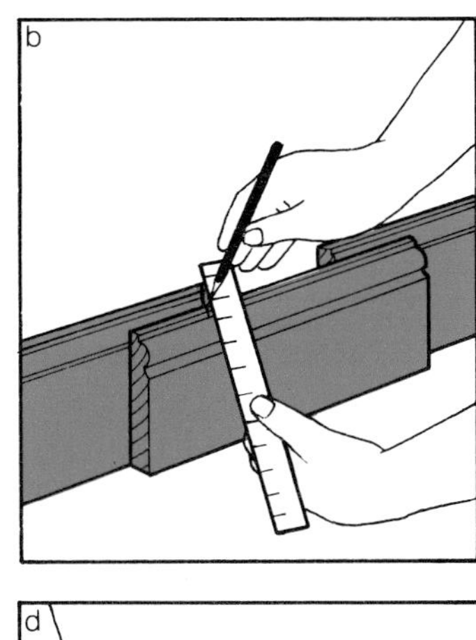

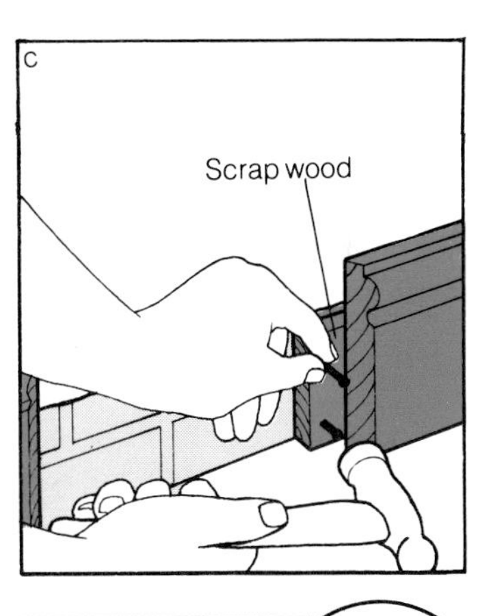

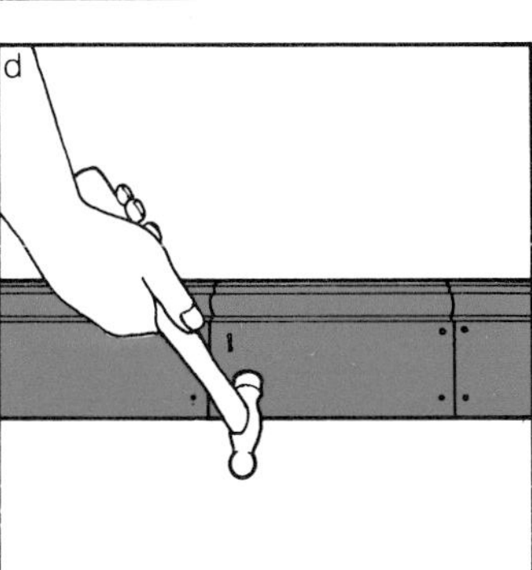

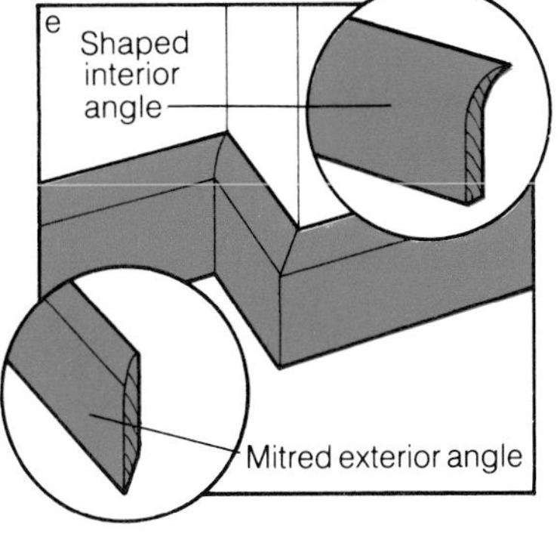

If you have sawn out the damaged timber with the aid of a mitre box, use this same guide to cut new timber at exactly the same angle. If you have used the second method, place a length of new moulding in front of the gap. Place a ruler on top of the existing skirting. Align the ruler accurately along the cut so that it overlaps the new skirting. Draw a pencil line along the ruler on top of the new moulding. Cut to this line and you should get a perfect fit.

To provide fixing points for the new mouldings, you need two pieces of scrap wood the same thickness as the plaster (you may have to plane them down to get an exact match) and the same height as the gap between floor and bottom of the plaster. Push these timber packing pieces behind each cut end of the existing skirting, and drive masonry nails through them and into the wall behind. Nail the new skirting to this timber.

Where the damaged portion is near the end of a run of skirting, such as in the corner of the room, you will need to cut through the skirting only once – on the side of the damaged portion furthest from the corner. Prise the damaged piece free. Cut the replacement so as to get a neat join at the corner as well as to fit the angle of the cut you have made. An external corner will probably be mitred – any variation from a 45° joint is due to inaccuracies in the angle of the wall. So, using a mitre box, saw at the angles that give an accurate fit.

At an internal angle, cut one length square to butt up against the wall. Shape the end of the other length to fit the contours of the first. It is much easier to do this before you cut the pieces finally to fit.

PICTURE RAILS

Besides providing an anchorage on which to hang pictures, picture rails provide an important visual break in the walls of high rooms. They are not usually fitted in modern rooms, which are rarely tall enough to take them, but they are widely found in older houses. Many such rails are beautiful additions to the charm of rooms built in a more graceful era, and to remove them would be an act of wanton destruction. Some picture rails, however, are not especially attractive, and even the best can become so badly damaged, or affected by woodworm or rot, that their removal becomes necessary.

Removing picture rails

Picture rails are fixed by means of cut nails driven through them into wooden plugs set into the masonry at centres varying from 450 to 600 mm (18 to 24 in). Prise them away as described for skirting boards, with either a claw hammer or an old chisel. Concentrate your efforts at the locations of the fixing nails. Once you start to lever, you will see their position at a glance. The wall will be damaged as you pull the rail away, but you can make good afterwards with plaster or decorator's filler.

If it is difficult to move the rail, perhaps because the nails have rusted, scrape off the paintwork until the nails are revealed, then punch them through the rail into the wall behind. The rail will then simply fall away. Or just split the rail along the line of the nails with a carpentry chisel, then lift it clear.

Whichever of these two methods you adopt, pull the nails out afterwards, otherwise they might rust and discolour any subsequent decorations. Take them out with a claw hammer, protecting the plaster by placing a small piece of thin waste wood on it. If the nail cannot be withdrawn, drive it well below the surface of the wall, so that it can later be covered with a thick layer of filler.

New picture rails

You may want to replace a damaged rail. Alternatively, you might like the elegance of a rail and the convenience it offers to hang pictures on the walls. Just as with skirting, it is often possible to buy old picture rails from firms that specialize in salvaging period timber from buildings about to be demolished. Otherwise new timber can be used.

If the rail is to replace a damaged one that has been removed, try to make use of the wooden plugs to which the original rail was fixed. Aim to get a rail long enough to cover a wall in one span, to avoid having untidy joins. Cut the rail to size. Hold it just below the plugs on the wall, and mark on the face of the rail where the fixing nails should go. Drill clearance holes for these, especially in old valuable timber, to lessen the risk of splitting the wood. Hold the rail in place, and hammer home the nails, taking care not to mark the face of the timber. Punch the nails home, and disguise the heads with filler.

If there are no timber plugs you can use, fix the rail with screws driven into plastic wall plugs. The heads of these will be more difficult to cover up on more intricate mouldings, but that cannot be helped.

To make your own picture rail, you can buy ornate modern moulding, or merely use a straight batten – timber 45 × 13 mm (1¾ × ½ in) is suitable. There needs to be a space behind the timber into which the hanging clips can locate. To provide such a space, glue small neatly-cut blocks to the back of the rail (Fig. 5:18). The blocks should be of the same size as the main rail and be placed at 900 mm (3 ft) intervals.

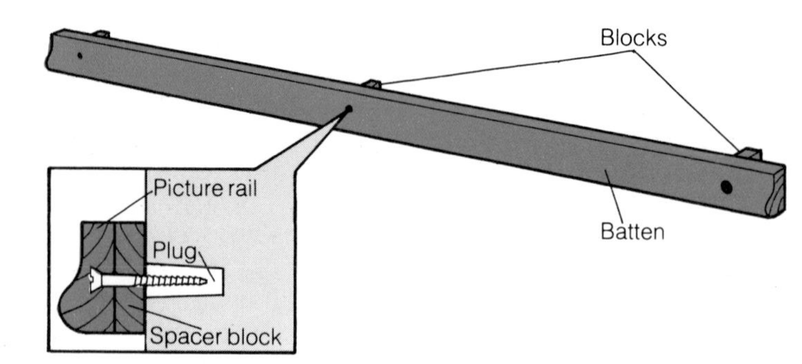

5.18 *Making a new picture rail by screwing a batten to spacer blocks.*

Fix the rail to the wall by means of screws driven through it and the spacer blocks into plastic plugs inserted in the wall. It is easy to paint such a rail without getting paint on the wall.

STAIRCASES

The type of staircase fitted will depend on the plan of the house. Simplest of all is a straight flight, which just goes up from ground to first floor in a single, straight run. Sometimes, however, the staircase changes direction. A half-landing may be fitted if the staircase doubles back on itself. There may be a quarter-landing when the turn is a right-angled one. As an alternative to a quarter landing, there may be angled steps, known as winders.

It is amazing how little appears to go wrong with most staircases when you consider the pounding they take from so many passing feet, and how comparatively slender their construction seems. It pays, though, to take care of staircases, and to rectify faults as soon as they appear, so that they can go on giving trouble-free service.

Avoid carrying out conversions to a staircase – for instance, to make an old-fashioned one look modern – because you might weaken the structure, besides the fact that you will destroy the character of your home.

How staircases are built

Traditionally, staircases were built on the spot by master carpenters working on the construction of the house. This practice has long been discontinued. Instead staircases are supplied to the site as factory-made units.

Usually the staircase is fitted in the hall, with one side against a wall and the other side open.

The part of the stair on which you actually walk is the tread, and the vertical timber that closes the gap between two treads is the riser. The riser is usually merely butted up to the treads and fixed by screws or nails. A better but rare practice, however, is for the riser to be joined by means of tongues and grooves. Sometimes, too, a length of moulding is fitted to the top of the riser, just underneath the projection of the tread, to mask any gap that may develop as the wood shrinks. The front edge of the tread – the nosing – is usually rounded off.

Some modern staircases are of an open-tread design – to make it seem less bulky in the confines of the hall of a small house. It is dangerous to attempt to convert a conventional staircase into an open-tread one, however, for structural reasons.

At each side of the staircase is a long length of timber, called a string. Two types of string are found – open and closed. An open string has a cut-out profile, into which the treads and risers are fitted. A closed string has straight edges, and the treads and risers fit into grooves cut into its side. Wedges are fitted to hold the tread and riser tightly in the groove. The two strings in a staircase need not necessarily be of the same type. It is not uncommon for the wall string (the one against a wall) to be closed, and the outer string (the one away from the wall) to be open.

A safety barrier or balustrade (also called a banister) is fitted to the open side (or sides) of a staircase. The length of timber which you hold as you climb a stairway is a baluster rail and the large upright members into which the baluster rail joins at each end are newel posts. The rail is supported by uprights known as balusters. Modern staircases have fewer balusters than older ones, but you should never alter the number of balusters, because you risk weakening the structure.

A balustrade can also be fitted to the landing, if required. When a staircase has a wall on both sides, there is no balustrade, but instead a handrail is fitted to the wall by means of metal brackets.

Underneath, the staircase is supported on lengths of timber on edge known as carriages. There may be just one central carriage, or there may be an additional two – one near each edge. Lengths of timber, called brackets or sometimes cleats, are fixed to the carriages, to give extra support to the treads. In addition, triangular pieces of wood, known as glue blocks, are fixed to strengthen the join between tread and riser. For the general structure of a staircase see Fig. 5:19.

In many small houses it is customary to have a cupboard under the stairs. In some instances, the underside of the staircase is in full view from within the cupboard. More usually, however, the underneath is covered with either plaster (plasterboard in modern homes, lath and plaster in older ones) or some form of board, such as hardboard.

General repairs to staircases

Major faults that develop in a staircase often require the services of a builder. There are, however, several types of maintenance that the do-it-yourselfer can carry out.

If the underside of the staircase is accessible, maintenance is easy, because you can see at a glance when anything is wrong. It pays to have a look at it from time to time to see that everything is all right. For instance, glue blocks may have fallen off. If so, fix them back with glue and nails. Similarly, a bracket may have worked loose, and should be properly fixed again. Any members that are damaged should be repaired. If the treads or risers are loose in the grooves in a string, make small timber wedges, smear glue on them, and drive them into the groove. You can also nail these wedges in position, using fine pins. Remedial work is much more difficult if the underside is covered. Do not remove the covering, except to repair a major fault.

Creaking stairs

One of the most common and irritating faults that can develop in staircases is creaking. The reason for this is that a tread or riser is not securely fixed and is flexing under the weight. If you can get at the underside, look to see if any blocks are missing, and re-fit them. The wedges holding the treads and risers in the grooves of the strings may have dropped out. Fit new ones if necessary (Fig. 5:19). If the whole staircase creaks, it may be well worth fixing an extra carriage. Indeed there may not be a carriage there at all, and in that case you should fit one.

It is not worth the bother of removing an understairs covering just to silence a few creaks, but makeshift remedies can be tried. Look if there is a gap between the noisy tread and the riser above or below it. If there is one, the simplest remedy could be to puff in a little talcum powder, which would act as a lubricant. Or you could squirt a little woodworking adhesive into the gap, then tap some thin nails down through the tread and into the riser below. Thin section moulding, fitted to both tread and riser just below the nosing of the tread (assuming that none is there already) might also stop the movement. You would, however, probably want to fit it to every riser to maintain continuity of appearance.

5.19 *How a staircase is built (a) and how to repair it: (b) New wedges stop creaks. (c) Mend worn nosing. (d) Re-fix a loose string. (e) To fit a new tread, remove the balusters so that you can free the damaged tread. (f) Make and fit a new riser. (g) Make a new tread, cutting out mortises to fit round the balusters. (h) Fit wedges, if needed, to hold the new tread in the string. (i) The mortises round the balusters should be closed off with moulding fitted after the balusters have been inserted.*

Worn nosing

The nosing on the front edge of a tread can become worn. Besides looking unsightly, this can be dangerous. To repair it, use a straight edge and pencil to draw a line on the tread parallel to the undamaged front of the nosing. Remove any

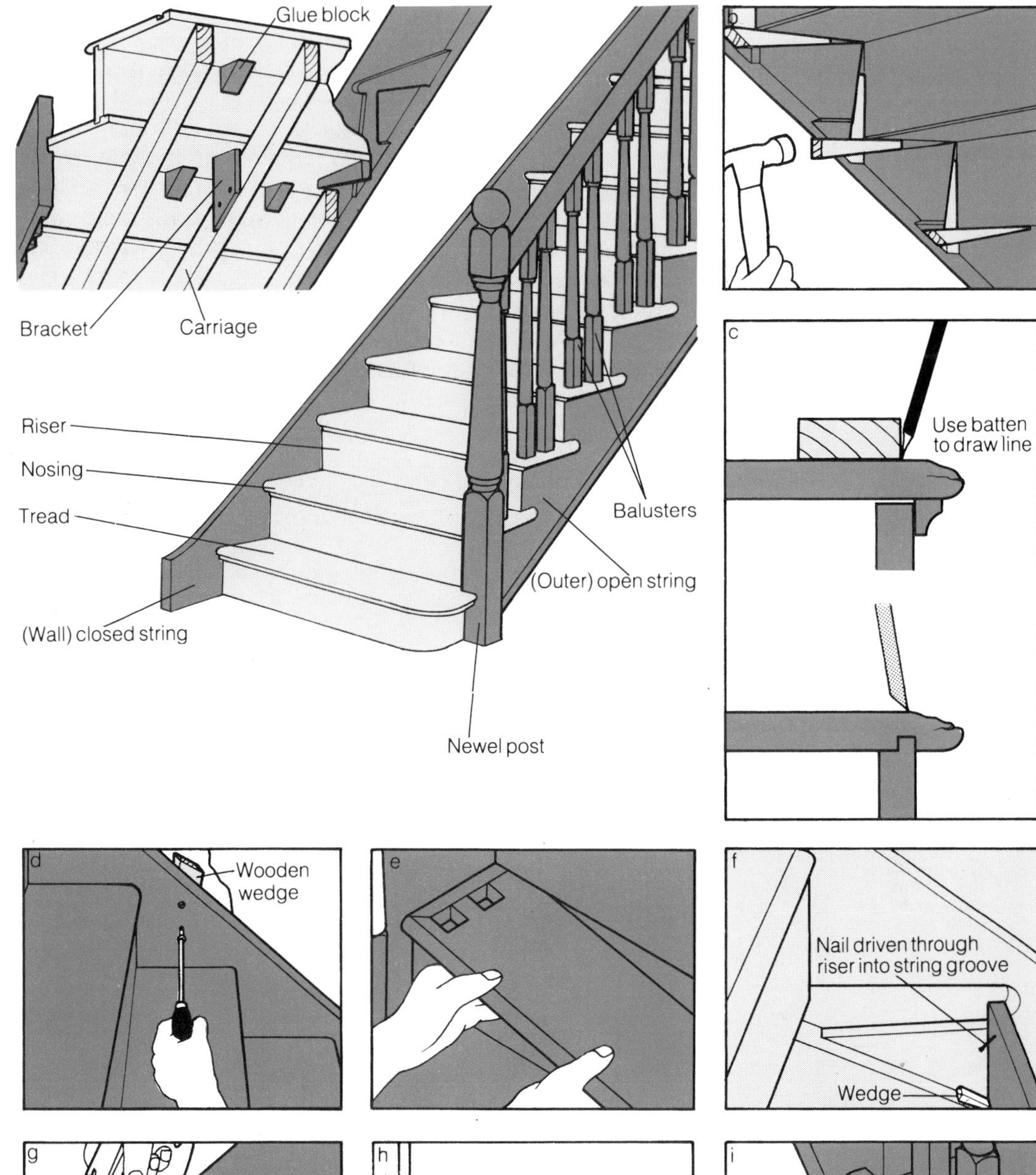

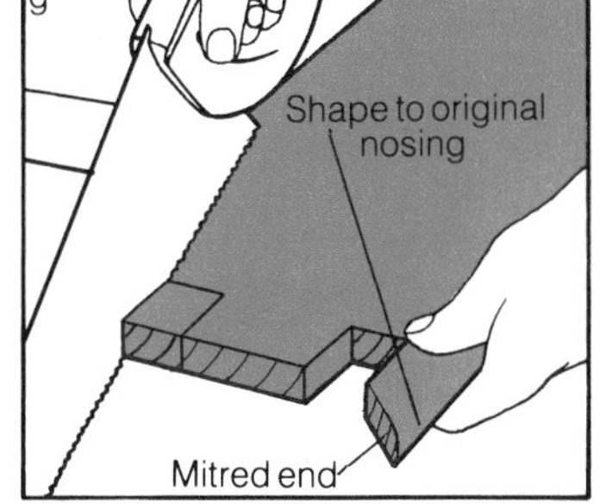

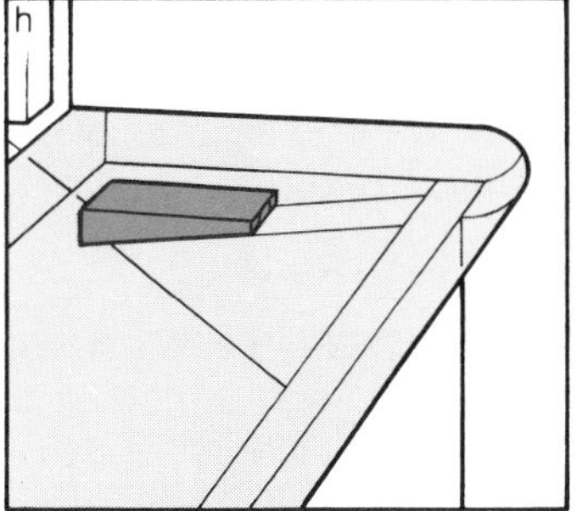

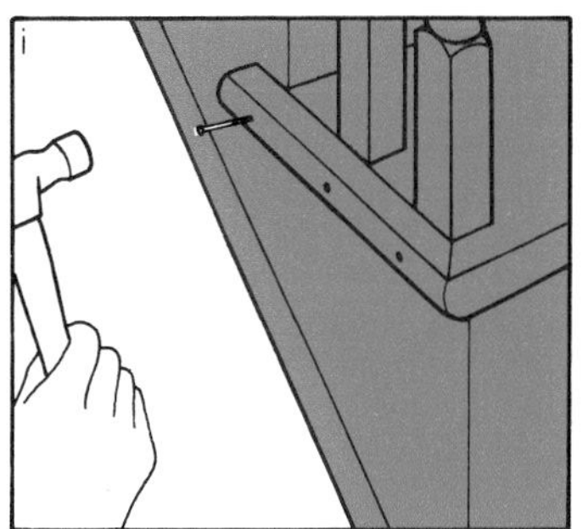

g

Shape to original nosing

Mitred end

h

i

moulding covering the join between tread and riser, then, with a hammer and broad chisel, chop along the pencil line to remove the nosing. Finish with a clean, straight line.

You should aim to have about 13 mm (½ in) of the edge of the riser exposed. If the tread and riser are joined by a tongue projecting from the riser into a groove in the tread, this tongue will have to be removed. Cut a length of softwood to match the width of the stair, and shape one edge to match the profile of the original nosing. You can do this shaping with a file, finishing off with glasspaper. Glue and screw this softwood to the front edge of the tread. Allow the glue to set, then, if necessary, plane the top of the new nosing down to the level of the tread. Replace any beading removed from the join between tread and riser.

Loose treads and risers

Settlement of the building may pull the string away from the treads and risers. Where the gap between the two is not large – up to, say, 19 mm (¾ in) – you could remedy the fault by driving wedges between the string and the wall, and these will force the string back on to the treads and risers. To do this, hack off plaster from the wall above the string near where the gap between string and tread has developed. Take a piece of timber about 300 mm (1 ft) long, 38 mm (1½ in) wide and 25 mm (1 in) thick. Taper one end to form a wedge, then tap it into the gap between the string and the wall as far as it will go. Fit as many wedges as are needed to reposition the string correctly. Saw off the protruding tops of the wedges so that they are flush with the string. Drive screws through the front of the string and into the wedge – you will need to drill pilot holes for the screws. Cover the screw heads with filler and paint. A wide gap – greater than 19 mm (¾ in) – indicates a more serious conditon, and you ought to call in a builder.

Loose balusters

Movement of the staircase can make a baluster loose at its joint with the string or the handrail. To wedge it back into place, smear matchstick-size pieces of timber with glue and push them into the enlarged hole. Top off with filler and paint.

Sometimes, too, a secure fixing can be obtained if you drill a pilot hole at an angle through the baluster and into the string below or rail above, then drive a nail through it.

New treads and risers

You may need to fit a new tread or riser, because one is damaged. Equally likely is that a gap larger than 19 mm (¾ in) may have developed between a tread or riser and the string so that a wider step is needed. If both strings are closed a repair will involve the virtual dismantling of the staircase and so should be left to a builder. If at least one string is open, however, it is possible for a skilled do-it-yourselfer to do the work. Remember, though, that a badly made staircase is a hazard, so if in doubt, leave the work to an expert.

Begin by removing the balusters from the affected tread. Tap them with a block of wood until any nails holding them in position are revealed. Remove the nails, then bend the balusters to spring them out. The tread will be joined to the riser above. Make a few test borings with a small drill bit to determine whether the joint is by means of a tongue and groove. If it is, saw through the tongue with a padsaw. If there is no tongue, the tread and riser will be joined with screws or nails. Saw through these with a hacksaw blade. Prise the tread from the string. Then prise out the riser, if it is to be removed. Cut a piece of softwood to size to make a new riser, and glue and nail it into place. If the joint between the riser and the string is mitred, then mitre the end of the new riser. In a closed string, the riser is held into the groove by means of a wedge.

Cut a tread to size, using the old one as a pattern, and shape the nosing. Cut out mortises in the balustrade edge to take the balusters. Pack the groove of a closed string with wedges if necessary, and fit glue blocks where the treads meet the riser below, then glue and nail the tread into place. Fit the balusters in the mortises, and close off the front of these with a piece of moulding.

A new staircase

The staircase may have so many faults that complete renewal is the only solution. If you have any doubts about your stairs, it is safest to seek the advice of a surveyor.

If a new staircase is to be fitted into an old house, it is unlikely that a factory-made replacement will be available, so a new one will have to be built on site. This is not a job for the do-it-yourselfer, because it requires expertise that only a craftsman has. If a staircase in a modern house is damaged, however, you may be able to buy a factory-built one to replace it yourself.

Spiral staircases

Spiral staircases are an old idea that has been revived for modern homes. All but the most minor repairs should be left to an expert. So if you spot any defects in a modern staircase, consult the supplier or manufacturer.

If you want to install a spiral staircase in an existing house, make sure that there is sufficient room for it. Contrary to popular belief, they do not require less space than conventional staircases; just space of a different shape. They also impose a heavy strain on the floor where the central pillar rests, and this area may need strengthening. Fitting a spiral staircase is a job for a specialist.

ENEMIES OF TIMBER

The joinery of your home, including timber floors, window frames and the wooden structural members of the roof and walls, is liable to be attacked by two main enemies – woodworm and rot. Whenever you are carrying out maintenance (lifting floorboards, for instance) or decorating, always look for signs of woodworm and rot. Indeed, it is a good idea to make periodic inspections to see if they are present anywhere. This is especially true of those parts of a house that are rarely seen – the loft, for instance, and any part of the foundations and underside of the floor that you can get at. If tackled early, an outbreak of woodworm or rot can be cured fairly easily, but if they are left to develop they can seriously damage the structure of your home.

Because it has become possible to calculate accurately the amount of stress that a piece of timber can withstand, modern buildings can be made from much less sturdy timber than previously. These calculations hold good so long as the structural timber is not weakened – and weakening is most likely to be caused by woodworm or rot.

Woodworm

Woodworm is not a worm at all, but a beetle that bores its way into timber, causing damage and unsightly holes. There are, in fact, several varieties of wood-boring insect, but the one commonly referred to as woodworm is *Anobium punctatum* – the common furniture beetle.

It is called the furniture beetle because at one time it attacked the traditional hardwoods from which furniture was made. It has now become more widespread and developed a taste for the structural softwoods used in house building. It used to be thought, too, that the furniture beetle went only for old timber, but in fact it attacks new wood as well.

The female beetle mates in the spring and early summer, then looks for a safe, hospitable place to lay her eggs. Holes or cracks in the wood, badly fitting joints, even stretches of especially rough timber, are all ideal. There she will leave as many as 60 eggs at a time.

The eggs hatch within a few weeks, and grubs emerge. It is these, in fact, that cause the damage. To feed on the wood, they bore into it and move in the direction of the grain. For two or more years they chew their way along the grain, leaving behind them what looks like brown sawdust. This debris (known as frass) consists of tiny pellets. Eventually, the grub prepares to enter the chrysalis or pupal stage. To do so, it scoops out a small chamber near the surface of the timber, where it lies for a few weeks, gradually turning into a beetle. When the change is complete it bites its way out, leaving behind one of those holes that are the principal sign of an attack of woodworm.

As soon as they emerge, the beetles mate, and the female lays her eggs – this time in old borings as well as in cracks and joints. So, once an infestation starts, there is a good chance that it will continue.

The adult beetle can fly, so they may have come into your home on the wing. In general, however, beetles do not move very far from their original flight holes, so it is more common for a ready-made infestation to be brought into a beetle-free home – perhaps in a piece of old furniture or a wooden box. A typical example occurs if there is woodworm in a loft; someone puts an old chest there; then you buy the chest, bring it home and the woodworm continues to breed.

There are several other wood-boring insects in addition to the furniture beetle, but it is this particular creature that causes most worry in the home.

Preventive measures: the most obvious way of keeping woodworm out of your home is to be wary of what you bring into it. By all means buy antiques and snap up bargains in second-hand furniture shops, but give them a thorough examination, and if you suspect the presence of worm carry out remedial treatment immediately.

In particular, be careful about what you store in the parts of your home that you seldom visit, such as lofts and cellars. Even though no sign of attack may be evident, eggs might have been laid there recently, and the grubs may be burrowing out of sight. The beetles like the glue used in old plywood, for instance, and many attacks can be traced to old tea chests pushed up into a loft and forgotten.

The beetles always seek bare wood on which to lay their eggs; they will not attack timber that is polished or treated with preservative, although the adult beetles will emerge through polished surfaces. They will not bite through paint, although paint is not a woodworm killer. The unfortunate aspect of this is that they might well emerge through the back of such parts of the joinery as a skirting board, so that there would be no outward signs of the infestation.

The beetles like wood that is slightly damp. They find decayed wood more nutritious than sound wood, so a dry home is less likely to attract them. The installation of central heating, with its warm pipes going under floorboards, is thought to discourage them.

If you ever introduce new structural timbers into your home, use only timber that has been factory-impregnated with preservative.

Looking for woodworm is not a pleasant task. Wood-boring beetles strike in the least accessible, dirtiest, coldest and most uncomfortable parts of the house – the loft and the cellar, for instance. However, it has to be done. Wear old clothes, and take a torch and a magnifying glass. Look at the roof joists, rafters and other timber in the loft. Do the same in the cellar. The most obvious signs of infestation are the flight holes left by the adult beetle. The may indicate an attack that is no longer active, however. Woodworm sometimes extract all the goodness they can from a length of timber, then abandon it – but do not rely on this. Signs of frass – which you would detect with a magnifying glass – are evidence that the attack is still active.

If you come across signs of infestation in the loft or under the floor of a terraced or semi-detached house, tell your neighbours. The worm might have strayed next door.

Getting rid of woodworm can be complicated by the difficulty of reaching likely sites of infestation. Modern woodworm killers are effective, and not particularly difficult to apply. The work, however, has to be done in some of the most uncomfortable parts of your home, and the disturbance to family life will be considerable. The furniture must be moved, floor coverings disturbed and floorboards lifted.

The advantage of calling in a specialist firm is that you can be sure they will be thorough, because they normally give a guarantee against re-infestation. They know exactly how much liquid to apply and where. They are trained to look for signs of attack, and know from experience exactly where the treatment ought to be carried out. They will finish the work more quickly than you, and will have less difficulty working under the eaves or down in the cellar. Moreover, a home-loan may depend on a certificate to show that eradication has been carried out by professionals, and loans to help pay for the work may be available. Make sure that any company with which you deal is reputable and is well-established. A guarantee from a company that is no longer trading is not worth having.

There is no doubt, however, that you can reduce the cost by doing the work yourself. For small, local attacks, the fluid can be applied to the wood by brush, and even injected in the holes by means of the small nozzle that can be fitted to the tins of the liquid. Where the infestation is on a large scale, the liquid must be sprayed on.

Suitable sprayers can be hired, but most types of garden spray will do provided they give a good pressure, and will hold a couple of litres (4 pints). You also need a nozzle that gives the correct type of spray. Ideally, you need a fairly coarse, fan-shaped spray. If the spray is too coarse, excess liquid will soil the plaster. If it is too fine, liquid will vapourize and pollute the air, making the work unpleasant. Furthermore, the spray should have a long lance – at least 600 mm (2 ft) – so that you can reach under the eaves and into the apex of the roof in the loft, and get a good distance under the floorboards.

Take care, too, about how you dress. Although you should wear old clothes that you do not mind getting dirty and stained, they should also offer you protection. Cover your arms with long sleeves and tuck your trousers into your socks. Wear gloves and goggles, and a light fume mask – sold at DIY shops and in some chemists – so that you will not inhale any vapour in a confined space. Do not smoke while spraying.

If you are going to work in a loft, lift up any insulation material to reveal the timbers. If your loft has no insulation, do the spraying just before you install it. The liquid cannot easily penetrate the layers of dust and cobwebs that will undoubtedly be lying on the timber, so clean the area. Use a vacuum cleaner, preferably a cylinder type with a hose. The heavy duty, industrial-style cleaners are ideal for this work – they can be hired.

If the cold water tank is insulated with expanded polystyrene lagging, this must be protected from the fluid, and in any event the tank itself must be covered so that no vapour from the spraying gets into the water. Look, too, at any wiring in the loft. If it is of the rubber-coated type, make sure no liquid gets on it. In any event, this type of cable is nearing or past the end of its useful life, so you ought to get it renewed. Even modern pvc-sheathed cable should be inspected for signs of wear. Fluid getting on to bare wire could cause a short circuit, but even more important is the fact that damaged cable is dangerous and should be replaced immediately.

When you start spraying, pay special attention to the affected areas, but treat all exposed timber. Apply sufficient fluid to wet all the surfaces thoroughly, but not so much that any runs through to stain the ceiling below. There will be a certain amount of fine spray falling as a mist as you work on the ceiling joists, and this should be sufficient to treat the laths on a lath-and-plaster ceiling.

When the floorboards and joists need treatment, lift up every fourth board, and clean the area below with a vacuum cleaner before spraying. Treat the area below the floor, not forgetting the undersides of the boards. When you have finished this, apply fluid to the undersides of the boards you have lifted, then replace them. Finally spray the top.

The floorboards will need at least six months to dry out thoroughly. While they are moist they could damage synthetic floor coverings, such as vinyls. In the meantime, use a temporary covering, or use a natural material such as cork, which would be immune to chemical attack. It has been suggested that lining a floor with hardboard will give sufficient protection, so you could lay any floor covering you like on top of it, but in fact the woodworm killer is so penetrative that it will work its way up through the nail holes and stain the top of the hardboard.

Rot

An occasional splashing, or even dousing, does no harm to timber, provided that it is allowed to dry out thoroughly. Timber that is continually and excessively moist, however, will eventually rot. Most people can recognize the signs of rotting wood. It warps and the surface starts to break up. Press it and it feels soft and spongy. By itself, the moisture in the timber does not cause rot. Rot is caused instead by fungi that are encouraged to grow in the dampness. A house that is well maintained, free from damp and well ventilated will not harbour rot.

Rot is usually classified into two types: wet rot and dry rot. Do not be misled by the name of the latter; it, too, is caused by damp. It gets it name because it reduces the timber it attacks to a dry powdery surface. Wet rot is much more common than dry rot, but fortunately is easier to cure. Both are serious conditions – much more so than woodworm. They can destroy the timbers of your home, reducing it to a dangerous, unhealthy and unsightly condition.

Identifying rot is not difficult. Dry rot causes a musty smell and a lot or rust-red dust. The dust is, in fact, spores from a fungus. In advanced cases, deep cracks will break up the surface of the wood into cubes, some of them quite large.

The surface of badly affected timber will be covered by a web of matted fungus. This web grows rapidly in humid conditions and generally looks like cotton wool. If it comes into contact with drier air, or is exposed to light, bright yellow patches appear. When the fungus is growing in damp conditions, globules of water-like drops are formed. The fungus also produces a thin, pancake-like fruit. The centre is ridged and rust red in colour, but the edges are white. The wood darkens in colour, is powdery when rubbed between the fingers and loses its resinous smell. If you pick it up, it feels much lighter than it should.

The most damaging parts of the fungus are the strands of the web. They spread, often unseen, and convey water to wood farther away that is dry and sound. Thus the condition spreads. Even if you remove defective wood, these strands could be left behind to continue spreading the fungus. As well as infecting the wood, they can pass through soft mortar and brickwork and find their way around stone and metal.

The fungal strands of wet rot are never as thick as those of dry rot, and they do not spread with the same ease. They cannot, for instance, penetrate brickwork. Moreover, they are dark brown in colour and, when growing over the surface of wood or damp plaster, form a sort of fern shape. A thin veneer of surface wood may conceal a soft dark mass of rot underneath.

Keeping rot at bay is better than treating it once it already has a hold. Rot is caused by damp. Dry rot cannot form in timber containing less than 25 per cent moisture, and wet rot requires a moisture content in the timber of between 50 and 60 per cent. To prevent rot, therefore, make sure your house is dry. If you suspect damp to be present anywhere, treat it as described earlier. Keep the gutters and downpipes in good order, so that the walls of the house do not become saturated.

Moreover, the fungi do not spread so easily when there is good ventilation. Check that air bricks and grilles are not blocked and keep the paintwork, especially that on outdoor timber, in good condition so that rainwater cannot penetrate it.

Getting rid of rot. Wet rot is the easiest to deal with. As soon as you remove the damp, it will die out. You are, however, left with the job of replacing all the damaged timber. If these are important structural members, then seek professional advice. Non-structural timbers, such as skirting, window frames, picture rails, door frames and floorboards can be replaced as described elsewhere in this book.

Prod the surface of the timber with a sharp instrument to determine the extent of the rot. Cut out and burn all affected wood, and remove all dust, dirt and debris. Make sure the new timber you use is sound, thoroughly dry and well seasoned. Also treat it, and the nearby timber, brick and concrete areas with dry rot fluid, to prevent that developing.

Dry rot is much more difficult to eradicate, and dealing with extensive attacks is beyond the scope of the average do-it-yourselfer. A thorough knowledge of building techniques is required, as well as a full acquaintance with the behaviour and symptoms of the fungus. Moreover, the disturbance caused can be tremendous and the house may be uninhabitable during the work. You can, perhaps, cope with small outbreaks yourself. As with wet rot, it is essential to remove the conditions that cause the fungus to develop in the first place: make sure the house is dry and well ventilated.

To tackle the infestation, inspect your home minutely for

evidence of the rot. Wherever you see any sign of attack, consider that point as being the centre of a sphere with a radius of 900 mm (3 ft) and make a close examination in every direction within that area. If you find any sign of decay, carry on with the sphere principle, until eventually you get to the limits of the attack.

Cut away affected timber to a point 900 mm (3 ft) beyond the visible limits of an attack. If this involves the structural timbers, seek expert advice.

The timber you cut out should be taken out of the house and burned. If strands have penetrated plaster, it must all be hacked off, taken outside in plastic bags and sprayed with dry rot fluid, before being taken away. Clean the whole area of the wall behind the plaster with a wire brush to make sure no strands are left. The debris from cleaning must also be taken outside in plastic bags and sprayed before disposal.

Where masonry has been affected, drill holes into the wall and fill them with dry rot fluid. The holes should be 13 mm (½ in) in diameter, 150 mm (6 in) deep, and at an angle of 45°. They should cover the contaminated area at 600 mm (2 ft) staggered intervals.

Working from the top downwards, spray all brick, block, concrete and earth surfaces until they are saturated, using a spray with a coarse nozzle. The precautions about clothing and a mask suggested in the section on woodworm should be observed. If the strands have gone through the brickwork, deal with both sides similarly.

Two coats of dry rot fluid must be applied to timber around the decayed timbers that have been cut away. The treatment should extend to a distance of 1500 mm (5 ft) from the last affected spot. Treat the new timber with a fungicidal wood preservative. Brush on liberal applications, and stand sawn ends in a pot of the liquid for a good five minutes.

Allow the wall to dry out properly before re-plastering and decorating. As an extra precaution, you may apply zinc oxycholoride plaster before the wall plaster.

The whole essence of the treatment of dry rot is thoroughness. Leave any of the strands behind, and it can go on spreading. So you must carry on looking for further signs of the attack, and be sure that you have removed every trace. It would be a pity to go to all that trouble, then find in a short while you are having to carry out the remedial treatment all over again. It is because of this – in addition to the scale of the work involved – that perhaps the work should be left to the experts, even though the cost of doing so can be high.

DECORATING THE JOINERY

The joinery discussed in this chapter needs to be well protected, both to keep it looking attractive, and to prevent it from deteriorating. This is especially true of timber that comes into contact with the weather outside. Doors, in particular, should be well cared for, since if they warp they will not operate properly. Protection is particularly necessary to keep rot at bay.

The best type of paint to use on joinery is a gloss. It is a little more troublesome to apply – and cleaning the brushes afterwards can be a chore – but it gives better protection. If you are starting off with bare wood, treat all knots and resinous areas with knotting, to prevent the resin form "weeping" through and spoiling the finished result. Then apply a wood primer. Follow this with an undercoat, then one or two coats of gloss.

Paintwork that is in good condition need merely be washed down, rinsed and allowed to dry, then have two coats of gloss brushed on. If you are changing the colour apply an undercoat.

Repainting should be carried out regularly – and ideally just before it is necessary. It will then be a much easier job, because less preparation will be required.

Chapter 6
INTERNAL WALLS

CONSTRUCTION

Some internal walls serve a structural function in that they actually help to support the house. These are called load-bearing walls. Others offer no support; they merely divide the space. Such walls are termed partitions. The distinction between the two is essential especially if you wish to re-arrange the interior layout of the house.

Solid walls

A load-bearing internal wall that gives major support will usually be built like an external solid wall: 230 mm (9 in) thick. Where it is of minor constructional importance, it may be only half that thickness – the width, rather than the length, of the brick. In modern homes, some types of building block are used instead of brick to make solid walls. Not all solid walls, however, are load-bearing – partitions may be solid.

Hollow partitions

In general, partitions are hollow structures, and are built on a frame of timber, with an outer covering of either lath and plaster in older houses, or plasterboard in more modern buildings. Alternatively, some form of factory-built system may be used for partitions in modern homes.

Where there is a room on both sides of the partition, there will be lath and plaster – or plasterboard – on each side of the framework. The void in the middle of the wall is often used to carry electric cables around the home.

If the partition is dividing, say, a store room from a habitable room, only the room side of it may have been faced.

Lath and plaster walls

Hollow walls in an older house may be of lath and plaster. A lath and plaster wall (Fig. 6:1) is constructed on a framework of timber, the size of which is variable, but will probably be about 75 × 50 mm (3 × 2 in). There will be a horizontal member (a ceiling plate) at the top, and a corresponding floor plate at the bottom. Between these two there is a series of vertical members, called studs. The spacing between the studs can vary between 300 and 600 mm (1-2 ft). The framework may also be strengthened by other horizontal members known as noggings, approximately halfway up the studs. Sometimes the noggings are fixed to the studs by means of half lap joints, or they can be skew-nailed. Another method is for them to be staggered, so that nails can be driven through the studs and into the ends of the noggings.

Across the studs are nailed narrow, thin timbers – the laths. These act as a key for the plaster, which is skimmed onto them.

Plasterboard walls

Hollow walls in modern homes are usually made up of plasterboard. There are two ways in which a plasterboard partition can be built. It can consist of sheets of the board, fixed on one or both sides of a timber framework (Fig. 6:2). This framework is similar to that of a lath and plaster wall, except that the vertical studs are usually spaced wider apart. Alternatively, it can be constructed of factory-built sections, made up from plasterboard sheets around an inner core, which slot together (Fig. 6:3).

How partition walls are made up: 6.1 *Lath and plaster* 6.2 *Plasterboard on studs and noggings* 6.3 *Factory-built sections*

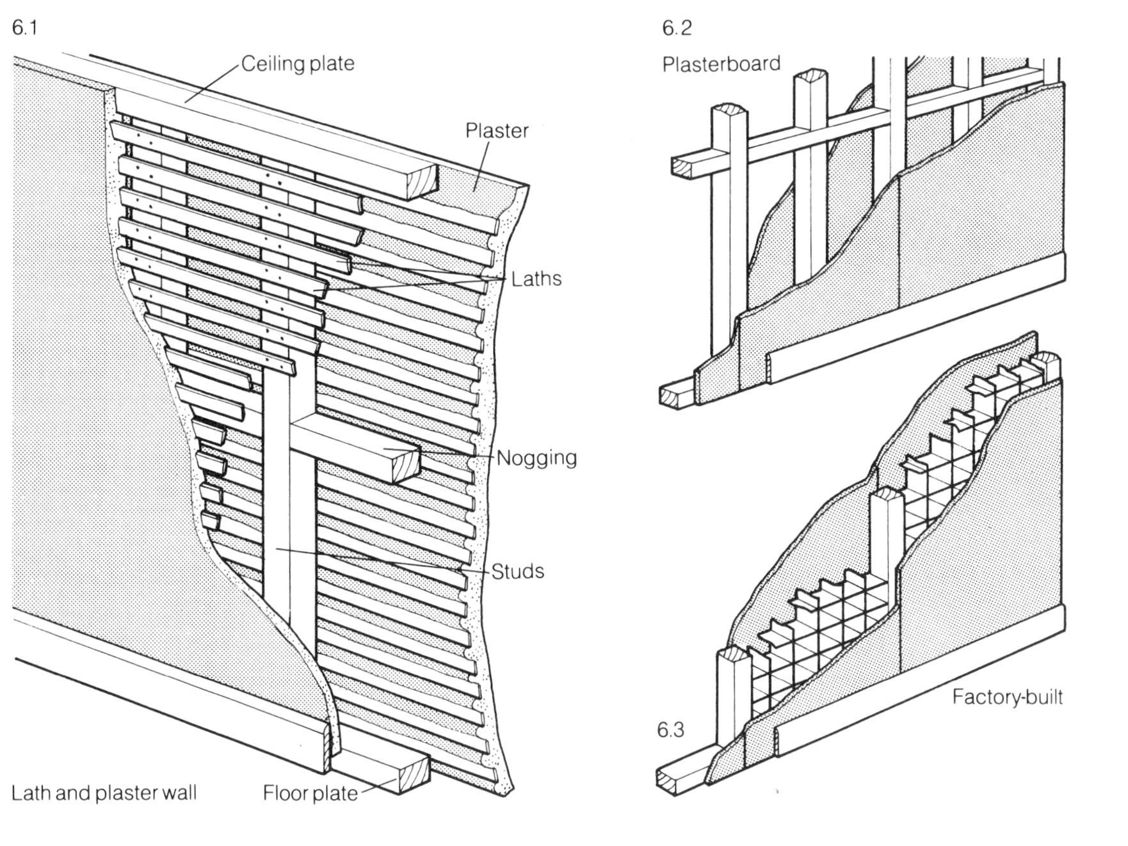

Telling the difference

To tell whether a wall is solid, or of plasterboard or lath and plaster, try tapping its surface with your knuckles. A plasterboard wall will have a hollow sound, unlike a solid wall. The surface of a lath and plaster wall will not be as true and flat as those of the other two types of wall, and there will be a certain amount of give if you press the surface.

If you are unsure of the type of wall, make a test boring in an inconspicuous spot. As the drill bit pentrates beyond the plaster of a solid wall, it will throw out red dust, if it is of bricks, or grey or black dust if it is made from building blocks. On a lath and plaster wall, you will get a slight amount of sawdust from the laths, before the bit bursts through into the void beyond. On plasterboard, there will be no lath, just the void. In both the latter cases, you might strike a stud, indicating that the wall is hollow. If you want to know which type (plasterboard or lath and plaster) move along the wall slightly, and drill in another place.

KNOCKING DOWN WALLS

The way that the builder – or some subsequent owner – has arranged the interior of your home might not suit you. You may prefer to have fewer, but larger rooms. Probably the wall most people wish to remove is that between two main ground floor rooms, to combine a dining room and a lounge, for example. Both load-bearing and partition walls can be removed, but the procedure is totally different for each type. So it is most important to recognize the type of wall with which you are dealing.

In any event, before carrying out a conversion of this kind, you may need permission from a local authority. So your first action should be to consult an expert about possible local regulations.

Load-bearing or partition?

To say with certainty whether an internal wall is load-bearing or a partition is not always easy. There are, however, certain guidelines. Determine the type of materials from which the wall is built. For instance, a lath and plaster or plasterboard wall is likely to be a partition. Similarly, a brick or building-block wall may be a partition but is more likely to be load-bearing. Next look at the position of the wall. If it is in the middle of the house and parallel to the floorboards of the room above (which would mean it is at right angles to the joists), then it is almost certain to be load-bearing. On the other hand, a wall at right angles to the boards, and therefore parallel to the joists, and positioned to one side of the building, could probably be just a partition. In the last resort, only an expert can tell with certainty, so always take advice on this point.

Removing any wall is a major job that will disrupt your domestic life considerably. Take precautions – for instance, put sheets over the room doors, to keep the dust as far as possible to one room. In very dusty conditions, keep the window open, wear a mask, and go outside for fresh air as often as necessary.

Decide beforehand where you are going to put all the rubble. You might bury it if you have a large garden, or you may decide to hire a skip. In either event, have a wheelbarrow to move it away.

Removing the joinery

Most walls will have at least a skirting board attached. If there is a door in the wall, there will be its architrave and door stops. The joinery is the first thing to be removed. Full instructions for doing this are given in Chapter 5.

Even if you are removing only part of a wall – as will definitely be the case with a load-bearing wall – prise away the skirting from the whole length of wall, because it is likely to be in one piece. Even if it is not, the lengths that make up the run are unlikely to coincide with the stretches of wall you want to remove.

Avoid damaging the skirting so that you can put it back in place. This is of particular importance in an old house, where it will be impossible to buy new skirting to make a precise match. Store the old skirting you do not put back, so that it can be used for any repairs that are needed in future.

Removing lath and plaster walls

Your first job is to remove the lath and plaster covering. Push a sharp instrument – an old chisel or stout screwdriver will do – into the plaster, and locate the studs. Using a lever, such as a large claw hammer or the same chisel or screwdriver, wrench the laths from the studs, bringing the plaster with them. Carry on in this way until all the laths and plaster are removed, and you are left with just the framework. Dispose of the rubble.

To complete the job, take out the framework. How you do this will depend on the way it has been fixed to the floor and ceiling joists. If, as is most likely, nails have been used, simply prise it free.

Examine the plates, studs and noggings for signs of rot or woodworm. If you detect any, then burn them immediately. If they are sound, keep them for future use elsewhere.

Removing plasterboard walls

Locate the studs as described for a lath and plaster wall. Wrench the boards away from the studs. You should be able to pull most of them away intact, which will mean there is less dust and less rubble to dispose of. Remove the framework.

Removing solid walls

To remove a minor solid wall, which you have been assured by an expert is non-load-bearing, hack off a bit of plaster at the top to reveal a brick, or some form of building block. With a bolster chisel and club hammer, chop away at the mortar joints round the brick or block until you can free it and remove it. Tackle the bricks on each side of it until the top row is clear. Now go on to remove the rest of the wall below it.

Making good

Whatever the type of wall, its removal will cause a certain amount of damage to neighbouring walls, ceilings and floors. In the case of hollow partitions, there may not be too many marks – certainly none to the ceiling and walls that cannot be made good with decorator's filler, or a bag or two of plaster. The damage might be more severe, however, where a solid wall has been hacked away, and you might have to carry out a repair with plasterboard.

Partition walls are usually built on top of the floor – they are erected after the floor has been laid. Scuffs and knocks to boards on a suspended timber floor will usually be covered up by the new floorcovering. If you want to have a sealed timber floor, with the boards on view, you might have to take up and replace a board or two.

A solid direct-to-earth concrete floor might have been covered with tiles, laid after the partition was built. You will probably find it difficult to buy new tiles to match the old. Lay down tiles of any colour or pattern, but of the same thickness, so that the floor throughout is of one level.

If there was parquet flooring in the two rooms on each side of the wall, you might be able to place strips of hardwood in the gap where the wall previously stood, to make an attractive disguise.

Taking down load-bearing walls

Since a load-bearing wall is helping to hold the house up, you cannot remove it without putting something else in its place. That something else is invariably a rolled steel joist (known to builders as an rsj). Right at the start, enlist the help of an expert – an architect or surveyor – who will work out the size of the rsj you require and submit plans to your local authority as necessary.

Removing a wall in the average small house involves leaving a short stretch of wall (a nib) at each side of the proposed opening. The nib, probably about 450 mm (18 in) long, provides support for the rsj which is fixed just below the ceiling. This is the reason for the arch effect in a room that was converted from two small ones. In some instances further strengthening may be needed.

Support must be provided for the structure, during the removal of the wall until the rsj has been installed (Fig. 6:4). It is best to use adjustable steel props, which can be hired. For an average-sized opening, you will need three or four props on each side of the wall, but your expert will advise you on this. Place a 150 × 25 mm (6 × 1 in) board on the floor and stand the props on this. Similarly, you need a board of the same size at ceiling level, and the props should be braced between the two.

With a piece of chalk, mark on the wall the area you plan to remove, and hack away the plaster with a bolster chisel and club hammer. Now look at the wall and adjust the chalk line slightly, if necessary, so that you need to cut a few bricks as possible. Some will certainly need cutting, be-

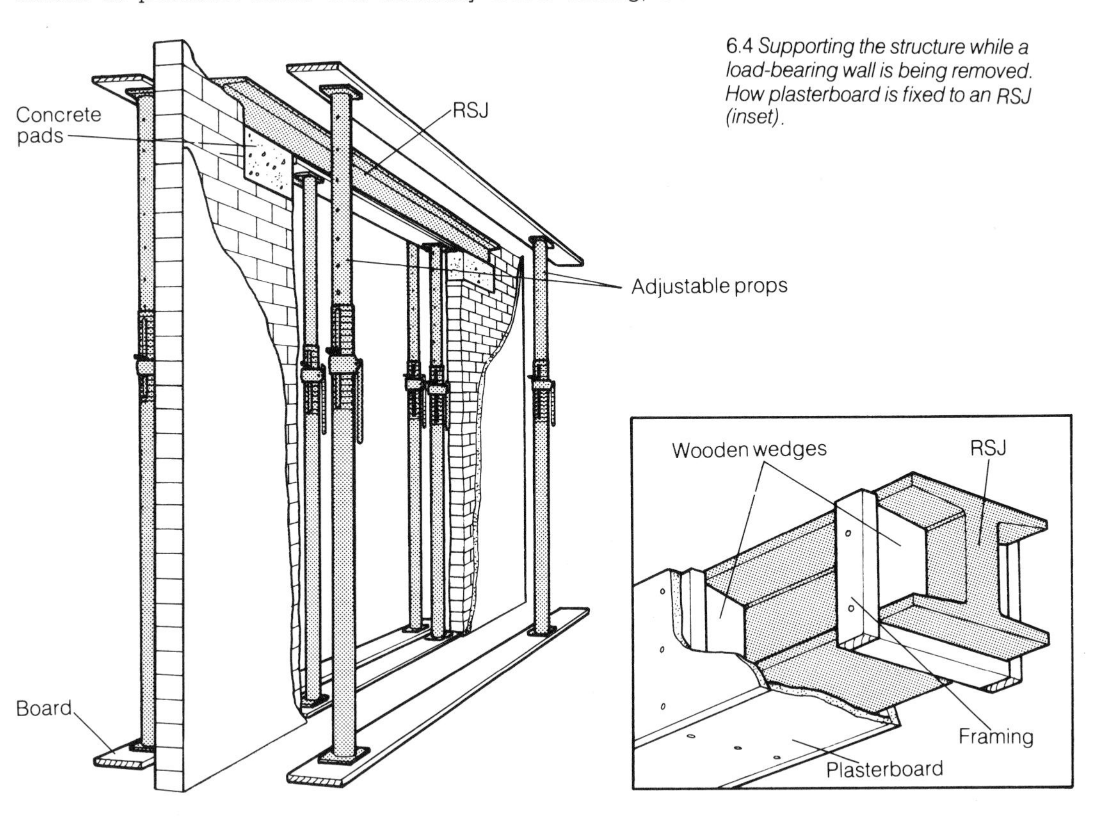

6.4 *Supporting the structure while a load-bearing wall is being removed. How plasterboard is fixed to an RSJ (inset).*

cause of the bonding of the brickwork, but by moving the line slightly, you can reduce this number to the minimum.

When you have determined the exact position of the opening, use the bolster chisel to cut a line in the brickwork around its limits on both sides of the wall. This will help to give a clean edge to the bricks when the wall is demolished, and will reduce the amount of making good that will be required later. Cut carefully through the ceiling plaster where it meets the wall.

Begin to demolish the wall by removing the bricks at the centre of the top course of the proposed opening. To do this, chisel out the mortar all round the centre brick. Then hack out the one next to it, and so on. Once you have freed a couple of bricks, the work will become progressively easier, and you can go on to take out the whole opening.

Since the wall is load-bearing, it will not rest on top of the floor, but rise up from the foundations. If the floor is of suspended floorboard, the joists will pass right through the wall below floor level. Chop out sufficient of the wall below floor level to allow extra floorboards to be fitted in the space once occupied by the wall. You will probably find it easier to do this if you take up a floorboard or two on each side. Take care not to damage the joists as you work. See Chapter 9 for details of how to take up boards and fit new ones.

On a direct-to-earth floor, remove enough of the wall to allow new tiles or parquet to be fitted so that there will be an uninterrupted run of floor through the new enlarged room.

Cut out a recess from the top of the nibs at each end to provide support for the rsj. Your expert should have worked out the exact size of these. Most probably, you will be required to allow the rsj to project into each nib by 225 mm (9 in).

It is not sufficient for the rsj to rest on brickwork. Make concrete pads on top of the masonry to provide firmer support. Your adviser will determine the exact dimensions. It is likely that the pads will be at least 150 mm (6 in) thick, so cut out sufficient of the wall to allow for this. The rsj has to be in position before the pads are formed.

Hauling up the rsj is a strenuous task, and is a job that will take at least three fit men. Raise it up into its correct position under the ceiling, and place two or three props underneath to hold it in place. Now form the concrete pads. Mix the concrete, and trowel it into place. Make sure it is well formed and compacted under the rsj, otherwise it will not offer enough support. Leave all the props – those supporting the rsj, and those each side of the opening – in place for about a week to allow the concrete to set properly.

When you remove the props, there comes the task of making good. The rsj should be covered with plasterboard.

Cut wooden wedges to make a tight fit, and hammer them in between the flanges with no more than 600 mm (2 ft) between their centres. To these wedges nail a timber framing of 50 × 25 mm (2 × 1 in) battens. Nail plasterboard to these battens (Fig. 6:4).

A builder would cover the raw edges of the brickwork round the opening, and make good any damage caused elsewhere, with plaster. You will probably find it easier to use plasterboard, doing the final filling with either plaster, bought in small bags, or decorator's filler.

BUILDING A PARTITION

A simple non-load-bearing partition can be built to divide a large room into two smaller ones. The best method is to use plasterboard on a timber framework.

Plasterboard is available in two thicknesses: 9.5 mm (about 3/8 in) and 12.7 mm (about 1/2 in). The thinner board is less expensive, but needs more timber supports, so is not necessarily cheaper in the long run. Furthermore, it does not offer such an effective degree of sound insulation. Plasterboard sheets are 1200 mm (47 1/2 in) wide and either 1800 mm (71 in) or 2400 mm (94 1/2 in) long. You will need the larger size to get sufficient height for a room partition. The board can also be bought with either squared or tapered edges. Use boards with tapered edges, then it is easier to disguise the joins. The material has an ivory coloured face. It should always be worked, and fixed, with this face outwards.

Plasterboard can be cut to size with an ordinary fine-toothed woodworking saw. Or you can remove short lengths by scoring the face with a sharp knife, and snapping off the waste over a straight edge. To cut a hole in the middle of the board – usually to accommodate an electrical fitting such as a switch or socket outlet – draw the shape in pencil, drill a starting hole, using an ordinary twist bit, at each corner, and saw out with a pad saw. Lightly sand all cut edges.

The framework

The framework for the partition should be in 75 × 50 mm (3 × 2 in) softwood. Use unplaned material, because it is cheaper and thicker than prepared softwood.

Begin by fixing a length of the timber along the floor. This member is known as the sole plate, and should be continuous and unbroken, except to form a door opening. To ensure it is positioned accurately, draw a line along one outer edge of the plate before you fix it. The fixing should be with nails, but if there is a ceiling below which might be damaged by the vibration caused by nailing, fix the plate with screws instead. If the partition is to be parallel to the floor joists, place the nails or screws at 200 mm (8 in) centres; if it is to run across the joists, fix the nails or screws into each joist.

Now fix a corresponding frame member to the ceiling. This is known as the head plate and you should ensure that it is exactly above the sole plate. Do this by using a plumb line and bob or a perfectly true batten and a spirit level with a vertical. If the head plate runs across the ceiling joists, fix it with nails or screws into the joists. If it is parallel to the joists, you cannot just fix it to the plasterboard or lath and plaster of the ceiling. There are two choices. The first is that you can fix short pieces of timber (noggings) to span between two joists and receive the fixing of the plate. This job is not too difficult if the loft is tall, with no floor above, but it is very disruptive if floorboards have to be raised first. The other choice is easier, but not always workable: it involves altering the position of the partition slightly so that it is immediately below a joist. Fixing should be at the same intervals as for the sole plate.

Now fit a series of vertical members (studs) between the two plates. The studs should be of the same section timber as the plates, and they are fixed by means of skew-nailing. Drive a nail into the side of a stud, but at an angle so that it goes into the plate below or above. If you think that the vibration of nailing might cause damage, use screws instead.

Place a stud at each end of the wall and at each side of door and other openings. Then, working from one end, fit them in between so that the centres are 400 mm (15¾ in) apart, for 9.5 mm (⅜ in) thick plasterboard, or 600 mm (23½ in) apart, for 12.7 mm (½ in) thick board. The last stud will almost certainly be nearer to the end than the recommended spacing. Follow these measurements closely, because they are necessary not only to give proper support to the wall, but also to match up the width of board.

A series of horizontal members (also called noggings) is needed halfway up the studs. These too can be fixed by skew-nailing. If you are likely to fix items to the wall later – built-in furniture, for instance – then try to plot its exact position at this stage, and fit noggings at the right place to receive its fixing screws. Cut the plasterboard to a length 25 mm (1 in) less than the height of the room, and place the cut edge at the bottom of the wall. Hold the board against the framework and jam it tightly up against the ceiling. A good way of ensuring this is to make a footlifter. Place one end of this under the board, press on the other end, and it will force the board up to the ceiling.

Fix the board to the frame with galvanized plasterboard nails at 150 mm (6 in) centres along every member of the

frame and about 13 mm (½ in) from the edges. Butt the boards tightly against each other along the edges. The gap at the bottom will be covered with skirting board later on and any at the top can be hidden by a cove.

If the wall divides two rooms, fix plasterboard to both sides. If there will be something such as a store room on one side, however, you need fix board to the room side only. Board of 12.7 mm (½ in) thickness on boths sides of a partition wall gives good sound insulation. If you want better sound insulation, fit two layers of 12.7 mm board on each side, making sure that the vertical joins are staggered, but

6.5 Building a partition wall: (a) How to deal with an internal and (b) an external corner. (c) Nail the plasterboard (held in position by a footlifter) to the framework of studs and noggings. Covering the joins between sheets of plasterboard using (d) filler, (e) tape, and (f) more filler.

that each edge is nailed to a frame member. In addition, fill the gap with insulating material.

Your wall may form an angle. Two types are possible. The way to deal with both of them is shown in Fig 6:5.

There is a sound method of disguising any gaps between the boards, using a special filler, tape and tools. These can be bought where you buy the plasterboard. The technique consists of applying the filler, pressing the tape into it, and covering with more filler. Full instructions are given with the pack.

If there is to be a doorway in the partition, base it on the width of a standard door, bought from a joinery supplier – it simply is not worth the time spent making your own. The inside of the door opening – both sides and the top – will need to be lined by a plate. This should be 25 mm (1 in) thick, and of a width to suit the plasterboard and studs – you may have to get one slightly oversize and plane it down. Then fit door stops. They should be about 38 × 32 mm (1½ × 1¼ in). Next, fit the architrave. All these items are simply nailed into place. Finally fit the door.

If the wall forms the outer shell of, say, a loft conversion, you will need to add insulation. Fix insulation blanket on the loft side of the wall, or fix a plasterboard that incorporates insulating material. You will also need a vapour check to prevent condensation from soaking the insulation. Such a check could consist of polythene, or a brush-on liquid.

Chapter 7
INTERIOR SURFACES

The interior surfaces of the walls of some historic buildings are left bare, and in recent years, when there has been a vogue for a return to natural materials, it is not uncommon for bare brick or stone to be used as a form of decoration. Most walls, however, are covered on the inside, usually with plaster. This material is strong, durable and presents a smooth surface that can take a wide range of decorative materials. From the do-it-yourselfer's point of view, however, plaster has one overwhelming disadvantage – applying it is probably the most skilled of the building trades, and far beyond the abilities of the average person. If you do want to give bare walls a plaster surface, however, you could apply plasterboard. This is known as dry-lining and is well within the scope of the do-it-yourselfer.

Other possible interior surfaces included timber cladding and ceramic tiles. Until timber became expensive in recent years, it was often used as a decorative covering instead of wallpaper. At one time, however, it used to be an alternative to plaster for covering bare walls and can still be seen in some old buildings. Ceramic tiles can be fixed to plaster or, provided the surface is smooth, directly on to brickwork.

THE NATURAL LOOK

If you have seen bare brickwork as a form of decoration in modern interiors, do not imagine that you can hack off the plaster in one of your rooms to reveal a similar surface. You never know how good a wall under the plaster will be. You might even find breeze blocks or some other building block there. Even if test borings with a drill in an inconspicious spot confirm that the wall is built of bricks, the wall is not likely to be attractive. The type of wall you have admired has to be specially built; it is known in the trade as fair face brickwork.

If you want natural brickwork in your home, leave the plaster intact, and apply small brick-like tiles, called 'slips', to it.

DECORATING PLASTER

Plaster is chosen as a coating for interior walls because it takes decorative treatments so well. At one time new plaster had to be allowed to dry out for several months before it could be decorated. Modern plaster settles down much more quickly, and six weeks to two months after being applied it is ready to receive any decorative finish.

In a brand new house this period would have elapsed by the time you occupy it, so you could decorate the walls as soon as you move in. If you are having a wall in an occupied house plastered – as would be the case, for instance, when you have a home extension built – it would be better to allow the plaster to dry for about a couple of months before decorating. If you are in a hurry to decorate it before then, use a thin emulsion paint, through which moisture can escape.

Plaster will take both gloss and emulsion paints, but it does not require the same protection as wood, so there is little point in applying anything other than emulsions, which are cheaper, easier to apply, and in general more convenient to handle.

Plaster also takes wallpaper readily. Especially when new, the plaster should be treated with size before you hang the paper so that the surface will have more slip. The manufacturers of some of the heavier papers suggest that walls should be cross-lined (see below) before the paper is applied.

Old plaster can sometimes become powdery, and will need to be sealed. Apply a stabilizing solution to the plaster surface and allow it to dry thoroughly before you decorate the wall.

Plasterboard can be decorated as soon as it is installed. No special preparation is required before painting it – treat the surface just as ordinary plaster. If you decide to hang wallpaper, however, apply a plasterboard primer first. This not only helps you when you are hanging the paper; it also makes it easier to strip off the paper when you come to redecorate.

REPAIRS TO PLASTER

It is unlikely that you will be able to plaster a wall satisfactorily starting from scratch, but you might well carry out repairs to a plastered surface.

Cracking caused by shrinkage of the plaster as it dries out, or even by settlement of the building, is the most common fault in a plastered wall. Stop up the cracks with decorator's filler, applied with a filling knife. This, incidentally, is often confused with a scraper, but the two are in fact totally different. The knife has a flexible blade, whereas the scraper is rigid.

Begin by running one corner of the knife blade down the length of the crack, to dislodge any loose material, and also to make the crack wedge shaped – narrower at the surface of the wall. Brush loose material from the crevice, and saturate it with water – using a brush to make sure that the water penetrates right into the crevice.

Now apply the filler. Mix it in an old cup or saucer and do not make it too runny – it should be a stiff paste. (Always add water to the filler, never the filler to water; use a wet sponge, so you can then control the flow of water easily). Take some filler on to the knife, and spread it across the width of the crack, flexing the blade as you do so, pushing the filler well into the crack. Draw the knife lengthwise along the crack, again flexing the blade, to wipe the filler flush with the surface and smooth it down. Cracks that are deep and wide should be filled in two stages. When the filler is dry, give it a light sanding, and the crack should then be undetectable when painted over. Fill small holes similarly.

If you propose to paint the wall a dark colour, you might have difficulty in obliterating the whiteness of the filler, which could persist in showing through even after two or three coats. To prevent this, add a few drops of the paint to the filler to tint it to about the final colour you have chosen for the wall.

In older houses, where the plaster is more brittle, the surface can become crazed with tiny cracks. Filling each crack individually would be impractical. The best course is to decorate the wall with a material that will cover the cracks: a heavy embossed paper, or even a woodchip paper, which you can paint, can be used. If you want a smooth, painted surface, however, line the wall first. The lining paper to apply as a base for paint has a shiny, impervious surface that does not soak up paint. If you try to paint lining paper intended for wallpapers, the surface will look like blotting paper.

Cross-lining

When lining is done as preparation for wallpaper, the lining paper should be hung horizontally – this is called cross-lining. Lining paper that you intend to paint can be hung vertically, in the normal manner. Some walls are in such bad condition that they need two layers of lining paper – the first in horizontal strips, the top one in vertical strips.

The defects in the plaster may be more serious than just a few cracks. There may, for instance, be large holes, or stretches of crumbling plaster. Hack away crumbling plaster, starting in the middle of the patch, and working outwards until you reach a firm sound edge. If the hole is small, fill it with decorator's filler, but for a large area it will be cheaper to use plaster, which is sold in small bags.

Apply the filler or plaster with a float trowel or a filling knife. Fill deep holes in two stages. First fill about half the depth of the hole. As this first layer or undercoat begins to harden, scratch it with the edge of the trowel to provide a key for the next coat. Leave for 24 hours, then apply the top coat.

Whether you fill in one or two stages, the filler should be applied so its surface is slightly raised. Then remove the excess with a batten, as described for repairs to rendering outside the house (see Chapter 3), leaving the repair level with the surrounding surface. Smooth off with the trowel or filling knife, keeping it moistened by dipping it in water.

You may not be too successful at smoothing off. This does not matter if, as is likely on a wall with crumbling patches, the rest of the surface is rough and you intend to cover it with lining paper, or if you plan to hang a heavy paper.

If the wall is generally in good condition, however, and you wish to paint it, there is a way to bring your repair up to the standard of the rest. Let it dry thoroughly then apply a sizing paste to the repaired area. Now apply wallpaper adhesive, making sure it is brushed only on the area of wall you have treated. Cut a piece of heavy-duty lining paper, so it is bigger all round than the repair. Apply it over the repair, smooth it down into place with a wallpaper brush, and let the adhesive dry. Then take hold of one corner of the paper and gently tear it round the edge of the patch. The paper will tear along the border where it is stuck, leaving an irregular and feathered edge that will not be noticed once you have painted over it.

The new plaster on internal walls can become covered with patches of a white powdery substance. This growth is called efflorescence, and it can also be seen on the external brickwork of new buildings. Efflorescence is caused by salts in the masonry drying out, and should eventually go away of its own accord. If its appearance bothers you, brush it off. On no account use water, for that will merely retard the drying-out process, and make the condition last longer. Do not decorate until the efflorescent has disappeared. If it does not disappear, this is an indication that you have a damp problem in the wall.

DRY-LINING A WALL

The easiest way for a do-it-yourselfer to plaster a wall is to cover it with plasterboard (Fig. 7:1). This is nailed to a framework of 50 × 25 mm (2 × 1 in) battens, screwed into

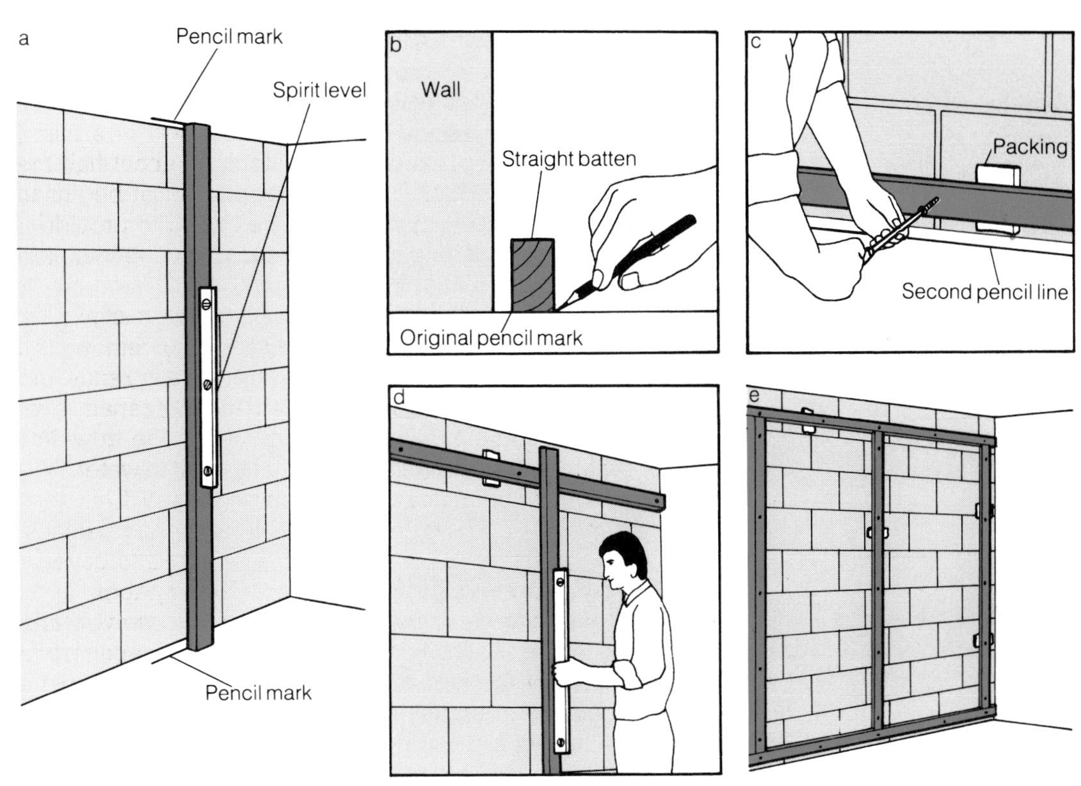

wall plugs. Much care is needed to fix the battens to the wall. The brickwork will never be flat, so if you screw the battens down hard they will follow the contours of the wall, and when you fix the plasterboard its surface will be full of 'waves'.

First find the part of the wall that bulges out farthest – known to builders as the high spot. You can do this either by moving a long, true batten together with a spirit level along the wall, or by using a plumb line and bob. When you have found the high spot, hold the batten on it, and use a spirit level to ensure that it is vertical. Make a pencil mark where the batten touches the floor on the side nearest to the wall, and a corresponding mark on the ceiling. Next, place a long true batten horizontally on edge along the floor. Position it so that it is parallel to the wall and with its inner face on the pencil mark. Now draw a pencil line on the floor along the side of the batten farthest from the wall and remove the batten.

Screw a single batten horizontally to the wall 25 mm (1 in) up from the floor, making sure that the batten is aligned accurately with the line on the floor. To ensure that you do not screw it too hard to the wall, and thus bend it out of alignment, place packing pieces of card or hardboard behind it at the point where you insert a fixing screw.

7.1 *Dry-lining a wall: (a) Mark the floor and ceiling with the aid of a batten and spirit level. (b) Use a pencil and batten to draw the line on the floor. (c) Screw a batten to the wall in alignment with the floor line. (d) Check that floor and ceiling battens are in alignment. (e) The framework is fixed to the wall and ready to receive the plasterboard.*

Now fix a corresponding horizontal batten 25 mm (1 in) from the ceiling, packed out so that it aligns with the pencil mark on the floor. You can ensure that it does so by using a vertical batten and a spirit level. Now fix vertical supports at both edges of every board. Fix additional vertical supports at 400 mm (16 in) centres if you are using 9.5 mm (3/8 in) thick plasterboard, or 600 mm (24 in) centres for 12.7 mm (1/2 in) thick board. The battens must be vertical and aligned with the two horizontal battens already fixed. Pack them out as necessary. Now is the time to fit battens to receive the screws of any built-in furniture you may wish to add later. If at a later date you wish to fix items where you have not made such provision, it is a simple matter to drill through the plasterboard and into the masonry, where you can insert a wall plug. Nail the plasterboard to these battens in the same way as to the framework for a partition (see pages 125-6).

TIMBER CLADDING

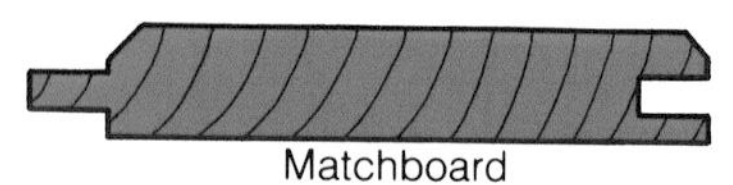

7.2 Matchboarding (above) and tongued and grooved

Timber cladding can be fixed directly to the bare brickwork of a wall as a substitute for plaster, or it can go on top of existing plaster as a form of decoration. The cladding can be matchboarding – lengths of shaped natural timber – or in sheets of hardboard or thin plywood with a surface pattern that simulates matchboarding.

Matchboarding is often confused with tongued and grooved boards (Fig. 7:2). Tongued and grooved boards have squared sides so that when two boards are joined they fit snugly together. Matchboarding has additional moulding, so that a V-shaped groove is formed where two boards meet. Tongued and grooved boards are, in general, fitted as flooring, matchboarding being unsuitable because of its grooves.

Matchboarding, however, is more suitable for cladding because the heat of the room will in time make the boards shrink, and cause gaps to appear between them. Such gaps look unsightly in tongued and grooved boards, but because of the V-shape they are not noticeable in matchboarding.

7.3 Matchboarding nailed to wall battens

The planks of matchboading are fixed to horizontal battens screwed to the wall. You need one batten at floor level, another near the ceiling, and a third half-way between. If you are fitting the timber to a wall that has a skirting board, use this instead of the bottom batten (Fig. 7:3). The two higher battens should then be of the same thickness as the skirting. A width of 50 mm (2 in) is suitable. If there is no skirting board, use 50 × 25 mm (2 × 1 in) battens.

The battens must be level with each other and with the skirting so that the cladding will present a flat surface. Pack out the battens as necessary when you fix them to the wall.

The planks are fixed to the battens by 'secret nailing', so that no fixing nails are visible. Pins are driven into the front of the tongue, but emerge on the other side through the main body of the plank to pass into the batten (Fig. 7:4). When the next board is fitted, its groove locates on the tongue, which holds it into place. On the other edge it is fixed by pins driven through its tongue, and so on.

Begin by fitting the first plank with its groove towards the end of the wall. Make sure, by using a plumb line or a spirit level, that this first plank is vertical, for its alignment will determine that of the rest. If the surface of the other wall at the corner (the return wall) is badly out of true, tack the first plank slightly away from it, making sure it is vertical. Place a small block of wood so that it touches the return wall and overlaps the plank. Place a pencil along the block and move both to trace out the profile of the return wall on to the plank (Fig. 7:5). Trim the plank along the pencil line.

To trim to the correct width the plank at the other end of the wall, place it on top of the last whole plank, and lightly tack it in place. Now take a short offcut of plank plus a pencil. Jam the offcut hard against the return wall at the top, and hold the pencil tightly against the offcut. Now move offcut and pencil slowly downwards to the bottom, tracing a line on the plank to be trimmed. Saw or file the plank to this line and it should be a tight fit in the gap.

When you use secret nailing, the planks at each end are not held in place on their outer edges. Usually, this does not matter. Tap the face of the planks lightly to check that they are firmly fixed. If not, drive three pins – one for each batten – through their face. These pins will not be hidden, but can be punched home and covered with stopping.

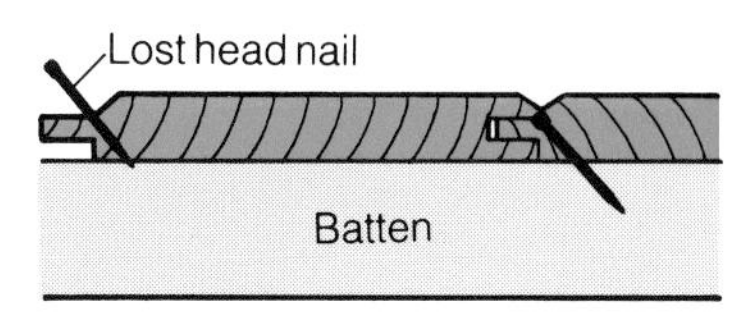

7.4 Secret nailing

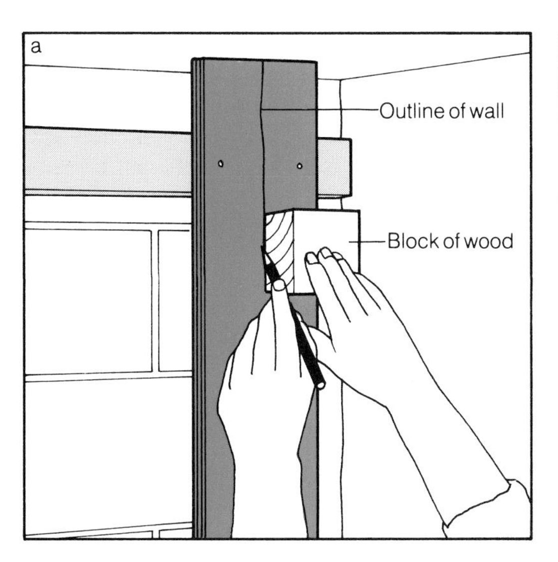

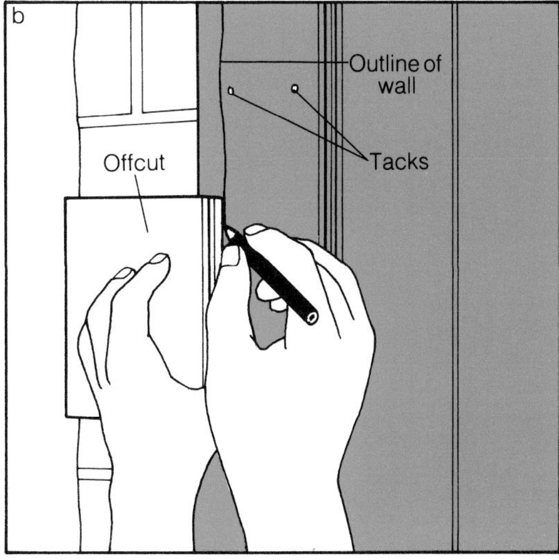

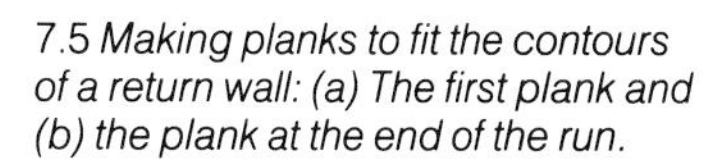

7.5 Making planks to fit the contours of a return wall: (a) The first plank and (b) the plank at the end of the run.

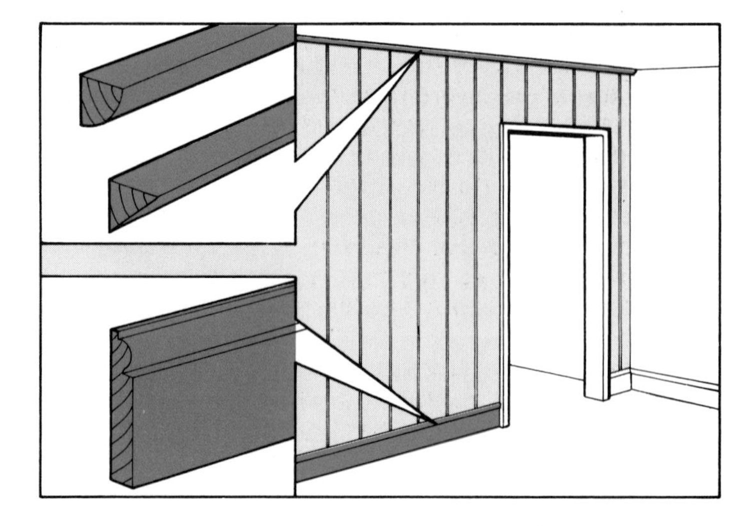

7.6 *Moulding, quarter round or triangular (top inset), neatens the top of timber cladding, and skirting (bottom inset) is fitted at the base.*

The floor, and especially the ceiling, may be out of true, as well as the return walls. Measure the height required for each plank individually. Even so, there will be slight gaps top and bottom. Disguise the bottom one by fitting skirting, which you can buy at wood yards. The skirting is nailed to the bottom of the planks. You can also use skirting turned upside down, at the top, or you might prefer a smaller moulding (Fig. 7:6).

If you are cladding adjacent walls and the angle where they meet is an internal one, a vertical length of quarter-round or triangular section moulding will neaten the join. Fig. 7:7 shows two methods of treating an external angle.

Fixing sheet cladding

Sheet cladding, since it is based on hardboard or plywood, comes with a maximum length of 2440 mm (8 ft). It is not suitable for rooms with a ceiling height greater than that dimension.

There are two ways in which it can be fixed. The first is to

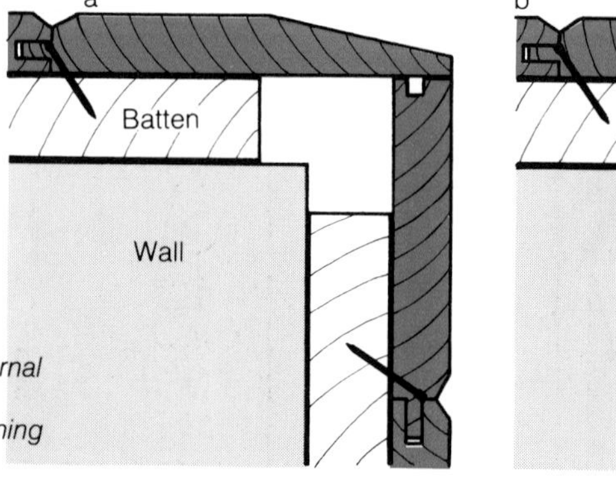

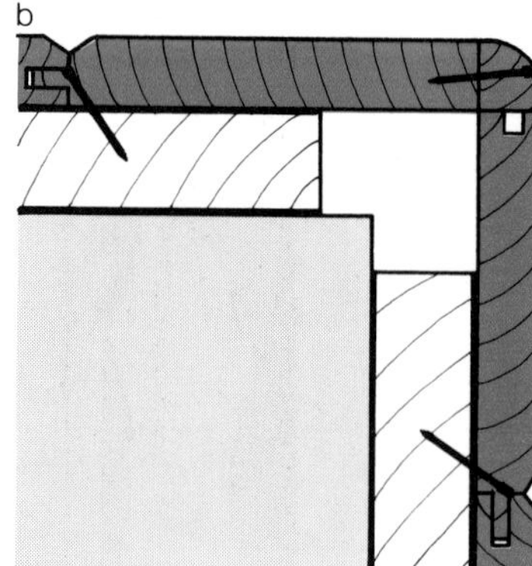

7.7 *Two ways of neatening an external corner in timber cladding:*
(a) Chamfering a plank and (b) pinning quarter round moulding.

fit a framework of battens to which the sheets can be nailed. You need a batten on each edge, an intermediate vertical one, and two intermediate horizontal ones. To make sure these are all in the same plane, pack them out as necessary.

The second method is to stick the sheets directly to the wall, provided you are working on a flat plaster surface. Remove any skirting, spread the adhesive on the wall and on the back of the sheets in a pattern similar to that suggested for the battening. You can use a glue gun with which to apply the adhesive to speed up the work. Fig. 7:8 shows both methods.

It is not easy to cut a large sheet to fit the irregularites of a floor and ceiling, so aim to disguise these with skirting at ground level and moulding at the top.

To fix this type of cladding in an alcove that is narrower than the width of a sheet, first cut the sheet to the correct height. Using a plumb line and bob, or a spirit level and true batten, draw on the alcove wall a vertical line about 75 mm (3 in) from one end of the alcove (Fig. 7:9). Place the sheet flat on the floor nearby, and on it draw a pencil line a little more than 150 mm (6 in) from one edge. At about 150 mm (6 in) intervals, measure the gap between the line on the wall and the end of the alcove. Transfer these measurements to the sheet, then join up the marks, and you have a line to which to saw or file. This edge of the sheet should now be a perfect fit against one end wall.

Now draw a second vertical line on the wall 150 mm (6 in) from the other end of the alcove. Measure the gap between the two lines. Use this measurement to draw a second line on the sheet, the same distance from the first line. Then measure the narrow gap between the second vertical line

7.8 Timber cladding can also be carried out with sheet material, glued and pinned to a timber framework. Inset shows glue being spread on back of sheets, and a mastic gun which can also apply the adhesive.

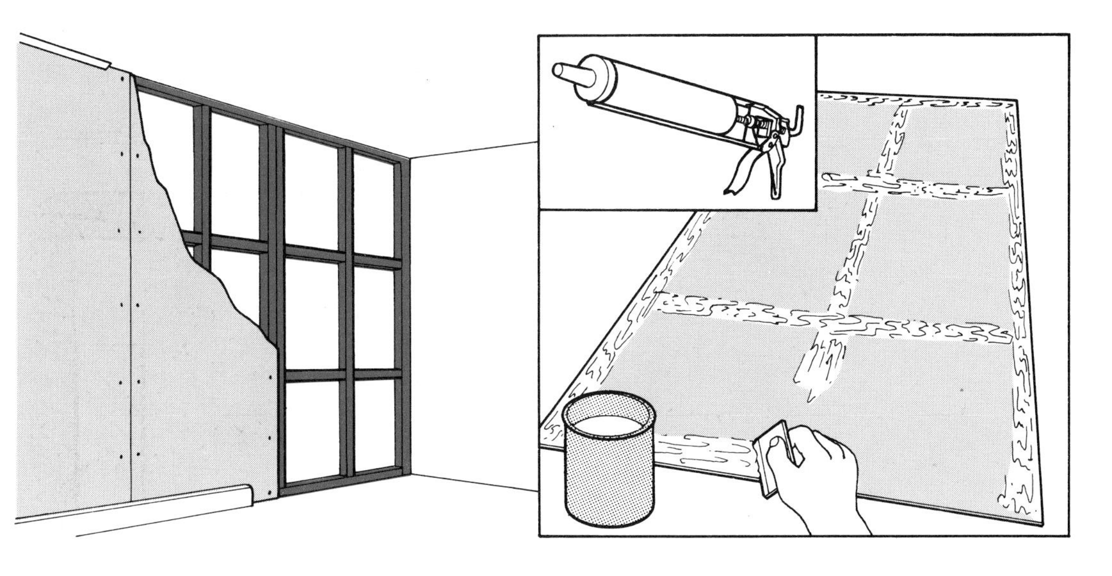

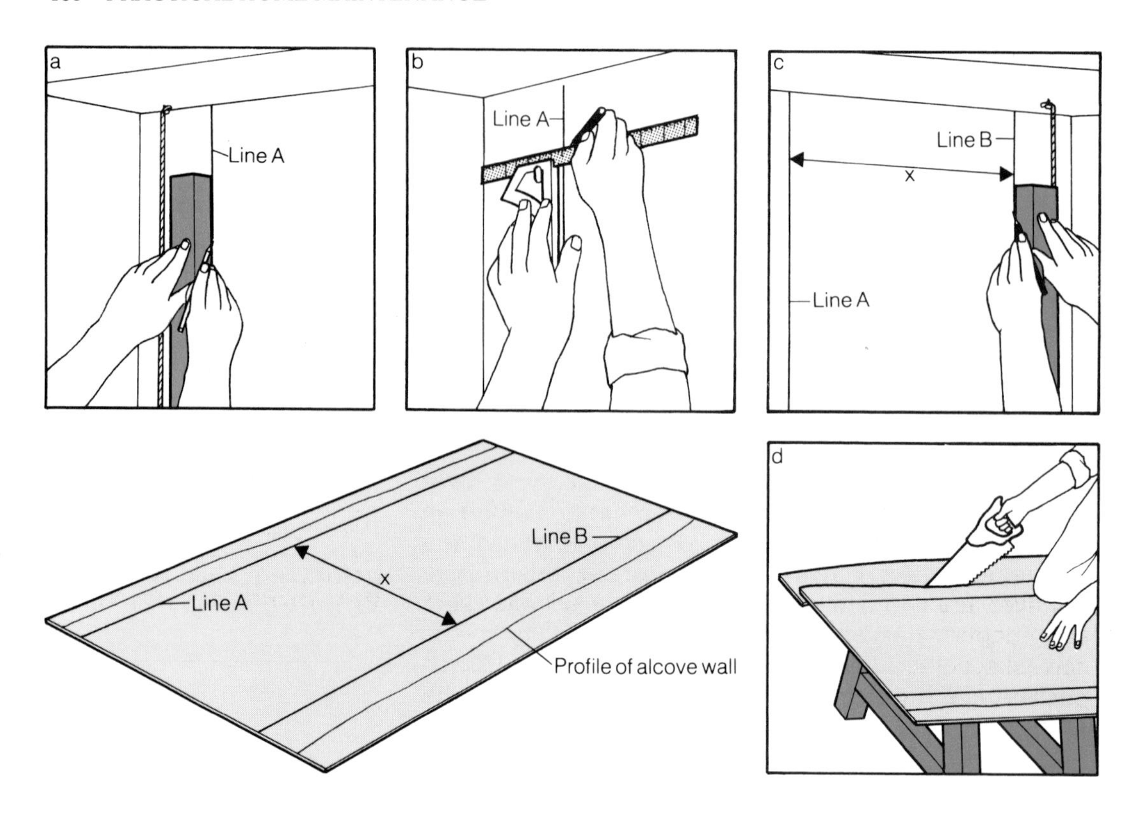

7.9 Cutting sheet cladding to fit an alcove: (a) Draw a vertical line (Line A) on the alcove wall. (b) Measure the distance between Line A and that end of the alcove wall at 150 mm intervals. (c) Draw a second line (Line B) 150 mm from the other end of the alcove. Measure the distance (x) between the two lines on the wall. (d) Transfer these measurements to the sheet. (e) Saw along the two outer lines and the sheet should be a perfect fit in the alcove.

on the wall and the end of the alcove. Transfer these measurements to the sheet, join them up, and saw to the line. The whole sheet should now be a perfect fit in the alcove, with only minor adjustments necessary here and there with a file.

When timber cladding was fixed in old cottages as an alternative to plaster, it used in general to be painted – normally white. One of the objects of installing timber cladding in modern interiors, however, is to introduce the beauty of natural timber into the home, so it is usually treated with a polyurethene varnish.

CERAMIC TILES

Ceramic tiling gives a permanent, hygienic, easily cleaned surface that is particularly suitable in kitchens, bathrooms and lavatories. Tiles can be fixed to a wide range of materials, including plaster, brick, synthetic boards, and even old ceramic tiles. In fact, they can be fixed to any flat surface that is clean and free from flaking material, except wood. If tiles are fixed to wood, the movement caused by gain or loss of moisture will cause cracks to appear in the tiles.

Fixing the tiles into place is easy, using modern adhe-

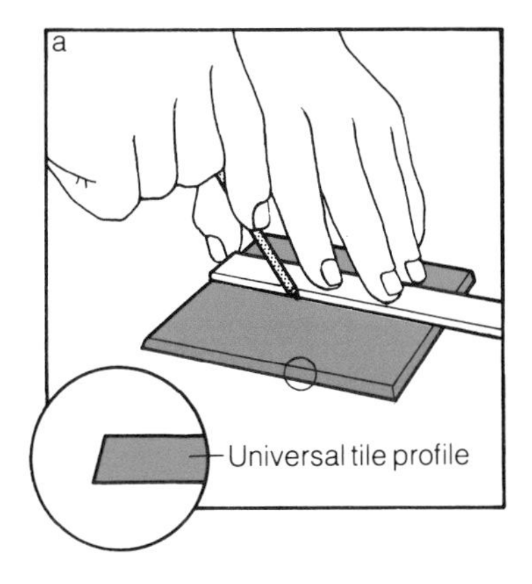

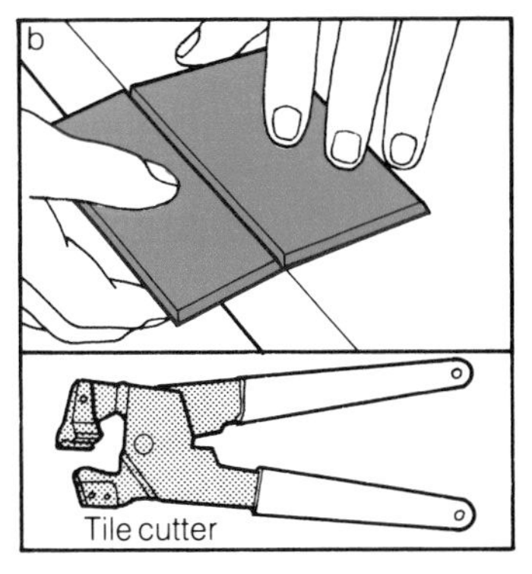

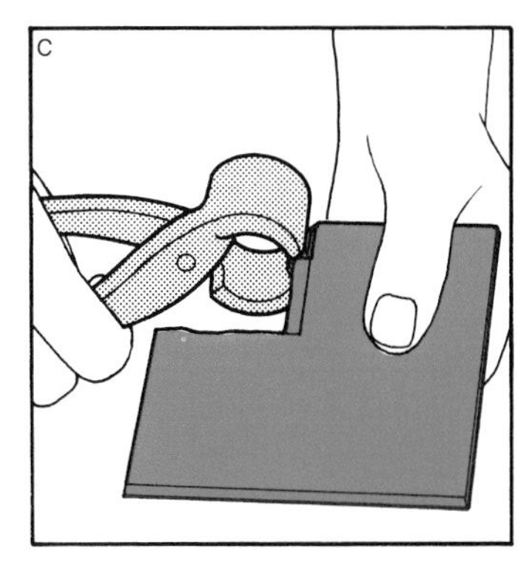

7.10 *How to cut a tile: (a) Score its face with a tiler's spike. (b) Place it on the bench and press. Alternatively place it in the jaws of a tile cutter (inset). (c) To make an L-shaped tile, snap out the waste with pincers.*

sives. A space needs to be left between the tiles to allow them to expand and contract with temperature changes. Until recently, most tiles have had lugs on the edges to ensure that the spacing is equal. A new development, however, is the Universal tile. This has a slightly chamfered edge, tapering towards the face of the tile to provide the correct spacing for expansion and grout. This tile also dispenses with the need for specially-made border tiles, because it is glazed on two adjacent edges, so can be used where these will be exposed. The adhesive is spread on the wall, and you merely place the tiles in their correct position on it. Do not slide them into position, however, as this forces adhesives up between the cracks.

To cut a tile (Fig. 7:10), place it on a flat surface, with a straight edge on its face. Draw a tiler's spike along the straight edge, to cut through the glaze. Press firmly to make sure the glaze is cut, but not so hard as to break the tile. Also score the glaze on the edges. Now place the tile with the cut line accurately on the edge of a bench, with just the waste overhanging. Press on the waste with a short sharp jerk, and the tile will break cleanly along the line.

Alternatively, use a tile cutter. One type looks like a pair of pliers with enlarged jaws. Grip the tile in the jaws and press. The tile will split along the line. If a tile has to be cut to an L-shape, or any other irregular pattern, score it, then snip off the waste bit by bit with a pair of pincers.

The tricky part in tiling comes in making sure the tiles will be arranged neatly on the wall – the 'setting-out'. On a plain, straight wall, you merely arrange the tiles so that the cut ones at each end of the wall are not too small, and are of equal size. Where there are obstructions – doorways, windows, bathroom or kitchen fittings – make sure that your setting-out does not leave small unsightly cut tiles round their edges.

Tiling a simple wall

First, prepare the wall. Plaster surfaces should be washed down and rinsed, and allowed to dry. High spots should be sanded off, and any large holes or cracks filled. Remove grease and dirt from other surfaces and fill any large holes or depressions.

Find the lowest point of the floor – or skirting board, if this is to be retained. Make a pencil mark on the wall one tile's height up from this point (Fig. 7:11). Cut a long, true batten to the length of the wall. Tack the batten in place on the wall, its top edge level with the pencil mark. Use a spirit level to ensure that the batten is truly horizontal. Tile adhesive is not a contact adhesive – it takes a short time to act. The batten gives a true line to which you can work, and it also prevents tiles from sliding down the wall before the adhesive has started to grip.

Measure the batten, and mark its centre. You can set out your tiles to ensure that the centre tile is located centrally on this point, or that there are two centre tiles, one each side of it. Adopt the arrangement that will give the largest cut tile at the edges. To find out the best arrangement, make a measuring staff from a long true batten, just over half the length of the one on the wall. Lay it flat on the floor or bench, and on it place a run of dry tiles. Mark off with pencil the width of a tile (including the spacer lugs if any) along the entire length. Place the measuring staff along the batten that is tacked to the wall, and determine which arrangement to adopt. Begin tiling at one edge of the batten – right-handed people will usually find it more convenient to begin on the left, but it is up to you.

Measure the width of the cut tile that will be needed at this edge. Mark this distance from the edge of the wall. Draw a vertical line at the mark, using a true batten and a spirit level.

Usually a combed spreader is supplied with the adhesive. Hold the spreader at an angle of 45° to apply the adhesive, in a series of combed ridges. Cover as much of the wall as you think you can conveniently cope with – a square metre (10 ft) is about right for most people. Place the tiles on the wall one by one. Position the first with extreme accuracy, and butt the others carefully against each other. Make sure the spacer lugs on the side just meet. If any adhesive oozes out, wipe it off before it dries.

Cover the wall with all the whole tiles needed. When the adhesive has set, remove the wall batten and fill in the border with cut tiles. Measure the space for each one individually – inaccuracies in the plaster and floor will make each space slightly different. The cut tiles should not butt up

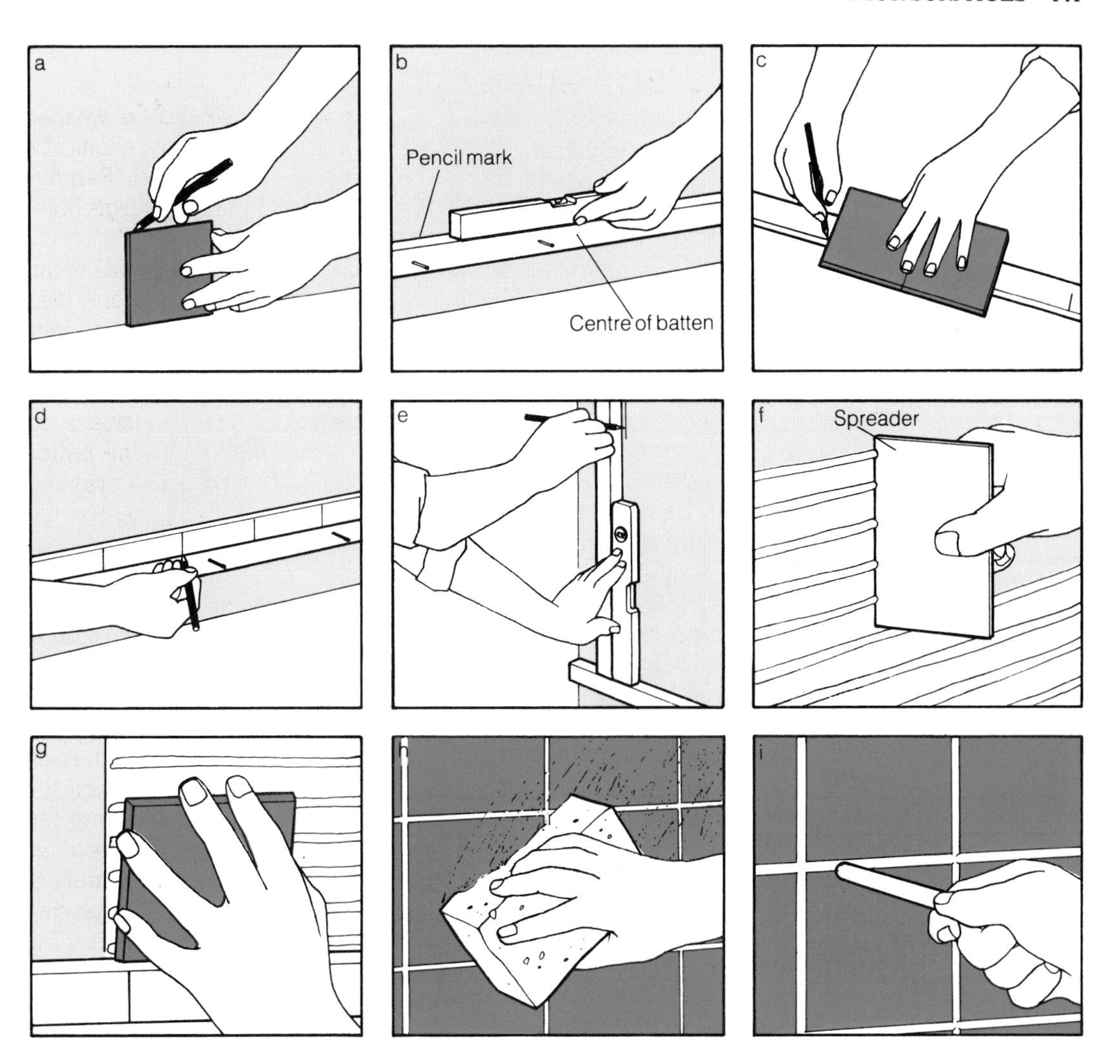

against the end walls, but should be the width of the spacer lugs away from it. The cut edge should go to the wall. As each tile is cut, spread adhesive on the back and place it on the wall, tapping it accurately into position. Wipe away any surplus adhesive.

Leave the tiles for at least 12 hours, then apply the grout. This is necessary to fill the space between the tiles. The grout usually comes as a powder to which you add water. You can buy ready-mixed grout, and there is a mixture that can be used as combined adhesive and grout. Apply the grout with a sponge, which you draw across the face of the tiles, pushing the grout well into the spaces. Wipe off the excess grout with a damp sponge. Draw a round pointed length of wood along each joint to give a really neat finish, then polish up the tiles with a dry cloth.

7.11 *Tiling a wall: (a) Mark one tile's height up from the floor. (b) Tack a batten at this height, using a level to ensure that it is horizontal. (c) Make a measuring staff. (d) Use the staff to determine the best starting point. (e) Draw the vertical line near the end of the wall. (f) Apply the adhesive with a combed spreader. (g) Place the tiles in position. (h) apply the grout. (i) Neaten the grout.*

7.12 Tile arrangements: (a) Tile round a washbasin (b) Support the tiles over a window opening. (c) How to take tiles round an external corner.

Complex tile arrangements

Walls with obstructions are tackled in much the same way as simple walls.

Plan the setting-out thoroughly. Make several trial runs with the measuring staff. Your aim should be not only to get the largest possible cut tiles at the ends of the rows, but also to avoid small cut tiles round the fixtures. In many instances you will have to compromise. Once you are satisfied you have the best setting-out possible, you can start to tile. When you come to a fitting such as a washbasin, continue to tile to the nearest full tile. Such a fixture cannot be relied on to be level, so nail a short horizontal lath (Fig. 7:12) above it, checking with a spirit level that it is true. Lay tiles on top of this batten. The cut tiles can be filled in later along with the border tiles.

If you are tiling only half-way up a wall and not using Universal tiles, border tiles – which have an edge without space lugs, and are slightly rounded – should be used on the top row. They are also required when you are tiling into a doorway or window reveal. Use ordinary tiles up to the edge of the reveal, and border tiles in the reveal with the rounded edge covering the edge of the standard tile. If you wish to tile on the underside of a door or window opening, fix the tiles and hold them in place with a batten wedged underneath with long lengths of timber.

Seal the gap round a basin or bath with ceramic bath trim. This is fixed with a sealant that acts both as flexible adhesive and grout. Alternatively, apply silicone bath sealant, which is available in different colours.

Chapter 8
CEILINGS

Domestic ceilings are normally covered with plaster. If the floor above is of concrete, as in modern high-rise buildings, the plaster is applied to the underside of the concrete. Where the floor above is laid on joists the ceilings are fixed to the joists. Traditionally such ceilings are of lath and plaster, but in modern homes plasterboard is often used instead.

Occasionally other materials, such as tongued and grooved boards or matchboarding, are used to form a ceiling. In many older cottages, the timber is fixed directly to the joists, and takes the place of plaster. If you came across a tongued and grooved ceiling in a modern house, however, it will usually have been installed as a decorative measure, and will be a false ceiling, with the original plaster one more than likely still above it.

Another type of ceiling that you will occasionally come across is the hollow-joisted ceiling. In this, the joists are fully on view. If there is a room above, you are likely to see the underside of its floor. On top storeys, plasterboard may have been fixed over the joists. On lower floors, the space between the joists under the floor might have been lined with plasterboard, to give a good, clean effect; although fitting it would be a very tedious job. The advantage of such a ceiling is that, in order to comply with building regulations, the room height may be measured to the underside of the top covering, not the bottom edge of the joist – an important point in some loft or basement conversions.

REPAIRS

You might be surprised to learn that ceilings have to withstand stresses. If there is a room above, then as feet pass across the floor they cause the joists below to move, even if only slightly, putting a strain on the fixings of the ceiling. Even on top storeys, there can be natural movement of the timber that might cause problems. Moreover, older ceilings would be fitted in the days when no one bothered about insulation, and the extremes of heat and cold in the loft could cause the joists to move. Rainwater getting through defective roofs and snow blown through the eaves are other hazards.

Lath and plaster ceilings are usually the ones that give the most trouble, if only because they are older, but you can also have problems with modern, plasterboard ceilings.

Cracks in the ceiling

Because of the problems of movement, ceilings are much more likely to have cracks than are walls. You can often, too, get rough surfaces caused by extensive cracking, or by areas where the smooth surface skin of the plaster has fallen away, leaving porous patches.

Small defects can be filled with ordinary filler, as part of the process of redecorating. Where the blemishes are widespread, however, it is better to use heavy-duty decorative material, such as thick ceiling paper applied over lining paper, or a textured finish when you decorate.

A ceiling needs more thorough washing and rinsing prior to redecoration than does a wall, because the movement of air in a room carries dirt and tar upwards.

Powdery surfaces

The surface of old lath and plaster ceilings is often perpetually dusty; brush your hand across it, and it will leave a powdery deposit on your palm. Seal the surface before carrying out any decorative treatment. Use a stabilizing solution, sold in paint shops or builders' merchants.

Ceilings that bulge

A common defect with lath and plaster ceilings is that they bulge away from the joists – they 'belly out'. The remedy for this depends on the cause. If the laths have worked loose, nail them back to the joists, using galvanised clout nails. The nail heads will be disguised later in subsequent redecoration. If the bulge has come about because the plaster has separated from the laths, nailing back will not work.

One method that is often effective is to work from above – either in a loft, or by raising floorboards in the upstairs room. Brace the bulge back into place by placing a wide length of timber under it, held by a stout timber prop wedged against the floor. Trowel new plaster from above over the laths so that it bonds with the old.

Such treatment might not give a smooth surface on which to paint, but you will get a satisfactory result if you cover it with a thick paper. In fact, thick paper, or textured finishes, are often the best solution to the problem of defective ceilings.

If the ceiling is not easily accessible from above you will have to scrape bulging plaster off, then fill the hole with decorating filler or plaster, according to the extent of the damage (Fig. 8:1).

Loose plasterboard

Structural stress can cause the nails holding plasterboard to pop, leaving an ugly edge where the board parts from its neighbour, and spots where the nail heads break through. Brace the board hard against the joist – a helper can do this for you – and re-fix the board by driving in extra galvanized plasterboard nails about 38 mm (1½ in) from each loose one. Drive home the loose nails. Fill in the cracks and disguise the nail heads with ordinary filler before you redecorate.

Patching plasterboard

Plasterboard ceilings are not unduly difficult to repair.

Begin by locating the joists at each side of the damage. You might see them from above in a loft. If you cannot, then tap the ceiling and listen to the sound. From below, push up a saw through the damage (Fig. 8:2), and cut sideways in each direction until you meet the joists. Make up a frame from 50 mm (2 in) square timber, half-lapped at the corners and strengthened with screws. The width of the frame should be such that it will just fit between the joists; its length should allow it to cover the entire damaged area. A frame longer than 600 mm (2 ft) should be strengthened with a cross member in the middle.

Offer up the frame to the ceiling, position it carefully between the joists, and pencil a line round its outer edges over the damaged area. Now saw out the area you have marked, beginning perhaps with a pad saw and finishing up with a handsaw.

You need a piece of plasterboard to fill this cut-out. To cut a piece to the right size, place the frame on a sheet of plasterboard (you might be able to buy an offcut, if you need only a small patch), draw a line round it, and cut 3 mm (⅛ in) inside this line.

Nail 50 × 25 mm (2 × 1 in) battens to the sides of the frame so that the battens will not touch the joists. Position the frame inside the hole you have cut in the ceiling, and fix it into place with 75 mm (3 in) screws driven through pre-drilled holes and into the sides of the joists. The frame should be positioned on the joists so that the new patch will be level with the old ceiling.

Place the patch in position on the frame, and fix it with galvanized plasterboard nails. Fix down any free ends of the plasterboard of the existing ceiling, by nailing to the joists or the battens fixed to the frame. Disguise the join between new and old plasterboard as detailed in Chapter 6.

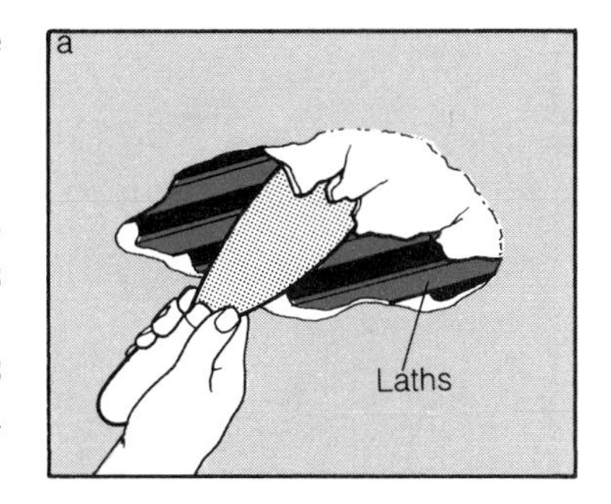

8.1 *Repairing a bulge in a lath and plaster ceiling: (a) Scrape off bulging plaster. (b) Fill the hole with decorating filler or plaster.*

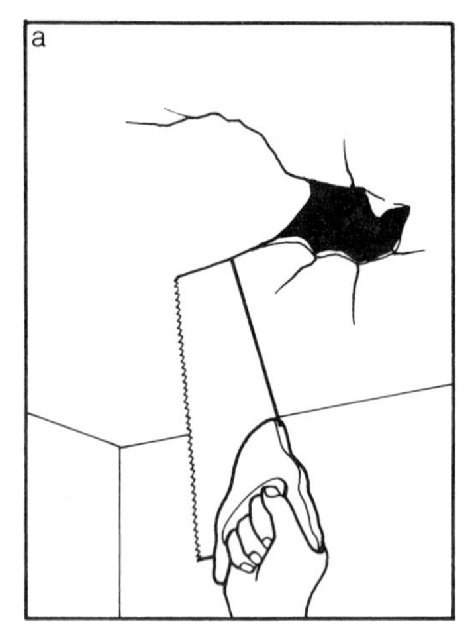

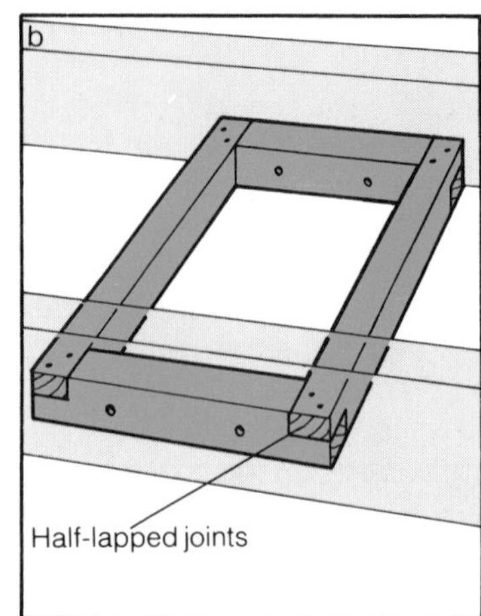

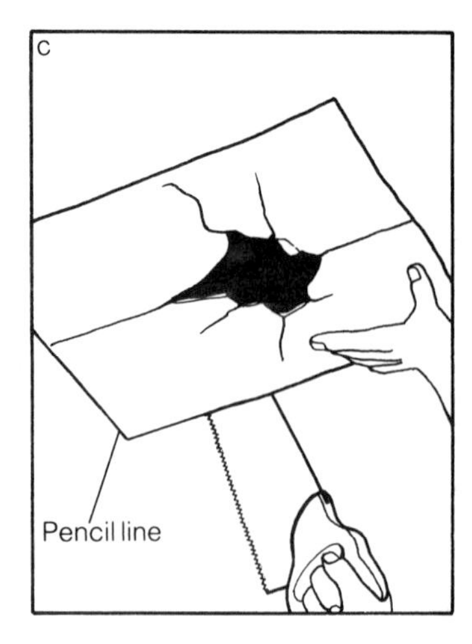

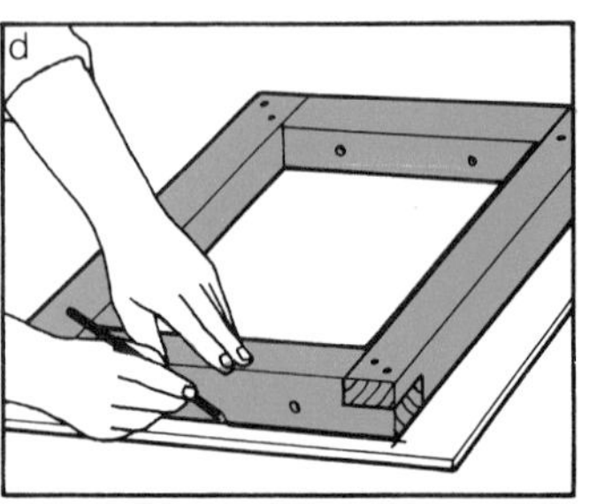

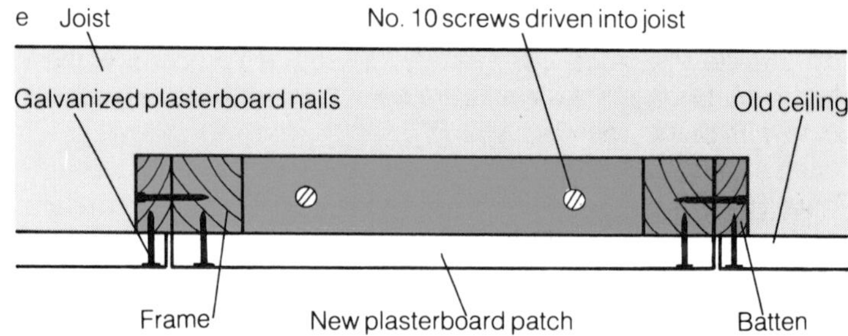

8.2 Patching a plasterboard ceiling: (a) Locate the joists with a saw. (b) Make up a frame that will eventually fit between the joists and cover the damaged area. (c) Mark and saw out area covered by frame. (d) Use frame as pattern for marking out plasterboard patch. (e) The patch is nailed to the frame, free ends of the main ceiling to the joists or battens fixed to the side of the frame.

Pulling down a ceiling

An old ceiling, particularly a lath and plaster one, can get into such a bad state that complete replacement becomes necessary. The first stage is to take down the old ceiling. This is not a job that calls for any particular skills, but it is not one to be undertaken lightly. Especially in an older house, you will be showered by a large amount of dust as the ceiling, along with the debris of 100 years or more lying on top of it, pours down. Do not underestimate the amount of dust there will be, especially on top floors: the cloud can be so dense that visibility can go down to a couple of feet.

Begin by opening the window. Warn the neighbours what you propose to do. Dust will billow out to such an extent that they might think it is smoke and that you have a fire. Wear goggles and a mask – improvise this from a handkerchief, if need be.

Work with an old stout chisel, screwdriver, small crowbar or any similar blunt instrument or even a large claw hammer. Push the tool up through the plaster and try to locate the joists. When you have found the joists, wrench the laths free, letting them and the plaster fall to the ground. Finding the joists will be easier as the work proceeds.

When the entire ceiling is pulled down and the dust has

settled, inspect the joists and pull out any nails or remnants of lath.

This is a good opportunity, too, to inspect the joists for damage or decay (see Chapter 9). Look particularly for signs of woodworm attack, both in the joists and in the underside of the floor above.

Decide whether you are going to put up a new ceiling, or leave the joists on view. Much depends on the condition of the joists and on the underside of any floor above. Only if these are attractive will you want to have them on view.

If you decide to leave the joists uncovered, you can get a pleasing effect by staining the joists a dark colour, and painting the underside of the floor above white.

A NEW CEILING

Modern ceilings are nearly always made of plasterboard. If you decide to put up a new ceiling, then this is the obvious choice. A timber ceiling is an alternative, but for most purposes it is prohibitively expensive.

Erecting a plasterboard ceiling

As already explained, plasterboard comes in two thicknesses. For joists spaced with the centres up to 450 mm (18 in) apart use 9.5 mm (3/8 in) board; if they are wider apart – up to 600 mm (24 in) – use 12.7 mm (1/2 in) board. Plasterboard incorporating an insulating material is available, and this is particularly suitable for top-storey ceilings. Choose a length of board that suits the spacing of the joists.

The boards should be fixed with the longest edge across the joists, and the ends should lie along the middle of a joist. They must not be left flapping free. Noggings (intermediate strips) should be fixed between the joists along the sides of the board, so that each is supported on all edges (Fig. 8:3).

Plasterboard is a heavy material, especially the larger thicker sheets, so you will need a helper. You must have proper access so that you can reach the ceiling. Do not attempt to balance on a pair of household steps: rest each end of a scaffold board on a strong support.

With the aid of a helper, lift a sheet of board and carry it on edge to a corner of the room, which is where the first one should be fixed. Turn it flat, and hoist it up. The helper should stand at one end, supporting the board with the head and outstretched hands. You stand at the other end, also using your head for support, and drive in the first few fixing nails. When sufficient nails have been driven in for the board to stay in place you can both drive home the fixing nails. Nails should be driven in at 150 mm (6 in) centres, and no closer than 13 mm (1/2 in) from the edge.

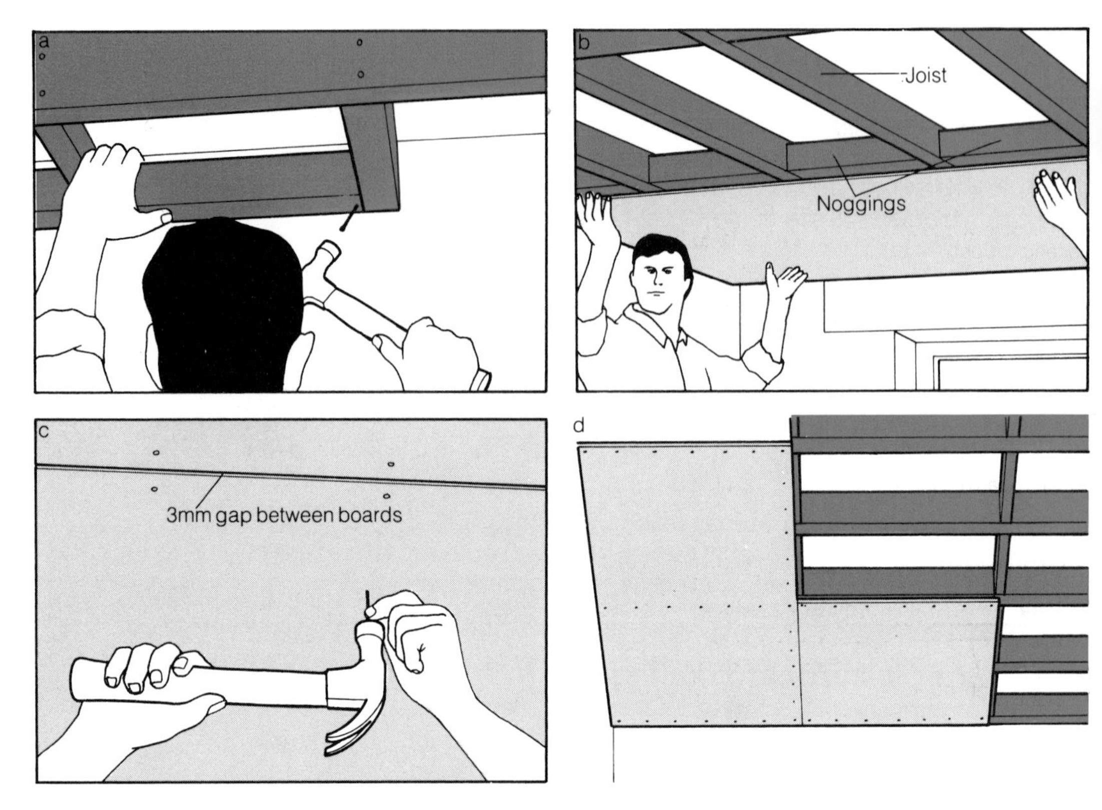

8.3 Erecting a plasterboard ceiling: (a) Fix noggings between the joints. (b) Lift up the plasterboard. (c) The board is nailed to joists and noggings. (d) Start off second row with a cut piece in order to stagger the joins.

Leave a gap of 3 mm (⅛ in) between this board and the next one you erect. Eventually, when you come to the end of a row, cut a board to fit. Use the waste from this to start off the next row, so the cross joins of the boards will be staggered. If an exact number of whole boards make up a row, start off the second row with half a board, in order to stagger the joints.

Full instructions for working with plasterboard and disguising the joins are given in the section on internal walls.

A false ceiling

Pulling down an old defective ceiling is extremely messy and disruptive so, where the ceiling height permits, it might be better to erect a false ceiling just below the existing one. The way to do this is to fix a network of battens to the ceiling, with screws driven through them and the plaster into the joists (Fig. 8:4). If you decide on a plasterboard ceiling, the network should go both along and across the joists, to give the necessary fixing points, as detailed in the previous section.

Finding the ceiling joists can be difficult, but in cases such as this – where there will be a good cover-up – you can make a series of test borings. Once you have determined

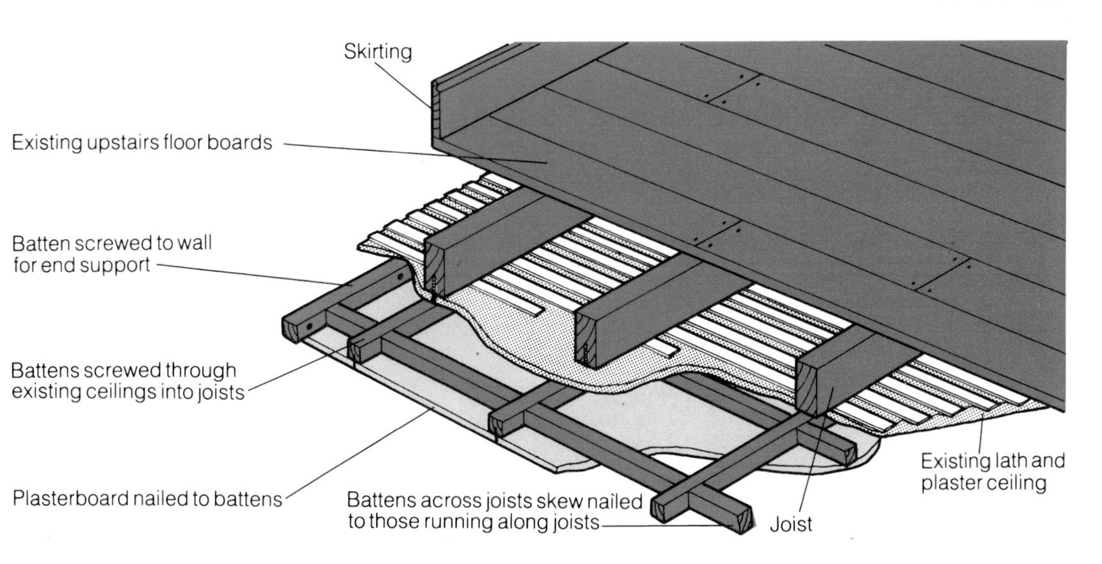

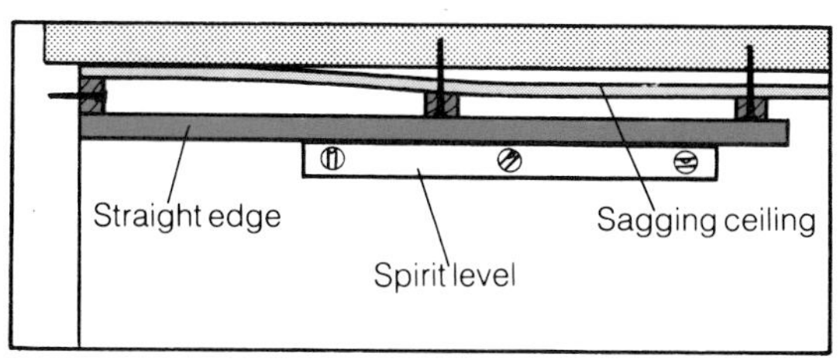

8.4 *Battens screwed through existing lath and plaster and into joists provide fixing points for a false ceiling. (Inset) Check with a spirit level and true batten that the fixing battens are all level. Those at a room's perimeter may have to be fixed to the top of the wall, instead of to the ceiling, to ensure that they are true.*

the position of two joists you should easily locate the others, because usually the spacing between them is regular.

To get a good, level ceiling, all the battens should be at the same height. Check that they are by placing a long, true batten, with a spirit level held against it, across them. To adjust the level, withdraw the battens' fixing screws or drive them in further as necessary. Where the ceiling joists have twisted badly out of true, and the ceiling bows heavily in the middle, fix the battens at the perimeter of the room to the top of the wall, rather than the ceiling (Fig. 8:4 inset).

The battens should have a cross-section of about 50 mm (2 in) square, so long screws will be required – a minimum of 100 mm (4 in) to get through batten, plaster and lath, and give a good, firm fixing.

A false ceiling serves a useful function in a top-storey room, where there is no accessible attic space above. You can place insulation materials above the plasterboard, to make the house warmer, and so reduce heating bills.

Timber ceilings

Many do-it-yourselfers putting up a false ceiling prefer to use lengths of matchboarding instead of sheets of plasterboard, because these are much easier to handle. Be

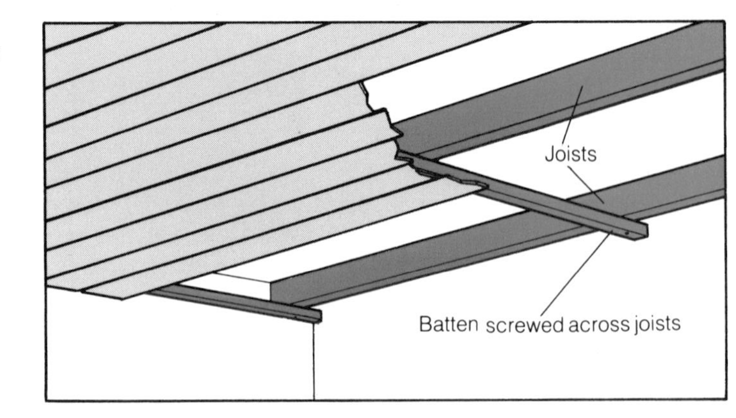

8.5 *False ceiling of matchboarding 'secret nailed' to battens screwed to joists*

warned, however, that many authorities feel that this represents too much of a fire risk.

Matchboarding used on a ceiling (Fig. 8:5) should be fixed to battens at each end and at spacings of about one metre (40 in). It will probably be easier to fix the battens across the joists, rather than along them, with a screw driven into each joist. The planks should be fixed to the battens with secret nailing (see page 135).

Illuminated ceilings

Until recently, illuminated ceilings were to be found mainly in shops and supermarkets, but they have become increasingly popular in the home. They consist of a series of plastic panels, suspended below a set of fluorescent tubes. The light from these ceilings is not suitable for living rooms and bedrooms, but is ideal for kitchens and bathrooms. Moreover, the warm surface of the plastic can help to reduce, if not eliminate, condensation – a problem to which such rooms are prone. An illuminated ceiling is also a good means of hiding one in a bad condition. It is particularly suitable for high-ceiling rooms, but could be a problem with rooms that already have a low ceiling.

Plan the height of the ceiling carefully. It should not be so high that there is no room for the tubes, or so low that the light becomes diffused. The manufacturers give advice on suitable heights. Many people think it a good idea to paint the original ceiling in brilliant white gloss before fixing the panels. With some brands, the panels can be used to change the colour of the light from the tubes. Using a combination of plain and coloured panels it is also possible to build up interesting patterns.

A TRAP DOOR TO THE LOFT

Many homes, especially those built in the last century, have no means of access to the loft, which is often necessary nowadays to lay insulation, fit a cold supply tank, or carry out electrical work.

A landing is usually the best place for a trap door, because you can enter the loft without inconveniencing anyone in a bedroom, and without showering the bedroom with dust when the door is opened.

Draw in pencil on the ceiling the shape of the opening you wish to cut. Ideally, this should be close to a joist on two sides, so be prepared to adjust its position if necessary. Push a chisel through the middle of the piece of plaster you wish to remove, and make a slot. Push a saw through the slot and cut out the shape with a saw. Get a helper to stand by as you do so, to support the cut-out. Lower it gently to the ground to minimize dust.

If you are dealing with plasterboard, it will be easy to take down the cut-out in one piece, and with the minimum of dirt; lath and plaster will be more messy, so saw through each lath carefully.

If the space between two joists is not big enough for a hatch, support the ceiling, then saw out a section of the joist in the middle of the opening. For the support use a stout post wedged between two lengths of timber (at least 50 mm (2 in) thick) – one on the floor and the other on the ceiling. These pieces of timber should be long enough to span at least two joists on both floor and ceiling. Saw through the joist squarely.

At each end of the opening fit a 'trimmer' (Fig. 8:6). This is

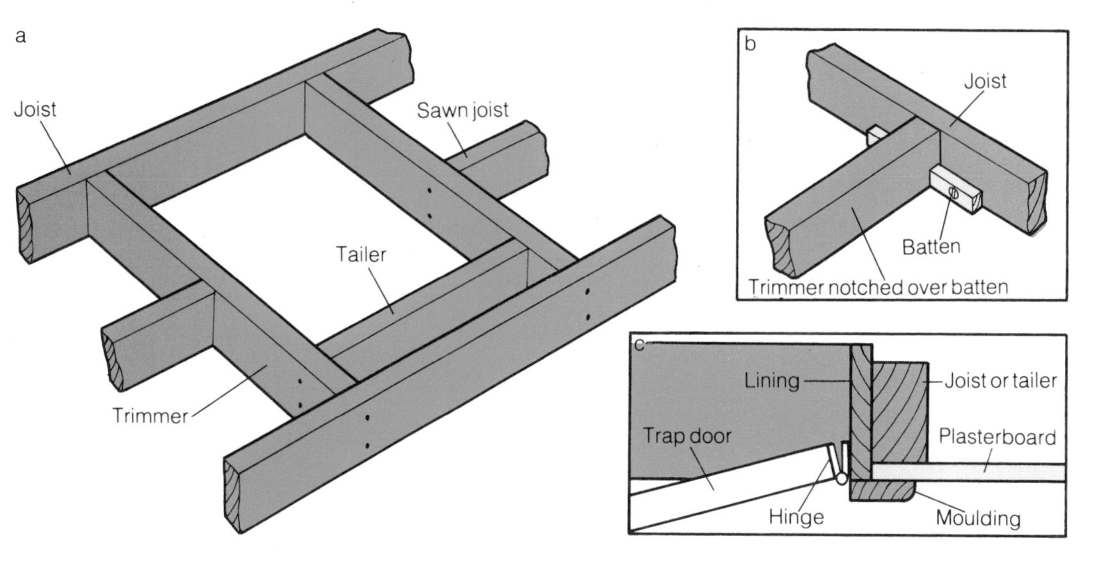

8.6 *(a) Framework for door to left (b) How to fix trimmers and tailers to sides of joist (c) Detail of how opening is lined with planed timber, and underside framed with moulding*

a length of timber (of the same size as the joists) that spans the gap between the two uncut joists. Butt the trimmer up against the end of the cut joists. If you want an opening narrower than the space between two joists, fit a 'tailer' – a similar piece of timber spanning the gap between the two trimmers.

Professionals would fix the trimmers and tailers with 100 mm (4 in) round wire nails. This will be secure enough only if the ends of the cut joists are square. If in doubt, screw battens to the sides of the cut ends of the joists, and notch the trimmers over them.

When the timber framework forming the opening is fixed securely, remove the timber supports. Line the inside of the opening with planed timber about 19 mm (¾ in) thick. Frame the underside with moulded timber, then make good any damaged plaster. Cut the door from a sheet of blockboard.

If the door will be used infrequently, you can line the loft opening with timber to form a ledge. The door can merely rest on this ledge, and be pushed up when you want to enter the loft. You might prefer to hinge the door instead. To enable you to fit a loft ladder you should fix the hinges so that the door opens downwards. Then you need a catch to hold the door closed when it is pushed back into place.

Chapter 9
FLOORS

There are two entirely distinct types of floor – those that actually rest on the ground below, and those that are fixed some way above it. These are known as 'direct-to-earth' and 'suspended' floors. Floors on the first storey and above must, by their very nature, be suspended; those on the ground floor can be either. In general, however, only direct-to-earth floors are found in basements.

SUSPENDED FLOORS

In small homes suspended floors are nearly always of timber, and that usually means floorboards. However, because of the high price of timber, some modern homes have floors of chipboard. Suspended floors can also be of concrete, but these are usually confined to high-rise buildings. There is little to go wrong with this material, and if cracks do develop they indicate faults way beyond the scope of the do-it-yourselfer. If tamping marks are visible on the surface of this sort of floor, a floor-levelling compound should be applied before fixing any floorcovering; no other repair should be attempted.

The joists

Suspended wooden floors are supported by, and fixed to, a network of joists. The normal fixing of each board is by floorboard nails, two driven into each joist.

The spacing between joists and their size will have been determined by the architect according to their span (the length across which they are unsupported) and the load they would be expected to carry. It is important to bear in mind that domestic suspended floors may have been designed to support only normal furniture and living stress. They can be damaged if subjected to excessive strain – unusually heavy furniture, for instance (water beds have recently been found to be a problem in some situations), or dancing. Natural stone fireplaces that spread beyond the chimney breast to incorporate shelves and so on can also pose a threat: they should never be installed on a sus-

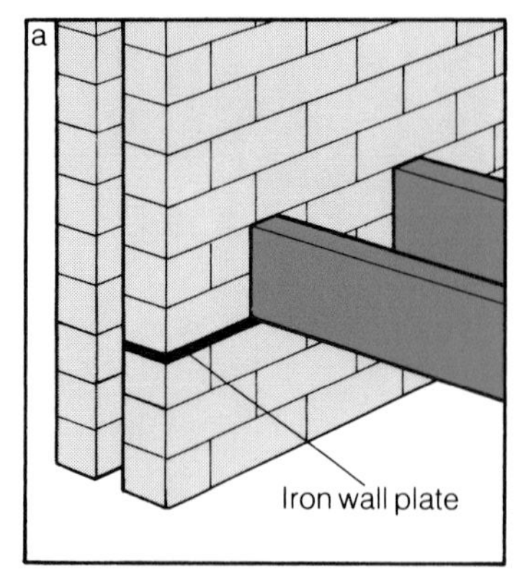

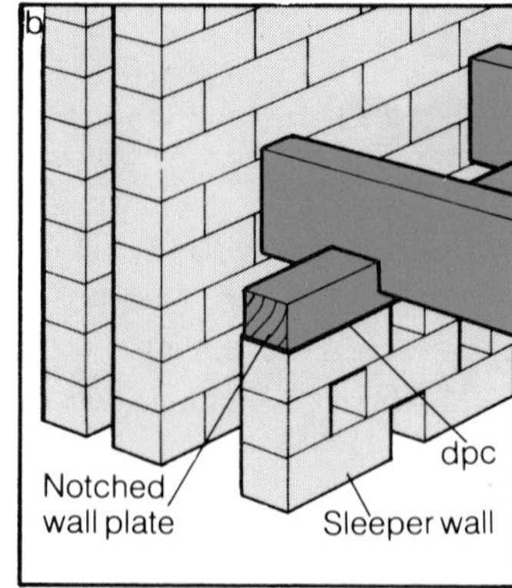

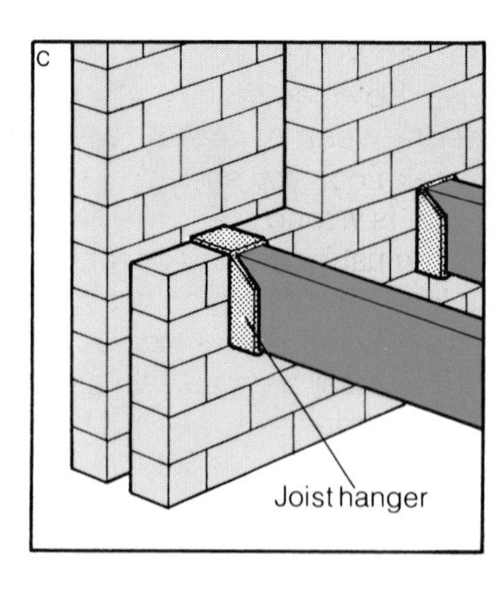

9.1 *Three ways in which the ends of floor joists can be supported: (a) In sockets, (b) on a sleeper wall and (c) in joist hangers.*

pended timber floor without extra support being added. The joist spacings will be at centres of from 300 mm (1 ft) upwards – you can see at a glance the spacing in your case (if the boards are not covered) by looking at the heads of the fixing nails. The size will usually be 100 × 50 mm (4 × 2 in) or perhaps 150 mm (6 in) depth and 38 mm (1½ in) width.

Fig. 9:1 shows three ways in which a ground floor joist can be supported at the ends:

1 It can be let into a socket left for this purpose in the brickwork. In such instances, there will often be an iron wall plate running under the joists, to spread the load along the entire wall.
2 It may rest on a low wall, built just inside the main walls of the house, and known as a sleeper wall. On top of the sleeper wall will be a damp-proof course (dpc) strip, then a length of timber known as a wall plate. The joist will usually be notched into and over the wall plate (although some just rest on top of it) and be held in place by skew-nailing.
3 It might rest in a device known as a joist hanger, a sort of galvanized metal stirrup built into the brickwork.

Any intermediate support that is necessary will be provided by extra sleeper walls in the middle of the span. Such sleeper walls have gaps to allow extra circulation of air, ventilation being an important factor in keeping damp at bay.

The ends of upper floor joists can also be fixed in sockets or joist hangers; intermediate support will be provided by an internal wall in the house.

Repairing joists

Fortunately, joists do not develop as many faults as floorboards, but defects can occur, especially if unseasoned wood was used in the first place. A joist can twist out of true. A symptom of this would be that a floorboard would be seen to be twisted, but could not be nailed down flat. Or a joist can be attacked by woodworm or dry rot. The floor will seem weak or unstable if this is the case. If you suspect a weak floor you should always lift a board or two to discover what is wrong.

It must be stressed that repairs to joists are a major undertaking, and not to be embarked upon lightly. They involve a great upheaval, especially on upper floors, for your work will almost certainly damage the ceiling below. Since each joist carries every board in the room, a large part of the floor – if not the whole lot – will have to be taken up, which will mean the room will be unusable, as will any room below if you interfere with its ceiling.

A joist might be damaged along part of its length – a tendency for the floor to sag, or feel unstable at one point is an indication of this. In such a case, saw out the damaged section as detailed below, buy a new length of timber of the same size, and bolt it to the cut ends of the old joist.

If a joist is twisted or bowed it is often possible to straighten it by fitting struts between it and the joist on each side. Should all the joists be twisted, struts of fairly strong timber, 25 mm (1 in) thick, and almost as wide as the joists are deep, will have to be fitted between each of them. They are cut to a length equalling exactly the spacing between the joists, and are fixed by skew-nailing. If this remedy does not work, the joists will have to be replaced.

Replacing joists

Begin by taking up all the boards fixed to the joist. If the joist is in an upper storey, you will need to free the ceiling below by pressing gently on top of the ceiling to push the fixing nails down. One way of finding these nails is to push a very thin blade under the joist and move it along until the nails are located. If the ceiling is made of lath and plaster you will probably have to cut a large area, if not take down the whole lot.

If the joist is supported at its end on joist hangers, or fixed to the top of a wall, it can be lifted clear. The new joist, which obviously should be of the same size as the old, can then be dropped into place. Should the joist be resting on wall plates, withdraw any fixing nails, then once again remove it and fit the new joist. If the joist is built into a slot, get someone to hold it while you saw through it near its ends. Lift the main body of the joist away, then pull out the short stub still in the slot. You cannot push a new joist back into these slots, so they will have to be bricked up and joist hangers mortared into the brickwork.

An electric cable may have been passed through a joist you are replacing. Disconnect it – having turned the supply off at the mains first – from the nearest connection and draw it clear. Bore a 19 mm (¾ in) diameter hole in the new joist 50 mm (2 in) from its top to accommodate the cable.

Timber floor surfaces

Floorboards, nowadays, are often tongued and grooved ('t and g') so that as shrinkage of the timber occurs over the years there will not be a gap for dirt and draughts to pass through. But this was not always so: in the last century, and occasionally in this, boards without tongues and grooves – 'square-edged' boards – were fitted.

Warped floorboards

Warping can cause boards to curl up at the edges, making it difficult to lay floorcoverings. If this is not too pronounced, overlaying it with hardboard will be a sufficient cure. Alternatively, you can sand the boards flat again with a floor sander, using a course abrasive belt. Normally when sanding boards you should work along – not across – their length, because crosswise sanding causes score marks that are difficult to remove. Work at an angle of 45° to the side of the boards. If you mean to seal the boards and leave them uncovered, treat them along their length in the normal way first with a medium, then with a fine abrasive.

Lifting and replacing floorboards

The commonest reason for having to lift a floorboard is to work on plumbing or electrics below. First check whether your boards are 't and g' or square-edged. Push a knife blade down between two boards, but not so far that you might strike a cable. If there is no resistance, the board is square-edged; if the blade will not pass through, there is a tongue. If there is a tongue you will have to remove it on both sides of the board. The traditional tool for doing this is the floorboard saw, but a powered circular saw is just as good (Fig. 9:2).

You must set the saw blade so that it protrudes just below the tongue you are going to cut, for not only does this ensure that the saw teeth strike the work at the best angle for sawing, but also that there is less risk of cutting into the joists or striking cables and pipes. The tongue occupies the middle third of the side of a board, so its lower edge would be about 8 mm (⅓ in) below the surface of a 25 mm (1 in) thick board, and 6 mm (¼ in) below that of a 19 mm (¾ in) board. When you have removed the tongues, you must saw across the width at each end of the section of board you wish to raise. These cuts should be done with a pad saw, for which you might have to drill a starting hole; the cut should be made immediately to the side of a joist – you will be able to locate

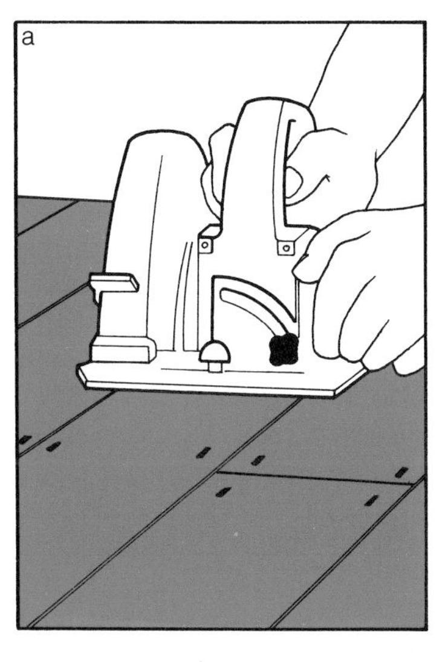

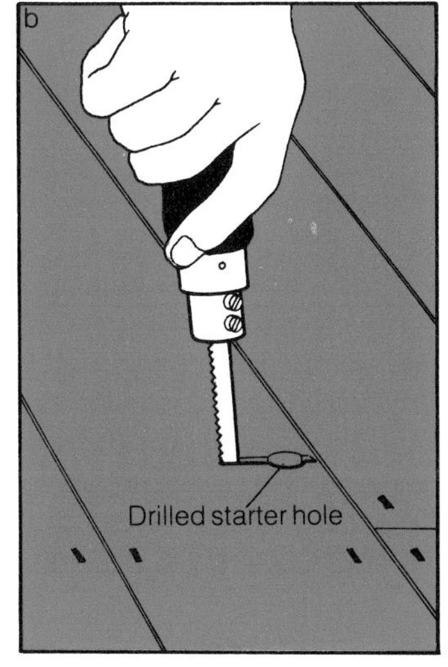

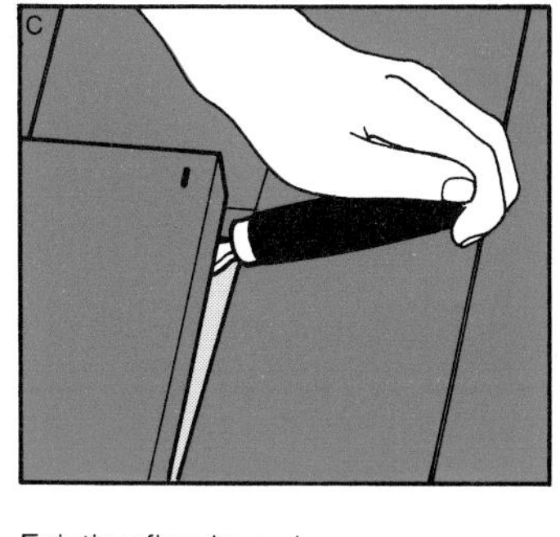

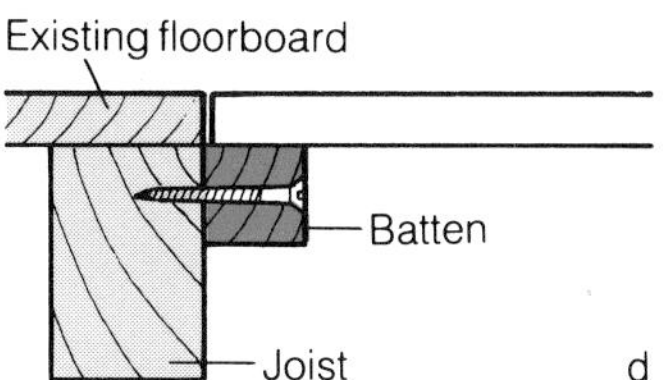

9.2 Lifting up a floorboard: (a) Cut off tongues with a circular saw. (b) Saw across width of board. (c) Prise board from cut end. (d) When board is replaced, its end is nailed to a batten screwed to side of joist.

these easily with a knife once the board tongues have been removed.

The board now has to be wrenched up. You can shove a strong screwdriver, old chisel, or small crowbar under the fixing points and heave, but you risk marking the boards this way. On an old floor that you intend to cover up completely this may not matter, but if you want the board to be on view, a better way is to wrench up a set of nails near a cut end, then push a hammer handle flat under the board and press down sharply on the free end. This will send a shock wave down the length of the board that will loosen nails further along. You will then be able to push the hammer farther along and repeat the process. The farther you push the hammer, the more effective this method will be, for you will be able to exert greater leverage. Pull the nails out as they loosen with either a claw hammer or pincers.

With one board up and out of the way, it is easier to remove subsequent boards. If you need to take up boards that are side by side, it will probably be enough to remove the tongues on each outer edge, leaving the ones between intact.

When you come to refix the board, you cannot nail it to the joists at the end since you have to cut just to the side of them. You must screw a small length of timber – 38 mm (1½ in) square is suitable – to the side of the joist. The length of the timber should be greater than the width of the board. Fix it with its top edge hard against the underside of the boards on each side, and it will be in the correct position to make the replaced board level.

If you have raised the board to install an electrical or plumbing connection, fix it back with screws, so that it will be easy to raise should you need access again. Otherwise use floorboard nails, unless it is an upstairs floor over a dubious ceiling, in which case hammering might loosen the ceiling's key.

A floorboard that is badly damaged can be replaced. Take it up and discard it. If just one board is involved, the replacement should be square-edged – a 't and g' board cannot be fitted. You may not be able to buy a board of exactly the right width, so get one larger and plane it to a close fit. Your new board should be of the same thickness as the old, but if it proves impossible to buy one of the correct thickness, you can choose one slightly thinner and place a little packing – hardboard, perhaps – on each joist. Or buy a thicker one and plane it to size – this is not too much trouble if you have a power planer.

Squeaking boards

A board squeaks because, as you walk over the floor, it moves and rubs against its neighbour. To stop such movement you must refix it. At its simplest, such refixing could consist of punching home nails properly. However, the movement of the board may have so enlarged the hole round the nails that this will not be effective. The obvious remedy then might seem to be to drive in extra nails elsewhere in the board. But you have to be careful to avoid cables and pipes.

Electricity cables are not such a problem because, if they have been properly installed, the holes in the joist through which they pass will be at least 50 mm (2 in) below the floor. Pipes are a different matter, however, because they are likely to be sitting in notches cut in the joist immediately below the boards. To find out where pipes are likely to be, look at whatever items supplied by gas or water are in the room and try to work out where the pipe runs. If all else fails, take the loose nails out of the loose board and replace them with screws driven in exactly the same holes.

Gaps between boards

Gaps that develop due to shrinkage or bad fitting between the boards can be a problem. Even if there is a tongue the gap makes it difficult to lay a floorcovering smoothly. There are several ways in which these gaps can be plugged. For instance, you can take thin strips of wood, taper them slightly with a sander on the lower edge, and tap them down into the gap. They should be left slightly proud, then smoothed down flush with a plane or, better still, a floor sander. Another method is to make papier mâché with old newspapers to fill the gap, but this, although cheap, is tedious. In both cases, if the floor is left bare it will be obvious what you have done.

The best method is probably to overlay the floor with hardboard. This presents a superb surface on which to lay floorcoverings and, if sealed, or even painted, can make an attractive flooring in its own right.

Hardboarding a floor

Hardboard comes in a range of sheet sizes, the biggest normally being 2440 × 1220 mm (8 × 4 ft). The bigger the sheets the more quickly you can work, but large sheets can be unwieldy and you might prefer to settle for a sheet 1220 mm (4 ft) or even 900 mm (3 ft) square.

Hardboard should always be conditioned before use, and this process is essential when it is to be laid over floorboards. Brush a litre (1⅘ pints) of water into the reverse side of each 2440 × 1220 mm (8 × 4 ft) sheet (use correspondingly less water on smaller sheets), then stack them flat, back to back, in the room where they will be laid. Leave them for approximately 48 hours – not much less or much longer. The sheets then dry out once they are fixed, and tighten up like a

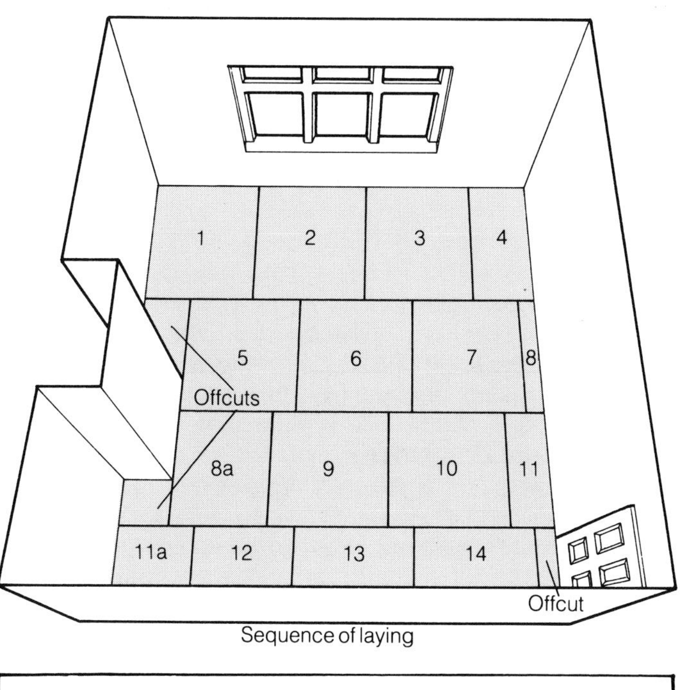

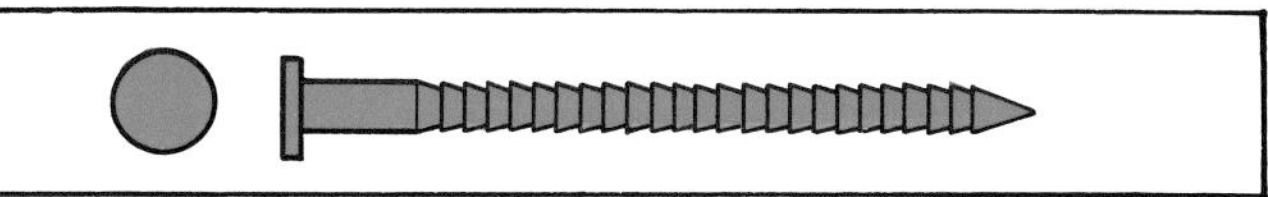

9.3 *Order in which sheets of hardboard are fixed to a floor. Fixing is best done with ring shank nails (inset).*

drum skin to form a perfect surface on which to lay a floor-covering.

Hardboard is fixed with ring-shank nails (Fig. 9:3). Lay it smooth-side down if you intend to cover it, so that the mesh will hide the nail head and present a good surface to receive the covering. You need a nail at 225 mm (9 in) centres in the middle, and 150 mm (6 in) centres round the edges.

Begin laying the sheets in the corner of the room farthest away from the door. This corner will probably not be a perfect right angle because most rooms are out of true, but it does not matter if the sheet does not fit perfectly against the wall. Butt the next sheet up against the first, and fix that. Eventually you will come to the end of the row, where you will have to cut a sheet to the size of the gap – again it does not have to be a perfect fit. Take the waste from this sheet and use it to start the next row. Not only is this an economical use of the material, but also it staggers the joins – breaks the bond – between the sheets thus making for a better job. The final row of sheets at the end of the room will probably need to be cut to width.

Re-laying a floor

Where large gaps have developed between floorboards, often the only remedy will be to take the floorboards up and re-lay them. Begin at the side of the room away from the door. Take up about seven or eight boards, but leave the one under the skirting undisturbed. The tongues should remain intact where possible. Clean off the edges and undersides of all the boards you left, and get rid of any dust or dirt on top of the joists. Take out any nails or tacks still left in the boards.

Now take one of the raised boards and push it into position up against the board still remaining under the skirting. Follow with about five more boards. You now need sets of two wedges cut from softwood and preferably slightly thicker than the floorboards. The wedges should be about 150 mm (6 in) long, and tapered from, say, 50 mm (2 in) at their widest to a narrow point. A set of wedges is required for every metre (39 in) of board length.

Place the wedges in pairs on their sides up against the last row out from the skirting, then nail a spare board to the joists hard against the wedges. Use two hammers to knock the wedges so they slide against each other, working on each set alternately. This will drive the boards as close as possible against each other. When you are satisfied they are tight, nail them in place, beginning with the one nearest the wedges. Use floorboard nails, two per board per joist.

Now you can remove the wedges and take up further boards to allow you to re-lay the next half dozen. Eventually you will come to the far side of the room. Once again leave the board half under the skirting alone. When you have re-laid all the rest, there will be a gap between this board and the rest of the floor. Fill it with a new board that will have to be cut to size.

Repairing and installing chipboard floors

In many modern buildings chipboard is used on top of the joist instead of floorboards, because it can be up to 30 per cent cheaper. It must, however, be a special type of chipboard suitable for the job. Chipboard is a good base for all types of floorcovering and can be an attractive surface in its own right when sealed.

Flooring-quality chipboard can be bought in three different edge profiles – square-edged, tongued-and-grooved on two sides or four, or loose-tongued. It is available in two thicknesses – 18 mm (11⁄16 in) and 22 mm (7⁄8 in) – and in various sheet sizes, 2440 × 1220 mm (8 × 4 ft) and 2440 × 600 mm (8 × 2 ft) being the most common. It is fixed to the joists with nails.

Chipboard has one other big advantage over floorboards, apart from cost: it is a more stable material than natural timber,and therefore less likely to twist, shrink or warp. It is not, of course, as strong, but is perfectly adequate for the job.

If any of the panels that make up a chipboard floor become damaged, replace them. Should the panel be a large one, you might be able to minimize costs by replacing just half of it.

First ascertain by probing as before, whether a 't and g' board has been used. If it has, the tongues on all sides will have to be removed, in the same way as for floorboards. Prise up the board, using a large, old screwdriver or chisel. Begin along one edge. Once you work this free, the rest will come up easily.

When the board is raised, measure its thickness, and buy a replacement of the same dimension. In the meantime, leave the damaged board loosely in place so that no one will fall down the hole. No matter what type of edge profile was used previously, the replacement will have to be square edged. Chipboard can also be used to replace a damaged plank floor. As already mentioned, flooring-grade chipboards come in two thicknesses – 18 mm (11⁄16 in) and 22 mm (7⁄8 in). For the former the joists must be no more than 450 mm (18 in) apart, while for the latter they can be up to 610 mm (24 in). Local building regulations may specify minima.

Square-edged boards should be supported on every edge (Fig. 9:4). Their long edges go parallel to – and should

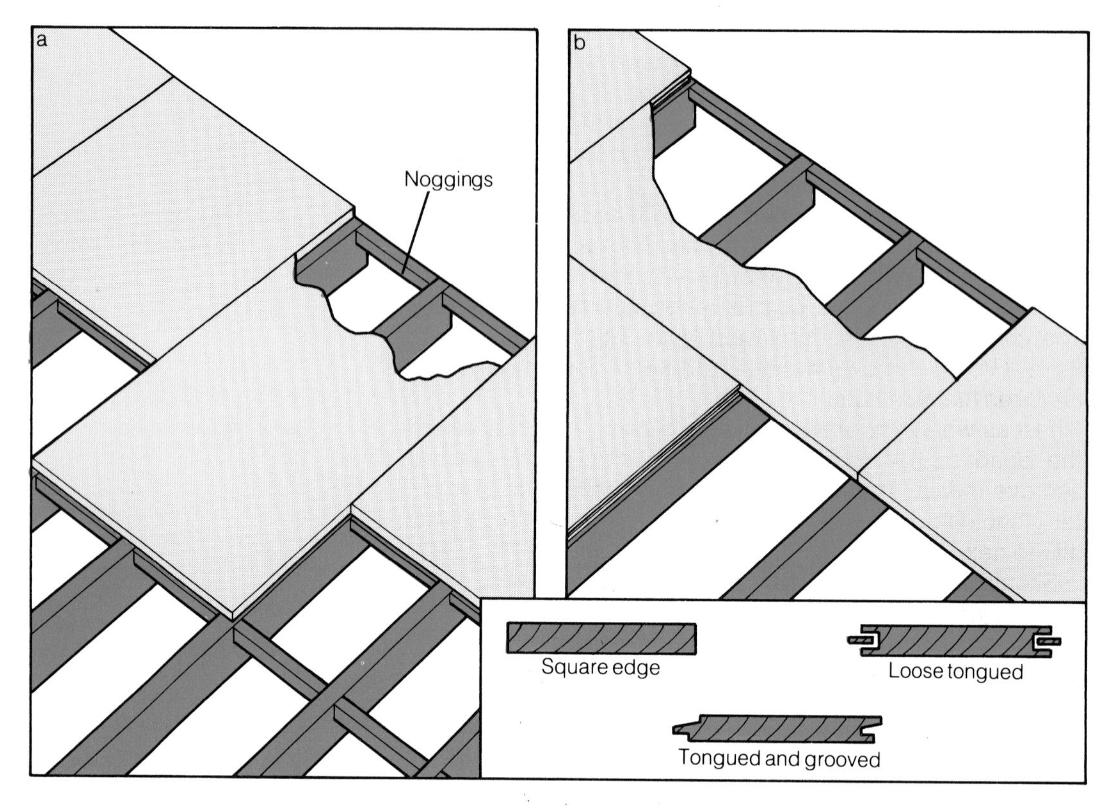

9.4 *Fixing a chipboard floor: (inset) Three types of board – square edged, loose-tongued, and tongued and grooved. (a) Square edged boards fixed parallel to joists with ends supported on noggings (b) Tongued and grooved boards run across the joists.*

fall in the middle of – the joists. This means that, if you cannot buy a standard sheet size to match your joist spacing, you will have to cut the sheets to width. The ends of the sheets are fixed to short lengths of timber, skew-nailed to the side of the joists. These lengths of timber are known as noggings, and they should be 38 mm (1½ in) wide. The boards should be nailed in place, the nails being about 9 mm (⅓ in) from the edge of the board, and 200-300 mm (8-12 in) apart round the perimeter, 400-500 mm (16-20 in) on intermediate joists.

Tongued-and-grooved boards go with their long edges across the joists. They must, however, be supported at the ends, so cut them to a length that ensures their short edges fall in the middle of joists, one 25 mm (1 in) from each edge, the others spaced between.

Study the foregoing information, look at the joist spacing in your home, get from your supplier a list of the sizes of board he can offer you, then work out which it would be best for you to buy.

The temptation will be to get the biggest boards possible because that would speed up the work. However, do remember that chipboard is such a heavy material that some of the larger sheets are unwieldy, so unless you can be sure of help, you might get along better with a smaller size.

When your chipboard arrives, it must be properly stored until you are ready to use it – bad storage can cause permanent distortion of the boards. Stack them flat, indoors. It is a good idea, too, to loose-lay them in the room where they will be fixed for at least 24 hours in order to condition them to the moisture content of the room.

The edges of all types of board should be tightly butted up against each other, and you will get a stronger result if you smear a pvc woodworking adhesive on the meeting surface. But where the boards meet the walls of the room you should leave an expansion gap. This gap should be 2 mm (1/12 in) for every metre (40 in) of floor, with 10 mm (2/5 in) as the minimum.

Just as when you are laying hardboard, you should break the bond so that the cross joins are staggered, and you achieve this in just the same way: when you saw a board to length to complete the end of the row, use the waste to start off the next row.

Should there be electrical or plumbing connections under a chipboard floor it is a good idea to form a trap above them. Make sure it is supported by joists or noggings on all edges, and fix it with screws rather than with nails so that it can be raised easily.

You can bond all types of flooring, both sheet and tile, directly to chipboard. If you will be using an adhesive with a high water content, seal the floor first with a polyurethane lacquer.

DIRECT-TO-EARTH FLOORS

A direct-to-earth floor, sometimes known as a solid floor, is one that is laid directly on the ground beneath. At one time most ground floors were of this type: typical were floors consisting of flagstones or quarry tiles embedded in mortar directly on the earth. They suffered from one overwhelming defect: they were subject to rising damp.

Timber direct-to-earth floors were a little more sophisticated. They consisted of timber floor plates lying on the earth, to which would be fixed a series of joists, with floorboards on top. The resulting cavity made for a warmer, drier floor than was possible with flagstones or quarry tiles, but it was still subject to damp. In some cases, large-section timber, looking something like railway sleepers, would be bedded directly to the earth. This type was very prone to damp.

Because of these considerations, direct-to-earth floors fell out of favour for many years, and were revived only after 1945. Two factors made for the revival. First, at that time timber was so scarce as to make the joist-and-boarded floor prohibitively expensive. Second, improved methods of

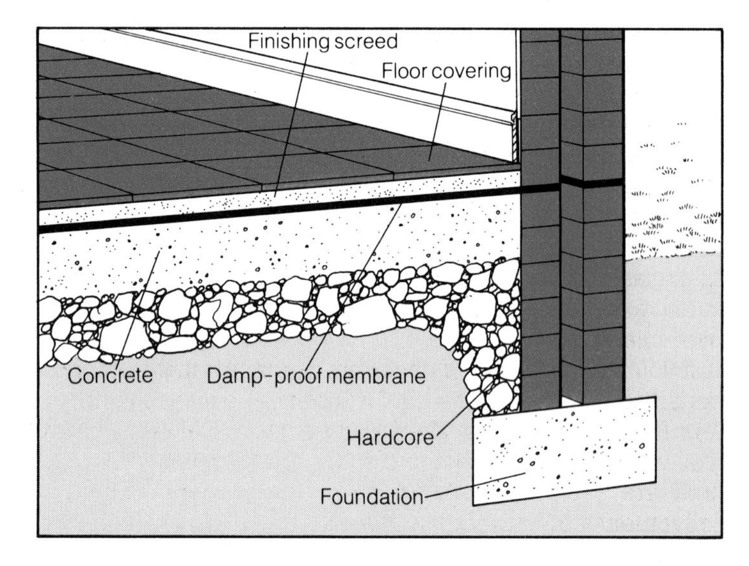

9.5 *Construction of a modern direct-to-earth floor*

damp-proofing meant that the rising damp could be kept at bay. And so homes with tiles – usually thermoplastic – throughout the ground floor made their appearance (or reappearance).

The modern direct-to-earth floor (Fig. 9:5) will be laid on well compacted earth. It will consist of a layer of hardcore, topped by concrete; then will come a damp-proof membrane, which will tie in with the damp-proof course of the walls; and finally there will be a finishing screed, with a floorcovering on top of that. Such a floor will be perfectly dry.

However, just because a floor has a concrete screed, you cannot assume that it has been correctly built. Before 1945 and, indeed, on occasions since, concrete floors were laid without proper damp precautions being taken.

Damp

If you have a direct-to-earth floor that was built before the last war, damp may be patently obvious, with marks covering the floor, and evidence of rotting in the floorcovering. In other cases, damp may be there without your being aware of it, and its presence would not matter unless you wanted to lay a floorcovering. There are various rough-and-ready tests you can carry out.

For instance, heat a brick in the oven for about an hour, then place it on the floor (so long as it is not a decorative one that can be damaged by heat). If the floor becomes stained, damp is present. Or you can take a sheet of metal, heat it on a blowlamp or gas ring, and lay it on the floor – again provided that it is one that will not be damaged by heat. Moisture beads will gather on the underside of the plate and a patch will appear on the concrete if the floor suffers from damp. Another test is to place a piece of glass on the floor and seal its edges with putty. Damp will cause moisture to form underneath it.

The snag with these tests, however, is that if they are negative you still cannot be absolutely sure that the floor is dry. Some floors are wet only during very damp weather, and in some cases the level of the local water table can vary. In the last resort, the only way to be absolutely sure is to call in an expert to make tests with special instruments – a hygrometer or protimeter.

If you have a floor – of concrete, perhaps – that is in good condition (level and smooth, for instance) except that it suffers from rising damp, then a cure can be effected fairly easily. Liquid preparations that can be brushed on to the floor are available at builders' merchants and home improvement centres. These can then be over-laid with the normal floorcoverings such as carpet, linoleum, or vinyl, and some can be left exposed as a floor surface in their own right. Follow the manufacturer's instructions when using them.

Laying a new floor

An old direct-to-earth floor, of flagstones, quarry tiles or timber, if damp or defective in some other way, has to be taken up and a concrete one built in its place. You must first of all remove the existing flooring (if you wish to retain the period flavour of an old house, this can be removed carefully, then re-laid on top of the new floor).

To lift flagstones, ram a crowbar or stout garden spade in between the joins, and lever up. The first quarry tiles should be chipped up with a cold chisel and club hammer, although later on you may get on faster with a garden spade. Quarry tiles that are cemented in place will be more difficult to lift without breakages. Timber can be prised up with a claw hammer, bolster chisel, or old screwdriver. There is no need to be gentle with this wood, as when dealing with floorboards: timber from a direct-to-earth floor will probably be so wet – and more than likely affected by rot or woodworm – that it will be fit only for burning.

Now you must excavate to get sufficient depth for your new floor. You will probably find it convenient to make this on the same plane as the original one, otherwise you will run into trouble with door openings and perhaps a change of level from other rooms.

The base of the excavation should be well compacted, and of the same depth throughout. You can ensure the latter by hammering in a series of timber pegs 25 mm (1 in) or 38 mm (1½ in) square. Span a batten from one peg to the next, and use a spirit level to ensure the tops of the two are level. Dig down to the same depth round each peg. The base on which the concrete slab rests will vary according to the site condition, and in particular to the relationship of the floor to the level of the soil outside the house and the nature of the soil. It could be that hardcore dressed with sand, or graded granular material, would be suitable. In some cases wet lean concrete – i.e. a very weak mix consisting of from 1:16 to 1:20 of cement to aggregate – would be best. Get expert advice from someone with detailed knowledge of local conditions.

The concrete should be at least 100 mm (4 in) thick, and consist of a mix of 2½ parts of sharp sand to 4 of coarse aggregate, by volume. It should be well compacted to obtain maximum density and strength, and be finished to a smooth surface. It is normal to top it off with a sand and cement screed, on which you can lay virtually any type of flooring.

A vapour-resistant membrane should be fitted between the concrete and the screed, and this should tie in with the damp-proof course of the walls. The damp-proof membrane (dpm) is necessary because although watertight, concrete is not vapour-tight, and vapour could pass through the slab to attack the floorcovering, or the adhesive with which it is fixed.

The dpm can be in either liquid or sheet form. However, the most effective liquid dpms must be hot-applied, and are really only for professional use. Of the sheet materials, polythene is probably the most convenient for the do-it-yourselfer.

A sheet 0.12 mm thick (500 gauge) is sufficient to keep out the damp, but might tend to get damaged in subsequent operations, so it is often as well to use material of twice that thickness. Joins in the material should overlap by at least 150 mm (6 in) and be taped down with vapour-resisting tape. The screed should be of Portland cement and clean sharp sand in a mix of 1:3 by weight, where the flooring finish will be of thin or flexible material (e.g. thin tiles or carpet); and 1:4 by weight if thick or rigid flooring, such as concrete or quarry tiles, are planned. Because it cannot be bonded directly to the concrete below, the minimum thickness of the screed should be 50 mm (2 in).

There is no need to split the floor into bays when dealing with domestic-sized rooms – you can cover the whole floor at one go. However, place down battens temporarily to give a depth to which to tamp down the screed. You must make sure that the material is well compacted, and that there are no hollows in the concrete. To help in this you can make a tamper from scraps of timber and a broom handle. Smooth off finally with a float.

When finished the floor should be cured for four days by being covered with a 0.12 mm sheet of polythene 500 gauge, well lapped and held down all round the edges. Since the floor is inside a building, there will normally be no need to provide protection against frost.

Chapter 10
PLUMBING

The plumbing system of your home has two distinct functions: it supplies water to the points where it is needed and it carries away waste water when you have finished with it.

Any work you do on the plumbing must comply with the regulations of your local water authority. You are not required to get permission beforehand, but the authority can inspect the work and demand changes if they are not satisfied. The rules vary from area to area, and are changed from time to time.

You do not need to consult anybody to carry out minor maintenance work, such as re-washering a tap, but if you plan major additions or alterations, check on the requirements first with your local water authority; this is equally true of changes to drains.

THE SUPPLY

The main supply pipes are under the street, and an underground branch line runs from them to bring water to your property. From the point at which the pipes leave public property (Fig. 10:1), they become the responsiblility of the householder. So a stop tap is fitted, usually at the limit of a private property – perhaps somewhere near the garden gate – in order that the supply can be turned off by the supplier whenever necessary. The pipe then continues into the building and usually surfaces near the kitchen sink, where there will be another stop tap. Just beyond this stop tap there will be a branch line to the cold tap at the kitchen sink so that water drawn there for cooking and drinking will be pure from the main. The supply pipe continues upwards, and from this point on is known as the rising main. It feeds a cold supply tank, which is usually, though not necessarily, in the loft – it is the one that freezes up in winter if it is not lagged properly. Like all storage tanks, this one has an overflow pipe to carry water away harmlessly, should the tank ever overfill.

The entry of water into this tank is controlled by a ball valve. This comprises a lever connected at one end to the

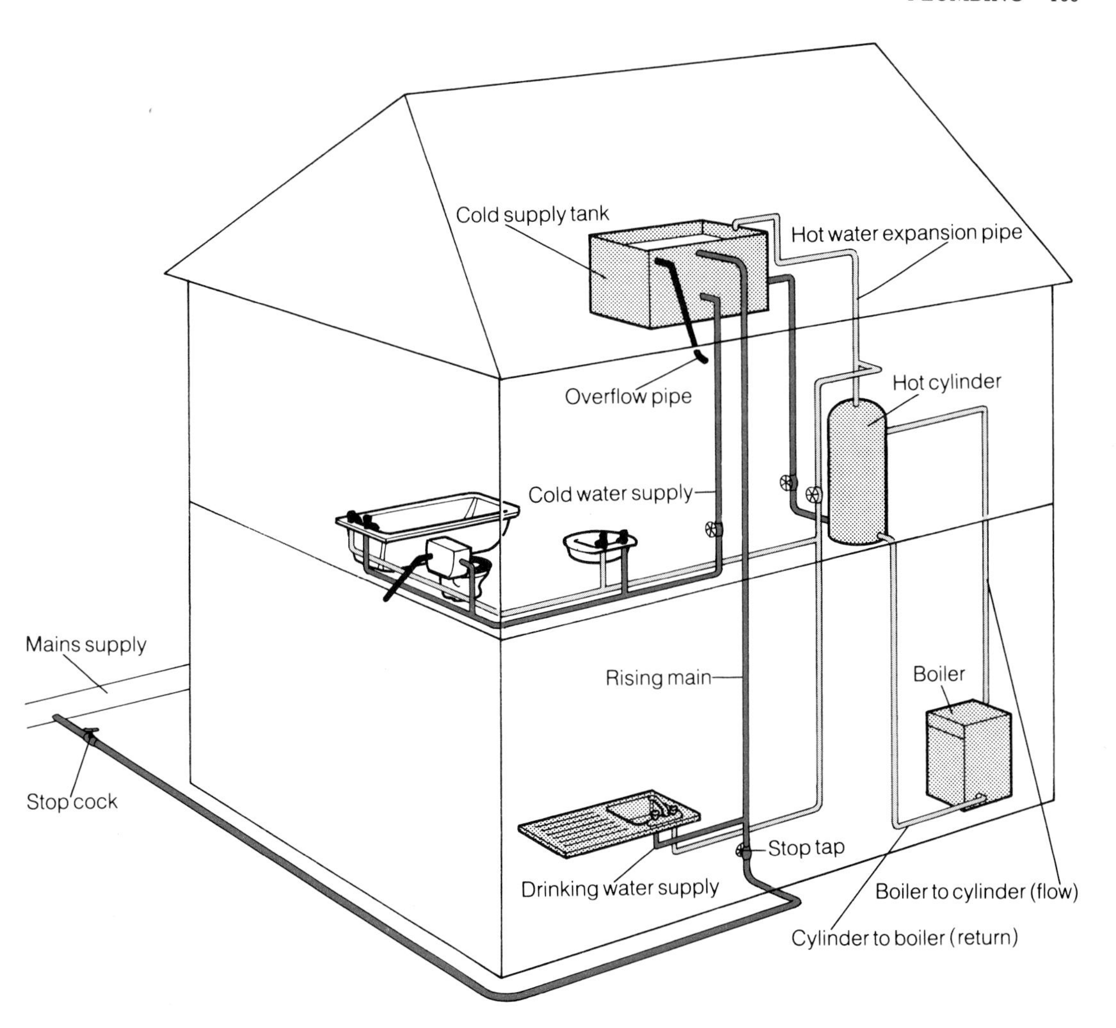

10.1 *Typical supply system in modern domestic plumbing*

inlet valve and a ball on the other end. The ball floats on the water. When water is drawn from the tank, the water level drops, taking the ball with it and opening the valve. As the tank fills the ball rises and shuts off the valve when the correct water level is reached. If the valve fails to close, excess water will be carried away via the overflow.

The cold supply normally feeds all the cold outlets in the house, except for the kitchen sink. These outlets include the cold taps at all baths, washbasins, and lavatories (collectively known as fittings), as well as washing machines. To save on pipework the builder of the house might have connected all or some of the cold outlets – most probably cold taps of basins and baths, perhaps even a lavatory cistern – directly to the rising main. This practice is frowned on by some water authorities, however.

Water reaches the cold tank because of the pressure in

the main. It flows from the cold tank because of gravity. The cold tank must, therefore, be high up in the house, which is why it is usually located in the loft. Water stored in this tank can be contaminated by dust and insects, for example, and become unfit for drinking, so the kitchen cold tap must have a direct pure supply from the main.

The height at which the tank is installed determines the strength of the flow of water at the various outlets: the greater the height, the faster water will gush out. Plumbers refer to the differences in height between the bottom of the cold tank (you do not measure from the top, in case the tank is half empty) and the water outlet as the head of water.

At various points throughout the system there may be other stop taps so that parts of the system can be turned off for maintenance without depriving the whole house of water. Such stop taps might be fitted to the supply to a lavatory, for instance, or to the hot water system.

Hot water

Domestic hot water (plumbers use the word 'domestic' to distinguish it from the water in a radiator system) is usually heated by a boiler. This may be free-standing in a kitchen or boiler house, mounted on a wall, or incorporated as a back boiler behind, say, a living room fire. Hot water for heating and domestic use is provided by the same boiler. When it has been heated it is stored in the hot cylinder, which may be housed in an airing cupboard.

Various fuels can be used to power the boiler, including gas, solid fuel and oil. Electric boilers are also being introduced. Whatever fuel is used, it is a wise economy to maintain the temperature of the heated water, and to achieve this the hot cylinder should be well insulated. Special jackets are sold for this purpose. At one time a jacket 25 mm (1 in) thick was considered adequate, but with escalating fuel costs a thickness of 75 mm (3 in) or more is now the rule. If your cylinder has only a thin jacket, do not discard it, but place a new one on top of it. You cannot have too much insulation on a hot cylinder, and lower fuel bills will soon cover the cost of an insulation jacket.

In normal circumstances, the water heating system will be of the gravity type, which works because hot water is lighter than cold. Water heated in a container will lie in layers of different temperatures, with the hottest at the top. So water heated by the boiler will rise to the hot cylinder through one pipe (the flow primary), and water that is cooler than this will fall to the boiler by another pipe (the return primary), to be heated in turn.

For such a gravity system to work effectively, the hot cylinder must be sited at a higher level than the boiler, and, indeed, in the average home it is customary for the boiler to be downstairs, with the hot cylinder in an airing cupboard conveniently by the bedrooms on the first floor. Even in bungalows and flats it is usually possible to raise the hot cylinder to a high enough level for the gravity system to operate.

For greatest efficiency, however, pumped primaries can be installed. Water from the cold tank (to replace the hot drawn off at the taps) is fed into the system at the bottom of the hot cylinder, where it will quickly drop down to the boiler through the return primary, and be heated. The draw-off point for water from the hot cylinder needs to be near its top, because that is where the water will be at its hottest.

Modern boilers are self-regulating (thermostatically controlled) so they maintain the water at a required temperature without overheating. In case a regulating thermostat fails, however, overheated water would rise up a pipe (known as the vent pipe) from the top of the hot cylinder to the cold tank, and would discharge there harmlessly. Should the cold tank become overfull as a result, excess water would run away through the overflow. Even so, if you ever hear water boiling in the hot cylinder (something that used to be more common when thermostats were not so general), shut down the heating immediately and draw off hot water by opening a hot tap somewhere in the house. Then have the system serviced by a heating engineer.

An immersion heater may be fitted to the cylinder, occasionally as a sole form of heating, but more usually as a standby if the boiler system fails.

The hot cylinder may be either 'direct' or 'indirect'. In a direct system the water heated in the boiler goes direct to the cylinder where it is stored until it is drawn off at the domestic taps. In an indirect system, water in a heating circuit is circulated through the boiler and a coil of piping within the cylinder. This coil serves as a heating element for the main body of water. Thus the water in the boiler and that for the taps are kept quite separate. Normally indirect cylinders are found where there is a radiator system of central heating, so that domestic and radiator water are never mixed, but you do come across them where the boiler is used just for domestic hot water.

Instant hot-water systems

The system described above is very common in modern homes because it makes use of the boiler that is necessary to heat water for radiators. If, however, there is an alternative form of space-heating, the hot water supply may be of the instant type. With such a heater, which can work off gas or electricity, no hot water is stored and there is, therefore no hot cylinder. Instead, the gas jets or electric elements come into play only when you turn on the tap and water passes across them.

Instantaneous heaters may be multi-point, with one heater serving all (or most) of the house. Or they can be single point, placed over a sink, washbasin or bath, for instance.

Such heaters are usually installed in conversion and modernization schemes because they simplify, and therefore usually reduce, installation costs, and because they are space-saving – one heater takes the place of a boiler and hot water cylinder. They can also save money in operating costs, because you heat up only as much water as you need; and they have the further advantage that they can supply unlimited hot water, whereas a hot tank once emptied of hot water takes time to reheat. In a home with this type of system it is often the case that all cold outlets are fed directly from the rising main, so that a cold storage tank will not need to be installed either.

Your own system

You should aim to get to know the plumbing system of your home, so that you will be ready to deal with emergencies. Try to trace the run of the pipes from the point at which the rising main starts. And, with the boiler or other water heater shut off, turn off one at a time any stop taps you come across. Then turn on the taps and flush the lavatories to determine which outlets are controlled by each stop tap.

Lagging

If the water in your supply pipe freezes you lose your supply temporarily. As the water freezes it expands, and may burst the pipe. Therefore any pipes in your supply system that are exposed to the weather should be lagged.

Lagging for pipes is available in two principal forms. One comes as a roll, and is wrapped like a bandage with large overlaps round the pipes. The other consists of cylindrical lengths of foam plastic, split lengthways so that they can be fitted round a pipe, then taped or clipped in place.

The cold tank, too, needs to be protected by lagging, especially if it is in the loft. Lagging kits consisting of four sides and a top are available. Also, never insulate the area of the loft below a cold tank because warmth rising from the house below helps to keep the tank from freezing.

Copper pipes

The first metallic plumbing systems were made of lead (the word plumbing comes from the Latin word *plumbum* for lead). Later on iron was used for a time. Today copper is used extensively; and plastic is gaining favour.

Most people altering or extending their plumbing system will be working with copper. If your supply pipes a.e in lead or iron, your whole plumbing system is out of date, and needs to be renewed – this is a job for a professional.

Pipes of three dimensions are found in modern plumbing systems. At one time they were in imperial sizes, which you will still come across when working on older installations. The modern (metric) sizes are 28 mm (used for the primaries), 22 mm (for the main runs), and 15 mm (for branch lines). The former imperial sizes were 1 in, ¾ in, and ½ in. If you convert pipe dimensions, it is important to note that the metric dimension refers to the external diameter, whereas the imperial refers to the internal.

Working copper pipe (Fig. 10:2) may involve cutting, joining, connecting up (a type of joining) or bending.

In any job using pipe, it will probably need to be cut to length. Copper is so soft that this can be done easily with a hacksaw – even a junior one. You will find, however, that there is a tendency to flatten the pipe with this method. You might also fail to make the cut square. Either distortion will make it impossible to achieve a fully watertight connection. The solution is to use a pipe cutter, which cuts squarely and does not flatten. Small portable ones are available. When you are cutting into a pipe that is already installed, however, there may not be enough room to wield a pipe cutter, and you will have to use a hacksaw. If so, take care not to flatten the pipe; and once the pipe has been cut, use a file to get rid of any burr on the end and also to square it up properly, if this is necessary.

In many plumbing jobs, pipes have to be joined – for instance to connect up two short lengths or to take off a branch line at a T-junction. Ready-made joints are needed for this and there are two kinds – compression and capillary. With both types of joint the 28 and 15 mm pipes can be connected up directly to the old 1 in and ½ in. However, to join 22 mm to ¾ in you must use an adapter.

A compression joint consists of a threaded body, known as a union, a small chamfered copper ring, called an olive, and a nut, the cap nut.

To fit a compression joint, slip first the cap nut, then the olive, with its shortest chamfer pointing towards the nut, on to the end of the pipe. Push the pipe as far as it will go into the union, and slide first the olive then the nut towards the body. When the nut is tightened it will crush the olive, forming a watertight joint. It is important to get just the right degree of tightness, however: too much, and the olive will be crushed too much; to little, and it will not be crushed sufficiently. In both cases, the joint will leak. To ensure the correct tightness, tighten the nut as far as you can by hand,

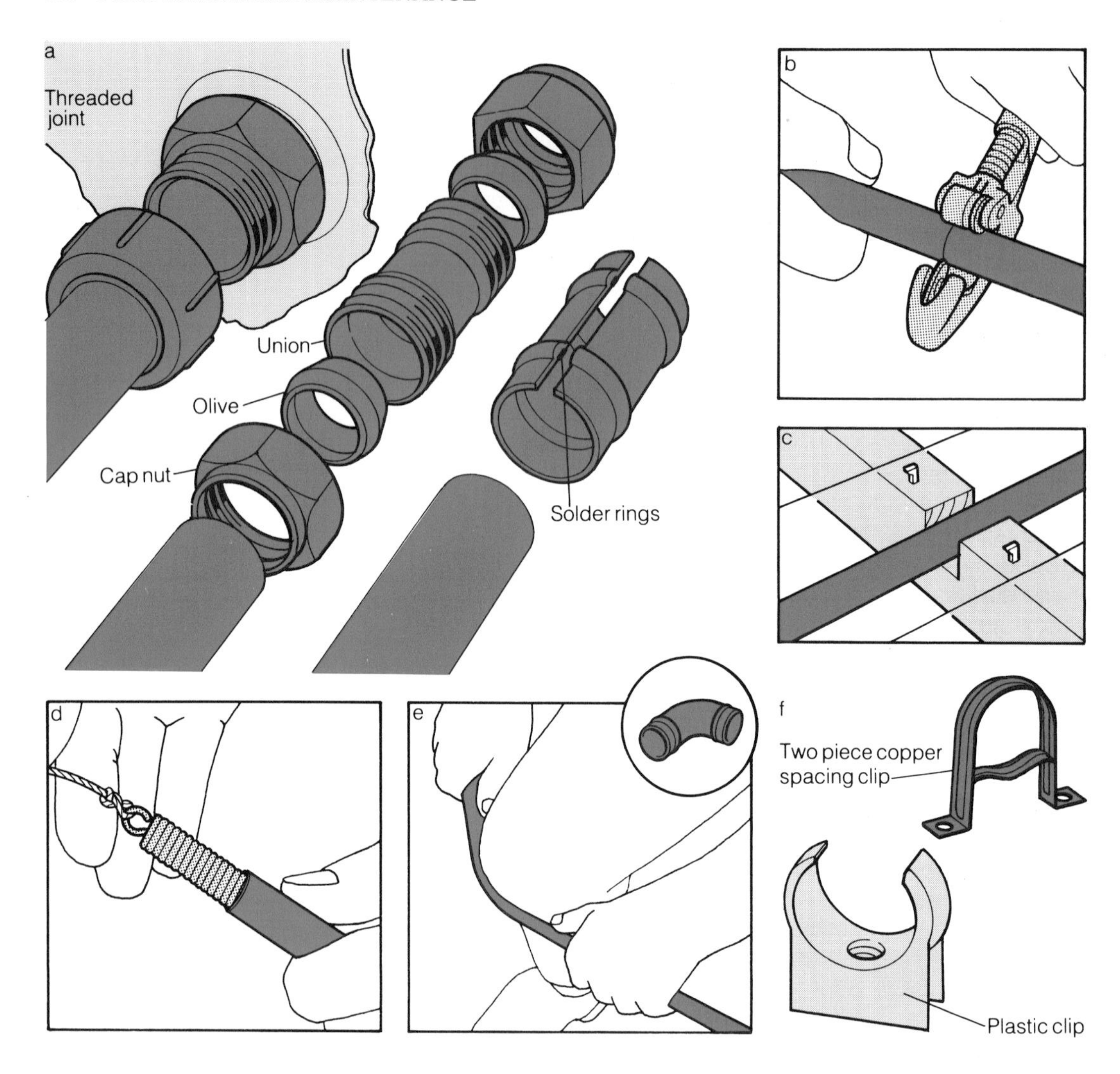

10.2 *Working copper pipe: (a) The three types of joint – threaded, compression and capillary. (b) Cut the pipe with a small portable cutter. (c) Pipe running under the floor is supported in joist notches. (d) A bending spring stops the pipe from flattening while being bent. (e) Bending a pipe on the knee as an alternative to using an 'elbow joint' (inset). (f) Two types of support clip.*

then give one complete turn with a spanner. When the water is turned on, inspect the joint for signs of weeping. If you find any, give quarter turns with the spanner until they stop.

One of the advantages of a compression joint is that you can make it while the pipes are wet, which enables repairs or additions to be made to an existing system. With capillary joints, you have to wait for all the parts to dry thoroughly.

A capillary joint is much smaller and neater, and less expensive than a compression joint, although it is a little more difficult to handle. It is sealed by solder, a small ring of which is inserted inside the joint during manufacture.

All the parts of a capillary joint must be spotlessly clean, so begin by burnishing both the end of the pipe and the inside of the joint with fine steel wool. Take care neither to damage the solder nor to grease any burnished surface with your fingerprints.

Apply soldering flux to the end of the pipe, push the end fully home, and apply a blowlamp flame on the joint. The heat will cause the solder to flow out and seal the joint, making it watertight. Once again, you have to make sure that you get things just right, for if you leave the flame on the joint for too long the solder will flow too far out, and if you do not heat the joint sufficiently, the solder will not flow far enough. The trick is to watch carefully until a ring of bright solder appears round the pipe, then withdraw the flame instantly. Allow the solder to cool off and harden before disturbing the joint. It is also necessary to make all parts of a capillary joint at one go, because heat will travel along the body of the joint causing all the solder rings to melt.

If a pipe needs to be connected up – to a radiator valve or some taps, for instance, a threaded joint is used. The joint is formed by screwing a 'male' part, which is threaded on its outer surface, into a 'female' part, which is threaded on its inner surface. The two parts cannot just be screwed together to make a waterproof joint, however. The joint must be reinforced with either plumber's hemp or PTFE tape, together with a jointing compound such as Boss White.

Plumber's hemp, which is sold by the hank, does not make such a neat joint as the tape, but it is more effective with deeper threads, such as you get on a boiler. To use it, first smear a little Boss White on the male fitting, then pull a few strands of the hemp off the hank. Wind the strands round the fitting in the same direction it will turn when being tightened, to ensure that it will be pulled into the fitting (rather than being unwound) when the joint is being tightened. Smear a little more Boss White on top of the hemp, insert the male fitting into the female, and tighten as hard as you can with a spanner.

Most of the hemp should be snugly inside the fitting. If much of it has pulled outside, there are three possible causes – you did not wind it on tight enough; you wound on too much; or you did not wind it in the right direction. In any case, you must unscrew the joint and make it again. Drawing a hacksaw blade lightly across the threads of the male fitting to form burrs that will grip the hemp may help keep it in place.

PTFE tape is easier to use, and is neater than hemp. Wind it on in the same direction as hemp, taking it two or three times round the fitting, and allowing it to overlap. Smear Boss White on the female thread, insert the male, and tighten.

Some thread should still be visible after the tightening, whether you have used tape or hemp. If it is not, you will probably find that the joint is too loose and will leak, so it will have to be remade.

Pipes can be bent into complicated shapes to pass round obstacles, or into simple curves to go round corners. If you are dealing with 22 mm and 15 mm pipe, bending is easy, but you must prevent it from flattening at the centre of the curve. You do this with a bending spring, which you can hire. Tie a length of string to one end of the spring, smear a little oil on its coil and push it into the pipe until its middle point is roughly at the centre of the required bend. Then take hold of one end of the pipe in each hand, place it on your knee at the centre of the proposed bend and give a short sharp tug. The pipe will then bend to the required curve.

Bend the pipe slightly more than required, then take it back to the required angle. If the process hurts your knee, tie a protective rag on it. Twist the spring clockwise, and you will be able to pull it out easily. You cannot make a bend near the end of a length of pipe in this way, so form a curve before cutting the pipe to length.

Pipe of 28 mm diameter is too strong to be bent by hand. Plumbers use a bending machine, but it is hardly worth hiring the pipe bender and a spring for one or two bends, so make use of elbow couplings instead. You can, in fact, always use elbow couplings instead of hiring a spring to bend narrow-gauge pipes, too, and although they are expensive it might pay you to use them for a small job, where only one or two bends are required.

Pipes should be supported by clips. Recommended spacings on vertical runs are 2.4 m (8 ft) for 28 mm and 22 mm pipes, 1.8 m (6 ft) for 15 mm pipes and 1.2 m (4 ft) for all three on horizontal runs. Use stand-off clips, which hold the pipes clear of the walls, rather than the kind that fits like a saddle over the pipe and holds it close to the surface. This is especially important for hot water pipes, which need to have air circulating round them to prevent them overheating the wall.

Pipes under floors and at right angles to floor joists can sit in notches cut in the top of the joists. Such notches should be directly under the middle of floorboards, so that when the board is nailed back there is no risk of puncturing the pipe.

Plastic pipes

Plastic pipes have been used for many years in waste systems, and for some time have been available as cold supply pipes. Because they were not suitable for hot water, there was little point in installing them just for cold. Now, however, pipes in cpvc (chlorinated polyvinyl chloride), which can be used for hot supply and for central heating, are available.

Plastic pipe has many advantages. It does not corrode, and scale does not form easily on the inside. It is a good insulator, so hot water does not cool so quickly and condensation does not form so readily on the outside. It is light and easy to handle, and does not dent easily.

A wide range of joints and stop taps is supplied for use with plastic pipe, and there are connectors to allow you to join it to copper. It is worked and joined, using the solvent welding method, in the same way as plastic waste pipe (see below).

There are some snags, however: plastic pipe cannot be used within 380 mm (15 in) of a boiler – you must use copper for this length, then connect it to the plastic; it is necessary to leave space for expansion under heat – about 6 mm (¼ in) per 3 m (10 ft) length; and an expansion loop, formed with two elbow couplings and a 300 mm (1 ft) length of pipe must be fitted to any run exceeding 10 m (25 ft). Nevertheless, plastic supply pipe will, in years to come, offer many advantages to DIY plumbers.

THE WASTE

Waste pipes, like supply pipes, were once made of lead, then of copper and are now almost exclusively of plastic. Each waste pipe must incorporate a trap, which is a loop of pipe filled with water, which stops drain smells coming back up into the home. Lavatories, too, have a trap, which may be a separate fitting or incorporated into the pan.

Two different systems are used to dispose of waste water to the drains. These are the two-pipe and the single-pipe (sometimes called the single-stack) systems (Fig. 10:3).

Two-pipe drainage

Two-pipe systems get their name because waste from fittings and appliances is kept separate from lavatory waste. Waste pipes from ground floor fittings and appliances discharge into open gullies that are connected to the drains. Baths, basins, bidets and other fittings on upper storeys empty into a hopper fitted to the top of a downpipe. This then conveys the water to an open gully at ground level – it may, in fact, be the one into which some or all of the ground floor waste discharges.

The lavatory in a two-pipe system is connected to a soil pipe leading to the sewer. It is easy to see at a glance whether a pipe on the outside wall of your home is a soil pipe or downpipe, besides looking for the connections from the lavatory. A soil pipe extends upwards above eaves level and well away from windows, to act as a vent for the escape of sewage smells. It should also be topped by a small wire

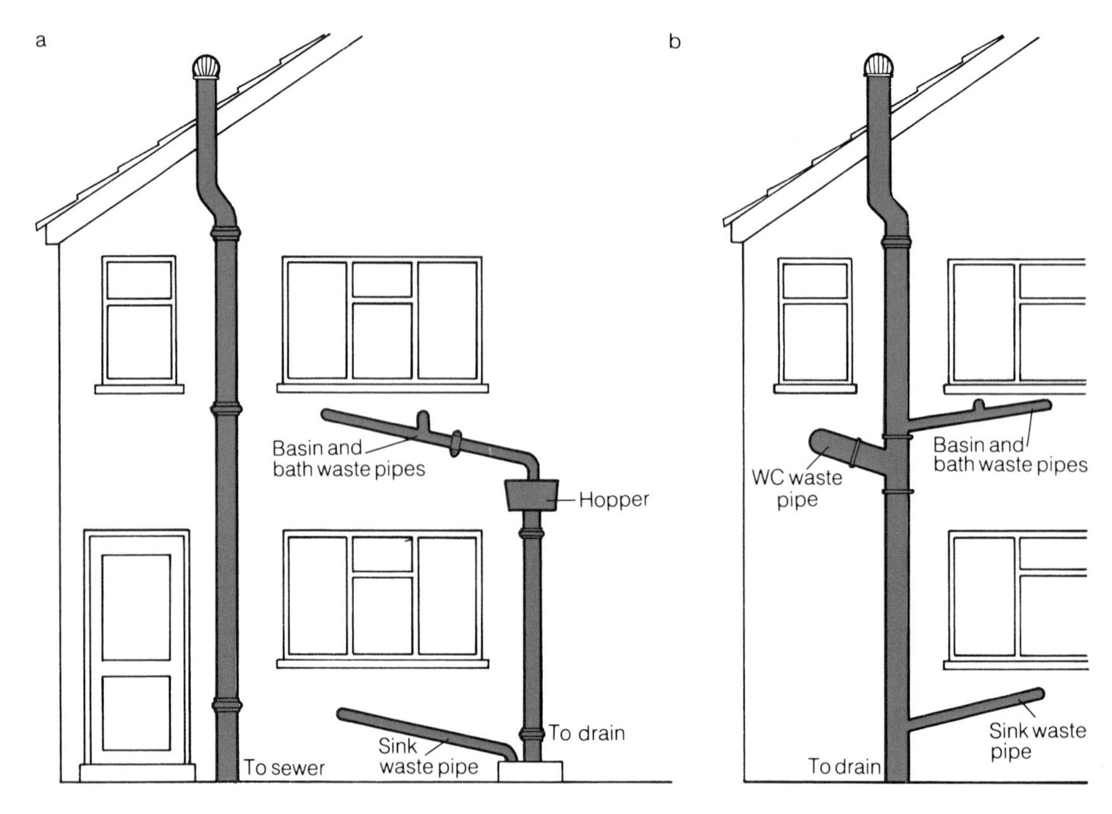

10.3 *The types of waste system: (a) Two-pipe and (b) one-pipe.*

cage to prevent rubbish getting in and causing a blockage. If this cage is missing from the soil pipe, you should fit a replacement.

To tell whether your home has a two-pipe drainage system, look ouside for a soil pipe, in addition to the downpipe, and for open gullies and hoppers.

Single-pipe drainage

In a single-pipe system one stack carries all the waste to the drains. It is fitted in high-rise buildings, and some modern two-storey homes. The stack will usually be inside the building. Older stacks were made of cast iron; modern ones are plastic.

Fittings and appliances in a single-stack system often need deep-seal traps, which prevent water being sucked out of them by back-siphonage as waste rushes down the stack. For the same reason, fittings may require larger diameter wastes (this is likely to be a matter of local regulation).

To test whether or not your home has single-pipe drainage, follow the course of the waste pipes to see if they end up at a stack, which you will usually find inside the building, and cross-check by the absence of gullies or open drains outside.

Installing plastic waste pipes

Modern waste systems are of plastic. Four types of plastic are used: upvc (unplasticized polyvinyl chloride); mpvc (modified polyvinyl chloride); abs (acrylonitrile butadiene styrene); and pp (polypropylene). Two sizes of pipe are used in domestic work – 43 mm (1½ in) diameter for baths and 36 mm (1¼ in) for fittings such as basins and sinks. As with supply pipes, the metric dimension is an external one and the imperial an internal one.

Plastic pipe is cut with a saw – a fine-toothed general purpose one is better than a hacksaw for ensuring a square cut (Fig. 10:4). As a guide to cutting, wrap a piece of paper with a straight edge round the pipe, making sure the ends line up. Once the pipe has been cut, clean off the burr both inside and out with fine glasspaper.

Lengths of pipe are connected up with small jointing pieces: a range of straight couplings and elbow fittings is available. Two methods are used – push-fit and solvent welding.

Push-fit joints have a small sealing ring inside. Usually this is inserted during manufacture but you may have to fit it yourself. In any case, you must make sure it is seated properly. To make a joint by this method, draw a line round the pipe about 10 mm (⅜ in) from its end, using a paper guide as described above. With a file, form a chamfer from the end back to this line. Clean the pipe and the inside of the socket and smear either a silicone jelly, supplied by the manufacturer, or petroleum jelly, on the end of the pipe. Push the pipe home as far as it will go, and make a pencil mark on it where it meets the edge of the fitting. Then pull it back by 10 mm (⅜ in) – using the pencil mark as a guide – to form an expansion allowance. The joint will now be fully watertight.

Solvent-welded joints are more difficult to make, but they are neater (note that pp cannot be solvent-welded, however). Use glasspaper to roughen the inside of the socket, and a file to roughen the part that will fit inside. To determine how much of the pipe should be roughened, push it fully home into the socket and draw a line all round the pipe. Apply the solvent with a small, clean paint brush both to the end of the pipe and to the inside of the socket. Make sure that the whole surface is covered – you will probably find this easier if your brush strokes go along the length of, rather than round, the pipe. Push the pipe home and hold the joint securely for about 15 seconds to allow the solvent to set, wiping off any that oozes out. Don't let hot water pass through a solvent-welded joint until 24 hours after welding.

One of the problems with solvent-welded joints is that, unlike the push-fit kind, they do not allow the pipe to expand

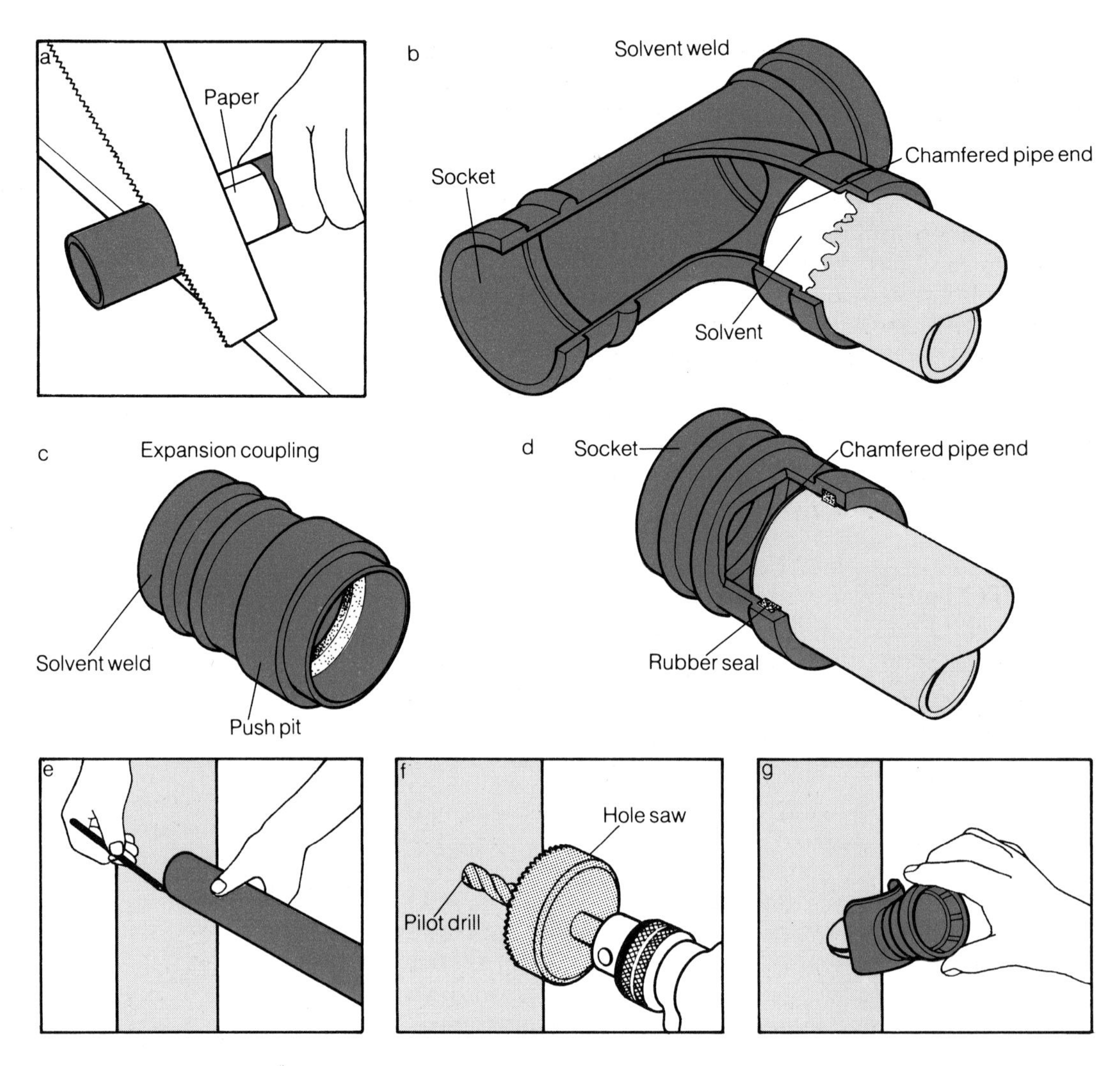

10.4 *Plastic waste pipe: (a) Cut it to size. (Note paper wrapped round pipe to act as a cutting guide.) Lengths of pipe are connected with jointing pieces. These can be (b) solvent welded, as with this T-fitting, (c) expansion coupling, or (d) push fit. To connect to a single pipe waster system, (e) mark where the waste will join the main stack. (f) Cut stack with hole saw. (g) Fit boss to which plastic waste pipe can be connected.*

as hot water passes through. So on long runs, fit expansion couplings at 1.8 m (6 ft) intervals. These are similar to ordinary joints but at one end they are push-fit, and at the other solvent-welded. It is unlikely that you will need to fit a coupling, however, because you do not get such long runs in the home.

Plastic waste pipe should be supported by clips at 750 mm (30 in) intervals. The pipe can be bent, but, even more than with supply pipes, it is not worth while; you would do better to use elbow couplings.

The pipe has to empty into the drains. With either a two- or one-pipe system, you may have nearby an existing waste pipe to which you can connect by means of a T-joint. If not, then in the case of a two-pipe system arrange for it to discharge into a convenient open gully or hopper. To reach one, chop a hole through a wall, using a club hammer and bolster chisel. Work from both sides of a cavity wall, making sure that debris does not fall into the cavity. With a solid wall, you can make the entire hole from inside.

On single-pipe systems, the pipe is joined to the stack by means of a boss. Various types are available; most are solvent-welded to the stack. Then the waste pipe is connected to the boss by either a push-fit or solvent-welded joint. A hole has to be cut in the stack for the boss, and this is best done with a hole saw fitted to a drill.

There are various rules about joining up to the stack, and this is one of the points on which you should consult your water authority. For instance, the boss must not be fitted within 200 mm (8 in) of a lavatory waste connection. And remember to slope the waste pipe, as you would slope a gutter, to allow the water to flow.

JOBS TO TACKLE

Before cutting into any part of the system, shut off the supply and open an appropriate tap to empty the pipe completely. Even so, a certain amount of water will come out, so be ready with bucket and mopping-up rags.

Fitting a stop tap

Few homes have enough stop taps, so whole sections of the system are deprived of water when even a minor job has to be done. In extreme cases the supply has to be shut off at the rising main and the whole system drained, just because a tap needs a new washer. A good system would have stop taps in the supply pipes from the cold storage tank, in the hot supply, and in the feed to lavatories. If your system lacks them, fitting one or two is a good introduction to simple plumbing.

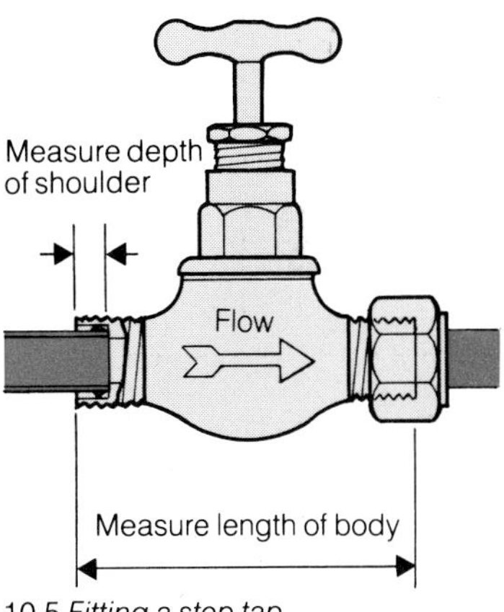

10.5 *Fitting a stop tap*

Begin by measuring how much of the pipe you must cut out to take the tap. In doing so, remember that the pipe must fit right up to the shoulder inside. So measure the length of the body, then the depths inside the shoulders (Fig. 10:5). The difference between these measurements is the correct dimension. The tap is fixed by means of a compression joint at each end; the arrow on its casing should point in the direction of the flow. Place it in position – you will be able to spring the pipes far enough apart to do this – and tighten the joints.

New taps for old

Fixing mixer taps at a kitchen sink or, indeed, just ordinary modern single taps in place of the old ones on any fitting, is a good way to update your kitchen or bathroom. If you plan to

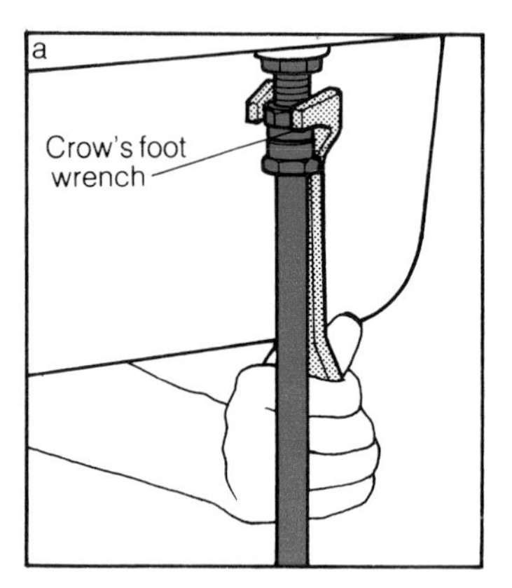

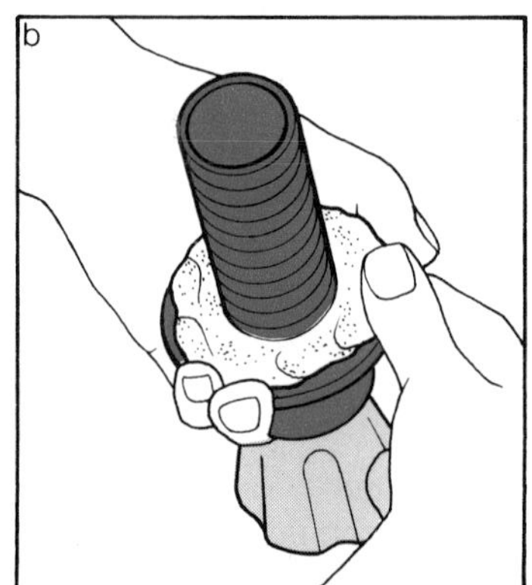

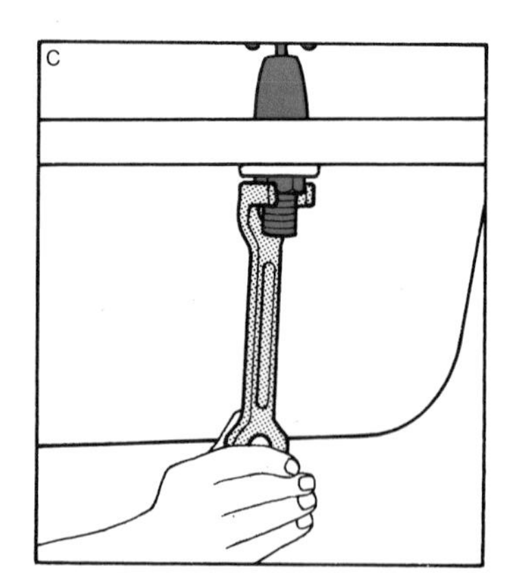

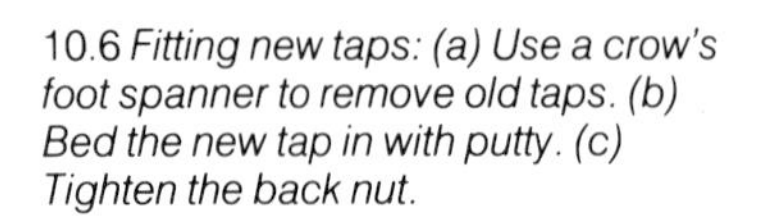
10.6 *Fitting new taps: (a) Use a crow's foot spanner to remove old taps. (b) Bed the new tap in with putty. (c) Tighten the back nut.*

fix a mixer, check before you buy one that it will locate in the existing holes of the sink.

The biggest difficulty lies in removing the old taps. Disconnect the supply from the taps. Unscrew the nut if a compression joint has been used, or saw through the pipe in the case of a capillary joint. There will probably not be enough room to use an ordinary spanner on the nut underneath, so you must use a crow's foot spanner, in which the jaws that grip the nut are at right angles to to the main body (Fig. 10:6). Even using a crow's foot spanner you may find that everything is so corroded that the nut will not turn. If so, apply penetrating oil, or one of the products designed to free corroded joints. Alternatively, grip the nut with the spanner, while a helper taps the spout of the tap with a rubber hammer – carefully so as not to damage anything. When the nut is loosened, remove the tap and scrape off the old putty that was underneath it.

Usually full instructions are given with the new tap – follow them closely. Place the tap in position, bedding it in putty, and with the washers in place (there may just be one for underneath the fitting, or one above and another below) tighten the back nut. A second locking nut may be supplied. A tap connector is fitted to the tail of the tap by means of a threaded joint, and this in turn is connected to the supply, usually with a compression joint.

Plumbing in a washing machine

It is much more convenient to have a clothes washing machine, or a dishwasher, plumbed in, rather than to have to connect its supply hoses to the taps every time you want to use it. The installation is easy, and kits containing all you need can be bought.

The instructions with the machine will tell you whether it takes both a hot and a cold supply, or just a cold. Find a convenient spot in the supply pipes and fit a T-joint there

(Fig. 10:7) – the technique is similar to that for fitting a stop tap. To the branch of the T fit a short length of pipe with a stop tap in the middle, so that you will be able to shut off the supply to the machine and remove it for maintenance and repairs without having to close down the whole system. At the end of this pipe, fit the coupling to which the hose of the machine is connected.

Another method is to use a self-cutting tap. This is fitted to the supply pipe; it has a piercing tip that cuts into the pipe and makes a connection. No water can escape during this process, so you do not even have to turn off the supply while you fit the tap. The device also acts as a stop tap. Self-cutting taps are sold at do-it-yourself shops, and full instructions are supplied.

Next fit a waste system to the machine (Fig. 10:8). This consists of a vertical length of pipe, open at the top, that runs to an existing waste pipe, out to a gully, or to a boss on a one-pipe stack. The instructions received with the machine specify what diameter of pipe to use, and the required height of the vertical section.

The machine has a flexible waste hose pipe with a permanent bend formed during manufacture. This hooks into the open end of the plastic waste pipe.

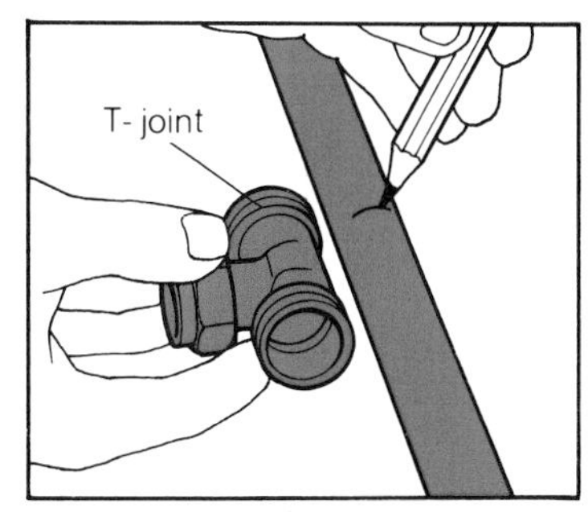

10.7 *Fitting a T-joint*

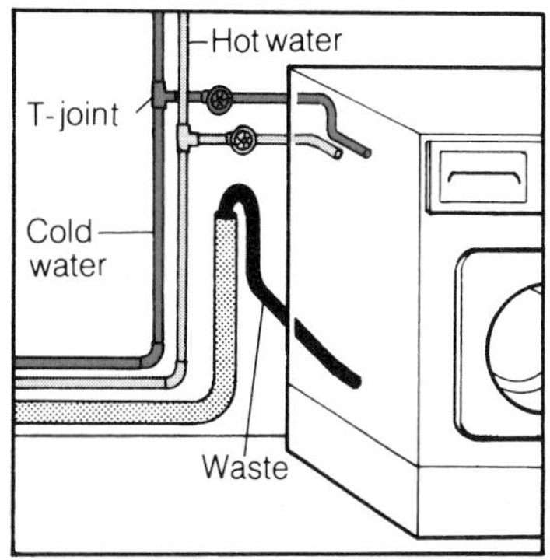

10.8 *Plumbing in a washing machine*

Fitting a shower

An electrically heated shower, which heats the water as it is being delivered, is the easiest (and usually the cheapest) to install. The heater unit should be positioned so it can discharge into a bath, and perhaps a basin as well, so it can be used for hair washing too. Fix it to the wall according to the manufacturer's instructions. Then connect it, by means of a T-joint, to the rising main.

Run pipe from this T-joint to the heater, and connect up according to the manufacturer's instructions. Carry out any final assembly – for example of the shower rose and flexible hose. The heater must then be wired up by a competent electrician.

Although the rising main should ensure that there is sufficient water pressure, the flow out of the rose of an electric shower is restricted by the heater. If you want a shower at a comfortable temperature, water can come out only as quickly as the heater can warm it.

If you have a cheaper means of heating the domestic hot water – especially if you have a radiator central heating system – your running costs would be lower with a shower unit fed from your existing hot and cold supply system.

For a shower unit to work effectively off the hot cylinder and cold tank you must have a strong enough head of water – probably at least 900 mm (3 ft). The greater the difference

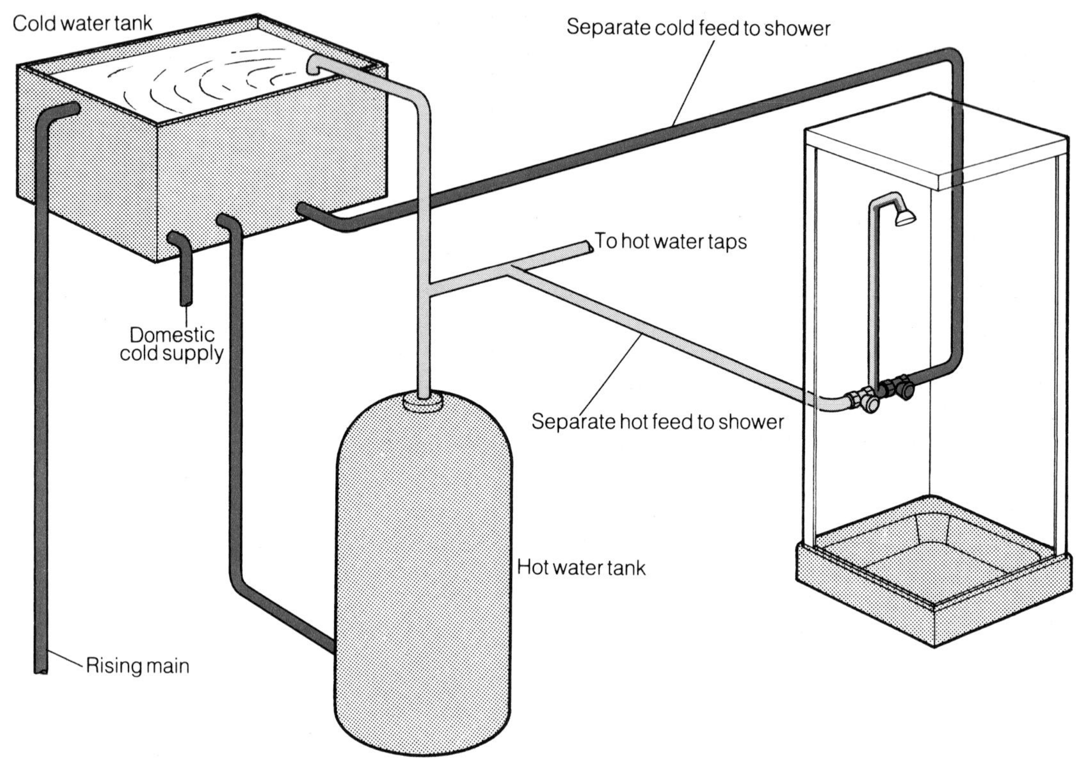

10.9 *How a shower is fitted*

in height between the shower rose and the bottom of the cold tank, the better the flow of water (Fig. 10:9). If you do not have such a head of water, consider re-siting the tank at a higher level (see next section) – or choose an electric shower, which will give a stronger flow than a shower unit with a poor head of water.

A shower unit can take the place of the existing bath taps, in which case the installation is similar to that of a kitchen mixer tap. Or you could install a separate unit, with its own supply.

There is, however, a caution to observe. A person might be taking a shower when somewhere else in the house someone turns on another tap – causing what the plumber calls an auxiliary draw-off that reduces, or indeed might cut off entirely, the flow of water to the shower. If the auxiliary draw-off is in the hot supply, then the bather gets a cold douche – uncomfortable, but not too serious. If the auxiliary draw-off is from a cold supply, however, scalding hot water might surge out of the rose (one of the advantages of an electric shower is that there can be no auxiliary draw-off).

The way to prevent auxiliary draw-off in a shower unit is to choose one that is thermostatically controlled. These are expensive, but they ensure that the temperature of the flow remains constant. If you fit a shower without such thermostatic control, give the unit its own direct cold supply from the cold storage tank. This will eliminate the most dangerous (scalding) type of auxiliary draw-off, by ensuring the cold supply is never interrupted. The direct cold supply must be fixed low down in the side of the tank by means of a tank connector (see next section).

A new cold tank

Cold supply tanks were at one time made of galvanized iron, a material that eventually corroded. Modern tanks are of either glass fibre or plastic. The plastic type is flexible, so can be squashed to go through a narrow loft opening, but may well need support under the entire base. Glass fibre tanks are rigid.

Your local water authority will have rules about the size of the cold tank, which it will express as something like 40/50. The latter figure (50 gallons/227 litres) is the amount the tank will hold when full to the brim; the former (40 gallons/181 litres) its capacity in practice.

When a tank is being replaced the house will be deprived of water for some time, so do as much of the preparatory work as you can beforehand. Begin by shutting off the rising main, and opening cold taps to empty the tank. The draw-off points are in the side, rather than the base, of the tank, so some water will be left behind. Beware later of spilling any of this. The tank needs to be disconnected from its various pipes. Do not bother trying to free corroded nuts to do this. The pipe runs will probably need modifying anyway, so just saw through them near the tank, making sure your cuts are square. Do not worry either, if the tank is too big to come out through the loft opening. Just leave it up there.

No holes are bored in the side of the tank when it is delivered – the manufacturer could not possibly know where you want them. You have to make them yourself, with a hole saw in either a hand drill or an electric drill. So decide on a site for the tank (remembering that if you want a shower it might be wise to site the tank on a stout platform as high as possible to increase the pressure of water at the rose). Plot the pipe runs, and determine the position of the holes in the tank (Fig. 10:10). The pipes are linked to the tank by pipe connectors. These have a threaded sleeve with a back plate. Push the sleeve through the hole from inside the tank, with a washer on each side, then tighten the fixing nut. The supply pipes are fixed to this connector with a compression joint.

You will need a cold supply from the rising main, a cold feed to the cold outlets, perhaps a special cold feed to a shower, and an overflow. Also the vent pipe from the hot cylinder must bend over the top of the tank. Modify existing

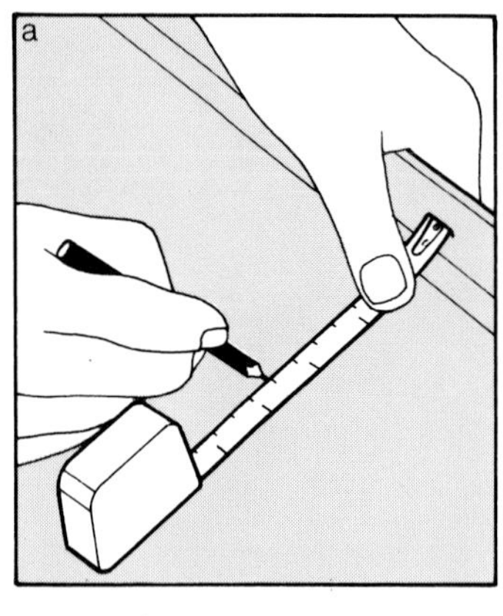

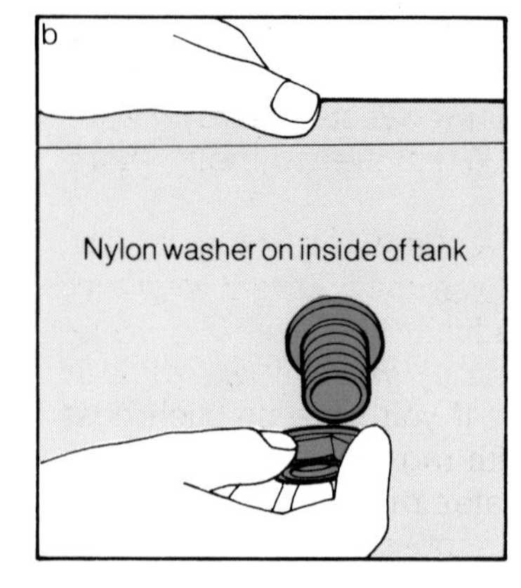

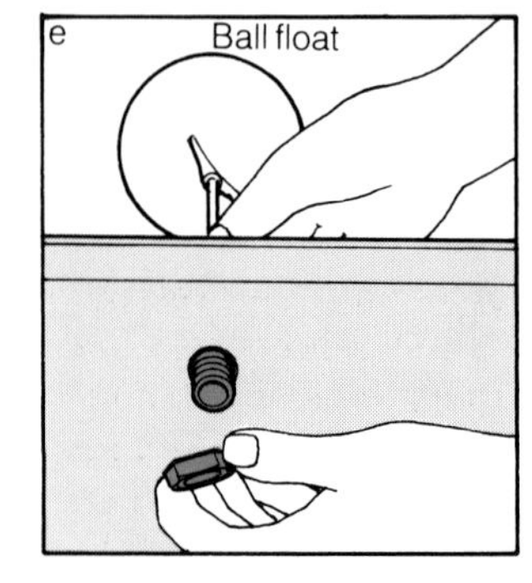

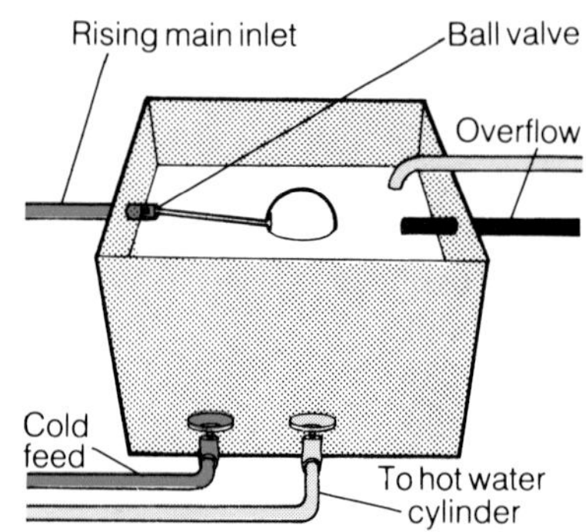

10.10 *Fitting a new cold tank: (a) Mark the position of the pipes on the side of the tank. The pipes are linked to the tank by pipe connectors on (b) the inside and (c) the outside. (d) Fit a stopcock. (e) A ball valve must be fitted. (f) The installation is complete.*

runs and add new ones as needed and connect them to the tank. A ball valve will be needed to control the entry of water from the rising main.

Your local water authority may have regulations about the position of the various pipes. A rule of thumb, however, is that the ball valve inlet should be 55 mm (2¼ in) from the top of the tank; the overflow should be 25 mm (1 in) below that (so that water from the tank cannot be sucked back into the main); and the various feeds to the supply should be 50 mm (2 in) from the bottom of the tank.

Finally, having connected up all the pipework, restore the supply and check for leaks.

EMERGENCIES

In even the best of plumbing systems, things can go wrong from time to time. One possible result is flooding, so deal with faults before any more serious damage is done.

Frozen pipes

This is one emergency that should never happen, because efficient lagging that will prevent it is readily available. The worst result of frozen plumbing is not so much that you are temporarily deprived of water at the particular taps affected, troublesome as that can be, but that when water turns to ice it expands and in so doing can fracture a pipe, or force a compression joint apart. When the ice melts, there will be a flood.

If you do have a frozen pipe, begin by opening the affected taps slightly and turning off the relevant stop tap. Working back from the tap, gradually apply heat (preferably with a hair dryer, but possibly with an electric fan heater) until water starts to flow. If you have no such heat source try wrapping the pipe with rags soaked in water as hot as you can handle. When water runs freely again, you can close the tap, and restore the supply.

As you work, look for signs of damage caused by the ice. If you find any, put a bucket underneath to catch the flow that will come as the ice melts. Then carry out the remedies suggested in the next section.

Bursts

When a supply pipe is burst, by frost or for any other reason, put a bucket underneath the pipe or get a helper to put his/her thumb over the hole. Then shut off the stop tap controlling the supply to that pipe, and open the tap at the end of the supply to empty the pipe as quickly as possible. When the flow has stopped, begin the repair. Fit a straight coupling compression joint at the break, in just the same way as a stop tap is fitted. If the damage (typically a split) is too long to be covered by one coupling, fit a short length of copper pipe with a coupling at each end.

If a leak occurs at a compression joint, try tightening the coupling nut a quarter of a turn at a time, until moisture stops oozing out. Do not test for this with your finger, because skin is always moist. Instead, wipe round the joint with a tissue or lavatory paper, and look to see if this gets wet. If you cannot stop the leak by tightening the joint, it may be that the olive has been damaged. If so, you will have to remove the joint and fit a new one.

If a leak develops at a capillary joint, remove the joint by cutting through the pipe on each side, and repair it as you would a damaged pipe.

Air locks

You will know there is an air lock in a supply pipe if the water comes in spurts instead of flowing out smoothly. There is a quick ploy that often clears it: run a length of hose pipe from the kitchen cold tap to the affected one, and secure both ends. This is simple when it is the adjacent hot pipe that is affected, but it can often be done with other taps too. Now turn on both taps and leave for a few minutes. The water from the kitchen cold tap, because it has the pressure of the mains behind it, will travel up the affected pipe and clear out the air bubble.

Some authorities frown on this procedure, saying there is a danger of impure water being sucked back from the air-locked tap into the main. Others argue that the pressure of the main is so strong that this cannot happen. Check with your own authority.

An alternative method is to use a pump operated through the appropriate outlet of the cold storage tank.

Blocked traps

The trap in a waste pipe can trap other things besides the pool of water it is designed to hold. Debris can collect there, especially from sinks, and block the waste. Two types of trap are in general use. First, there is the kind formed simply by a bend in the pipe, and known because of its shape as either the P or the U trap. The other kind is the bottle trap.

On modern plastic systems the trap can be removed by hand. P traps are held in place by a couple of nuts, bottle traps by just one. Unscrew the nut, remove the trap, empty out solids and wash it out (at another sink or basin).

It is more difficult to remove older, metal traps, so try to clear the blockage by using a plunger first. This consists of a rubber or plastic cup, with a short wooden or plastic handle. Run some water into the sink, block up the overflow with a rag bung, place the plunger's cup over the waste outlet, and pump the handle up and down. This will force water down the waste outlet, and ought to clear the blockage. If it does not, try poking wire down the waste pipe, then use the plunger again. If this still produces no result, tackle the problem from the base of the trap. There you will find a large nut. It may be knurled so that you can grip it by hand, or you may have to use a large spanner. In some cases there are small lugs against which you place a short length of wood and hammer it. Place a bucket under the trap, open it, and water should pour out, bringing debris with it. You might have to force debris along by poking around with a length of wire from below or above.

When a lavatory trap becomes blocked you have to clear it with a lavatory plunger. This looks something like a sink plunger, but there is a metal plate behind the cup to stop the cup from becoming inverted. Such plungers can often be hired. Place the cup in the lavatory pan and work it up and down to force water round the bend and drive the blockage away. Once it has gone, flush the lavatory to fill the trap again.

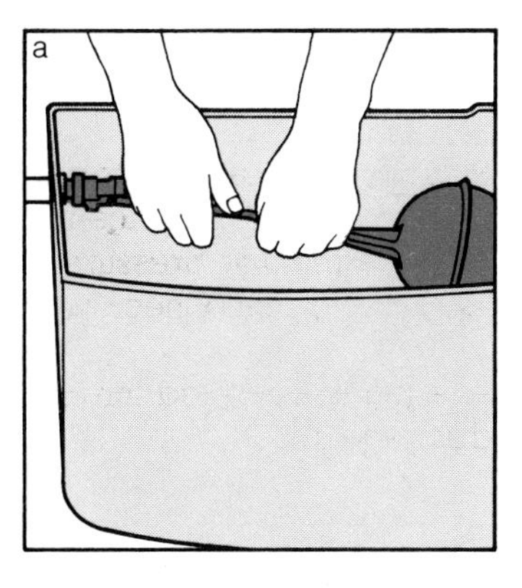

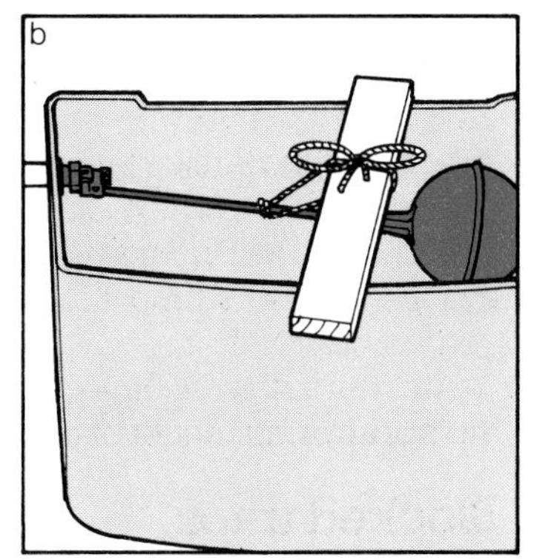

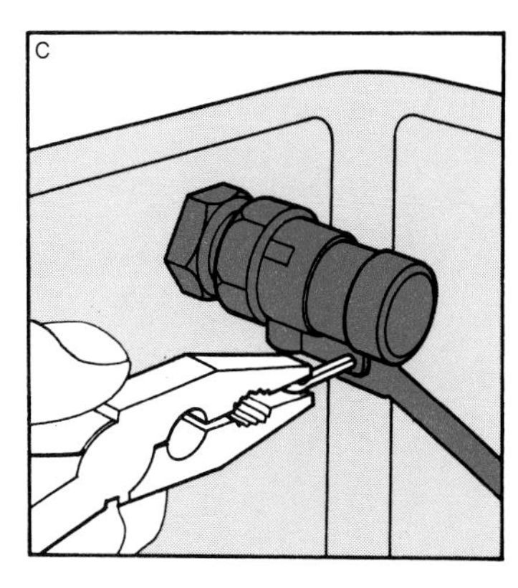

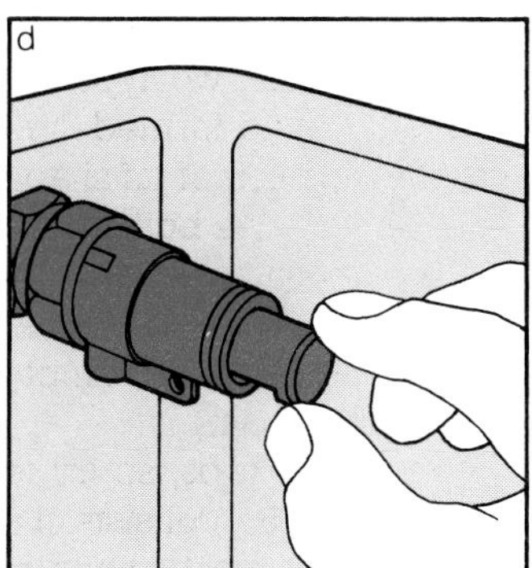

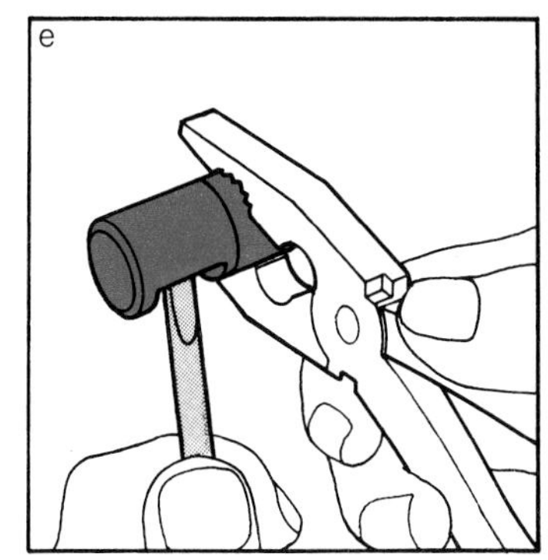

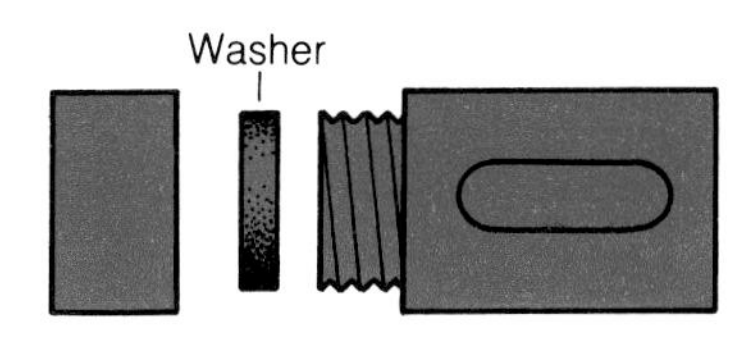

10.11 *Cures for a cistern overflow: (a) Bend the lever arm so the ball will be lower in the water. (b) The arm is tied to a stick to stop the entry of water as an alternative to shutting off the supply. (c) Withdraw the split pin holding the lever arm. (d) Remove the cap on the end of the valve case. (e) Unscrew the two parts of the piston. (f) Insert a new washer in the smaller end of the piston.*

Overflows

When you hear an overflow running from the cold tank or a lavatory cistern it may simply be that the ball is riding too high in the water, and as a result the water level has passed the overflow pipe before the inlet valve shuts off the supply. For this there is a simple remedy. Support the lever with one hand at the valve then bend the lever arm down so that the ball rides lower, shutting off the water at a lower level (Fig. 10:11).

If the ball is punctured it will take in water and be too heavy to float, so it will not rise enough to close the inlet valve. Do not bother trying to mend the puncture – you would never get the water out. Remove the ball, which is threaded on to the end of the lever arm, and fit a new one in its place.

While carrying out this – and, indeed, any other – repair you will have to shut off the water supply. If the cistern does not have its own stop tap, to avoid shutting down the whole system, place a stick across the top and tie string to it to hold the ball lever up high.

If the ball is neither submerged nor riding too high, raise the lever as high as it will go and notice whether water drips in through the inlet. If it does, the valve needs re-washering.

The whole mechanism may have become so damaged that a new one will have to be fitted. Unscrew the nuts and remove the valve. Slip one of the washers provided with the new kit over the threaded tail of the new valve, push the tail through the hole in the side of the tank. Fit the other washer on the outside, and tighten up the retaining nut. Connect the tail to the supply pipe.

Chapter 11

THE ELECTRICAL SYSTEM

The benefits that electrical systems provide are taken so much for granted that it is easy to forget that they are made and installed by fallible beings. It is also easy to overlook the fact that the components of the system tend to decay and therefore need replacement.

The dangers of a faulty or decayed wiring system are electric shocks and fires. The consequences of these are so serious that you should never allow your system to fall into disrepair. Do not wait to receive a shock before you heed the warning signs of a faulty system. And if a fire starts in the wiring, it can burn inside walls throughout a house before it breaks out, engulfing the entire structure. Always, therefore, treat electrics with respect.

THE SYSTEM'S CONDITION

A properly installed modern system should give no cause for concern. In some older homes, however, replacement is long overdue. In particular, cables insulated with rubber, which by now may well have perished, are hazardous. Also the insulating material of which old switches and sockets are made can become brittle and may crack, giving you a shock or even causing a fire. Moreover, the wiring systems of 20 or 30 years ago were rarely designed to cope with today's heavy loads.

Modern systems are insulated in plastic, which is extremely durable. If you are doubtful about the state of your system, judge its age by the appearance of the light switches and the socket outlets. If they are square or rectangular in shape, and the sockets are all the same size, then the system is modern. If the fittings are circular, with the sockets in two or three different sizes, then it is likely that the installation is due for complete replacement. This is not a job the average householder should tackle; it requires a professional electrician.

It is, however, possible for a do-it-yourselfer to work on a modern system – to improve, extend or repair it. Some of those jobs are detailed in this chapter. If you do not understand the instructions fully, and if you are in any doubt about what you are doing, call in an electrician.

Always switch off at the mains before you carry out any work on the system.

HOW THE SYSTEM WORKS

Electricity is brought into your home from the main supply by a service cable, which ends at a service terminal box. This box contains a fuse that protects the whole installation and allows engineers to switch off the supply when they need to carry out maintenance work. Close by the box is the meter. From the mains to the meter the installation is the property and responsibility of the supplier and you should not tamper with it. Beyond the meter the installation is the responsibility of the consumer.

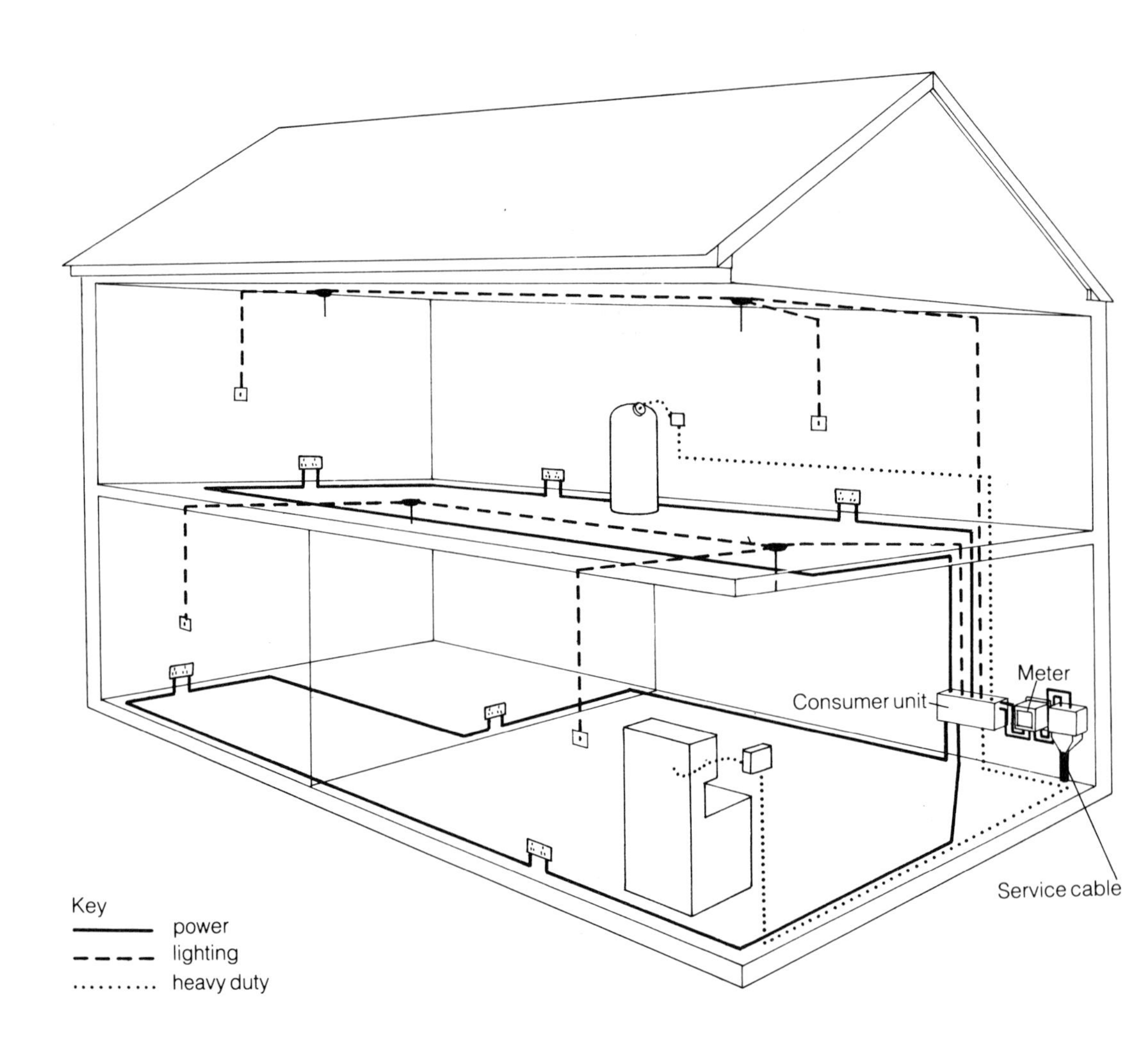

11.1 *Typical domestic wiring*

At the heart of the consumer's installation is a consumer unit or fuse box. This is a metal or plastic box housing the mains switch that governs the supply to the whole house, and the fuseways that protect each individual circuit within the house. The various power and lighting circuits lead off the consumer unit. It is normal, for example, to have an upstairs lighting circuit and a separate one for downstairs. Similarly, there would normally be separate power circuits – see Fig. 11:1.

Each of the circuits goes from a fuseway, which consists of a fuseholder housing a fuse. A fuse is a weak link inserted in the circuit so that it will burn through should anything go wrong, thus cutting off the supply of electricity before damage can be caused. Each circuit must have its own fuseway, unless it is fitted with a Miniature Circuit Breaker (MCB), also known as a 'trip-switch'. It is useful to have a unit with spare fuseways or MCBs because you will need these should you ever wish to install extra circuits.

There are two types of fuse. The most common is the rewireable fuse, in which a length of fuse wire is looped through a holder and connected to a terminal at each end. Less common are cartridge fuses which are similar to, but not interchangeable with, those in the plugs of portable appliances. It is much easier to change a cartridge fuse, but you cannot immediately see which one has blown, as you can with the rewireable kind.

Modern fuseholders have a small coloured dot so that you can tell their rating at a glance. The colour coding is; white – 5 amp (for lighting); blue – 15 amp (for power); red – 30 amp (for cookers and immersion heaters). Your consumer unit may have a fuseway for two or more of some of them.

The consumer unit is connected to the meter by two cables called meter leads – one live and the other neutral. The live one has pvc insulation coloured red, whereas the insulation of the neutral lead is black. There is also an outer sheathing. This in some cases is the same colour as the inner insulation, but in others it is grey. There is also a third cable, insulated in green or green and yellow pvc, but with no outer sheathing; this is the earth lead. In modern installations, it is good practice to provide an earth by means of a Residual Current Breaker (RCB); previously this was called an Earth Leakage Circuit Breaker (ELCB).

It is a good idea to mark on the back of the consumer unit cover which fuseway governs which circuit – in fact, there is often a small card on which to do this – so that you can immediately identify the various circuits.

The cable used in house wiring is described as being flat pvc – sheathed and insulated two core and earth. It's worthwhile knowing what that specification means. The fact that the cable is flat is stressed, because leads and non-domestic cables are circular in cross-section. The term 'pvc-sheathed' refers to the outer covering, which is white when the cable will be on view, but grey, which is slightly cheaper, when it will be out of sight. Some cables – those used out of doors, for instance – have a different kind of sheathing. The 'two-core' refers to the conductors – the wires that actually carry the electricity – which are, as the specification says, insulated with pvc. The live conductor has a red covering and the neutral a black (the international brown – live – and blue – neutral – coding is used only for flexes, not cables). Finally there is the earth, a bare strand of wire. When the outer sheathing is stripped off to make a connection, a sleeve of pvc sheathing must be slipped over the end of the earth wire. This earth sheathing used to be green, but is now green and yellow, just like that used to distinguish the earth wire on an appliance flex.

SWITCHING OFF

Before carrying out any job on the electrics of your home, you must shut off the supply at the main. There is no need to deprive the whole house of electricity. Turn off the mains switch at the consumer unit, remove the fuse controlling the circuit on which you will be working, then restore the supply.

But do check that it is the right fuse you have removed. If you are dealing with a lighting circuit, then even before going to the consumer unit, switch the relevant lights on to make sure the bulbs are working. Then turn off at the main, remove the circuit fuse and check that the lights are off. If they are, you can go ahead safely. If it is a power circuit you wish to check or change, switch off the supply, then plug in an appliance you know to be in good order and verify that it does not work. It is easy to forget as you become absorbed in your work, but you cannot be too careful about shutting off the supply.

THE CIRCUITS

There are three types of circuit – lighting, power (supplying socket outlets) and special heavier duty circuits for items such as cookers and water heaters. Cable of different size is used according to the kind of circuit. Ring circuits start out from the return to the consumer unit; radial circuits come to a stop when they reach the farthest points on their routes.

Power Circuits

The normal circuit used to supply the socket outlets into which portable appliances are plugged is the ring circuit. It consists of a loop of cable 2.5 sq. mm in cross-section, running from a 30 amp fuseway. The ring circuit can supply appliances up to a rating of 3 kilowatts – table lamps, televisions, washing machines, room heaters. Anything above that rating – for example, cookers and water heaters – must have its own circuit.

One advantage of a ring circuit is that only one size and type of plug is used no matter what the appliances (under previous systems, different sizes of plug were used for appliances of different ratings). There is, however, a cartridge fuse inside the plug, and this should be changed according to the amount of power the appliance takes.

For appliances up to a rating of 720 watts the fuse is 3 amp, coloured red; for those between 720 and 3000 watts (3 kilo-

11.2 *A domestic ring circuit*

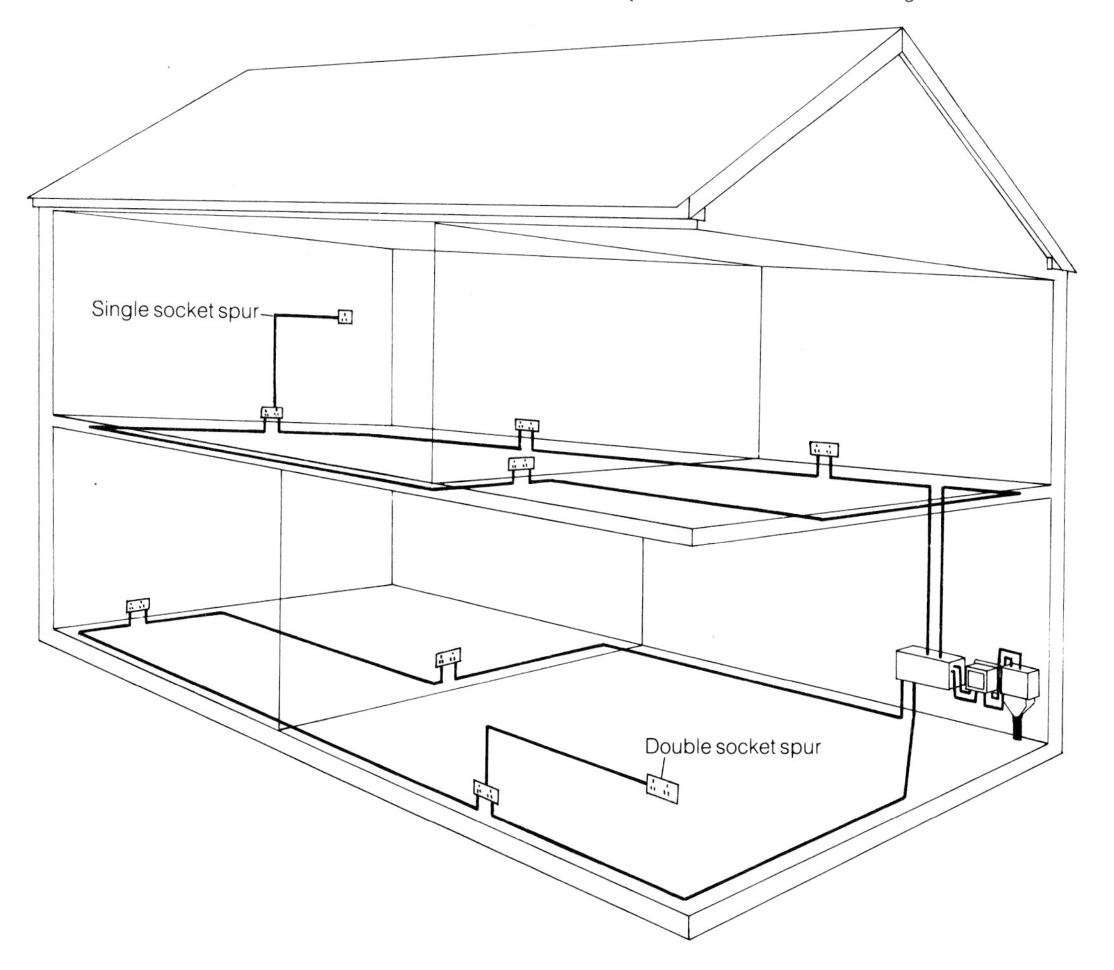

watts) the fuse should be 13 amp, coloured brown. When you buy a new plug it usually comes with a 13 amp fuse. The shopkeeper should change it for a 3 amp if you ask for one. It is a good idea to keep a stock of fuses of both sizes, because they may blow because of a fault, and if you transfer the plug from say, a table lamp to a room heater, you will need to uprate the fuse in the plug from 3 to 13 amps.

To prevent dangerous overloading, a ring circuit must not supply an area of your home greater than 100 sq. m (1000 sq. ft). In fact it is usual for small homes to have one ring for the ground floor and another for upstairs, even when it is not strictly necessary, so that the whole house will not be deprived of power if one circuit fails.

In addition to the main loop, a ring circuit can have branch lines, known as spurs, used for supplying outlets some distance from the main ring (Fig. 11:2). Each spur may supply only one socket, though this can be a double.

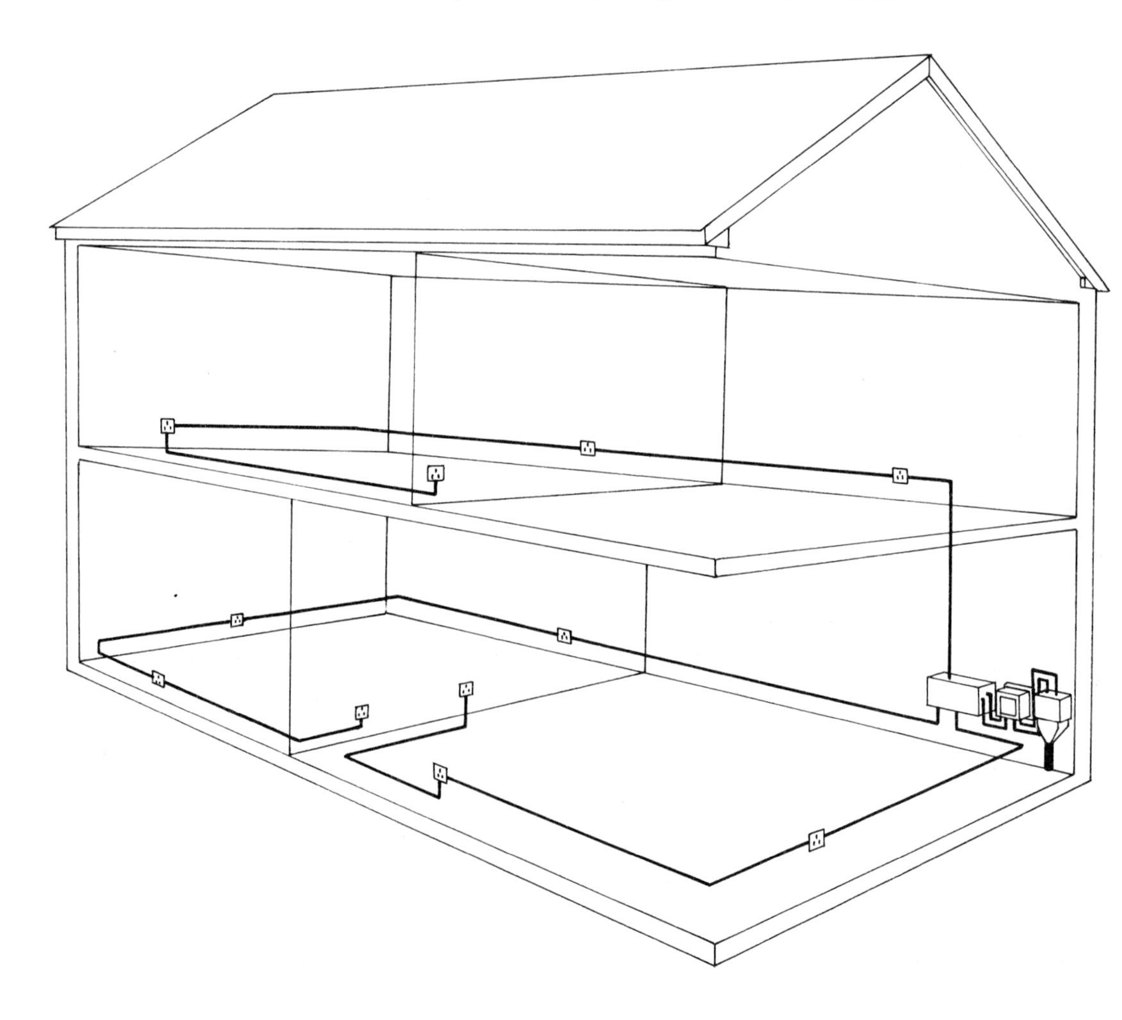

11.3 *Radial circuits supply socket outlets*

To supplement the sockets of the ring main, a radial circuit can also be used to supply socket outlets – this can be useful in small areas, such as a kitchen, where there are many appliances.

The number of outlets that can be connected to a radial power circuit (Fig. 11:3) is unlimited, but the area supplied by such a circuit must not be greater than 50 sq. m (500 sq. ft). The circuit must be in 4 sq. mm cable and run from a 30 amp fuseway, controlled either by a cartridge fuse, or by a miniature circuit breaker, not by a rewireable fuse. When the area is only 20 sq. m (200 sq. ft) the cable can be 2.5 sq. mm and the fuseway 20 amp. Moreover this circuit can be controlled by a rewireable fuse, instead of a cartridge or an MCB.

Besides socket outlets, a ring can have Fused Connection Units (FCUs), to which appliances are permanently wired and which have a fuse housed inside the unit. Such units are useful for appliances that you do not wish to keep unplugging – for example, waste disposal units, fridges, freezers and dishwashers. FCUs have a switch, and often a neon indicator as well to show when a current is flowing.

Lighting Circuits

There are two distinct types of lighting system, both of which use radial circuits. The more modern type is the loop-in system (Fig. 11:4). Cable goes from the consumer unit to each of the roses of the lighting system in turn, and is connected to them (or looped-in), hence the name. Separate cable connects the rose to the lampholder, and a third cable connected inside the rose leads to the switch – the 'switch drop'. So there will be at least three sets of wires inside each rose – the incoming and outgoing circuits and the switch

11.4 *Loop-in wiring*

11.5 *Junction-box wiring*

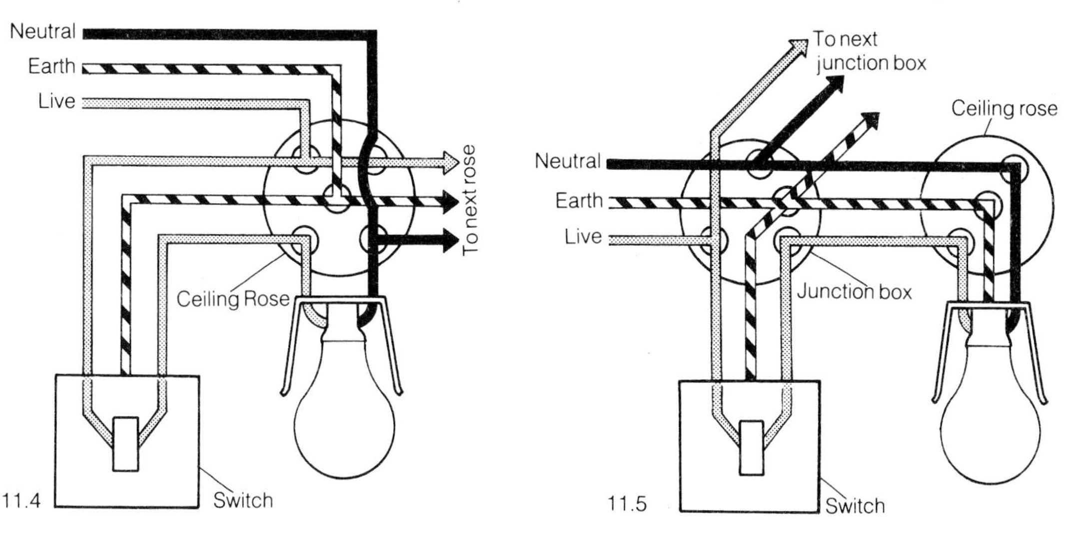

drop. There may also be a branch line leading to another lighting point, but the number of terminals available restricts such branches to only one per rose.

Lighting systems used to be wired according to the joint-box (or junction-box) system (Fig. 11:5). Cable passed from the consumer unit to a series of joint boxes. From each of these there was a lead to its light point and another to the switch.

The reason that the loop-in system is preferred is that all connections are made inside the rose, which is easily accessible, so it is much easier to check the system or add to it. Nevertheless, a joint-box system has advantages in some applications. For instance, if you cannot hide the cable to a lighting point it is better to expose just one cable (that from a joint box) rather than three – the cable to the rose, the return cable and that to the switch. Where a lighting point is a long way from the next light or the switch, it will involve less work and fewer materials if you connect it to the circuit via a joint box. There are hybrid systems that are mainly loop-in but incorporate elements of joint-box wiring.

Both types of system are wired in 1 sq. mm cable governed by a 5 amp fuseway. Previously, lighting circuits did not incorporate an earth wire, but because of safety considerations – especially in view of the increasing use made of metal light fittings – modern installations invariably do.

Since fewer connections are made inside a rose in a joint-box wiring, fewer terminals are needed, and so you might imagine that such a rose would cost less. For single or small purchases, however, it does not, and since there is much less demand for joint-box roses, most retail outlets do not stock them. Accordingly, roses intended for loop-in systems are found in joint-box wiring. But you can tell at a glance on which system a rose is wired. Unscrew its cover, and observe how many wires enter it. If there is only one set (live, neutral and earth, if the cable carries an earth wire) then, in general, the system is the joint-box one. If there are two or three cables, it will almost certainly be a loop-in wiring system.

Most of the points supplied by lighting circuits are known as plain pendants – they consist of flex hanging from a ceiling rose and supporting a shade held on a lampholder. There are, however, special pendant fittings, many of which carry more than one bulb and incorporate their own rose cover, such as close-mounted ceiling fittings (usually found in kitchens and bathrooms) batten fittings and wall lights. Switches are normally on the wall, but there are also cord-operated ceiling switches. These are fitted in bathrooms to minimize the risk of shock (a person who is wet is at greater risk from shock than one who is dry).

Installing cable

Cables can be hidden, according to need, in a variety of ways.

Under the floorboards is the normal place for running cable to socket outlets above skirting boards, or to lighting points in the ceiling below. To install cable here, lift up the floorboards (see page 156-7). If the cable is parallel with the joists it can lie loosely on the top of the ceiling below, if there is one. On ground-storey suspended floors, with just a void below, clip the cable to the side of the joists (Fig. 11:6). When the cable has to cross the joists pass it through holes bored through them at least 50 mm (2 in) from their tops. If this clearance is not possible, perhaps because the joists are not big enough, the cable must be protected by metal inserts sold for this purpose.

Above the ceiling is the normal place to run cable supplying roses in rooms. In a house with a loft, the installation is easy. Run the cable either parallel to the joists (tucked well down below the insulation at the side of the joist) or across. If it runs across, there is no need to bore holes through the joists unless you are going to floor the loft: fix the cable with clips on each side so that it lies neatly and close. If there is cable on top of the joists in any areas where you are likely to walk (for example, around the cold water storage tank) protect it with plastic channelling.

Even if there is no loft you can run cable parallel to the joists above a ceiling. Make a hole at the start of the run, feed the cable along, then bring it out through a hole at the end (see page 201 for the technique). Patch the holes with filler when you have finished. Running cable across the joists of such a ceiling presents problems, because you have to by-pass each joist. The method is to cut holes in the ceiling each side (Fig. 11:7), and then cut a channel in the bottom of each joist. Bring the cable out of one hole, pass it along the

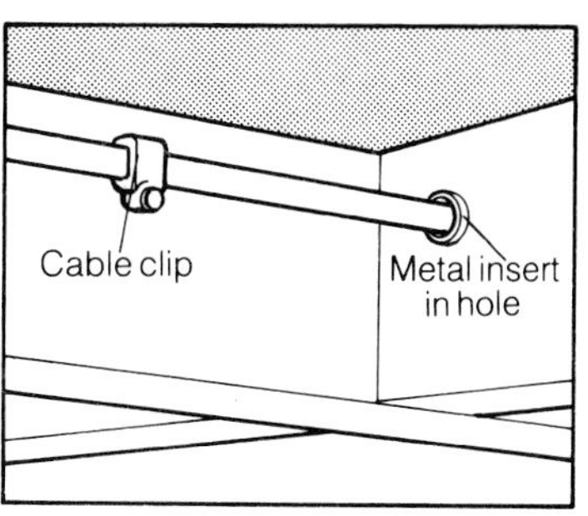

11.6 *Cable passing through and clipped to a joist*

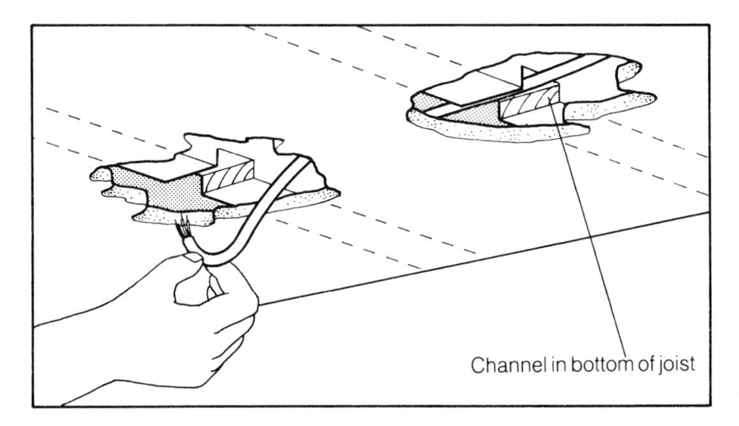

11.7 *Passing cable above a ceiling*

channel into the other, and then make good. Crossing joists is thus laborious and to be avoided except for short runs.

Inside hollow walls is the natural way to run cable from one floor to the next, when you can, or to feed socket outlets or wall lights. If the cable is to pass through the top member of a stud wall in the top storey, bore the hole from the loft; if it is to pass through the top member of a lower-storey wall you merely have to lift floorboards. Sometimes there are intermediate horizontal frame members, which can obstruct the cable's passage. Electricians have long wood augers with which to bore holes as much as 1 m (3 ft) from the top. It is not worth a do-it-yourselfer's while acquiring one, so use the method already outlined for passing across ceiling joists – pass the cable through a hole cut in the wall above the frame member, along a channel chopped out of its side and into a hole in the plaster below it. Since there will normally be one intermediate horizontal timber in a wall frame, this is not such a bothersome task as it is in a ceiling where there are many joists.

Inside cavity walls is a convenient place to hide cable – provided there is no insulation. If a vertical drop in a cavity wall exceeds 4.6 m (15 ft), however, regulations demand that it should have an intermediate fixing. Make this by boring a hole in the wall's inner leaf, under the first-storey floor, then loop the cable out and secure it to a joist.

Behind an architrave is a small gap between the timber lining the doorway opening and the wall itself. Cable can be pushed into this gap and covered by the architrave. This is an ideal place for hiding cable going to a switch, which can be next to the architrave, or for passing cable from one storey to another if there is no adjacent hollow wall.

Behind a skirting board the plaster of the wall does not usually extend to meet the floor, so there is a gap behind the skirting board where cable can be hidden. This is a convenient spot for hiding cable supplying socket outlets low down on the wall – indeed it is the only place if the floor is a direct-to-earth one, under which cable cannot be passed.

Buried in the plaster. Cable passing along a wall that is not hollow, or along a cavity wall filled with insulation, can be buried in the plaster. To do this, cut out a chase or channel. If there is paper on the wall, first trim away a strip about 25 mm (1 in) wider than the cables. Make two firm lines on the plaster surface, the width of the cable apart, using a craft knife and a straight edge.

Run the blade of an old wood chisel or screwdriver along the grooves cut by the knife, then use it to chop out the plaster back to the masonry behind. In many cases, a chase the depth of the plaster will be sufficient to take the cable; if not, deepen it by cutting into the masonry with a bolster chisel and club hammer. Place metal channelling, bought from electrical suppliers, over the cable and nail or screw it to the wall. This is to prevent the cable being pierced or cut accidentally. Make good with filler. If you want to run cable in two adjoining rooms there is no need to cut a chase on both sides of the dividing wall. Just make the chase on one side double width, put both cables into it, and feed the cable for the next-door room through a hole in the wall.

Making cable move

Cable weighs little, so when you want to drop it down a confined space – inside a cavity or hollow wall, for instance – you cannot always rely on gravity. To solve the problem devise a mouse, a weight tied to a length of string (see the section on renewing sash cords in Chapter 4).

Drop the mouse down the cavity then tie the cable to the weight end of the string, if you want to haul the cable upwards, or to the free end if you aim to draw it down. A mouse can also be used to determine how far down any obstructions – such as horizontal frame members of a cavity – may be, so that you know where to cut into the surface of the wall to make a bypass.

It can also be difficult to move cable horizontally – for instance, when you drop it under a suspended timber floor at one end of a room and want it to emerge at the other; or if you are trying to run it above a ceiling where there is no loft. This is accomplished by using a length of stout wire bent at one end into a hook shape. Form the cable into a loop and push it under the floor, or above the ceiling. Insert the wire from the other end, then push it along so its hook catches the loop of the cable. Then pull it back. Electricians refer to this as 'fishing' for cable.

Stripping the ends

The ends of the sheathing and insulation of cable must be stripped off to allow you to make connections to a terminal. To remove the outer sheathing, cut with a small knife drawn lengthways between the wires forming the inner core. It does not matter if you nick into the insulation at the start, for the ends of the core insulation will have to be stripped off anyway; as the cutting proceeds, however, you will be able to hold the cores far enough apart to avoid nicking the insulation. Peel the sheath back, and cut across its width.

The core insulation is best removed with a wire stripper, which you use to cut through the insulation and then bare the core – there is a depth regulator to stop the cutter's jaws from biting into the core itself.

SOCKETS AND SWITCHES

Socket outlets (sometimes incorrectly called power points) and the switches that control ceiling lights consist of two parts – a faceplate and, behind it, a box.

In the best installations, the box is buried flush with the wall's surface. Sometimes, though, the box is fixed to the surface of the wall, because this is easier. Surface-mounted boxes for use in homes are usually in white plastic. Flush-mounted ones are always in metal, usually aluminium alloy or black-coated steel.

Boxes come in three main sizes. For square-plate accessories (single switches and socket outlets) there is the 1-gang box. Such boxes usually have four lugs to take the accessory's fixing screws. There are only two screws, so it does not matter which way up you fix the box. Next there is the 2-gang box, used for double socket outlets. These have four fixing lugs positioned to take the four screws of a double socket outlet. The third type is the dual box, which you should not confuse with the 2-gang type. This has extra lugs so that you can fix two square-plate accessories to it.

Boxes also come in varying depths. The shallowest is a square-plate accessory box which is only 17 mm (about ⅝ in) deep. On most walls, that would be no more than the thickness of the plaster, and it is, in fact, often referred to as a plaster-depth box. It is designed to take room light switches only – there is not enough space for a socket outlet.

The normal depth for a box is 25 mm (1 in). There are, however, deeper boxes – at 35 and 46 mm (about 1½ and 2 in) – and the extra space can prove useful when you need to fit many cables inside a box, for instance when you are running a spur from a socket ring circuit. Special boxes are also available for such items as cookers, control panels and shaver sockets.

On the sides and back of plastic boxes there are thin sections, known as push-outs or knock-outs. You do as the phrase suggests – push them out to form a hole through which cable can pass. A metal box has perforated knock-out blanks. Once a blank has been pushed out for cable a small grommet, in plastic or rubber, must be inserted so that the cable's insulation will not be chafed.

The terminals to which the cable is connected are on the back of the faceplate. It is therefore important to draw enough cable through the box to allow the faceplate to be connected without undue labour, but not so much that it cannot fold comfortably into the space left in the box. In the case of switches, the earth wire is fixed to a terminal in the box.

When fixing a box to the wall, take care to make it hori-

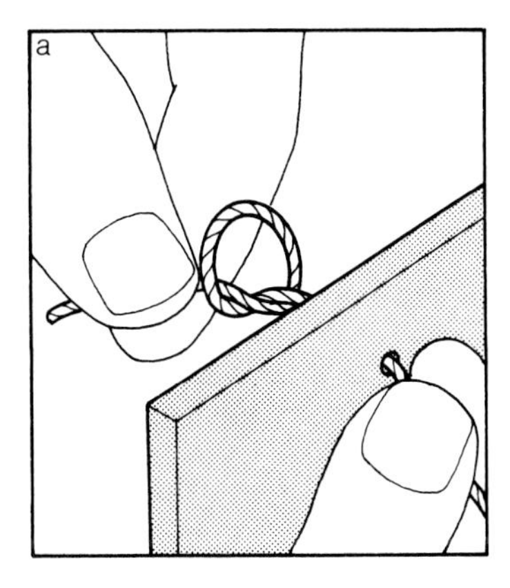

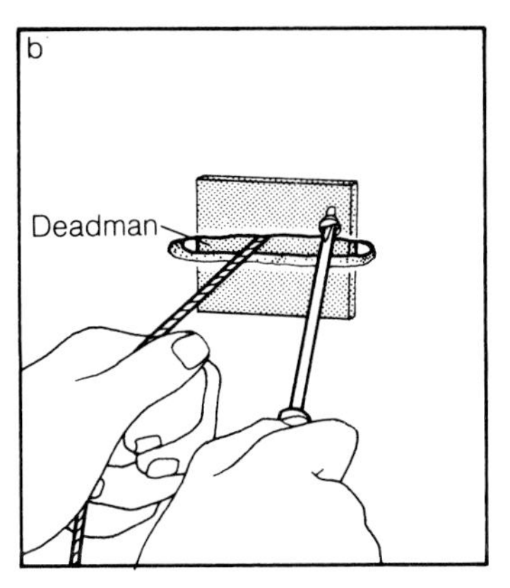

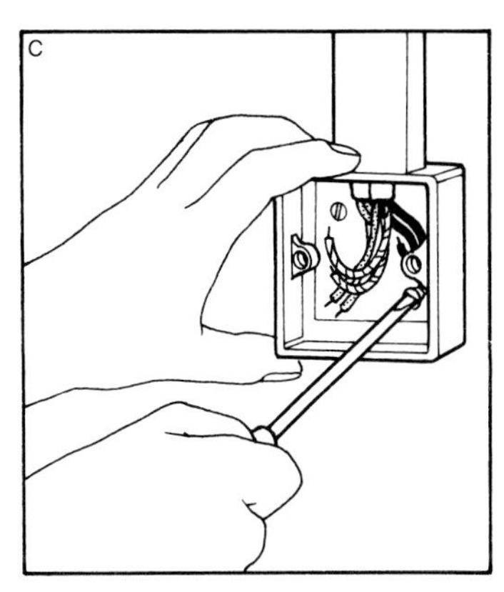

11.8 *Fitting a box in a hollow wall: (a) Tie the string to a small batten. (b) Pull the batten into place. (c) Screw the box to the batten.*

zontal, or at least parallel to some prominent feature, such as a skirting board, architrave or the grout pattern on a tiled wall.

Fixing surface-mounted boxes

On a brick or stone wall, the screws should be driven into wall plugs. Such a fixing might be suspect in breeze block, however, because the outlets need to withstand some force when plugs are withdrawn. It is better to cement or glue to the wall a thin piece of wood slightly smaller all round than the box, then make the fixing with woodscrews driven into this timber.

On a hollow wall, aim wherever possible to position the box so that you can drive its fixing screws into the timber framework behind the plaster. If you must have the box between pieces of the framework, fit a deadman – a thin batten inserted behind the plaster (Fig. 11:8). Drill a small hole at one end of the batten and thread a length of string through it. Hold the string in place with a knot tied at the back. Make an incision in the plaster, slip the batten through, and use the string to pull it to the correct spot. Drive screws through the surface of the lath and plaster or plaster-board to fix the deadman in place. Fixing screws for the box can then be driven through the plaster and into this timber. The box can be positioned to hide the incision. Otherwise make good with filler.

Flush-mounted boxes

On solid walls, make this job as easy as you can for yourself by choosing as shallow a box as you can get away with. Should a deep box be necessary, make sure the wall is thick enough to take it. Place the box on the surface of the wall and draw round its outline in pencil. Run a sharp knife along these lines, using a straight edge. If there is wallpaper, peel off the waste. Using a cold or bolster chisel and a hammer, carefully chop out the plaster to the masonry below. Check whether the hole is deep enough for your box. If it is not, cut into the masonry. Aim to make the bottom of the hole flat. Should this prove too difficult, chop out a hole that is too deep, cover its base with cement, then press the box into place to level off the cement. Remove the box, wipe off excess cement that has seeped through the holes, and let the cement set before drilling holes for the wall plugs.

Hollow walls constructed from plasterboard should pose no problem. In fact, on these walls it pays you to choose a site between frame members, for the fixing is then easier. You can buy special lugs that clamp on the side of a metal box, and are then fixed to the plasterboard. Should you want to site the box directly above a frame member, then you merely cut a hole in the board equal in area to that of the box. Where that does not give you sufficient depth, cut out a notch, making sure it is absolutely flat, in the frame member, and fix to the timber.

Lath and plaster walls present a problem. It is not too bad when you are fitting a shallow box to a stud or nogging, or when you have deep plaster. But if you have to cut into the laths, then the end of one or more will be left flapping free. The only way to remedy this is to push a thin piece of wood behind one or more laths and smear glue on the meeting surfaces to provide support.

Do not attempt to fix between frame members on a lath and plaster wall. There is no way of making the fixing firm enough to withstand use.

Extra socket outlets

There are rarely sufficient electrical socket outlets in a modern home. If your system is in good order, you can install extra ones.

Singles into doubles

One of the easiest ways to increase the number of sockets is to convert any existing singles into doubles. Any single socket on a ring circuit can be doubled, but if you are working on a spur with two sockets, you cannot convert either of them to a double. You can, however, double a single socket if it is the only one on a spur.

To establish whether a socket is on the ring, or if it is the only one on a spur, switch off at the main and remove the faceplate. If there are two sets of wires, the socket is either on the ring or it is the first one of two on a spur. To determine which, you need a continuity tester. This you can easily improvise from a battery and bulb holder (Fig. 11:9). Connect one lead of the tester to one of the red wires in the socket, and the other lead to the other red wire. The bulb

11.9 *A simple continuity tester*

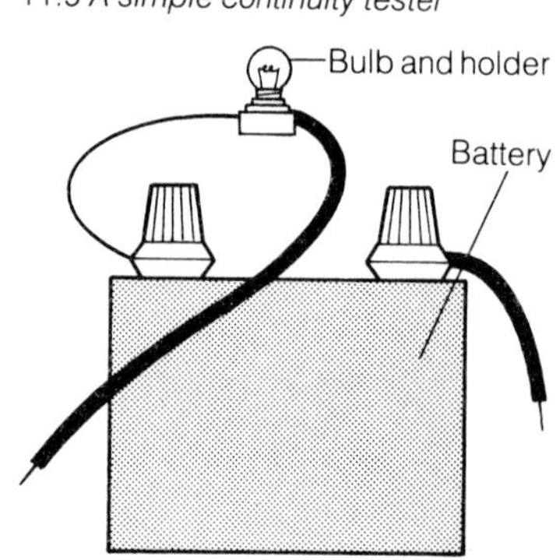

will light if the cable is part of a ring, but not if it is a spur.

If the socket has only one set of wires it is on a spur, but it could be the last of two. A test helps you to be sure. Call the first socket A. Look for another socket nearby that, because of its position, could be on the same spur. Call this socket B. Remove the faceplate of B and twist together the black and the red cores of the cable going towards socket A. Remove the faceplate of A and connect the bulb tester to its red and black wires. If the bulb lights, both sockets are on the same cable and you must not double either. Do be sure to reconnect all the cables properly before restoring the power.

Assuming that you can proceed, there are various possibilities. If the single socket is flush mounted, an easy conversion is to make the new double a surface one. Modern surface boxes do not protrude as far as the older kind, so the result need not be obtrusive. You can buy a 2-gang plastic box that can be screwed to the fixing points of the existing flush single box. Then draw the cable(s) through a knock-out in the back of the new box, connect them to the terminals of the new double faceplate, and screw this to the new box.

If you wish to retain the outlet as flush, remove the existing single box, enlarge the hole and fit a new 2-gang box. Then fix the double socket to the box.

When you are dealing with a surface-mounted box, the procedure will usually vary according to whether the cable is surface-run. If it is, there is nothing to gain by making the new outlet flush mounted. Merely fit a 2-gang box in place of the existing single, and fix the new double socket to it. If the wiring to the surface box is concealed, use the same method, but it might be worth while making the socket flush fitting. This involves chopping out a hole for the new 2-gang box.

Instead of one double socket, you can fit two singles side by side, but you must then use a dual box, not a 2-gang one. Buying one new single faceplate instead of a double would not be much less expensive. But if you are thinking of turning two singles into doubles you need buy only one double to put alongside the two singles in a dual installation.

Installing a spur

All the sockets in your rooms may be doubles already. And even converting all the existing singles may not give you sufficient socket outlets. Moreover, you may want a socket in an entirely new position. A new socket is installed by means of a spur. You can have only one socket on this spur, but it can be a double so you might as well make it that. Use 2.5 sq. mm cable for the spur.

Begin by switching off at the consumer unit and then fixing the socket either flush- or surface-mounted. Connect the cable to its terminals, and run it to the point at which you propose to connect it to the supply. There are three possible places at which you can make the supply connection.

The first is at an existing socket outlet to which no spur is already connected. Choose one that is conveniently situated. It need not be in the same room as your new socket. For instance, if you are fitting the new socket on the dividing wall between two rooms, consider connecting it to a socket on the other side of the wall. Fit the new socket directly opposite the existing one. If the wall is not thick enough, fit the new socket slightly to one side of the old. In either case you will get an easy installation.

Another possibility (though as a last resort only) is to connect to a socket on another floor. A short length of cable, for instance, dropping down from a bedroom to a living room, perhaps through a hollow partition wall, would also be an easy installation. You will have to remember, though, when carrying out work in the future that you remove the fuses controlling both the upstairs and the downstairs rings. This is a good example of why it is essential always to check that a socket or lighting point is dead before touching it.

To make the connection, first remove the supplying socket's faceplate. If the socket is flush-mounted, remove the mounting box from the hole to allow you to remove a knock-out blank, through which the spur cable will enter. Also, it is easier to fish for a new cable with the box out of the way. You may, however, be able to push out the blank of a plaster surface-mounted box without removing it from the wall.

Once the new cable is brought through into the box, connect its wires to the same terminals as those of the ring, making sure that the terminal screw grips all three. Replace the faceplate.

The second place at which you can make a supply connection is at a joint box inserted in the ring circuit. This is

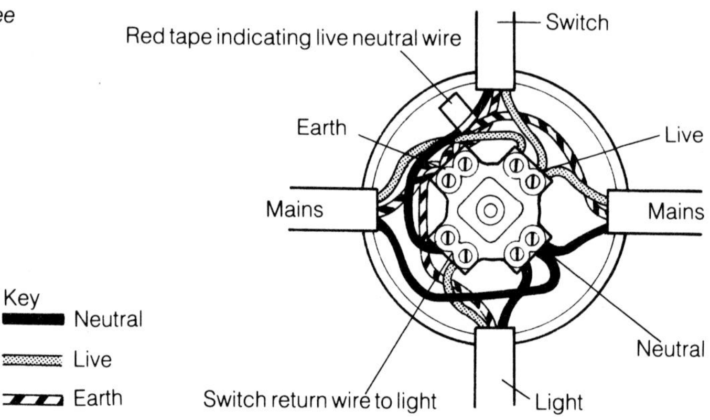

11.10 *Connections inside a three terminal joint box.*

worth considering only if the ring runs conveniently close by and under the floor. The ring is usually out of sight, so you have to make an inspired guess at its route, taking into account the position of existing sockets in the room. You can then remove the faceplate of a socket, and perhaps the box, too, to get an idea of where the cable runs before finally lifting a floorboard or two to confirm your guess.

Connect to the ring by means of a three-terminal joint box (Fig. 11:10). Fix this into place by screwing it to a length of 75 × 25 mm (3 × 1 in) timber spanning two joists, about 75 mm (3 in) from their top edge. Support this timber with screws on to two short battens nailed to the sides of the joist. There will be nine wires to be connected – six from the ring, and three from the spur. Make sure all three reds go to the same terminal, all three blacks to another, and all the earths to a third.

The third place to make a supply connection is at a ring circuit fuseway in the consumer unit. This is a method it might pay you to adopt if the new socket is near to the consumer unit.

Extra lights

If you wish to fit extra lights, make a simple check to ensure that the loading will not be too great. On a domestic lighting circuit the loading must not exceed 1200 watts.

To determine the loading you must first find out which lights are on the circuit. So switch on all the lights in your home, then switch off the mains at the consumer unit, and remove a lighting fuse. Restore the power and check which lights do not light up: these are all on the same circuit. Repeat with the second lighting fuse, then the third, until you have plotted all the lighting circuits in your home.

Now inspect the bulbs on the circuit you wish to work on and add up the total wattage. Bulbs of 100 watts and over should be taken at their face value; those of less than 100

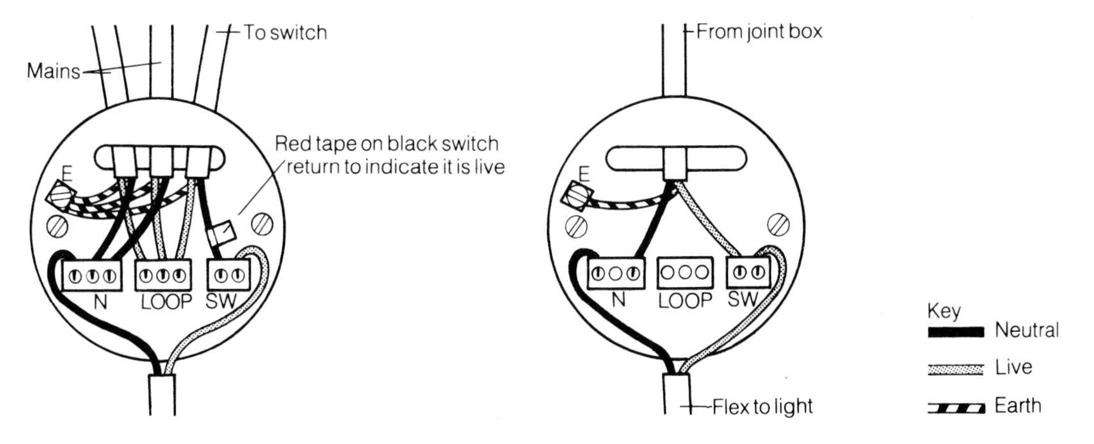

11.11 *Connections inside a loop-in rose (left) and a junction box rose*

watts should be counted as 100. Provided the extra light will not take the load beyond 1200 watts on that circuit you can go ahead. Use 1 sq. mm cable.

Fig. 11:11 shows typical connections inside a loop-in and a joint-box system rose. There is one point you should note about the switch drop: both of its cores are, in fact, live. One core (the neutral) goes straight to the light, and the other (the live) passes to it via the switch. Ordinary cable is used for the switch drop, so inside a loop-in rose or a joint box you will see a black core connected to a live terminal. To avoid any dangerous confusion, a piece of red sticky tape should be fastened to this black wire, but the electrician who worked on your home might not have bothered.

Your first job when installing a new light is to select the position for the rose, then fix it into place. To fix a rose, unscrew its cover and drive 38 mm (1½ in) woodscrews through two of the fixing holes in its base. The fixing must be completely secure, for the rose will have to bear the weight of the light fitting, which can be heavy. In a building with a concrete ceiling, a secure fixing presents no problem. The fixing screws can be driven into wall plugs fixed in the concrete, so the rose can be positioned almost anywhere you like. On a plasterboard or lath and plaster ceiling, you will make things simpler if you fix directly to a joist, by driving the fixing screws through the plaster and into the timber. There will be sufficient room to feed the cables through, although you may have to chisel a slight notch in the joist. Otherwise, provided there is access above, you can fit a short length of 100 × 25 mm (4 × 1 in) timber on top of the ceiling, immediately above the site of the rose, and attach it at each end to a joist. The fixing screws go into this timber.

A loop-in system. If you wish to have the new and existing lights controlled by the same switch, so that both come on and go off together, then connect up your new rose as for the joint-box in Fig. 11:10. Run the mains cable from this rose to the existing one. There connect its red wire to the SW terminal, the black to the N and the earth to the E.

You may wish to have the new light independently switched. In that case you can still loop-in to a rose in the same room, if there is one. Otherwise, look for the most convenient rose in another room nearby, on the same circuit. At the existing rose, the red wire of the new cable goes to the LOOP terminal instead of the SW one. The black goes to the N terminal, and the earth to the E.

You also need to install a switch, and the wiring at the new rose is as in Fig. 11:10.

A joint-box system. The job is still simple if the new light is not to be independently switched. Install the new rose, then run cable from it to the rose of the light with which it will work in tandem. The red, black and earth wires go into terminals already occupied by wires of that colour.

Installing a new independently switched light on a joint-box circuit is complicated – this is why the system has been superseded – and involves much disturbance to the house as you try to trace hidden lighting cables, so it is better to call in an electrician.

WHEN THINGS GO WRONG

Not much should go wrong with a modern electrical system. The most common fault is that the room light will not work when you turn on the wall switch. Usually, the fault is a defective bulb. Turn off the wall switch while you change it.

Occasionally, however, the bulb will not have been at fault. In that case check whether other lights in the same and adjacent rooms – those likely to be on the same circuit – are working. If all are out, the trouble is probably a blown fuse.

If none of the lights in the house works, look outside to make sure that the whole neighbourhood does not have a power failure.

Check at the consumer unit. If you have previously noted which fuse controls which circuit, you will know the fuseway you should inspect. Otherwise, deal with each one in turn. If, like most homes, yours has the rewireable type of fuse, you can see immediately if anything is wrong, for the wire will be broken, and there may even be charring. But you cannot tell merely by looking at a cartridge fuse if it is defective. You can, however, carry out a simple test using a metal torch. Remove the bottom end cap of the torch, place one end of the fuse on the metal casing and the other on the end of the battery. Switch on. The bulb will glow only if the fuse is sound. You can use this test on the cartridge fuse of an appliance plug. If you have an MCB system, you will be able to see immediately which switch has tripped.

It is easy to rewire a fuse, or to change it if you have the cartridge type. If the fault that caused the fuse to blow in the first place persists, however, the fuse will blow again immediately you restore the power. The most probable cause of such a fault is a short circuit brought about because one of the wires in the cable has become detached from a terminal and is touching the other wire. To check this, make sure all the lights in the circuit are switched off. Replace the fuse and restore the power at the main. Now go round the house switching on each light in turn to discover which causes the fuse to blow. Switch off at the main again and examine the connections inside the bulb holder, rose and switch. You may find a loose connection. If not, you had better call in a professional electrician.

Very rarely it may be that neither a bulb nor a blown fuse is at fault. If all the lights in the circuit are off, and there is no power cut, then there is a break somewhere in the circuit.

Dealing with this is probably a job for an electrician, although if you have surface-run wiring you might just as well inspect it to see if anything is obviously wrong. If just one light is not functioning, it might be that a terminal connection has come loose without causing a short. Check. If you can see nothing wrong, call in an electrician.

If you get no power when you plug into a socket outlet, the trouble is most likely to lie with the appliance rather than the circuit. The reason for this is that the fuse in the appliance plug will blow before the fuse controlling the circuit burns through.

If you plug in, say, a vacuum cleaner, and when you switch on the motor does not start, unplug it and plug in a table lamp. If this works, then (except for the extremely rare occurrence that a connection inside the socket has come loose, and is making contact only intermittently) you can be certain that the fault lies with the vacuum cleaner. If the lamp does not work, try it on an adjacent socket to test the circuit. If the lamp does not light, check the circuit fuse. If it does light, switch off at the main, remove the faceplate of the first socket and check its terminals. If there is nothing wrong with the connections, you need an electrician.

If the fault seems to lie in the appliance, replace the fuse in its plug with a fuse you have tested in another plug. If the appliance still does not work it needs repairing.

Glossary

A

Abutment wall: Wall at the end of, and projecting at least as high as, a pitched roof. It is square at the top, and is capped off with either stone coping or rendering.
Access tower: Metal framework for reaching high parts of the house.
Acoustic tiles: Sound absorbent material for fixing to walls or ceilings to reduce noise or improve the sound quality of a room.
Aggregate: Natural sand or gravel, or crushed stone that is added to cement to make concrete.
Air brick: Perforated brick, of earthenware or cast iron, built into a wall to provide ventilation.
Allen key: L-shaped steel tool, hexagonal in cross section and in various sizes, used to turn round-head bolts with hexagonal slot.
Anchor bolt: Device for making extra strong fixing in a wall – it has a steel, rubber or plastic sleeve that expands as the bolt head is tightened.
Angle bead: Right-angled metal strip reinforcing external corners in plasterwork.
Annular nail: Nail with ridged serrations along its shank which gives extra strong fixing. They are often used for fixing hardboard to a suspended timber floor.
Anodizing: Protective film – glossy, matt or coloured – given to metal, especially aluminium, by electro-chemical methods.
Architrave: Decorative moulded timber surrounding a door or window opening.
Arris: Sharp edge where two angled surfaces meet – for example, the corner of a brick or stone.
Arris rail: Triangular-section rail running horizontally between fence posts to provide a fixing for the fence boards.
Asbestos cement: Mixture of cement and asbestos fibres used in the manufacture of building materials – for example, corrugated roofing sheets and rainwater goods.

B

Back boiler: Boiler fitted behind an open fire – gas or solid-fuelled – used to supply heating or hot water.
Ball valve: Valve operated by a float at the end of a lever, used to control entry of water into a cold water tank.
Baluster: Vertical length of wood, often decoratively moulded, supporting the handrail of a staircase.
Balustrade: Row of balusters along the sides of a staircase.
Bargeboard: Length of timber fixed to the top of a gable wall where it joins up with the end of a pitched roof.

Barrel bolt: Surface-mounted bolt that slides open or closed in a cylindrical sleeve – the barrel.
Batten: Originally a long thin piece of squared timber used in flooring, and to support laths, tiles and slates. Now widely used to describe any small-section timber.
Beading: Originally, moulding carved like a row of beads, but now any small-section moulding of timber or other material.
Belly out: Bulging or bowing in a wall or ceiling.
Bending spring: Flexible former inserted in plumbing pipes, to stop them being flattened when bent.
Bleeding: Blemish on decorative surface caused by, for example, resins from knots, or colours of previous paints or wallpapers seeping through to the surface.
Blockboard: Manufactured board with a core of parallel strips of softwood faced on each side with one or more layers of veneer. Most commonly 19 mm (¾ in) thick.
Bond: Overlapping of bricks in a wall so that the vertical joints between courses are staggered.
Boss: Device for connecting waste pipes to a drainage stack.
Boss White: Compound for use with plumber's hemp and PTFE tape to make plumbing joints watertight.
Box gutter: Gutter built up on site, as opposed to being factory-made. It is found where, for instance, a pitched roof meets a parapet wall.
Bottle trap: See **Trap**.
Brace: 1. Carpenter's tool which, when fitted with a bit, is used to bore holes.
2. Length of metal or timber used to strengthen the construction of building.
Building block: Rectangular blocks, other than bricks, used in building. They can be solid, hollow or cellular and are sometimes used for the inside leaf of cavity walls, or for internal walls. Some are load bearing; others are lightweight. They have better insulating qualities, and are cheaper than bricks.
Butt joint: Joint formed when two squared pieces of timber meet without overlapping.

C

Came: Metal strip holding the glass in a leaded light window.
Capillary groove: Channel cut into, for example, a window frame, to stop water being forced up the frame by natural suction.
Capillary joint: Sleeve with internal rings of solder, for joining plumbing pipes.
Capping: Protective or decorative finish on the top of a wall or fence.
Cap sheet: Top layer of felt fixed to a roof.
Carriage: Length of timber that supports a staircase from the underside.
Chase: Groove cut in a wall or floor to take concealed cables or pipework.
Caulking: The act of filling the gap between door and window frames or a bath or kitchen worktop and surrounding walls. The material used for such filling.
Cavity fixing device: A sort of wall plug for hollow walls.
Ceiling plate: Horizontal member at the top of a timber framework for a hollow wall of lath and plaster, or plasterboard.

Cement: Material used as a binder with sand to form mortar, or with aggregate to make concrete.
Cess pit: Underground chamber (in brick, concrete or plastic) into which domestic sewage is discharged, to be emptied at intervals.
Chair rail: Moulding at the top of a dado, fitted to stop chair backs from scratching the wall.
Chamfer: Sloping surface of a bevelled edge or corner.
Chipboard: Manufactured board made from particles (and therefore sometimes known as particle board) of wood, or occasionally flax, bonded with resin and compressed to a high density.
Cill: See **Sill:**
Cladding: Material applied to a wall or vertical framework as either a decorative or protective covering (or sometimes both).
Cleat: 1. Piece of timber fixed under a staircase to provide extra support.
2. Metal or plastic anchorage to which cords, for example blinds or clothes lines, are tied.
Clout nail: Nail with extra large head. Used for fixing roofing felt and sash cord.
Coach bolt: Dome-headed bolt in which a short part of the shank nearest the head is of square-section.
Compression joint: Plumbing joint formed by tightening a nut to compress a ring-shaped seal.
Coping: Finishing detail on the top of a wall to make it look neater and protect it from the weather.
Corbelling: Courses of brickwork projecting from a wall in an inverted triangular pattern – the lower courses stick out less than the higher ones – usually to support masonry above.
Cornice: Ornamental moulding, usually in plaster, where a wall joins up with the ceiling.
Corrugated fastener: Short length of corrugated steel sharpened along one edge so that it can be driven into timber to strengthen a butt joint.
Coupled sash: Type of double glazing in which a pane of glass in a wood, metal, or plastic frame is fixed to an existing sash in the window.
Coving: Prefabricated cornice, in plaster or polystyrene.
Cramp (clamp): Tool for holding joined pieces of wood together while the glue sets.
Cross lining: Practice of applying lining paper horizontally so that its joins will not coincide with those of the top decorative wallcovering hung in the normal vertical manner.
Crow's foot spanner: Spanner in which the jaws are at right angles to the body.

D

Dado: Lower half of a room wall, often given a different decorative treatment from that above, and topped off with a decorative moulding, known as a chair rail.
Damp-proof course (dpc): Bed of impervious material running horizontally in a wall to stop moisture in the ground from rising up the structure.
Damp-proof membrane: Layer of waterproofing material in a direct-to-earth floor to stop damp from rising.

Dentil slip: Place of material used to fill the cavity under a deep-profile ridge tile (such as a pantile) on a roof. Dentil slips can be bought specially, or bits of broken tile can be used instead.
Direct-to-earth floor: Floor resting directly on the ground.
Door furniture: Accessories, such as handles, finger plates, locks, street numbers and letter boxes that can be fitted to a door.
Dog leg stair: A staircase with two non-parallel flights separated by a half-landing.
Door stop: Part of a door frame against which the door closes.
Down draught: Draught set up when a cold panel (usually a window) sets up a movement of air, as opposed to one caused by air passing through gaps around doors and windows.
Downpipe: Pipe that carries rainwater from the gutter down to the drains.
Drip bead: Shaped piece of timber that forms part of the top rail of a window frame, to throw off rainwater.
Drip channel: Groove in the underside of a window cill, cut out or formed with moulding, to prevent rainwater running back on to the house wall.
Drop: Length of wallpaper needed to cover the wall from ceiling (or picture rail) down to the skirting or chair rail.
Dry lining: Cladding an internal wall with plasterboard, as opposed to using plaster.

E

Eaves: Point where a roof meets the top of the house walls.
Efflorescence: White deposit on the surface of walls caused by soluble salts, which crystalize as brickwork or plaster dries out; it can be brushed off but will eventually disappear of its own accord.
Elbow coupling: Right-angled joint used in plumbing.
Escutcheon: Surround that neatens a keyhole.
Expanded metal: Mesh formed by perforating a sheet of metal then expanding it.
Expansion joint: A flexible joint that allows a structure to expand or contract as the temperature changes, without causing damage.
Expansion loop: Length of pipe inserted in a run to allow for expansion.
Expansion tank: Empty tank that accommodates water expelled from a radiator central heating system as the temperature rises, then feeds it back when the water contracts as its temperature falls.

F

Fair face brickwork: Interior brickwork laid particularly neatly to a decorative surface.
Fascia: Horizontal timber, to which the gutters are fixed at eaves level.
Fibre building board: Sheet material made by compressing wood or vegetable fibres. Hardboard and insulating board are different forms of fibre board.
Firring piece: Tapered length of timber fixed to the rafters to slope a flat roof and ensure that rainwater runs off.
Flashing: Strip of material fitted to give a waterproof joint where a roof joins up with a wall or chimney stack.

Flaunching: Mortar into which chimney pots are set on top of a chimney stack.
Flooring brad: Nail for fixing floorboards to joists.
Floor plate: Bottom horizontal member of the timber framework for a hollow wall.
Flow and return pipe: Pipe used to carry hot water from the boiler of a central heating system, round the radiators and back to the boiler.
Footlifter: Tool used to position wall boards when they are being fixed to a timber framework.
Frass: Tiny brown pellets, like sawdust, that are left behind by the grubs of wood-boring insects such as woodworm.
Frenchman: Improvised tool used for trimming mortar when repointing a wall.
Frieze: 1. Part of a wall between picture rail and ceiling.
2. Thin strip of wallpaper applied as a border – for example, horizontally below the ceiling or just above the skirting board.
Frog: Inset part on one face of a brick.

G

Gable wall: Wall at the end of a house with a two-way pitched roof; the top is triangular in shape, to conform with the shape of the roof.
Glazing bar: Small-section intermediate frame member that divides a window into small pieces.
Glazing spring: Small headless nail that holds a window pane in its frame before putty is applied.
Glue block: Small (usually triangular) piece of timber held in place by glue under a timber construction (for example, a staircase, chair or sideboard) to strengthen the joint.
Grout: Adhesive-like material used to fill the gaps between tiles after they have been fixed into place.
Gully: Opening in the ground through which rainwater is conveyed to the drains; usually a glazed earthenware fitting with a trap.

H

Hanger: Timber member of a roof truss.
Hardcore: Rubble such as broken bricks, stone and concrete, placed on the ground as a base for concrete.
Hawk: Tool used for carrying plaster or mortar. It consists usually of a small, square sheet of wood about 12 mm (½ in) thick attached to a short handle.
Header: Brick laid across a wall, usually to form a bond or coping.
Head plate: Top horizontal member of the framework for a stud partition wall.
Herringbone: Flooring pattern in which parquet, bricks, tiles or other materials are laid in a zig-zag arrangement.
High spot: Part of a surface (a wall or floor, for instance) that bulges slightly from the surrounding area.
Hinge bolt: Also known as stud or dog bolt. Fitted to the hinge edge of a door to locate in the frame to stop this edge from being forced by burglars.
Hip: Line where two slopes of a hipped roof meet.
Hip iron: Curved strip of iron at the foot of a hip, which prevents the hip tiles from sliding down before the mortar holding them has set.

Hip rafter: Main corner rafter of a hipped roof.
Hipped roof: Type of pitched roof that has a second slope at its end instead of a gable wall.
Hollow-joint ceiling: Ceiling without any cladding; the joists and the floor of the room above are fully on view.
Hollow wall: Partition wall with cladding (plasterboard, or lath and plaster) on a timber frame.
Hopper head: Open top of a downpipe into which waste pipes from baths, sinks and basins above ground level discharge.
Horn: Part of a window frame or door frame that projects beyond the main structure.
Hygrometer: Instrument used to test for damp.

I

Illuminated ceiling: False ceiling, usually in opaque plastic, above which are fluorescent lights.
Inspection chamber: Brick-built chamber in a drainage system (sometimes called a manhole).
Insulating glass: Another name for a double glazing sealed unit.

J

Jack rafter: Intermediate rafter on a hipped roof.
Jamb: Vertical member at the side of a door or casement window frame.
Joist: Horizontal structural timber supporting floors and ceilings.
Joist hanger: Galvanized metal stirrup built into brickwork of a house to support a joist at one end.

K

Keeper plate: See **Striking plate**
Knotting: Liquid, based on shellac, applied to knots and other resinous areas of timber to stop resin from oozing out later to spoil the paintwork.
Knuckle: Point where two leaves of a hinge join.
Kraft paper: Strong, smooth brown paper.

L

Ladder stay: Device to hold the top of a ladder away from a wall so it does not rest on a gutter or window.
Laminboard: High quality blockboard in which the core battens are thin and the structure strong.
Latch: Locking device in which the bolt is spring loaded and opened by the operation of a handle or key, unlike a lock, which can be opened and closed only by a key.
Lath and plaster wall: Internal partition wall built on a timber framework to which small horizontal pieces of timber (the laths) are nailed to provide a key for the plaster which is skimmed on to them.
Lead boat: Wooden tool, so-called because one end is shaped like the bow of a boat; used by glaziers to close the beading that holds the glass in leaded lights.
Lintel: Horizontal structural member, in stone, concrete or even wood, holding up the masonry above a door or window opening.
Lipping: Thin strip of timber or plastic used for disguising a raw edge.

Lock block: Block of wood fitted inside a flush door to take locks, handles and other furniture.
Lock nut: Second nut threaded on to the end of a bolt to stop the first one from working loose. A nut that incorporates a retaining washer.
Lock rail: Middle horizontal member of a panelled door.
Loose fill: Insulation material in the form of pellets or flakes.

M

Mastic: Non-hardening material used for sealing gaps, such as in rainwater fittings, round baths and between door and window frames and walls.
Matchboarding: Timber similar to tongued and grooved boards but with additional moulding so that a V groove is formed where two boards meet.
Melamine: Resin applied to synthetic boards (especially chipboard) to give a protective, easily-cleaned surface.
Microbore: System of radiator heating based on very small pipework – even smaller than those used in **Small bore.**
Mirror plate: Small, shaped piece of brass or chromium-plated metal used for hanging pictures, small cupboards and mirrors on a wall.
Mixer valve: A control valve that mixes hot and cold water so that it emerges from the tap at the desired temperature.
Mortise bolt: Bolt that is housed in a recess cut into the door.
Mortise lock: Lock housed in a recess cut into the door.
Mouse: Small weight, attached to the end of a length of string, that is dropped into gaps and cavities so that electric cable or sash cords, for example, can be drawn after it.
Mullion: Intermediate vertical member of a large window frame.

N

Newel cap: Piece of wood, often decorative, fixed to the top of a newel post.
Newel post: Stout post that forms the end of a staircase balustrade at the bottom of the stairs and on landings.
Nib: 1. Short stretch of wall left at each end to support the rsj that is inserted when a load-bearing wall has been removed.
2. Projection of a roofing tile that hooks on to the roofing batten.
Night latch: Rim latch operated by a key from outside the door and a small handle inside. A small catch stops the handle or key from turning the latch and can hold the latch open.
Nogging: Subsidiary supporting member in a timber framework – such as horizontal cross-pieces between the main uprights (or studs) in the framework of a wall, or a minor cross-member between the joists of a ceiling.
Nosing: A rounded front edge – especially of a stair tread.

O

Offset: Section of a downpipe that leads from the gutter to the main pipe under the eaves. Also called a **Swan's neck.**
Opening light: A window that can be opened.
Open tread: Staircase in which the risers (the vertical sections between the treads) are omitted.

Outer bead: One of three beads that form the channels in which vertical sliding windows run. See also **Staff bead** and **Parting bead.**

P

Pantile: A decoratively shaped roofing tile.
Parapet gutter: Gutter formed *in situ* between a roof and the back of a parapet wall.
Parapet wall: External wall that extends higher than the eaves of a pitched roof.
Pargetting: Decorative plasterwork on the outside of buildings.
Particle boad: See **Chipboard.**
Parting bead: Central bead that forms the channels in which sliding sash windows run. See also **Outer bead** and **Staff bead.**
Parting slip: Vertical piece of timber that divides the weight compartment of a vertical sliding window in two, keeping the two weights apart.
Penetrating damp: Caused by rainwater finding its way through the structure of a building.
Piano hinge: Long hinge, with several holes in each leaf, of the sort used on piano lids.
Pilot hole: Starting hole drilled for screw, slightly less in diameter than the screw itself, making it easier to drive home the screw without splitting the wood.
Planed all round (PAR): Term used to describe softwood that (as is the norm) is sold planed on every edge, and is therefore slightly smaller than its nominal size – reduced about 3 mm (⅛ in) in each dimension.
Plasterboard: Plaster-based material sandwiched between paper to form a hard rigid board, which is applied to walls and ceilings, instead of plaster.
Plasticizer: Compound added to mortar to make it more workable.
Plumber's hemp: Fibre used in making joints watertight.
Plunger: Wooden or plastic handled tool with a small rubber cup at one end, used for clearing blockages in waste pipes.
Pocket piece: Timber covering the weight compartment of a vertical sliding sash window.
Pointing: Facing of mortar applied to the joints between courses of brickwork.
Primaries: Plumbing pipes that carry water between a boiler and a hot water cylinder.
Protimeter: Instrument used to test for damp.
PTFE tape: Plastic used in plumbing to make joints watertight.
P-trap: See **Trap.**
Purlin: Intermediate cross-member of roof timbers.

Q

Quoin: Large stone inserted in the corner of buildings built mainly of brick.

R

Raft: A slab of concrete.
Rasp: Coarse file used to shape, reduce or smooth material.
Rebate: Small recess cut out along the edge of a length of timber. Used, for example, in window frames to provide housing for glass and in door frames.

Rendering: Facing of sand and cement applied to a wall.
Retaining wall: Wall built to hold back earth piled up behind it.
Reveal: The opening for a window on the room side of the frame.
Ridge: Point at which the two slopes of a pitched roof meet.
Ridge board: Timber support under the apex of a pitched roof.
Ridge tile: V-section tile fixed to cover and weatherproof the ridge of a pitched roof.
Rim latch or lock: Security device fitted on the surface of the door – not housed in a mortise.
Ring shank nail: Nail with raised ring along the shank; used for fixing hardboard to a timber floor because it is less likely to be shaken loose than a conventional nail.
Riser: Vertical section between the treads (steps) of a staircase.
Rising butt: Hinge that raises a door as it opens so that it is lifted clear of, say, a floorcovering.
Rising damp: Damp that rises up into the structure from the moist earth below.
Rolled steel joist (RSJ): Strong supporting member for buildings, usually inserted in the top of an interior load-bearing wall that is removed to convert two rooms into one.

S

Sash: Fixed, opening or sliding frame of any material holding a pane of glass and forming part of a window. Commonly describes a vertical sliding window.
Saw horse: Four legged trestle that supports large-section timber while it is being sawn.
Scratch coat: First coat of rendering on a wall; it is scratched just before it sets, to provide a key for the next coat.
Screed: Layer of sand and cement used to top off a concrete floor.
Secondary sash: Double glazing in which sashes are installed just inside, and separate from the existing ones.
Secret gutter: Gutter formed behind a parapet wall.
Secret nailing: Method of fixing tongued and grooved planks or match-boarding, by driving nails at an angle through the tongue and out via the main body of the plank, so that they are covered by the groove of the next plank to be installed.
Self-levelling compound: Viscous liquid applied to a floor to make it level before a floorcovering is laid.
Septic tank: Container in which sewage is purified by bacteria, before being filtered into the soil.
Shake: Split in timber.
Sharp sand: Coarse sand used in making concrete.
Shoe: Section at the bottom of a downpipe that directs the water into a gully.
Shuttering: Wooden formwork that makes a mould for concrete.
Sill: Bottom horizontal member of a window or door frame.
Skew nailing: Method of fixing timber framework by driving a nail at an angle through the side of one member and into another that meets it at right angles.
Skin coat: Smooth top coat of plaster or sand and cement rendering.
Sleeper wall: Low wall used to give intermediate support to the joists of a ground-storey suspended floor.
Slip: Thin piece of brick-like tile stuck to the surface of an interior wall to give the impression of natural brickwork.

Slurry: Mortar mixed to a cream-like consistency.
Small bore: Central heating based on small-diameter pipes.
Soffit board: Horizontal length of timber fixed under the rafters and behind the fascia board, at the eaves of a building.
Soft sand: A fine sand containing stone particles, used in mortar and certain renderings.
Soil pipe: Pipe leading from a lavatory to the drains.
Solvent welding: Use of adhesive to join plastic pipes.
Spalling: Surface flaking of bricks.
Stack: Main drainage pipe.
Staff bead: The inner of the three beadings that form the channels for a vertical sliding window. See also **Parting bead** and **Outer bead**.
Stile: Vertical side member of a door or ladder.
Stop bead: Part of the lining round a door opening.
Stopping: Material used to fill holes in woodwork.
Strawboard: Form of building board, often used on flat roofs.
Stretcher: Brick laid lengthways to bond a double-skin wall.
Striking plate (keeper plate): Housing for a bolt or latch in a door frame.
String: Timber member at the side of a staircase into which the steps and the vertical sections between them (risers) are fixed.
Stucco: Smooth external rendering with a painted finish.
Stud: Vertical member of the timber framework for a hollow wall.
Stud partition: Non-load-bearing hollow wall that consists of cladding (usually lath and plaster or plasterboard) on a timber framework.
Swan's neck: Term for an offset – a section of downpipe shaped to run under the eaves and connect the gutter with the main vertical run.

T

Tack rag: Fabric impregnated with slow drying varnish, used for dusting off surfaces prior to repainting.
Tail piece: Shaped piece of timber at the end of a **bargeboard.**
Terrazzo: Floor-finish consisting of marble chippings in cement.
Thixotropic paint: Jellied (non-drip) paint.
Threaded joint: Plumbing joint in which a threaded insert fits into a threaded hole.
Threshold: Strip (of wood, metal or plastic) across the foot of an external door opening to make it weatherproof.
Tile hanging: Roofing tiles used vertically on an external wall.
Tiling batten: Strip of timber fixed at right angles to the roof rafter to support tiles or slates.
Tilting filler: Triangular piece of wood used at the eaves to lift the slates or tiles of the roof slightly so that they bed properly on the nails.
Tongued and grooved ('t and g'): Lengths of timber moulded along both edges – one with a groove, the other with a matching tongue. Used mainly for floors, where the tongue of one board locates into the groove of the next to provide a draught- and dust-free seal.
Toothing: Brickwork in which alternate courses are left projecting (like teeth) so that the wall can be extended later.

Top-hung: Opening casement window hinged at the top.
Torching: Mortar used to fix slates and tiles to a roof and to seal the gap between rows.
Transom: 1. Horizontal part of a window frame that separates a fixed from an opening window.
2. Horizontal member between a door and a fanlight.
Trap: Bend in a waste pipe to contain a small pool of water that stops drain smells from coming up into the home.
Trimmer: Timber member used to support the ends of rafters that have been cut (for example, to make a window opening in the roof).
Trussed rafter: Roofing support in which the rafter joist, strut and other members are delivered to the site as one unit.

U

U-valve: Measure of the performance of insulation material. The lower the U-valve, the better the insulation.

V

Valley: Angle formed when two slopes of a pitched roof meet at the bottom.
Ventilating pipe: Open-ended pipe leading from a soil pipe.
Vent pipe: Pipe leading from the top of a hot water cylinder to allow excess overheated pressure to escape.
Vent stack: A ventilating pipe.
Varge: Roof projection beyond the gable.
Vermiculite: Loose-fill insulating material based on mica.

W

Wall plate: Horizontal length of timber fixed to a wall to provide anchorage for floor joists or rafters of a lean-to building.
Wainscot: Wood panelling on an interior wall.
Wall tie: Strip of metal, wire or plastic bedded into mortar courses in the middle of a cavity wall to hold the two leaves together.
Waste pipe: Pipe that carries water from sinks, basins and baths.
Water bar: Strip of metal under a door to stop rainwater finding its way through.
Waterhammer: Noise caused by vibration in water pipes.
Weatherboard: 1. Shaped piece fitted to the bottom of a door to throw rainwater clear; usually made of timber, but sometimes of metal or plastic.
2. Horizontal timber cladding on the outside of a building.
Weep holes: Holes left in a structure to allow moisture to flow out.
Weight compartment: Housing for the balancing weights of a vertical sliding sash window.
Welted apron: Overlap of roofing felt projecting from a flat roof to throw rainwater into the gutter.
Wet and dry: Abrasive paper that can be used dry, but is normally used wet so that it produces no dust.
Winder: Angled step used where a staircase changes direction.
Wire balloon: Metal cage that prevents debris from falling down a ventilation pipe.

Index